THE
# LIGHT AIRCRAFT
DATA BOOK

Copyright 2004 J. Blade

First printed July 1997
Reprinted December 1997
Second edition 1998
Third edition 2000
Fourth edition, complete revision 2004

A catalogue record of this book is available from the
British Library

ISBN 0-954834-60-7

Published by Small Plane Publishing\Flaydemouse
The Media Building, 8 Buckland Road,Yeovil, Somerset
BA21 5EA
Telephone 01935 479453

Printed by Octavo, Yeovil, Somerset

# THE
# LIGHT AIRCRAFT
## DATA BOOK

Fourth edition

Des Armour and Edwin Shackleton

Small Plane Publishing/Flaydemouse

# ABOUT THIS BOOK

Following on from the original Light Aircraft Data Book of 1997, the second and third editions appeared, revised and with additions, the number of types covered increasing from 214 to 328.

In 2003 I renewed my association with a long-standing friend, printers and publishers, Flaydemouse, who looked at the book and said 'let's do it in colour!'

So here you have it! The majority of photographs are not only in colour but new, and a batch of new or interesting types have been added. All the existing types have been checked and revised thanks to the indefatigable Edwin Shackleton (who is in the Gemini on the back cover).

Des Armour


# PREFACE TO FOURTH EDITION

## ERRORS, OMISSIONS AND ECCENTRICITIES
In the case of De Haviland Gipsy engines my computer argues with me – and wanted to spell Gypsy – sometimes I gave in  to it!

I have been economical with engine type numbers (on the grounds of space mainly) and have generally referred only to the maker and horse power.

My system of aircraft size/wight/power categorisation is the old one ie, Microlights: 859lb (390kg); AUW 5lb/sq ft (25kg/sq m) wing loading; Ultralights: 1200lb (545kg) AUW, 75hp max – all others are Light Planes. I include now 450kg microlights and certain SLA and VLA categories.

In the tables, where no 'official' figure was available I have calculated it an it is shown in italics.

'Climb' in the performance figure refers to 'initial climb'.

# PHOTOGRAPHS

Edwin Shackleton, Rod Simpson, Paul Kelsey and myself have supplied most of the photographs. Here and there I have slipped in my drawings. I am indebted to all the following who have helped me with photographs.


PHOTOGRAPH CREDITS
I would like to thank Air Britain, Chichester-Miles, Les Millen, Peter Huggett, Seawind Amphibians, Phil Stacey, Frank Maclean, Don Conway and Urban.

All original drawings by Des Armour.

COVER PHOTOGRAPHS
Front cover: Denney Kitfox Mk3
Back cover: Miles Gemini

# CONTENTS

Note: Within type sections above, the aircraft are in approximate age order.

The Aeronca two seat C3 – affectionately known as the 'flying bathtub' – was produced before WW2 by the Aeronautical Corporation of America Inc. in Cincinnatti. Production was briefly undertaken in the UK at Peterborough as the Aeronca 100 and 19 were made, eleven of both types survived wartime storage to fly again after hostilities ceased and three were still flying in 1993.

Of steel tube, wood and fabric construction, the Aeronca has been fitted with many engines in the past, the classic being the Company's own Aeronca E113 which developed 40 hp and in the British version was made by J. A. Prestwich as the FAP J-99.

Maybe not the most beautiful aeroplane ever designed, the C3 is nonetheless an enduring eye-catcher at fly-ins and in spite of its 'draggy' wire-braced wing still gives very economical flying at 3 gall/hr.

Six on UK Register, three flying and twelve in world museums.

# AERONCA C3

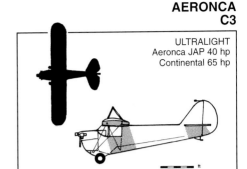

ULTRALIGHT
Aeronca JAP 40 hp
Continental 65 hp

| DATA | IMPERIAL | | METRIC | |
|---|---|---|---|---|
| Span | 36 | ft | 11 | m |
| Wing area | 142 | sq ft | 13.3 | sq m |
| Aspect ratio | 9.1 | | 9.1 | |
| Empty Weight | 569 | lb | 258 | kg |
| Loaded weight | 1150 | lb | 522 | kg |
| Wing loading | 7.4 | lb/sq ft | 36 | kg/sq m |
| Max speed | 107 | mph | 171 | kmh |
| Cruise speed | 87 | mph | 139 | kmh |
| Stalling speed | 48 | mph | 76 | kmh |
| Climb rate | 450 | ft/min | 138 | m/min |
| Range | 200 | mls | 320 | km |

The two-seat Coupe was the sole product of the Civilian Aircraft Company of Burton-on-Trent, the ABC Hornet powered prototype flying in 1929.

Five of the boxy Coupes were built between 1929-31 at the firm's plant at Hedon, the municipal airport of Hull. Apart from the prototype, all subsequent models had AS Genet major five-cylinder engines and were typed as Coupe Mk2.

The Coupe was of mixed wood and metal construction, skinned all over with plywood and was in its time considered 'state of the art' in an era of mainly wire braced bi-planes. All controls were push-rod operated and unique for its day, the main wheels were fitted with brakes. Coupes regularly took part in the inter-city air races of the period.

One aircraft, G-ABNT kept going until 1939 when it was stored for the duration of WW2. Restored to airworthy condition by Shipping and Airlines Ltd at Biggin Hill, this venerable machine may be seen again on the vintage air show circuit.

Parts of other Coupes, of unknown history are also in store at Biggin Hill.

# CIVILIAN COUPE

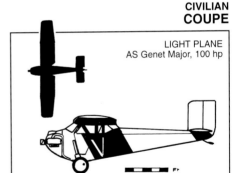

LIGHT PLANE
AS Genet Major, 100 hp

| DATA | IMPERIAL | | METRIC | |
|---|---|---|---|---|
| Span | 35.5 | ft | 11 | m |
| Wing area | 168 | sq ft | 15.7 | sq m |
| Aspect ratio | 7.5 | | 7.5 | |
| Empty Weight | 985 | lb | 447 | kg |
| Loaded weight | 1500 | lb | 681 | kg |
| Wing loading | 8.9 | lb/sq ft | 45 | kg/sq m |
| Max speed | 105 | mph | 168 | kmh |
| Cruise speed | 96 | mph | 154 | kmh |
| Stalling speed | 50 | mph | 80 | kmh |
| Climb rate | 816 | ft/min | 250 | kmh |
| Range | 360 | mls | 576 | km |

The Dessouter Aircraft Company of Croydon modified the Cirrus powered Dutch Koolhoven FK41 in 1929 and called it the Dolphin. Later, re-engined with a Hermes I, it was known simply as the Dessouter Monoplane. A Mk2 with a Gipsy III engine and a re-designed tail appeared in 1930.

Forty-one Dessouters (including thirteen Mk2s) were built up until 1931, ten of which went abroad.

Of all-wood construction with a plywood covered fuselage and cantilever wing the Monoplane was the first three-seat cabin monoplane built in the UK.

The Dessouter was operated by National Flying Services (National Aviation Day displays and the Red Cross) as an air ambulance. In 1933 G-AAPZ led the Kings' Cup air race but was beaten into fourth place in the last mile or so. A Danish Dessouter finished seventh in the Great England/Australian race in 1934.

Eight existed up to WW2, 5 were impressed and did not survive. G-AAPZ originally owned by R. O. Shuttleworth and kept at Old Warden is now airworthy. An Australian Dessouter was airworthy up until 1951 where another non-flying one exists.

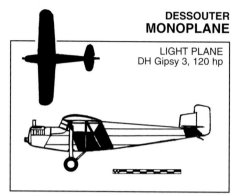

### DESSOUTER
# MONOPLANE

LIGHT PLANE
DH Gipsy 3, 120 hp

| DATA | IMPERIAL | | METRIC | |
|---|---|---|---|---|
| Span | 35.7 | ft | 11.3 | m |
| Wing area | 183 | sq ft | 17.2 | sq m |
| Aspect ratio | 7 | | | |
| Empty Weight | 1180 | lb | 535 | kg |
| Loaded weight | 1900 | lb | 862 | kg |
| Wing loading | 10.4 | lb/sq ft | 50.7 | kg/sq m |
| Max speed | 125 | mph | 200 | kmh |
| Cruise speed | 100 | mph | 160 | kmh |
| Stalling speed | 55 | mph | 88 | kmh |
| Climb rate | 1000 | ft/min | 308 | m/min |
| Range | 500 | mls | 800 | km |

Nick Comper founded the Comper Aircraft Co. at Hooton in 1930 and designed the CLA-7 Swift. Its type number refers to the Cranwell Light Aeroplane Club where Comper worked on his earlier designs.

A small sporty high winger with an open cockpit, the Swift was initially powered by an ABC Scorpion and 8 were produced in its first year. The 85 hp Pobjoy-geared radial engine became the favoured power unit for the 30 Swifts finally produced (Gipsy Majors were also fitted, giving a V max of 165 mph).

Swifts were great little racers, always performing well in the Kings' Cup air races and in 1931 with C. A. Butler at the controls, G-ABRE broke the England-Australia record in 105 hours.

Four are still on the British Register including one new home-built from original drawings. three are in museums abroad.

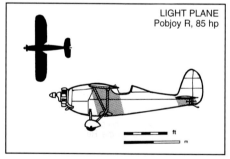

### COMPER
# CLA-7 SWIFT

LIGHT PLANE
Pobjoy R, 85 hp

| DATA | IMPERIAL | | METRIC | |
|---|---|---|---|---|
| Span | 24 | ft | 7.4 | m |
| Wing area | 90 | sq ft | 18.46 | sq m |
| Aspect ratio | 6.4 | | 6.4 | |
| Empty Weight | 540 | lb | 245 | kg |
| Loaded weight | 985 | lb | 447 | kg |
| Wing loading | 10.9 | lb/sq ft | 53.47 | kg/sq m |
| Max speed | 140 | mph | 224 | kmh |
| Cruise speed | 120 | mph | 192 | kmh |
| Stalling speed | 40 | mph | 64 | kmh |
| Climb rate | 1000 | ft/min | 308 | m/min |
| Range | 360 | mls | 576 | km |

A pioneering US kit-plane from the late 1920s designed by 'Ace' Corben and initially powered by motorcycle and Ford Model A car engines. The Baby Ace is a single seater with wooden wings attached to the welded tube fuselage by triangulated struts and a pair of parallel lift struts, powered these days by a Continental A65 (65 hp).

Corben had excellent build plans published in *Mechanix Illustrated* and was one of the first people to supply proper kits of parts.

Close relatives of the Baby Ace are the Junior Ace, side-by-side two seater (Model E) and the latest, first flown in 1956, a refined single seater of almost identical appearance apart from 'V' lift struts in place of the parallel pair. This is the Ace Aircraft Co. of Chesapeake's Model D Baby Ace available as a kit or plans.

Only two are on the UK Register (and one Model E) the Model D is PFA approved.

The Data below is for the Ace Aircraft Model D.

## CORBEN BABY ACE

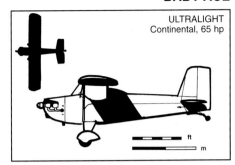

ULTRALIGHT
Continental, 65 hp

| DATA | IMPERIAL | | METRIC | |
|---|---|---|---|---|
| Span | 26.5 | ft | 8.05 | m |
| Wing area | 112 | sq ft | 10.5 | sq m |
| Aspect ratio | 6.3 | | 6.3 | |
| Empty Weight | 575 | lb | 261 | kg |
| Loaded weight | 950 | lb | 431 | kg |
| Wing loading | 8.5 | lb/sq ft | 41.4 | kg/sq m |
| Max speed | 110 | mph | 177 | kmh |
| Cruise speed | 100 | mph | 161 | kmh |
| Stalling speed | 34 | mph | 55 | kmh |
| Climb rate | 1200 | ft/min | 366 | m/min |
| Range | 350 | mls | 563 | km |

The Aircamper was designed by Bernie Pietenpol in 1932 one of the pioneers of the American light plane movement.

Of an extremely simple construction, the plans and instructions on how to build it were serialised in a pre-war flying magazine and many hundreds were made and are still being built.

Suitable aero engines were not available in 1932 so Pietenpol designed the Aircamper around a Model A Ford car engine and the first Aircampers flew with this heavy 40 hp unit. The most common motor became the 85 hp Continental and the performance figures below refer to this type.

It is an all-wood aeroplane with fabric-covered wings and tail unit, all the 'struttery' is metal and the large wheels are usually motorcycle wheels!

One example in the USA has just been retired to a museum after sixty years flying!

There are thirty-five on the Register and others being built.

## PIETENPOL AIRCAMPER

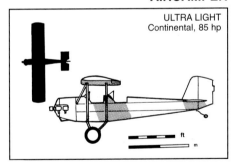

ULTRA LIGHT
Continental, 85 hp

| DATA | IMPERIAL | | METRIC | |
|---|---|---|---|---|
| Span | 29.5 | ft | 9.1 | m |
| Wing area | 140 | sq ft | 13.3 | sq m |
| Aspect ratio | 6.2 | | 6.2 | |
| Empty Weight | 620 | lb | 287 | kg |
| Loaded weight | 1020 | lb | 463 | kg |
| Wing loading | 7.3 | lb/sq ft | 35.6 | kg/sq m |
| Max speed | 85 | mph | 136 | kmh |
| Cruise speed | 75 | mph | 120 | kmh |
| Stalling speed | 40 | mph | 64 | kmh |
| Climb rate | 500 | ft/min | 154 | m/min |
| Range | 200 | mls | 320 | km |

A 1933 aeroplane that was in production at Fairchild's in Maryland, USA, until 1947 when around 1000 had been made. The first models, powered by a 145 hp Warner Scarab radial engine, were three seaters and in 1938 the four seater version with the Super Scarab and 'in line' Ranger engines of 165 and 175 hp went into production.

The fuselage is of welded steel tube with fabric covering over wooden framing and the wing, all wood with fabric aft of the plywood covered leading edge. The sturdy wide track undercarriage is a noteworthy feature.

During WW2 several hundred were delivered to the RAF and ATA under the Lease Lend deal, serving in many war theatres. With peace, many were bought for 'civilianisation' and were sold all over Europe – eight still remain on the UK Register, four of which are flying.

Twenty-five in world museums.

## FAIRCHILD
## F24 ARGUS

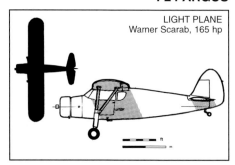

LIGHT PLANE
Warner Scarab, 165 hp

| DATA | IMPERIAL | | METRIC | |
|---|---|---|---|---|
| Span | 36.3 | ft | 11.2 | m |
| Wing area | 173.6 | sq ft | 16.3 | sq m |
| Aspect ratio | 7.6 | | 7.6 | |
| Empty Weight | 1482 | lb | 672 | kg |
| Loaded weight | 2562 | lb | 1163 | kg |
| Wing loading | 14.8 | lb/sq ft | 72 | kg/sq m |
| Max speed | 124 | mph | 198 | kmh |
| Cruise speed | 112 | mph | 179 | kmh |
| Stalling speed | 58 | mph | 93 | kmh |
| Climb rate | 500 | ft/min | 154 | m/min |
| Range | 720 | mls | 1152 | km |

First known in 1933, the three seat DH 85 Leopard Moth was designed as a replacement for the earlier DH 80 Puss Moth, of similar configuration but with a welded steel tube fuselage. In both these Moths the pilot sat centrally in front and the two passengers side by side in the rear.

The construction is all wood with fabric-covered wing and fuselage (over a stressed skin plywood box). The tailplane is wire braced and the 'V' bracing struts are arranged to allow the wings to fold alongside the fuselage.

A total of 132 Leopards were built, pre war, some going into storage but most into communications work with the armed forces during hostilities. Forty-four survived the conflict, many flying again in the immediate post war years and up to the present day.

Seven on the UK Register, four flying and three in world museums.

## DE HAVILAND
## LEOPARD MOTH

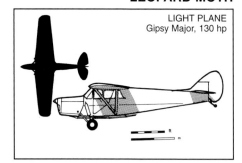

LIGHT PLANE
Gipsy Major, 130 hp

| DATA | IMPERIAL | | METRIC | |
|---|---|---|---|---|
| Span | 37.5 | ft | 11.55 | m |
| Wing area | 206 | sq ft | 19.4 | sq m |
| Aspect ratio | 6.8 | | 6.8 | |
| Empty Weight | 1405 | lb | 638 | kg |
| Loaded weight | 2225 | lb | 1010 | kg |
| Wing loading | 10.8 | lb/sq ft | 52.7 | kg/sq m |
| Max speed | 137 | mph | 219 | kmh |
| Cruise speed | 119 | mph | 190 | kmh |
| Stalling speed | 50 | mph | 80 | kmh |
| Climb rate | 625 | ft/min | 192 | m/min |
| Range | 715 | mls | 1144 | km |

G. N.Wikner, an Australian cousin of Edgar Percival set out to design and build a very cheap cabin two seater. In 1936 with the help of V. Foster the first Wicko was built in London at a furniture factory.

Wikner's cost cutting aims lead him to install a 3.5 litre Ford V8 car engine and it was so powered for its first flight. The 450 lb non-aero engine was an inevitable power/weight penalty and was shortly replaced by a Cirrus Minor of 90 hp.

The structure was all wood with a plywood covered fuselage and wings, dual controls and split trailing edge flaps were standard.

Nine production aircraft were built at Eastleigh fitted now with Gipsy Major engines of 130hp.

All the private Wickos were impressed at the start of WW2 (only one survived with the official name of Warferry!).

Wikner's prototype, stored during the war, was resurrected and flew again briefly, but is no more.

The surviving Wicko, G-AFJB is under restoration and is expected to fly in the year 2004.

## FOSTER WIKNER
# WICKO

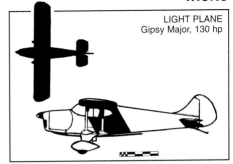

LIGHT PLANE
Gipsy Major, 130 hp

| DATA | IMPERIAL | | METRIC | |
|---|---|---|---|---|
| Span | 34.5 | ft | 10.62 | m |
| Wing area | 153 | sq ft | 14.4 | sq m |
| Aspect ratio | 7.8 | | | |
| Empty Weight | 1255 | lb | 570 | kg |
| Loaded weight | 2000 | lb | 908 | kg |
| Wing loading | 13 | lb/sq ft | 63 | kg/sq m |
| Max speed | 140 | mph | 224 | kmh |
| Cruise speed | 103 | mph | 165 | kmh |
| Stalling speed | 55 | mph | 88 | kmh |
| Climb rate | 800 | ft/min | 246 | m/min |
| Range | 480 | mls | 768 | km |

The Minor first flew in 1936 when it was manufactured by Luton Aircraft Ltd in Bedfordshire to the designs of C. H. Latimer-Needham who had adapted it from the earlier tandem wing experimental aircraft the LA-2. Several were built by home constructors prior to WW2 and in 1960 the design was overhauled and restressed to the latest British Airworthiness Requirements and plans marketed for homebuilders.

The PFA approved design is all wood with plywood and fabric covering.

Plans of this single seater have been sold world-wide and the straightforward construction of this docile aeroplane has attracted many builders with over thirty-two currently on the British Register. Various engines have been fitted, the data below is for the Aeronca JAP J99 hp model.

## LUTON
# MINOR

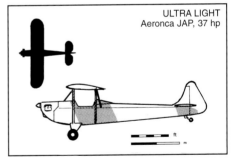

ULTRA LIGHT
Aeronca JAP, 37 hp

| DATA | IMPERIAL | | METRIC | |
|---|---|---|---|---|
| Span | 25 | ft | 7.6 | m |
| Wing area | 125 | sq ft | 11.6 | sq m |
| Aspect ratio | 5 | | 5 | |
| Empty Weight | 390 | lb | 177 | kg |
| Loaded weight | 750 | lb | 340 | kg |
| Wing loading | 6 | lb/sq ft | 29.3 | kg/sq m |
| Max speed | 69 | mph | 111 | kmh |
| Cruise speed | 63 | mph | 102 | kmh |
| Stalling speed | 28 | mph | 45 | kmh |
| Climb rate | 250 | ft/min | 76 | m/min |
| Range | 180 | mls | 290 | km |

The two-seat Silvaire first flew in 1937 a product of the New Jersey company, Luscombe, pioneers in the production techniques of small metal aircraft.

The components were accurately die cut and jigged for true fit and interchangeability. Over 1000 were built pre war (up to 1942) and when production was resumed a further 4660 were made, after various company changes.

The fuselage is an all metal monocoque with side-by-side seating and cantilever main legs, operating on under-floor oleos. Early models had fabric covered wings over metal spars and ribs with 'V' strut bracing. The later models had metal skinned wings and a single strut brace. All control surfaces are covered in a fluted light alloy skin and final variants had a squared-off fin and rudder.

A pretty aeroplane still, its metal structure aiding its longevity. There are an impressive eighty-two on the British Register.

# LUSCOMBE
# SILVAIRE 8E

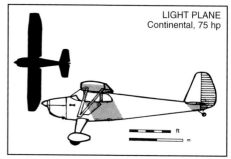

LIGHT PLANE
Continental, 75 hp

| DATA | IMPERIAL | | METRIC | |
|---|---|---|---|---|
| Span | 35 | ft | 10.7 | m |
| Wing area | 140 | sq ft | 13 | sq m |
| Aspect ratio | 8.75 | | 8.75 | |
| Empty Weight | 710 | lb | 322 | kg |
| Loaded weight | 1310 | lb | 594 | kg |
| Wing loading | 9.4 | lb/sq ft | 45.6 | kg/sq m |
| Max speed | 115 | mph | 185 | kmh |
| Cruise speed | 110 | mph | 176 | kmh |
| Stalling speed | 42 | mph | 67 | kmh |
| Climb rate | 900 | ft/min | 274 | m/min |
| Range | 500 | mls | 800 | km |

The Piper Cub range is extensive, all stemming from the E2 Cub of 1931. Manufactured by Taylor Aircraft up until 1937 and moving up to the re-designed J2 and J3, which first flew in 1937, all of which had two seats in tandem, Continental and Lycoming engines of 40 to 60 hp, good economy and small field performance (eighty percent of J3s were fitted with 65 hp Continentals).

The construction of the J3 comprised a welded steel tube fuselage, two wooden (later metal) sparred wings with metal ribs and fabric covering aft of the sheet metal nose, 'V' struts to the lower longerons, and a bungee sprung undercarriage.

20,000 J3 Cubs were made up to 1947, many of them being for the US forces (as the L-4).

105 are on the UK Register, most imported since the war.

Production was resumed after the war and the J3 became the PA 11 Cub Special with wing tankage and fully enclosed engine.

# PIPER
# J3 CUB

LIGHT PLANE
Continental, 65 hp

| DATA | IMPERIAL | | METRIC | |
|---|---|---|---|---|
| Span | 35.2 | ft | 10.8 | m |
| Wing area | 178.5 | sq ft | 16.8 | sq m |
| Aspect ratio | 7 | | 7 | |
| Empty Weight | 750 | lb | 340 | kg |
| Loaded weight | 1220 | lb | 554 | kg |
| Wing loading | 6.8 | lb/sq ft | 33.3 | kg/sq m |
| Max speed | 100 | mph | 160 | kmh |
| Cruise speed | 87 | mph | 140 | kmh |
| Stalling speed | 40 | mph | 64 | kmh |
| Climb rate | 514 | ft/min | 158 | m/min |
| Range | 300 | mls | 480 | km |

Introduced in 1938 the two seat Piper J4 was the first in the Piper range to have side-by-side seating.

Initially powered by a 50 hp Continental with the cylinder heads exposed and later 65 and 75 hp Continentals which were fully cowled.

Other refinements over its predecessor, the famous J3 Cub were hydraulic brakes, navigation lights and improved instrumentation. Trailing edge flaps were still a model or two away.

Production continued up to WW2 and twenty, then in the UK, were impressed into the RAF. Only five survived the war. Production was resumed after the war.

The structure, like the J3, comprises a welded steel tube fuselage, wooden sparred wings and built-up light alloy ribs under a fabric covering. Lycoming engines from 50 to 75 hp are fitted.

Many are still flying in the USA and though less numerous than the legendary J3 there are still a handful on our Register.

# PIPER
# J4 CUB COUPE

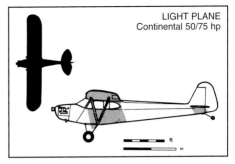

LIGHT PLANE
Continental 50/75 hp

| DATA | IMPERIAL | | METRIC | |
|---|---|---|---|---|
| Span | 36.15 | ft | 11.1 | m |
| Wing area | 183.75 | sq ft | 17.38 | sq m |
| Aspect ratio | 7.1 | | 7.1 | |
| Empty Weight | 865 | lb | 393 | kg |
| Loaded weight | 1400 | lb | 636 | kg |
| Wing loading | 7.6 | lb/sq ft | 37.2 | kg/sq m |
| Max speed | 100 | mph | 160 | kmh |
| Cruise speed | 96 | mph | 154 | kmh |
| Stalling speed | 42 | mph | 67 | kmh |
| Climb rate | 450 | ft/min | 139 | m/min |
| Range | 455 | mls | 728 | km |

In 1938 a British firm, Taylorcraft Aeroplanes (England) Ltd was formed to manufacture under licence the successful two-seat, side-by-side high winger designed and built in the USA by the Taylor Young Airplane Corp of Ohio.

The Taylorcraft company produced twenty-two before the outbreak of WW2 when, after Air Ministry trials, 100 were ordered for communication duties. About half of these survived the war to become civil registered again.

In 1946 the company name was changed to Auster Aircraft Ltd under who's initiative over 400 different Taylorcraft/Auster variants were produced in the immediate post war years.

Taylorcraft in the USA resumed production after the war and, after many management changes are still in business.

There are eight of the Plus Ds on the UK Register.

# TAYLORCRAFT
# PLUS D

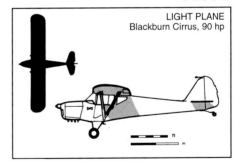

LIGHT PLANE
Blackburn Cirrus, 90 hp

| DATA | IMPERIAL | | METRIC | |
|---|---|---|---|---|
| Span | 36 | ft | 11.1 | m |
| Wing area | 167 | sq ft | 15.7 | sq m |
| Aspect ratio | 7.7 | | 7.7 | |
| Empty Weight | 890 | lb | 404 | kg |
| Loaded weight | 1450 | lb | 658 | kg |
| Wing loading | 8.7 | lb/sq ft | 42.4 | kg/sq m |
| Max speed | 120 | mph | 192 | kmh |
| Cruise speed | 102 | mph | 163 | kmh |
| Stalling speed | 45 | mph | 72 | kmh |
| Climb rate | 1000 | ft/min | 308 | m/min |
| Range | 325 | mls | 520 | km |

The American Taylorcraft company had been making small aeroplanes since 1936 with welded tube fuselages, wooden spar wings, all fabric covering which came in models A, B, C and D.

In 1939 a Model B was used as the basis for Taylorcraft (England) Ltd's first product, typed Model C but soon altered to Plus C. These were built on American jigs but with beefed up tubing to meet British ARB requirements. Initially powered by a 55 hp Lycoming, they were re-engined with Cirrus Minors of 90 hp for Army use and re-styled as the Plus C/2 and then Plus D.

The Lycoming models were clearly under-powered after the British modifications had increased the weight.

The blurring of Model C to Plus C to Plus C/2 and then D make tracing the history dependent on contract number identification rather than registration or engine type.

See page 17 for Auster history.

LIGHT PLANE
Lycoming, 55 hp

| DATA | IMPERIAL | | METRIC | |
|------|----------|--|--------|--|
| Span | 36 | ft | 11.1 | m |
| Wing area | 185 | sq ft | 17.4 | sq m |
| Aspect ratio | 7 | | 7 | |
| Empty Weight | 812 | lb | 368 | kg |
| Loaded weight | 1218 | lb | 553 | kg |
| Wing loading | 6.6 | lb/sq ft | 32 | kg/sq m |
| Max speed | 85 | mph | 136 | kmh |
| Cruise speed | 74 | mph | 118 | kmh |
| Stalling speed | 30 | mph | 48 | kmh |
| Climb rate | 350 | ft/min | 108 | m/min |
| Range | 210 | mls | 336 | km |

In production from 1944 as AOPs (Air Observation Post) over 1000 were built and many are still flying today in civilian guise.

The Auster 4 (or Model G) was powered by a Lycoming engine of 125 hp which gave it a cruising speed of 110 mph. Improvements over it's predecessor (the Mk 3) included, a third seat, improved cabin glazing involving lowering the top longeron for better rear view, a tail wheel in place of a skid and a 'proper' fuel gauge in place of the float and vertical wire poking up from the tank in front of the windscreen. The Auster 5 (Model J) was a Mk 4 with a blind flying panel and an elevator mounted trim tab replacing the trimming 'paddle' beneath the tailplane. When civilianised models were re-engined with Gipsy Major 1s (130 hp) they became Mk 5 Ds.

Of standard Auster construction, welded tube fuselage, wooden wing spars with metal ribs all fabric covered, they had split trailing edge flaps and navigation lights, but no engine starter.

The soundness of the basic Taylorcraft/Auster design and its enduring airworthiness have ensured that these veterans still grace our skies half a century after leaving the factory.

There are approximately forty-three still on the Register. Details below are for the Mk 5.

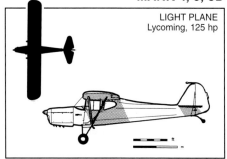

LIGHT PLANE
Lycoming, 125 hp

| DATA | IMPERIAL | | METRIC | |
|------|----------|--|--------|--|
| Span | 36 | ft | 11 | m |
| Wing area | 185 | sq ft | 17.4 | sq m |
| Aspect ratio | 7 | | 7 | |
| Empty Weight | 1160 | lb | 526 | kg |
| Loaded weight | 1850 | lb | 840 | kg |
| Wing loading | 10 | lb/sq ft | 48.8 | kg/sq m |
| Max speed | 130 | mph | 208 | kmh |
| Cruise speed | 110 | mph | 176 | kmh |
| Stalling speed | 30 | mph | 48 | kmh |
| Climb rate | 720 | ft/min | 222 | m/min |
| Range | 250 | mls | 400 | km |

A pre-WW2 design that first flew in 1939, the two seat Major was derived from the single seat Minor and used many of the latter's components.

Both aircraft were creations of C. H. Latimer-Needham the prolific pre-war British light plane designer.

The pre-war and immediate post-war aircraft were powered by 62 hp Walter Microns while later versions used 65/85 hp Continentals.

The design rights were acquired by Phoenix Aircraft in 1958 and after some Airworthiness hikes, marketed as a 'plans only' homebuilt.

Construction is all wood, the strut braced wings having two spars and fabric covering aft of the main spar, the nose being plywood covered. The fuselage is wooden with plywood covering and the tail surfaces are fabric covered.

A PFA approved design with only one on the Register, and is flying in Ireland and others are being restored.

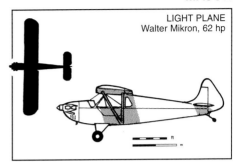

LIGHT PLANE
Walter Mikron, 62 hp

| DATA | IMPERIAL | | METRIC | |
|---|---|---|---|---|
| Span | 35.15 | ft | 10.72 | m |
| Wing area | 163 | sq ft | 15.3 | sq m |
| Aspect ratio | 7.6 | | 7.6 | |
| Empty Weight | 600 | lb | 272 | kg |
| Loaded weight | 1100 | lb | 500 | kg |
| Wing loading | 6.7 | lb/sq ft | 33 | kg/sq m |
| Max speed | 105 | mph | 169 | kmh |
| Cruise speed | 95 | mph | 153 | kmh |
| Stalling speed | 35 | mph | 56 | kmh |
| Climb rate | 700 | ft/min | 213 | m/min |
| Range | 300 | mls | 483 | km |

# AUSTER – AN OUTLINE

The roots of Auster are American. The North American firm The Taylorcraft Aviation Company was formed in 1936 and built side-by-side, two seat, high wingers with welded tube fuselages and wooden spar wings with metal ribs, all fabric covered. they came in Models A, B, C and D and just before WW2 a few were imported into the UK, six Model As with a 40 hp Continental and one Model B.

The type proved popular and British Taylorcraft was formed at Thurmaston to build the American Model A under licence, strengthened to British Airworthiness Standards and re-engined with a 55 hp Lycoming, as the Model C, soon renamed Plus C.

Twenty-three Plus Cs were built along with nine Plus Ds (90 hp Cirrus Minor 1) before the war began in 1939.

Practically all these early British Taylorcrafts were impressed into Army Co-operation work after all the American engines had been replaced with the Cirrus. An order for 100 was placed, initially, and the name Auster was coined – a gentle wind. Over 1600 followed that initial order, Marks 1, 3, 4 and 5 doing sterling work in the battlefields of Europe and North Africa. Mark 5s, a Mark 4 with a blind flying panel, were the most numerous with approximately 800 produced.

Note: Strictly classifying the war time Austers one should use Roman numerals for the Mark numbers, but I have stuck to Arabic throughout.

After the war the firm, renamed Auster Aircraft Ltd, entered the civilian market with the J1 Autocrat and became the only post war British firm to manufacture and export light aircraft in quantity.

Many WW2 4s and 5s are still flying along with the numerous later models, all enthusiastically watched over by the International Auster Pilots Club.

Investment and foresight in aviation were sadly lacking in the early 1960s and Auster began to break up, becoming, briefly Beagle-Auster and in 1962 the name Auster disappeared.

The AOP 6 is also designated Auster 6 and Auster Model K.

Powered by Gipsy Major of 145 hp the AOP 6 followed the Auster 5 in to military service, 379 being made during the years 1946 to 1953, a fair number of these retiring into civilian roles (fifteen on the UK Register).

The AOP 6 was the first production Auster to have the one piece moulded windscreen in place of the multi panelled type.

Operated as a two seater with a rear space taken up by a bulky service radio the AOP 6 had Mk 5 type rear glazing and metal auxiliary aerofoil flaps (permanently extended).

The type saw service in most of the post war hot spots including Palestine, Korea and Malaya.

A two seat dual trainer version was typed as the Mk 7 (or Mk 10) and 87 were made between 1949 and 1952.

Mk 6s and 7s were fitted with floats, skis and long range tanks for Antarctic exploration in the '50s. (The float planes have a ventral fin to counter the forward float area).

Sixteen Mk 6s were modified as glider tugs and called Tugmasters.

Six AOPs and six Tugmasters exist.

## AUSTER AOP 6

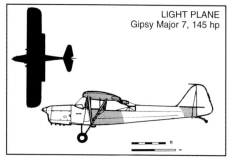

LIGHT PLANE
Gipsy Major 7, 145 hp

| DATA | IMPERIAL | | METRIC | |
|---|---|---|---|---|
| Span | 36 | ft | 11.1 | m |
| Wing area | 185 | sq ft | 17.4 | sq m |
| Aspect ratio | 7 | | 7 | |
| Empty Weight | 1423 | lb | 641 | kg |
| Loaded weight | 2147 | lb | 975 | kg |
| Wing loading | 11.6 | lb/sq ft | 56.6 | kg/sq m |
| Max speed | 124 | mph | 199 | kmh |
| Cruise speed | 107 | mph | 171 | kmh |
| Stalling speed | 37 | mph | 59 | kmh |
| Climb rate | 737 | ft/min | 227 | m/min |
| Range | 345 | mls | 552 | km |

Virtually a J2 with a Cirrus Minor 1 engine of 90 hp, it was a two seater with a straight topped rear fuselage and no flaps.

Only twenty-six were built over a period of twelve years (1946-1958) most going overseas. (Referred to as the J4 Archer, the J4 was, in fact, never officially named).

J4s followed the standard Auster construction practice, ie welded tube fuselage twin wooden sparred wings with fabricated metal ribs, all fabric covered and a bungee sprung undercarriage.

In 1951 a J4 made the headlines by taking off pilotless, whilst being started, and flying for two hours reaching 8000 feet and only crashing when it ran out of fuel! A tribute to its inherent stability. (A similar incident happened in Australia in 1955, also a J4!)

There are four on the UK Register.

## AUSTER J4 ARCHER

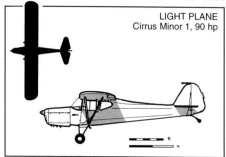

LIGHT PLANE
Cirrus Minor 1, 90 hp

| DATA | IMPERIAL | | METRIC | |
|---|---|---|---|---|
| Span | 36 | ft | 11.1 | m |
| Wing area | 185 | sq ft | 17.4 | sq m |
| Aspect ratio | 7 | | 7 | |
| Empty Weight | 957 | lb | 434 | kg |
| Loaded weight | 1600 | lb | 726 | kg |
| Wing loading | 8.6 | lb/sq ft | 42 | kg/sq m |
| Max speed | 110 | mph | 176 | kmh |
| Cruise speed | 95 | mph | 152 | kmh |
| Stalling speed | 37 | mph | 59 | kmh |
| Climb rate | 700 | ft/min | 215 | m/min |
| Range | 320 | mls | 512 | km |

After the hundreds of camouflaged spotter planes, Auster 3s, 4s and 5s , rolled out a Rearsby and Thurmaston during WW2, the peace came and with it the first civilian Auster, the J1 Autocrat.

Development from the Auster 5, the Autocrat had a one piece moulded windscreen, split trailing edge flaps, three seats and was powered by the economical Cirrus Minor 2 of 100 hp.

It was in production from 1946 to 1953, during which period 414 were made, many going for export.

An Autocrat that blazed the Auster name in the world of aviation was G-AERO, owned by the magazine *The Aeroplane*, it was seldom out of the news, ie for landing on HMS Illustrious, and must have been a great salesman.

The J1A version had a bench type rear seat making it the first four seat Auster and re-engined with 130 hp. Gipsy Majors or Lycomings it became the J-1N Alpha.

There are approximately seventy-six on the UK Register, details below are for the J1.

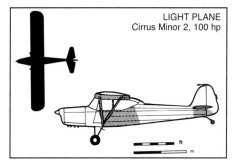

LIGHT PLANE
Cirrus Minor 2, 100 hp

| DATA | IMPERIAL | | METRIC | |
|---|---|---|---|---|
| Span | 36 | ft | 11 | m |
| Wing area | 185 | sq ft | 17.1 | sq m |
| Aspect ratio | 7 | | 7 | |
| Empty Weight | 1052 | lb | 476 | kg |
| Loaded weight | 1850 | lb | 840 | kg |
| Wing loading | 10 | lb/sq ft | 49 | kg/sq m |
| Max speed | 120 | mph | 193 | kmh |
| Cruise speed | 100 | mph | 160 | kmh |
| Stalling speed | 30 | mph | 48 | kmh |
| Climb rate | 560 | ft/min | 180 | m/min |
| Range | 220 | mls | 354 | km |

The charming little Nord 858 always makes me smile. A shoulder wing two seater from SNCAC which originated from a 1946 design competition as the NC 850. Though not the winner, an order for 100 was placed for the 853 variant which had twin fins and a Minie engine of 80hp.

Taken over by SNCAN in 1949 in mid production the 853 continued with the addition of an 'S' to its type number (NC858S) and ninety-five were finally completed. Various models followed with seating and engine changes but generally of the same configuration. The NC858, shown in the drawing and photos, is the model with the Continental C90 of 90 hp – the earlier 854 had a 65 hp Continental and many Minie powered 853s were re-engined with Continentals.

A single strut braces the round tipped wing to the steel tube, fabric covered, fuselage and the main identification feature, the twin finned tailplane, also braced with a single strut. Other features are the well glazed cabin and the external undercarriage shock strut.

There are nine 858s and variants on the UK Register.

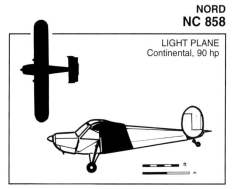

LIGHT PLANE
Continental, 90 hp

| DATA | IMPERIAL | | METRIC | |
|---|---|---|---|---|
| Span | 37 | ft | 11.3 | m |
| Wing area | 166 | sq ft | 15.6 | sq m |
| Aspect ratio | 8.2 | | 8.2 | |
| Empty Weight | 863 | lb | 392 | kg |
| Loaded weight | 1480 | lb | 672 | kg |
| Wing loading | 8.9 | lb/sq ft | 43.5 | kg/sq m |
| Max speed | 114 | mph | 182 | kmh |
| Cruise speed | 97 | mph | 155 | kmh |
| Stalling speed | 45 | mph | 72 | kmh |
| Climb rate | 850 | ft/min | 261 | m/min |
| Range | 280 | mls | 448 | km |

In production from 1946 to 1952 the J2 Arrow was a two seater with a fuselage that reverted to the straight top longeron (ie no fuselage tadpoling) and was powered by a 75 hp Continental engine.

Designed down, as a less expensive club and private-owner aeroplane the Arrow had no flaps and a production run of forty-four, the majority going abroad.

A pretty aeroplane that harked back to the pre war Taylorcrafts.

A 65 hp Continental engined version named the J2 Atom was under-powered. Only one was flown and that was destroyed in a gale at Rearsby in 1947.

Some later Austers had belly fuel tanks for increased range – the Arrow had a cylindrical tank in the cabin roof.

Two J2s are on the UK Register, two are airworthy and one won Best Classic Aircraft at the 1999 PFA Rally.

See page 17 for Auster history.

## AUSTER
# J2 ARROW

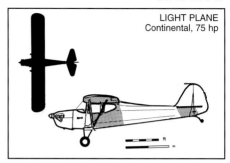

LIGHT PLANE
Continental, 75 hp

| DATA | IMPERIAL | | METRIC | |
|---|---|---|---|---|
| Span | 36 | ft | 11.1 | m |
| Wing area | 185 | sq ft | 17.4 | sq m |
| Aspect ratio | 7 | | 7 | |
| Empty Weight | 872 | lb | 396 | kg |
| Loaded weight | 1450 | lb | 658 | kg |
| Wing loading | 7.8 | lb/sq ft | 38 | kg/sq m |
| Max speed | 98 | mph | 257 | kmh |
| Cruise speed | 87 | mph | 139 | kmh |
| Stalling speed | 35 | mph | 56 | kmh |
| Climb rate | 510 | ft/min | 157 | m/min |
| Range | 320 | mls | 512 | km |

A post WW2 development of the 1940 J5 Cub Cruiser with increased tankage, cowled cylinders and tidier interior. As in the J5 the pilot sat in the front and the two passengers, side-by-side, behind him/her.

The PA 12 was in production from 1946 to 1948 during which time over 3500 were made, in spite of the recession of 1947. The fuselages were welded steel tube and the wings had metal ribs threaded over wooden spars, the whole being fabric covered. The PA 12 was the first Cub to have the less draggy gear with internal bungees rather than the external leather bungee strut bags.

The PA 14, a close relative, had seating for four and a 115 hp Lycoming engine.

Approximately 1700 are flying in the USA and eight are still on the UK/Eire Register. All the early Pipers have Fan Clubs and many books have been written about the company which was founded by Bill Piper in 1930 when he took over Taylor Brothers Aircraft Corp.

## PIPER
# PA 12 SUPER CRUISER

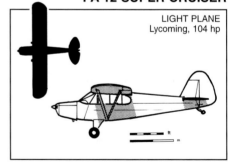

LIGHT PLANE
Lycoming, 104 hp

| DATA | IMPERIAL | | METRIC | |
|---|---|---|---|---|
| Span | 35.5 | ft | 11 | m |
| Wing area | 179.3 | sq ft | 16.8 | sq m |
| Aspect ratio | 7 | | 7 | |
| Empty Weight | 950 | lb | 431 | kg |
| Loaded weight | 1750 | lb | 794 | kg |
| Wing loading | 9.8 | lb/sq ft | 46.6 | kg/sq m |
| Max speed | 115 | mph | 184 | kmh |
| Cruise speed | 105 | mph | 168 | kmh |
| Stalling speed | *50* | mph | *80* | kmh |
| Climb rate | 510 | ft/min | 157 | m/min |
| Range | 600 | mls | 960 | km |

The all-metal Beaver which was produced by De Haviland of Canada carries a pilot and six passengers and is powered by a 450 hp Pratt and Whitney Wasp Junior.

A rugged bush aircraft capable of operating on floats, skis and wheels. The Beaver first flew in 1947 and was snapped up by the US Air Force who ordered 970 of them. Beavers were supplied to many other air forces and operators and 1,692 were built before production ceased in 1968. (This includes the later Turbo Beaver eleven seater).

Five acquired UK civil registrations, DH's own G-ALOW and the others, ex-military, included G-BUVF, currently based and flying in the Netherlands. Four are static in UK collections.

The sole Beaver 2, manufactured in 1953, G-ANAR, which has an Alvis Leonides of 550 hp returned to Canada in 1971.

The Beaver, a big success, led to demand for a Super Beaver, the DHC 3 Otter of which 465 were built.

# DE HAVILAND CANADA
# BEAVER

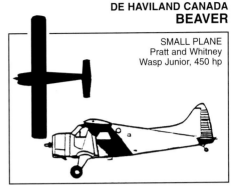

SMALL PLANE
Pratt and Whitney
Wasp Junior, 450 hp

| DATA | IMPERIAL | | METRIC | |
|---|---|---|---|---|
| Span | 48 | ft | 15 | m |
| Wing area | 250 | sq ft | 23.5 | sq m |
| Aspect ratio | 9.2 | | 9.2 | |
| Empty Weight | 2810 | lb | 1275 | kg |
| Loaded weight | 4820 | lb | 2188 | kg |
| Wing loading | 19.3 | lb/sq ft | 94.2 | kg/sq m |
| Max speed | 179 | mph | 286 | kmh |
| Cruise speed | 137 | mph | 219 | kmh |
| Stalling speed | 60 | mph | 96 | kmh |
| Climb rate | 1020 | ft/min | 314 | m/min |
| Range | 455 | mls | 728 | km |

One of the first of the long line of Cessna monocoque high wingers, the 170 was a four seater development of the two seater 120/140 and it first flew in 1947 with a Continental C145 engine of 145 hp.

Early 170s had fabric covered 'V' strutted, parallel chord wings and no dorsal in extension. From 1948 the 170As had all metal, single strut braced half span tapered wings and a fin dorsal extension.

With the 170B came bigger flaps and the 0-300 series Continental, still 145 hp and from 1955 amongst other refinements, larger rear windows.

Over 5000 170s were built between 1949 and 1956 and were to lead to the famous trike geared Cessna 172. it is interesting to note that a new 170 cost $8000 and today a forty year old one would set you back $20000. Bob Grimstead flew a 170 for *Pilot* and wrote '...this is a pilot's aeroplane, handling in the air is 'classic' as befits its generation... on the ground... in a cross wind, it is 'stimulating'.

There are four on the UK Register, two are airworthy.

# CESSNA
# MODEL 170

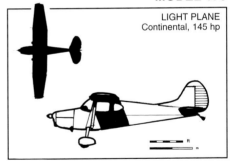

LIGHT PLANE
Continental, 145 hp

| DATA | IMPERIAL | | METRIC | |
|---|---|---|---|---|
| Span | 36 | ft | 11.1 | m |
| Wing area | 174 | sq ft | 16.3 | sq m |
| Aspect ratio | 7.4 | | 7.4 | |
| Empty Weight | 1425 | lb | 646 | kg |
| Loaded weight | 2200 | lb | 999 | kg |
| Wing loading | 12.6 | lb/sq ft | 61.5 | kg/sq m |
| Max speed | 135 | mph | 216 | kmh |
| Cruise speed | 120 | mph | 192 | kmh |
| Stalling speed | 52 | mph | 83 | kmh |
| Climb rate | 660 | ft/min | 203 | m/min |
| Range | 495 | mls | 792 | km |

Reminiscent of the big radial engined high wingers of the 1930s – the Stinsons, the Howard DGA 'Mr Muligan' – the Cessna 190/195 was a 'throw back'. It first appeared in 1947, an all-metal cantilevered wing, five seater that was in production for six years during which time about 1000 were made.

Powered by Continental or Jacobs radials in the 240-300 hp band, the C195 was, in its day, no sluggard, cruising at 170 mph and climbing at over 1000 fpm. The view from the cockpit is notoriously bad and the big radials are thirsty and take some looking after but they sound fabulous.

Although 1000 were made, this was a poor take up by Cessna standards and those that did sell went to commercial bush and survey operators, plus a batch of twenty to the US Air force. It was too clunky and thirsty for the private market.

There are two on the UK Register and are both flying.

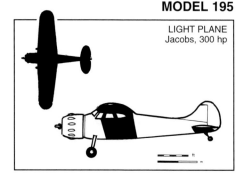

## CESSNA
## MODEL 195

LIGHT PLANE
Jacobs, 300 hp

| DATA | IMPERIAL | | METRIC | |
|---|---|---|---|---|
| Span | 36.2 | ft | 11.1 | m |
| Wing area | 218 | sq ft | 20.5 | sq m |
| Aspect ratio | 6 | | 6 | |
| Empty Weight | 2100 | lb | 953 | kg |
| Loaded weight | 3350 | lb | 1521 | kg |
| Wing loading | 15.48 | lb/sq ft | 75 | kg/sq m |
| Max speed | 200 | mph | 320 | kmh |
| Cruise speed | 174 | mph | 278 | kmh |
| Stalling speed | 62 | mph | 99 | kmh |
| Climb rate | 1135 | ft/min | 350 | m/min |
| Range | 805 | mls | 1288 | km |

The Aeronautical Corporation of America, or Aeronca was founded in 1929 and its most famous pre war design was the C3 'Flying Bathtub', of which many are still flying,

During the war they produced a tandem two seater, strut braced high wing monoplane, the L3B, for the American forces.

After the war they produced three models, the Champion, with tandem seats, the Chief with side-by-side seats and the Sedan, a four seater. Over 7000 of these types were made before Aeronca ceased production in 1951. The Chief has a fabric covered welded steel tube fuselage and wings with pressed aluminium ribs threaded over two fabric covered wooden spars. The undercarriage, in an era of bungee springing, had the luxury of oleo sprung legs and the cockpit has the air of a 1940s car with dual wheels and a glove pocket. A fifty year old gem!

Twenty-one are on the UK Register.

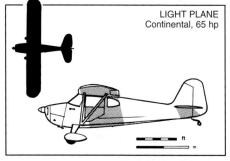

## AERONCA
## MODEL 11, CHIEF

LIGHT PLANE
Continental, 65 hp

| DATA | IMPERIAL | | METRIC | |
|---|---|---|---|---|
| Span | 36 | ft | 11.1 | m |
| Wing area | 175 | sq ft | 16.4 | sq m |
| Aspect ratio | 7.4 | | 7.4 | |
| Empty Weight | 770 | lb | 350 | kg |
| Loaded weight | 1250 | lb | 567 | kg |
| Wing loading | 7.14 | lb/sq ft | 34.8 | kg/sq m |
| Max speed | 95 | mph | 152 | kmh |
| Cruise speed | 85 | mph | 136 | kmh |
| Stalling speed | 42 | mph | 67 | kmh |
| Climb rate | 400 | ft/min | 123 | m/min |
| Range | 260 | mls | 416 | km |

A pre WW2 civil two seater that was adapted for military use as the L-5 Sentinel in which guise it was in production throughout the war with a bigger fin and extra cabin glazing.

In 1949 the original Stinson company having gone through several changes of management (Vultee, Consolidated, Convair) was finally tied in with Piper who updated and re-engined the Model 10 Voyager as a four seater and produced seven variants – building a total of approx 5,000 including the Flying Station Wagon two seat hauler.

The construction is standard 'rag and pipe' with a metal wing structure under fabric tail surfaces, ailerons and flaps are metal skinned. The undercarriage has hydraulic shock struts and disc brakes and flying controls are by push rod.

Now a bit of a collectors item (there are five variants on the UK Register) those who have flown it proclaim its good manners.

## STINSON VOYAGER

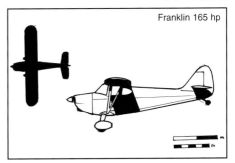

Franklin 165 hp

Stinson 108 Station Wagon

| DATA | IMPERIAL | | METRIC | |
|---|---|---|---|---|
| Span | 33 | ft | 10 | m |
| Wing area | 155 | sq ft | 14.6 | sq m |
| Aspect ratio | 7 | | 7 | |
| Empty Weight | 1294 | lb | 587 | kg |
| Loaded weight | 2400 | lb | 1089 | kg |
| Wing loading | 15.5 | lb/sq ft | 75 | kg/sq m |
| Max speed | 145 | mph | 232 | kmh |
| Cruise speed | 130 | mph | 208 | kmh |
| Stalling speed | 49 | mph | 78.4 | kmh |
| Climb rate | 1000 | ft/min | 304 | m/min |
| Range | 554 | mls | 886 | km |

After WW2 Cessna, allegedly, after taking a long look at the Luscombe produced two new models, the 120 and the 140. These were two seaters with stressed skin monocoque fuselages and fabric covered wings braced with 'V' struts. Both models had the then unique spring steel cantilever undercarriage legs (a Steve Wittman patent) and 85 hp Continental engines. The 140 was an up market version of the 120 and had additional windows, flaps and an electric starter.

The all metal wing, tapered from half span and braced by a single strut came in 1948 with the 140A and were to become a Cessna trade mark.

Over 7000 Cessna 120/140s were built plus 500 140As.

The Cessna 170, a four seater version of the 140A went on to become the 172, one of the all time world best sellers.

There are forty-two Cessna 120/140s on the UK Register and five of the much prized 170s.

## CESSNA MODEL 120/140

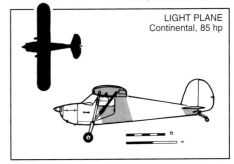

LIGHT PLANE
Continental, 85 hp

| DATA | IMPERIAL | | METRIC | |
|---|---|---|---|---|
| Span | 32.8 | ft | 10.1 | m |
| Wing area | 160 | sq ft | 15 | sq m |
| Aspect ratio | 6.5 | | 6.5 | |
| Empty Weight | 800 | lb | 363 | kg |
| Loaded weight | 1450 | lb | 658 | kg |
| Wing loading | 9 | lb/sq ft | 4.4 | kg/sq m |
| Max speed | 120 | mph | 192 | kmh |
| Cruise speed | 105 | mph | 168 | kmh |
| Stalling speed | 50 | mph | 80 | kmh |
| Climb rate | 550 | ft/min | 880 | m/min |
| Range | 450 | mls | 720 | km |

The T29 Motor Tutor first flew in 1948 and was intended for ATC use, though as a single seater this must have limited its training role.

The all wood wings and tail were those of Slingsby's T8 glider and the fuselage design and construction was carried out by Martin Heath Ltd, who built Slingsby gliders under licence. The glider skid was replaced by a conventional undercarriage.

Two prototypes were built and an order placed by the ULAA (the PFA predecessor) for six more. These were only partially completed when the order was cancelled. The fuselages of these incomplete aircraft were taken up by various other builders and appeared as complete aeroplanes in later years.

These hybrids were made without Slingsby drawings and embody many variations.

With the release of ex-ATC T31 Tandem Tutor gliders, several rebuilds to single seat Motor Tutor are current with others still under conversion mainly powered by VW 1834 cc engines.

There are seventeen Motor Tutor variants on the UK Register, only four of which appear to be airworthy.

**SLINGSBY**
# MOTOR TUTOR

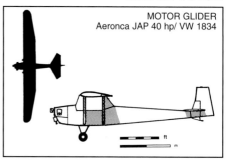

MOTOR GLIDER
Aeronca JAP 40 hp/ VW 1834

| DATA | IMPERIAL | | METRIC | |
|---|---|---|---|---|
| Span | 43.3 | ft | 13.3 | m |
| Wing area | 200 | sq ft | 18.8 | sq m |
| Aspect ratio | 9.4 | | 9.4 | |
| Empty Weight | 555 | lb | 252 | kg |
| Loaded weight | 800 | lb | 363 | kg |
| Wing loading | 4 | lb/sq ft | 19.5 | kg/sq m |
| Max speed | 75 | mph | 120 | kmh |
| Cruise speed | 654 | mph | 104 | kmh |
| Stalling speed | 28 | mph | 45 | kmh |
| Climb rate | 250 | ft/min | 77 | m/min |
| Range | 200 | mls | 320 | km |

Using war surplus Cub wings, shortened by six feet, the PA 15 Vagabond was Piper's first post war product. A utility design, powered by the economic Lycoming O-145-B engine of nominal 65 hp. The Vagabond, originally the Cub Vagabond, was only in production for two years in which time 387 were sold.

The PA 17 Vagabond Trainer, or Vagabond de Luxe, followed, having dual controls, improved instrumentation and comfort, plus a Cub type bungee sprung undercarriage (the PA 15 relied on low pressure tyres) and a Continental A65 engine of 65 hp.

Many original PA 15s were upgraded to PA 17 standard.

Construction comprised fabric covered welded tube fuselage, wooden or metal spar wings with pressed alloy ribs, fabric covered aft on the metal nosing. The tailplane is wire braced.

There are thirty PA 15/17s on the UK Register and the data below is for the PA 17.

**PIPER**
# PA 15 VAGABOND

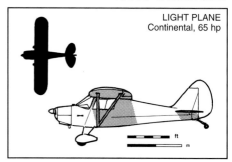

LIGHT PLANE
Continental, 65 hp

| DATA | IMPERIAL | | METRIC | |
|---|---|---|---|---|
| Span | 29.3 | ft | 9 | m |
| Wing area | 147.5 | sq ft | 13.8 | sq m |
| Aspect ratio | 5.8 | | 5.8 | |
| Empty Weight | 695 | lb | 315 | kg |
| Loaded weight | 1150 | lb | 522 | kg |
| Wing loading | 7.8 | lb/sq ft | 38 | kg/sq m |
| Max speed | 100 | mph | 160 | kmh |
| Cruise speed | 90 | mph | 144 | kmh |
| Stalling speed | 48 | mph | 77 | kmh |
| Climb rate | 500 | ft/min | 154 | m/min |
| Range | 247 | mls | 395 | km |

The family of Cubs, Super Cubs, Super Cruisers etc, is a legion and goes right back to 1931 when it was the Taylor E2 Cub and in 1938 with the everlasting, exposed cylinders, J3 Cub. Over the years 40,000 Cubs of all types have been produced and are flying all over the world.

PA 18 Cub was the first post WW2 design to roll out of the Piper factory in Pennsylvania in 1949 and went on to produce some 20,000 aircraft.

The Super Cub is a tandem two seater, like the pre war Cubs, and is built on standard American lines. Welded tube fuselage, two wooden wing spars, threaded with light alloy girder ribs, the whole being fabric covered. Trailing edge flaps were fitted on some models and the landing gear is a bungee sprung split axle with steerable tail wheel.

An easy and forgiving aeroplane to fly with a well proven airframe requiring the minium of maintenance.

There are 129 on the UK Register.

# PIPER
## PA 18 SUPER CUB

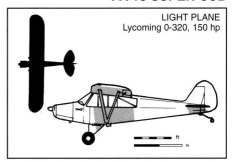

LIGHT PLANE
Lycoming 0-320, 150 hp

| DATA | IMPERIAL | | METRIC | |
|---|---|---|---|---|
| Span | 35.2 | ft | 10.8 | m |
| Wing area | 178.5 | sq ft | 16.8 | sq m |
| Aspect ratio | 7 | | 7 | |
| Empty Weight | 930 | lb | 422 | kg |
| Loaded weight | 1750 | lb | 794 | kg |
| Wing loading | 9.8 | lb/sq ft | 47.8 | kg/sq m |
| Max speed | 130 | mph | 208 | kmh |
| Cruise speed | 104 | mph | 166 | kmh |
| Stalling speed | 45 | mph | 72 | kmh |
| Climb rate | 960 | ft/min | 296 | m/min |
| Range | 460 | mls | 736 | km |

The military Bird Dog used the civil Cessna 170s wings, tail unit and undercarriage. It was a tandem two seater as opposed to a 2x2 four seater. The engine was a 213 hp Continental in place of the 170s 145 hp unit and it had a 'joy-stick' instead of a control wheel. The airframe was all metal with big flaps and good STOL performance with AOP style extensive cabin glazing to give 360˚ vision, and, in ground attack style, four under-wing rocket pylons.

First flown as Model 305A in 1950, its military designations were variations on 0-1 and L19 including turbo versions (XL19B and XL19C) and trainer (TO-1D).

Built under licence in Japan and used by many foreign air forces, the Bird Dog saw service in Korea and when production ceased in 1958 over 3000 had been made.

De-mobbed in 1967 this rugged, little leaper was snapped up by civilian buyers. Approximately 150 are still flying, but only two in the UK. One is static at Middle Wallop).

# CESSNA
## BIRD DOG

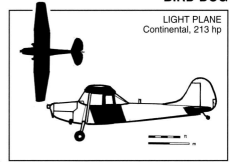

LIGHT PLANE
Continental, 213 hp

| DATA | IMPERIAL | | METRIC | |
|---|---|---|---|---|
| Span | 36 | ft | 11.1 | m |
| Wing area | 174 | sq ft | 16.3 | sq m |
| Aspect ratio | 7.4 | | 7.4 | |
| Empty Weight | 1614 | lb | 7322 | kg |
| Loaded weight | 2430 | lb | 1103 | kg |
| Wing loading | 13.9 | lb/sq ft | 68 | kg/sq m |
| Max speed | 115 | mph | 184 | kmh |
| Cruise speed | 104 | mph | 166 | kmh |
| Stalling speed | 35 | mph | 56 | kmh |
| Climb rate | 1150 | ft/min | 354 | m/min |
| Range | 530 | mls | 848 | km |

The two seat, 65 hp Vagabond, the first of the short winged Pipers, was joined by a four seat version, initially named PA 16 Clipper – Pan Am objected and the type was re-designed and re-named the PA 20 Pacer. The Pacer, as well as four seats, had flaps, a larger tail plane with horn balanced elevator, increased tankage and dual control wheels in place of sticks. In production from 1950 to 1954, over 1000 Pacers were built, initially with the 125 hp Lycoming, a few later models had a 115 hp Lycoming. The PA 20-135 had a 135 hp Lycoming engine and a two position Aeromatic prop.

The Tricycle gear version, the PA 22 Pacer, in production from 1951-63, is often regressed to tail wheel configuration, such is the lure of the tail dragger.

The Pacer airframe follows standard Piper practice, welded steel tube fuselage frame, wooden spar wings with metal ribs, all fabric covered – the wings braced with 'V' struts.

There are nineteen on the UK Register and many hundreds in the USA.

# PIPER
## PA 20 PACER

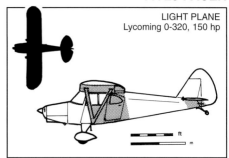

LIGHT PLANE
Lycoming 0-320, 150 hp

| DATA | IMPERIAL | | METRIC | |
|---|---|---|---|---|
| Span | 29.3 | ft | 9.02 | m |
| Wing area | 147.5 | sq ft | 13.8 | sq m |
| Aspect ratio | 5.8 | | 5.8 | |
| Empty Weight | 900 | lb | 408 | kg |
| Loaded weight | 1650 | lb | 749 | kg |
| Wing loading | 11.2 | lb/sq ft | 54.8 | kg/sq m |
| Max speed | 141 | mph | 225 | kmh |
| Cruise speed | 134 | mph | 214 | kmh |
| Stalling speed | 50 | mph | 80 | kmh |
| Climb rate | 800 | ft/min | 246 | m/min |
| Range | 536 | mls | 856 | km |

A four seater, in production from 1952 to 1958 the J5G Autocar had a new look fuselage, the rear decking was humped to follow the curve of the domed perspex cabin roof. It also sported a horn balanced rudder of increased area, fuel tanks in both wing roots, landing flaps and a sloping engine bulkhead that permitted the luxury of an electric self starter.

Powered by a Gipsy Major 1 of 130 hp the Autocar fulfilled many roles and was fitted with both floats and skis and with a large tank in the passenger space it performed as a crop sprayer. When fitted with the more powerful Cirrus Major 3 of 155 hp the designation became the J5G and ninety-two of this model were made (the Gipsy engined J5B had a production run of eighty-two).

It is staggering to note that these Autocars sold for £1500 new, you could only buy a good prop for that today.

Many were sold abroad including a batch for the Australian navy and others for dusting and pest control in developing countries.

Ten are on the UK Register, most are airworthy. Details below for J5G.

# AUSTER
## J5G AUTOCAR

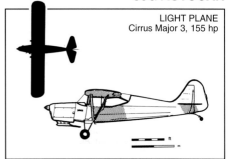

LIGHT PLANE
Cirrus Major 3, 155 hp

| DATA | IMPERIAL | | METRIC | |
|---|---|---|---|---|
| Span | 36 | ft | 11.1 | m |
| Wing area | 185 | sq ft | 17.4 | sq m |
| Aspect ratio | 7 | | 7 | |
| Empty Weight | 1367 | lb | 620 | kg |
| Loaded weight | 2450 | lb | 1112 | kg |
| Wing loading | 13.2 | lb/sq ft | 84 | kg/sq m |
| Max speed | 127 | mph | 203 | kmh |
| Cruise speed | 110 | mph | 176 | kmh |
| Stalling speed | 35 | mph | 56 | kmh |
| Climb rate | 710 | ft/min | 218 | m/min |
| Range | 485 | mls | 776 | km |

The Aiglet Trainer had the standard Auster wing reduced in span by four feet and improved ailerons to bring it into the semi-aerobatic category (-3 to +4.5g).

The windscreen is of the one piece moulded type, the cabin is 4ins (10cms) wider and the seat backs raised to facilitate a four point harness. The fuselage was a basic J5 up-stressed for aerobatics not to be confused with the J1B Aiglet a non aerobatic crop sprayer with a J1 fuselage.

Ninety-two were made during the period 1952-56 with many going overseas.

One J5F, G-AMOS set up no less than twenty-eight point to point world records for its category in the early 1950s and G-AMLR flew to Australia and back.

When fitted with a 36 ft span (Autocar) wing the name changed to J5R Alpine.

A famous Alpine was G-APAA owned and operated by the AA and used for traffic reconnaissance.

There arefourteen on t he UK Register, mostly airworthy.

# AUSTER
# J5F AIGLET TRAINER

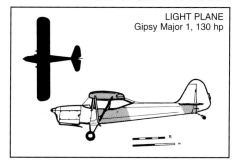

LIGHT PLANE
Gipsy Major 1, 130 hp

| DATA | IMPERIAL | | METRIC | |
|---|---|---|---|---|
| Span | 32 | ft | 9.8 | m |
| Wing area | 164 | sq ft | 15.4 | sq m |
| Aspect ratio | 6.24 | | 6.24 | |
| Empty Weight | 1324 | lb | 601 | kg |
| Loaded weight | 2200 | lb | 999 | kg |
| Wing loading | 13.4 | lb/sq ft | 65.4 | kg/sq m |
| Max speed | 125 | mph | 200 | kmh |
| Cruise speed | 107 | mph | 171 | kmh |
| Stalling speed | 33 | mph | 53 | kmh |
| Climb rate | 670 | ft/min | 218 | m/min |
| Range | 270 | mls | 432 | km |

The AOP 9 was the last aeroplane produced in quantity by Auster, 150 being supplied to the AOP squadrons and thirty-five going to the Indian Air Force.

The AOP 9 has an all metal airframe but retains fabric covering. It has hydraulically operated flaps combined with drooping ailerons and a 180 hp Cirrus Bombardier fuel injection engine. The semi cantilever undercarriage legs have hydraulic shock absorbers and the tailplane, abandoning the traditional Auster flat plate section became a proper aerofoil. The wing has a single strut bracing instead of 'V' struts.

A dorsal fin extension and fuselage strakes were additions that appeared after some hair raising spinning trials.

AOP 9s saw service in the trying conditions of the Malayan jungle, where they served with credit.

An AOP 11 was made, an AOP 9 with a 260 hp Lycoming for military trials but by 1962 helicopters were taking over the AOP role.

There are fourteen AOPs on the Uk Register, most airworthy.

# AUSTER
# AOP 9

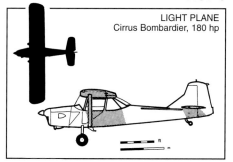

LIGHT PLANE
Cirrus Bombardier, 180 hp

| DATA | IMPERIAL | | METRIC | |
|---|---|---|---|---|
| Span | 36.5 | ft | 11.2 | m |
| Wing area | 198 | sq ft | 18.6 | sq m |
| Aspect ratio | 6.7 | | 6.7 | |
| Empty Weight | 1558 | lb | 707 | kg |
| Loaded weight | 2350 | lb | 1064 | kg |
| Wing loading | 11.8 | lb/sq ft | 58 | kg/sq m |
| Max speed | 118 | mph | 189 | kmh |
| Cruise speed | 100 | mph | 160 | kmh |
| Stalling speed | 44 | mph | 70 | kmh |
| Climb rate | 920 | ft/min | 283 | m/min |
| Range | 242 | mls | 387 | km |

Designed by air race pilot and pioneer of the post war North American home-building movement Steve Wittman, the Tailwind first flew in1953 and still looks trendy after fifty years.

The Tailwind's construction is along what was standard American lines for its day, ie welded steel tube fuselage with fabric covering, a single strut braced wooden wing, part fabric covered.

The single raked back cantilever undercarriage leg is a distinguishing feature, and at the time, fairly unique.

Seating two side-by-side, the Tailwind is a small aeroplane (22ft span) that looks and flies like a bigger one.

Over the years a range of motors from 85 to 140 hp have been fitted and earlier models did not have the raked fin and rudder.

A PFA approved type with fourteen on the Register and several being built.

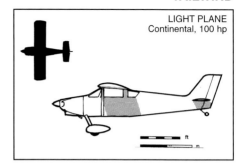

LIGHT PLANE
Continental, 100 hp

| DATA | IMPERIAL | | METRIC | |
|---|---|---|---|---|
| Span | 22.6 | ft | 7 | m |
| Wing area | 90 | sq ft | 8.46 | sq m |
| Aspect ratio | 5.7 | | 5.7 | |
| Empty Weight | 750 | lb | 340 | kg |
| Loaded weight | 1300 | lb | 590 | kg |
| Wing loading | 14.4 | lb/sq ft | 70.3 | kg/sq m |
| Max speed | 170 | mph | 272 | kmh |
| Cruise speed | 155 | mph | 248 | kmh |
| Stalling speed | 55 | mph | 88 | kmh |
| Climb rate | 900 | ft/min | 277 | m/min |
| Range | 450 | mls | 720 | km |

Derived from the Auster J1/N Alpha, the Husky was the last in the range, finally being produced by Beagle Aircraft Ltd in 1960, the year of its first flight.

The Austers are all based on the pre WW2 American Taylorcraft and have welded steel tube fuselages, covered in fabric and two wooden sparred strut braced wings with metal ribs under a fabric skin.

The Husky, powered by a 160 hp Lycoming engine, is a full four seater and out-performs its stable mates the Alpha, Arrow, Alpine etc.

The large dorsal fin is a distinguishing feature of the Husky as is the Lycoming engine, most other Beagle/Austers having Gipsy and Cirrus.

The Auster family is numerous and ageless, though Huskys are fairly rare, six on the UK Register, six flying.

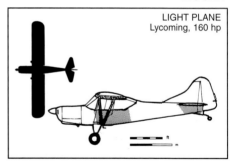

LIGHT PLANE
Lycoming, 160 hp

| DATA | IMPERIAL | | METRIC | |
|---|---|---|---|---|
| Span | 36 | ft | 11 | m |
| Wing area | 185 | sq ft | 17.2 | sq m |
| Aspect ratio | 7 | | 7 | |
| Empty Weight | 1450 | lb | 658 | kg |
| Loaded weight | 2450 | lb | 1111 | kg |
| Wing loading | 13.2 | lb/sq ft | 64.6 | kg/sq m |
| Max speed | 124 | mph | 198 | kmh |
| Cruise speed | 108 | mph | 174 | kmh |
| Stalling speed | 55 | mph | 88 | kmh |
| Climb rate | 640 | ft/min | 197 | m/min |
| Range | 460 | mls | 740 | km |

Taylorcraft Aeroplanes (England) Ltd. became Auster Aircraft, which became Beagle -Auster, and finally, Beagle Aircraft, the family resemblance is plain to see!

The Terrier, which first flew in 1961, was a civilian version of the Auster AOP 6, a British Army 'air observation post' of 1945 vintage which was a Gipsy engined version of the AOP 5 with a Lycoming.

300 AOP 6s were made including the T7 Trainer.

The Terrier, of which only sixty-five were produced, is still well represented in the lists with twenty-eight currently shown on the UK Register.

Differing from its military predecessor in having larger tail surfaces, three seats, luxurious seating and trim, and a long exhaust pipe and silencer below the fuselage (this is deleted on some aircraft).

Construction is standard Auster, welded steel tube fuselage, metal wing ribs and wooden spars, fabric covering.

A glider tug version was also produced called the Tugmaster.

## BEAGLE
## A 61 TERRIER

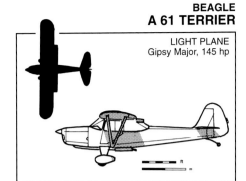

LIGHT PLANE
Gipsy Major, 145 hp

| DATA | IMPERIAL | | METRIC | |
|---|---|---|---|---|
| Span | 36 | ft | 11.1 | m |
| Wing area | 184 | sq ft | 17.3 | sq m |
| Aspect ratio | 7 | | 7 | |
| Empty Weight | 1490 | lb | 676 | kg |
| Loaded weight | 2400 | lb | 1089 | kg |
| Wing loading | 13 | lb/sq ft | 63.6 | kg/sq m |
| Max speed | 124 | mph | 198 | kmh |
| Cruise speed | 108 | mph | 173 | kmh |
| Stalling speed | 50 | mph | 80 | kmh |
| Climb rate | 600 | ft/min | 185 | m/min |
| Range | 300 | mls | 480 | km |

The Polish Wilga, or Thrush in English, is a versatile aircraft with a STOL performance being equally at home as a sports tourer, or in an agricultural role, a parachutists hack, towing gliders or an air ambulance.

Though fairly rare in this country, eight on the UK Register over 900 have been built and sold all over the world in many variants and is still in production

First flown in 1962 the all metal Wilga has a distinctly insect like look about it, the trailing link mounted main wheels definitely owe something to the praying mantis!

The main plane, rather surprisingly for a low speed utility aircraft are cantilevered, though the tail plane is strut braced.

The fuselage makes much use of external fluting as do the flying control surfaces.

In its day the Wilga held the world altitude record for its class with 33,428 ft. (6836 m.)

A special export version, The Wilga 2000 has a 300 hp Lycoming large leg fairings and an extended dorsal fin.

Data below is for Ivchenko Wilga.

## PZL
## WILGA

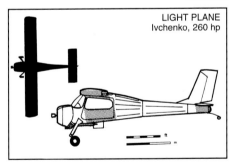

LIGHT PLANE
Ivchenko, 260 hp

| DATA | IMPERIAL | | METRIC | |
|---|---|---|---|---|
| Span | 36.5 | ft | 11.14 | m |
| Wing area | 170 | sq ft | 16 | sq m |
| Aspect ratio | 7.8 | | 7.8 | |
| Empty Weight | 1874 | lb | 850 | kg |
| Loaded weight | 2755 | lb | 1250 | kg |
| Wing loading | 16.2 | lb/sq ft | 79 | kg/sq m |
| Max speed | 120 | mph | 192 | kmh |
| Cruise speed | 104 | mph | 166 | kmh |
| Stalling speed | 50 | mph | 80 | kmh |
| Climb rate | 1245 | ft/min | 380 | m/min |
| Range | 370 | mls | 592 | km |

First flown in 1963 the Maule M4 Rocket, designed by Belford Maule and manufactured at Moultrie, Georgia, has been the basic airframe for all the subsequent variants, mainly engine size changes. (A seaplane and turboprop version are available).

The M5 Lunar Rocket has a 210 hp Continental engine, four seats and a genuine STOL performance, the M6 has 235 hp and the M7 is the first Maule to have a tricycle undercarriage.

The fuselage is of welded steel tube with fabric covering and a large integral fin; the wings are all metal and braced with 'V' struts, as is the tailplane.

Maules are distributed in the UK by Aeromarine and the Moultrie plant has produced 1700.

Popular with South American bush operators thanks to its tough capacious fuselage and STOL feature.

Thirty-three are on the UK Register, including M4, M5, M6 and M7s.

# MAULE
# M5 LUNAR ROCKET

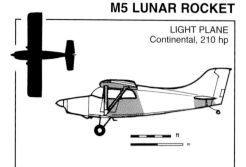

LIGHT PLANE
Continental, 210 hp

| DATA | IMPERIAL | | METRIC | |
|---|---|---|---|---|
| Span | 30.8 | ft | 9.5 | m |
| Wing area | 138 | sq ft | 12.9 | sq m |
| Aspect ratio | 6.9 | | 6.9 | |
| Empty Weight | 1300 | lb | 590 | kg |
| Loaded weight | 2400 | lb | 1089 | kg |
| Wing loading | 17.4 | lb/sq ft | 85 | kg/sq m |
| Max speed | 170 | mph | 272 | kmh |
| Cruise speed | 160 | mph | 256 | kmh |
| Stalling speed | 40 | mph | 64 | kmh |
| Climb rate | 1500 | ft/min | 462 | m/min |
| Range | 700 | mls | 1120 | km |

British designed and built by E. Clutton and E. Sherry, the FRED (Flying Runabout Experimental Design), first flew in 1963 powered by a 500cc Triumph motor cycle engine. A variety of engines have been fitted since, mainly 1500 cc VW, though some flew with the American Lawrence radial.

Plans have been available since 1970 and have proved very popular with the home builder.

The structure is all wood with a plywood and fabric covering and the thick wing is wire braced. The tail unit consists of a cantilever tail plane with push rod operated elevator and an aerodynamically balanced finless rudder (Ed fixed fin mod is recommended). The long undercarriage legs, attached to the top longerons have coil springs at the top and scooter wheels at the bottom.

The wings fold easily along side the fuselage for ease of storage or towing, which can be done with a motor cycle!

There are twenty-nine FRED on the Register and they are PFA approved.

# CLUTTON
# FRED

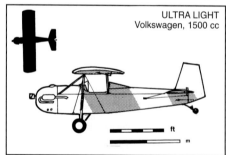

ULTRA LIGHT
Volkswagen, 1500 cc

| DATA | IMPERIAL | | METRIC | |
|---|---|---|---|---|
| Span | 22.5 | ft | 7 | m |
| Wing area | 110 | sq ft | 10.3 | sq m |
| Aspect ratio | 4.6 | | 4.6 | |
| Empty Weight | 533 | lb | 252 | kg |
| Loaded weight | 773 | lb | 351 | kg |
| Wing loading | 7 | lb/sq ft | 34 | kg/sq m |
| Max speed | 75 | mph | 120 | kmh |
| Cruise speed | 55 | mph | 88 | kmh |
| Stalling speed | 40 | mph | 64 | kmh |
| Climb rate | 400 | ft/min | 122 | m/min |
| Range | 200 | mls | 360 | km |

The charming single seat Sky Scooter is an American design by Ken Flaglor, which first flew in 1967. It is designed for home building and plans are available from Headberg Aviation Inc of Longwood, Florida.

Construction is all wood with Ceconite covered wings, rear fuselage and control surfaces. The wing centre section and engine mount are steel tube and the wing leading edge is light alloy sheet.

The wings are wire braced to the lower longerons and to a steel pylon above the centre section. The tailplane is strut braced and the rudder is fin-less.

A short spring leg carries the main wheels and a sprung and steerable tail wheel brings up the rear.

The design power unit is a Volkswagen 1500 cc flat four developing about 40 hp.

The design is PFA approved, though none are currently under construction.

The one Sky Scooter currently on the UK Register (G-BOWE) turned many a head when it flew in to the big PFA Rally at Cranfield in 1999.

## FLAGLOR
# SKY SCOOTER

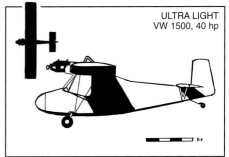

ULTRA LIGHT
VW 1500, 40 hp

| DATA | IMPERIAL | | METRIC | |
|---|---|---|---|---|
| Span | 27.9 | ft | 8.5 | m |
| Wing area | 115 | sq ft | 10.7 | sq m |
| Aspect ratio | 6.7 | | 6.7 | |
| Empty Weight | 390 | lb | 177 | kg |
| Loaded weight | 625 | lb | 283 | kg |
| Wing loading | 5.4 | lb/sq ft | 26.5 | kg/sq m |
| Max speed | 80 | mph | 129 | kmh |
| Cruise speed | 65 | mph | 105 | kmh |
| Stalling speed | 34 | mph | 55 | kmh |
| Climb rate | 325 | ft/min | 100 | m/min |
| Range | 175 | mls | 282 | km |

The two seater, in tandem Aeronca 7 Champion first flew in 1944 and was produced in considerable quantities.7,200 of the 7 AC Champion and 509 of the military variant the L-16A.

In 1954 Champion Aircraft got the rights from Aeronca and made 733 Model 7s as the 7EC Traveller and 472 of the nose wheeled Tri Traveller, also the aerobatic Citabria. Bellanca bought Champion in 1970 and re-engined the 7 AC with a 60 hp Franklin, they also produced variants of the Citabria culminating in the the fully aerobatic Model 8, Decathlon. American Champion Aircraft took over when Bellanca closed in 1980 and are producing Decathlons and Citabria's.

A few tricycle gear converted Champions are to be seen rejoicing in the name of Tri-Champion.

There are fifty-five Champion/Bellanca/Citabria on the UK Register.

## AERONCA/BELLANCA
# CHAMPION-CITABRIA

LIGHT PLANE
Lycoming, 150 hp

| DATA | IMPERIAL | | METRIC | |
|---|---|---|---|---|
| Span | 33.5 | ft | 10.2 | m |
| Wing area | 165 | sq ft | 15.5 | sq m |
| Aspect ratio | 6.8 | | 6.8 | |
| Empty Weight | 1067 | lb | 484 | kg |
| Loaded weight | 1650 | lb | 749 | kg |
| Wing loading | 16 | lb/sq ft | 78 | kg/sq m |
| Max speed | 125 | mph | 200 | kmh |
| Cruise speed | 117 | mph | 187 | kmh |
| Stalling speed | 51 | mph | 130 | kmh |
| Climb rate | 725 | ft/min | 223 | m/min |
| Range | 509 | mls | 814 | km |

Designed by Jim Bede, the *enfant terrible* of the American kit plane scene, the BD-4 is an eye-catching, angular, two or four seater with, unusual for a high winger, a cantilever wing.

The fuselage of all metal construction, is of extremely simple geometry for ease of construction, and the wings have tubular spars that double as fuel tanks, with composites forming the wing section profile.

BD-4s may be seen with either nose wheel tricycle or tail-dragger undercarriages.

A variety of engines are fitted ranging from 100 to 200 hp. The data below is for the 180 hp Lycoming model which has a very useful cruising speed and range.

Four are on the UK Register and is approved by the PFA in the two seat version.

## BEDE
## BD-4

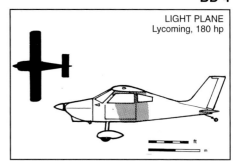

LIGHT PLANE
Lycoming, 180 hp

| DATA | IMPERIAL | | METRIC | |
|---|---|---|---|---|
| Span | 25.5 | ft | 7.85 | m |
| Wing area | 102 | sq ft | 9.6 | sq m |
| Aspect ratio | 6.4 | | 6.4 | |
| Empty Weight | 1080 | lb | 490 | kg |
| Loaded weight | 2000 | lb | 908 | kg |
| Wing loading | 19 | lb/sq ft | 92.7 | kg/sq m |
| Max speed | 183 | mph | 293 | kmh |
| Cruise speed | 174 | mph | 278 | kmh |
| Stalling speed | 63 | mph | 101 | kmh |
| Climb rate | 1400 | ft/min | 431 | m/min |
| Range | 750 | mls | 1200 | km |

Originating in Australia in the mid 1980s the side-by-side two-seat, three-axis control thruster microlight is now built and marketed in the UK by Thruster Air Services of Ginge, Oxon.

Early models were typed as T300 but production ceased in the early 1990s.

The new breed of Thrusters, the T600s are available with nose or tail wheel undercarriages (nose – T600T, Tail T600N) and a range of engines including Rotax's 503, 582 and 912 plus the flour stroke HKS.

Of light, alloy construction with fabric covering the Thruster is a very popular club trainer with over 100 on the UK Register. The main undercarriage legs are sprung and have low set wide tracked braked wheels and the T600T, a steerable nose wheel.

The latest development is the Sprint, which has a fully enclosed cockput and faired rear fuselage to boom – this version being offered with a Jabiru engine.

## TNT
## THRUSTER

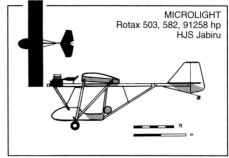

MICROLIGHT
Rotax 503, 582, 91258 hp
HJS Jabiru

| DATA | IMPERIAL | | METRIC | |
|---|---|---|---|---|
| Span | 31.5 | ft | 9.7 | m |
| Wing area | 161.5 | sq ft | 15.2 | sq m |
| Aspect ratio | 6.14 | | 6.14 | |
| Empty Weight | 330 | lb | 150 | kg |
| Loaded weight | 816 | lb | 370 | kg |
| Wing loading | 5 | lb/sq ft | 24.4 | kg/sq m |
| Max speed | 92 | mph | 147 | kmh |
| Cruise speed | 69 | mph | 110 | kmh |
| Stalling speed | 37 | mph | 59 | kmh |
| Climb rate | 500 | ft/min | 154 | m/min |
| Range | 172 | mls | 276 | km |

The Avid Flyer, a side-by-side two seater, comes in many variants, STOL, Heavy Hauler, Speedwing, Aerobatic and Commuter.

All versions have tail wheel or nose wheel options. Of fabricated tube with Dacron covering, the kit containing all aluminium and foam items and can be built, it is claimed, in 800 man hours.

First flown in its country of origin, the USA, in 1983 where ten years of development and build experience have produced a reliable and popular aeroplane with 1000 built in the USA and forty-one in the UK at the time of writing.

The original design team included Dan Denney who went on to design the Kitfox, some parts of which are indeed interchangeable with the Avid Flyer.

A special Jabiru engined version has been built and is flying in the UK.

| DATA | IMPERIAL | | METRIC | |
|---|---|---|---|---|
| Span | 29.8 | ft | 9.2 | m |
| Wing area | 122 | sq ft | 11.5 | sq m |
| Aspect ratio | 7.3 | | 7.3 | |
| Empty Weight | 400 | lb | 181 | kg |
| Loaded weight | 911 | lb | 413 | kg |
| Wing loading | 7.44 | lb/sq ft | 36 | kg/sq m |
| Max speed | 95 | mph | 152 | kmh |
| Cruise speed | 85 | mph | 136 | kmh |
| Stalling speed | 32 | mph | 51 | kmh |
| Climb rate | 1400 | ft/min | 422 | m/min |
| Range | 350 | mls | 560 | km |

# LIGHT AERO
# AVID FLYER

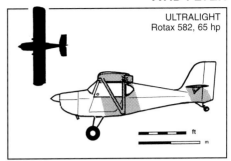

ULTRALIGHT
Rotax 582, 65 hp

SPEEDWING

Probably the most popular kit plane yet marketed, with over 1500 sold since it was introduced in 1984 and is still being produced at the rate of twenty-thirty a month by Denney Aircraft Co. at their works in Idaho.

Designed by Dan Denney, the Kitfox has a welded steel tube fuselage (supplied complete in kit) and a wing based on two dural tube spars with plywood ribs and fabric covering, as on the fuselage.

The wings fold easily for towing or garaging and the landing gear options available include floats, skis and amphibian floats. Push rods operate the full span flaperons and elevators whilst the rudder relies on cables for its motion.

At the time of writing there are 101 on the UK Register, plus others being built.

The Kitfox 3 is identical in appearance to the Kitfox 2 but is stronger to accommodate the Rotax 912. Kitfox models now go up to MkVII and one has been fitted with a Rotec, seven cylinder radial engine. The data below s for the Rotax 582, 64 hp.

| DATA | IMPERIAL | | METRIC | |
|---|---|---|---|---|
| Span | 31.5 | ft | 9.7 | m |
| Wing area | 130 | sq ft | 12.2 | sq m |
| Aspect ratio | 7.6 | | 7.6 | |
| Empty Weight | 440 | lb | 200 | kg |
| Loaded weight | 950 | lb | 431 | kg |
| Wing loading | 7.6 | lb/sq ft | 35.6 | kg/sq m |
| Max speed | 114 | mph | 182 | kmh |
| Cruise speed | 105 | mph | 168 | kmh |
| Stalling speed | 25 | mph | 40 | kmh |
| Climb rate | 1300 | ft/min | 400 | m/min |
| Range | 230 | mls | 368 | km |

# DENNEY
# KITFOX

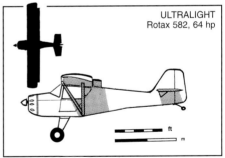

ULTRALIGHT
Rotax 582, 64 hp

Reality Aircraft and Just Aircraft of Idaho are partners in light aircraft kit production. Their Easy Raider is a tandem two-seater, tail dragger with one set of controls. A requirement for a dual conrol, side-by-side version still in the microlight category involved the two US companies and UK based Reality Aircraft of Amesbury.

Using all the Easy Raider wing and under carriage a side-by-side fuselage, with dual controls, was designed – the resulting aircraft being the Escapade.

The Escapade's fuselage is of welded steel tube with fabric covering and the wing has two tubular spars with metal ribs – also fabric covered. The under carriage may be simply switched from nose to tail wheel type by turning the main gear through 180° and the locating aft and fitting a nose wheel unit to the fire wall. The main gear is bungee sprung. Designed to take either the Rotax 912 or Jabiru 2200 the Escapade first flew in February 2003 and in the same year was the 'outstanidng light plane' award at Sun'N Fun. The type is BMAA approved, one is flying and nine are being built in the UK.

# REALITY
## ESCAPADE

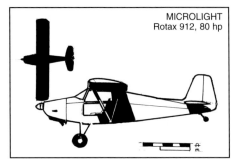

MICROLIGHT
Rotax 912, 80 hp

| DATA | IMPERIAL | | METRIC | |
|---|---|---|---|---|
| Span | 28.5 | ft | 8.7 | m |
| Wing area | 13.5 | sq ft | 12.7 | sq m |
| Aspect ratio | 6 | | | |
| Empty Weight | 550 | lb | 250 | kg |
| Loaded weight | 990 | lb | 450 | kg |
| Wing loading | 7.3 | lb/sq ft | 35.8 | kg/sq m |
| Max speed | 100 | mph | 160 | kmh |
| Cruise speed | 85 | mph | 136 | kmh |
| Stalling speed | 41 | mph | 66 | kmh |
| Climb rate | 880 | ft/min | 268 | m/min |
| Range | 350 | mls | 560 | km |

Fisher Aero of Ohio produce plans and kit build light planes including the Celebrity biplane and the interesting Culex twin engined two seater. The Horizon 1 first flew in 1990 having a strut braced high wing with two seats in tandem and a tail dragger undercarriage. The construction is all wood with fabric covering (with welded tube option) and easy one-man operation wing folding.

The Horizon kit is offered with either floats, skis, wheel fairings, hydraulic or mechanical brakes and a variety of engines of 65-115hp.

The Horizon 2 an improved version of the Horizon 1 has slotted flaps, revised fin and cut down rear fuselage and therefore has better slow flying characteristics and a higher cruising speed. The Horizon though PFA approved is a rare UK sighting.

# FISHER
## HORIZON 2

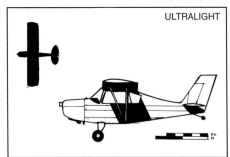

ULTRALIGHT

| DATA | IMPERIAL | | METRIC | |
|---|---|---|---|---|
| Span | 26 | ft | 7.92 | m |
| Wing area | 113.6 | sq ft | 10.55 | sq m |
| Aspect ratio | 6 | | | |
| Empty Weight | 450 | lb | 204 | kg |
| Loaded weight | 1050 | lb | 476 | kg |
| Wing loading | 9.2 | lb/sq ft | 45 | kg/sq m |
| Max speed | 110 | mph | 177 | kmh |
| Cruise speed | 95 | mph | 153 | kmh |
| Stalling speed | 35 | mph | 57 | kmh |
| Climb rate | 1200 | ft/min | 366 | m/min |
| Range | 250 | mls | 402 | km |

Fisher Flying Products of Edgeley, North Dakota have produced a range of aeroplanes including the Koala. Skybaby, Classic, Dakota Hawk and recently the R80 eighty percent Tiger Moth replica. In 1984 the two seat version of the Koala, the Super Koala made its first flight, since then over 1000 kits have been sold.

A Mike Fisher design, the side-by-side Super Koala first flew in the UK in 1996 with a Rotax 532 of 64 hp and at an all up weight of 830 lb, comes within the Ultralight category.

The kit, which comes in Standard or Quick Build form, is all wood with a geodetic type structure on the wings and fuselage sides. In the Quick Build version the spars, ribs, fuselage, sides and empennage are ready assembled. Electric engine start, wheel brakes and spats are optional extras.

The Super Koala's performance is noteworthy. With two up it will cruise at 85 mph, stall at 32 mph and climb at 1100 fpm, all on a modest 64 hp. Update: a 80 hp Jabiru 2200 is being fitted.

Available from Alastair Malcolm Aviation Ltd, Park Farm, Throwley, Faversham, Kent the Super Koala is PFA approved. There are three on the UK Register.

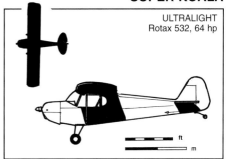

ULTRALIGHT
Rotax 532, 64 hp

| DATA | IMPERIAL | | METRIC | |
|---|---|---|---|---|
| Span | 31 | ft | 9.5 | m |
| Wing area | 140 | sq ft | 13.2 | sq m |
| Aspect ratio | 6.9 | | 6.9 | |
| Empty Weight | 400 | lb | 181 | kg |
| Loaded weight | 830 | lb | 377 | kg |
| Wing loading | 6 | lb/sq ft | 29 | kg/sq m |
| Max speed | 95 | mph | 152 | kmh |
| Cruise speed | 85 | mph | 136 | kmh |
| Stalling speed | 32 | mph | 51 | kmh |
| Climb rate | 1100 | ft/min | 339 | m/min |
| Range | 150 | mls | 291 | km |

A Canadian light plane, UK Group A, from the drawing board of Daryl Murphy, with a little help from Dick Hiscocks who designed the DH Beaver. The Rebel looks a bit like a little Beaver.

The Rebel first flew in 1990 and the manufacturers of this smart all metal kit plane claim that 400 kits have already been delivered. There is an ultralight version sold as the Maverick.

The wing has three spars, stamped L.A. ribs and is braced by a single strut to a fuselage strongpoint. Wings and semi monocoque fuselage are covered in aluminium sheet and they are stressed for +9-6g. Three engine options are available, Rotax 582, Rotax 912 and the Lycoming 0-235, which is the version the data below refers to.

With detachable wings and an upward folding tailplane the Rebel can have a narrow storage profile. The Rebel is PFA approved and there are twelve on the UK Register plus others being built.

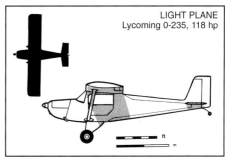

LIGHT PLANE
Lycoming 0-235, 118 hp

| DATA | IMPERIAL | | METRIC | |
|---|---|---|---|---|
| Span | 30 | ft | 9.24 | m |
| Wing area | 150 | sq ft | 14.1 | sq m |
| Aspect ratio | 6.1 | | 6.1 | |
| Empty Weight | 850 | lb | 386 | kg |
| Loaded weight | 1650 | lb | 749 | kg |
| Wing loading | 11 | lb/sq ft | 53.7 | kg/sq m |
| Max speed | 120 | mph | 192 | kmh |
| Cruise speed | 110 | mph | 176 | kmh |
| Stalling speed | 32 | mph | 51 | kmh |
| Climb rate | 800 | ft/min | 304 | m/min |
| Range | 400 | mls | 640 | km |

Another light plane from the Mike Whittaker stable. First flown in 1987 the MW 7, the smallest of the MW range, follows the well proven configuration of the earlier MW 5 and MW 6 and continues the use of large diameter light alloy tubes to carry the main loads.

A good looking single seater which may be seen with various cabin configurations, dependent on the constructor and on later models a larger fin and rudder (this is now standard).

As with all previous MW models the motor is mounted at the front end of the main boom and the rudder and all moving elevator at the other, but unlike earlier models the MW 7 is a tail-dragger with a well sprung tailwheel mounted below the fin.

Ten are on the UK Register and are PFA approved.

## WHITTAKER MW 7

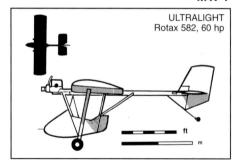

ULTRALIGHT
Rotax 582, 60 hp

| DATA | IMPERIAL | | METRIC | |
|---|---|---|---|---|
| Span | 22 | ft | 6.8 | m |
| Wing area | 88 | sq ft | 8.3 | sq m |
| Aspect ratio | 5.5 | | 5.5 | |
| Empty Weight | 300 | lb | 136 | kg |
| Loaded weight | 600 | lb | 272 | kg |
| Wing loading | 6.8 | lb/sq ft | 33.2 | kg/sq m |
| Max speed | 92 | mph | 147 | kmh |
| Cruise speed | 74 | mph | 118 | kmh |
| Stalling speed | 40 | mph | 64 | kmh |
| Climb rate | 1000 | ft/min | 308 | m/min |
| Range | 100 | mls | 160 | km |

The German Ikarus C22 ultralight first appeared in 1986, a product of Ikarus Comco. Very popular in Germany where several hundred of this factory built, two seater are flying. As it is a factory built, two seater it is approved for dual instruction and is therefore widely used in flying schools on the continent and many hundreds have been built. The Rotax 912 (80 hp) version has been built in smaller numbers and includes a rear fuselage, fairing as shown in the photo.

Developed from Ikarus Comco Fox-D, a single seater, the airframe is of aluminium tube with fabric covering, rugged, easy to inspect and repair.

A C22 won the German ultralight Championship in 2002.

The C22 has not been marketed by the UK Ikarus agent. This class of three axis ultralight with the Rotax engine and ultra-simple construction in a very competitive class.

## IKARUS C22

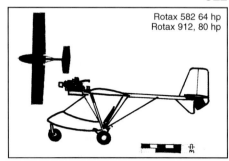

Rotax 582 64 hp
Rotax 912, 80 hp

| DATA | IMPERIAL | | METRIC | |
|---|---|---|---|---|
| Span | 34 | ft | 10.4 | m |
| Wing area | 161 | sq ft | 15.2 | sq m |
| Aspect ratio | 7.2 | | 7.2 | |
| Empty Weight | 568 | lb | 258 | kg |
| Loaded weight | 991 | lb | 450 | kg |
| Wing loading | 6.15 | lb/sq ft | 30 | kg/sq m |
| Max speed | 90 | mph | 145 | kmh |
| Cruise speed | 81 | mph | 130 | kmh |
| Stalling speed | 35 | mph | 56 | kmh |
| Climb rate | 984 | ft/min | 300 | m/min |
| Range | 280 | mls | 448 | km |

First flown in 1936... the legendary WW2 German STOL three seater has been built in several countries since the war, with and without a nod in the direction of its original manufacturers, Fieseler.

Nestor Slepcev, Yugoslav by birth, Australian national designed the three-quarter scale Storch and flew a single seat version powered by a Rotax 912 in 1991. In 1994 the two seat version flew successfully and was offered as a kit. (Factory built models are available). Three versions are now available, the Ultra, Ultralight, the Muster a utility model and the 'Criquet' a Rotec radial-engined version.

The fixed leading edge slotted Slepcev Storch has separate ailerons and flaps whereas the original had somewhat surprisingly combined elevons. All controls, except rudder, are push-rod operated and the gawky undercarriage has a ten-inch stroke. The kit comes with a fuselage ready welded up and all controls in position. This Storch is a STOL performer, landing at 22mph with everything hanging out and pulling up after forty feet or so. Storch Aviation, Australia pty Ltd is in Beechwood, NSW.

# SLEPCEV
# STORCH

ULTRALIGHT
Rotax 912, 80 hp

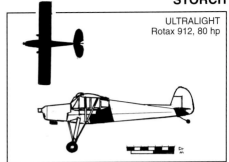

| DATA | IMPERIAL | | METRIC | |
|---|---|---|---|---|
| Span | 32.8 | ft | 10 | m |
| Wing area | 172.6 | sq ft | 16.2 | sq m |
| Aspect ratio | 6.25 | | 6.25 | |
| Empty Weight | 700 | lb | 318 | kg |
| Loaded weight | 1200 | lb | 545 | kg |
| Wing loading | 7 | lb/sq ft | 34 | kg/sq m |
| Max speed | 103 | mph | 164 | kmh |
| Cruise speed | 80 | mph | 128 | kmh |
| Stalling speed | 22 | mph | 35 | kmh |
| Climb rate | 800 | ft/min | 244 | m/min |
| Range | 400 | mls | 640 | km |

The Chrislea CH3 Ace first flew at Heston in 1946. It was powered by a 130 hp Lycoming and had a single fin and rudder (soon changed to twins). The fuselage was a welded tube structure and the wings had steel spars and aluminium ribs, all fabric covered.

Chrislea's big idea was to simplify the flying controls by doing away with the rudder bar and moving the rudder with a sideways movement of the 'steering wheel'.

The Super Ace (Gipsy Major 10) was produced at the re-located Chrislea works at Exeter and first flew in 1948, initially with the 'all purpose' steering wheel, but later models reverted to orthodoxy. A tail-dragger version the Skyjeep followed in 1949 with a Blackburn Cirrus Major (155 hp) and an upward hinged rear decking for awkward loads (ie. a stretcher).

Lack of orders caused the firm to fold in 1952 when twenty-three Super Aces and three Skyjeeps had been built. Most of the Super aces finished up in foreign lands, one survivor is in Japan and another in Australia. Two British Super Aces are flying, one Sky Jeep being restored.

# CHRISLEA
# SUPER ACE

LIGHT PLANE
Gipsy Major 10, 145 hp

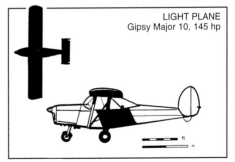

| DATA | IMPERIAL | | METRIC | |
|---|---|---|---|---|
| Span | 36 | ft | 11 | m |
| Wing area | 177 | sq ft | 16.6 | sq m |
| Aspect ratio | 7.3 | | 7.3 | |
| Empty Weight | 1350 | lb | 673 | kg |
| Loaded weight | 2400 | lb | 1090 | kg |
| Wing loading | 13.2 | lb/sq ft | 64 | kg/sq m |
| Max speed | 126 | mph | 202 | kmh |
| Cruise speed | 112 | mph | 179 | kmh |
| Stalling speed | 43 | mph | 69 | kmh |
| Climb rate | 750 | ft/min | 231 | m/min |
| Range | 400 | mls | 640 | km |

First flown in 1950 the four seat Tri Pacer is the tricycle gear version of the PA 20 Pacer and is the only Piper high wing trike.

Of traditional Piper construction, welded tube fuselage, two spar wing, fabric covered and fitted with a variety of Lycoming engines ranging from 125 hp to 160 hp.

The main variants are the 1958 PA22-150 Caribbean, not so fully equipped as the original model, and the two seat 108 hp Colt of 1961 a two seat trainer. Float plane and ski versions also appear.

Production of all PA 22s ended in 1963 when over 9000 had been made, many hundreds of which are still flying world-wide, including over fifty-seven on the British Register.

Details below are for the 160 hp PA22 Tri Pacer.

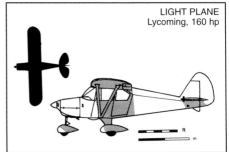

LIGHT PLANE
Lycoming, 160 hp

| DATA | IMPERIAL | | METRIC | |
|---|---|---|---|---|
| Span | 29.2 | ft | 8.9 | m |
| Wing area | 147.57 | sq ft | 13.7 | sq m |
| Aspect ratio | 5.8 | | 5.83 | |
| Empty Weight | 1110 | lb | 504 | kg |
| Loaded weight | 2000 | lb | 908 | kg |
| Wing loading | 13.6 | lb/sq ft | 66.3 | kg/sq m |
| Max speed | 141 | mph | 226 | kmh |
| Cruise speed | 134 | mph | 214 | kmh |
| Stalling speed | 55 | mph | 88 | kmh |
| Climb rate | 800 | ft/min | 246 | m/min |
| Range | 655 | mls | 1055 | km |

Alfons Putzer KG, the German company, began building sailplanes in 1953 and in 1958 a motor glider, from this the two seat Elster (Magpie) was developed.

First flown in 1959, twenty-one of the all wood Elsters were purchased by the German government for flying club use.

The prototype was powered by a Porsche 678/3 engine but production aircraft had 95 hp Continental C90-12F and were designated Elster B. A glider towing version the Elster C was powered by a 150 hp Lycoming O-320.

About thirty Elsters in all were built and in the mid sixties Putzer became Sportavia Putzer GmbH.

The fuselage is an all wood plywood skinned monocoque and the high, semi elliptical wing has a single wooden spar braced by a metal strut. The tricycle undercarriage is rubber block sprung, the nose wheel is steerable and the main wheels have mechanical brakes. The side-by-side seats are reached via upwards hinged doors.

Three Elsters are on the UK Register, all ex-German registered, only one of which is currently airworthy.

An interesting 'Super Motor Glider'!

LIGHT PLANE
Continental C90-12F, 95 hp

| DATA | IMPERIAL | | METRIC | |
|---|---|---|---|---|
| Span | 43.3 | ft | 13.2 | m |
| Wing area | 188 | sq ft | 17.7 | sq m |
| Aspect ratio | 10 | | 10 | |
| Empty Weight | 1014 | lb | 460 | kg |
| Loaded weight | 1543 | lb | 700 | kg |
| Wing loading | 8 | lb/sq ft | 39 | kg/sq m |
| Max speed | 104 | mph | 180 | kmh |
| Cruise speed | 93 | mph | 150 | kmh |
| Stalling speed | 46 | mph | 74 | kmh |
| Climb rate | 720 | ft/min | 220 | m/min |
| Range | 280 | mls | 450 | km |

Thirty five thousand Cessna 172 Skyhawk buyers can't be wrong! One of the most successful 'planes ever built, the 172 first flew in 1955 and was a tricycle gear version of the model 170 of 1945, so the basic design is fifty-nine years old! The 170 differed from the 172 in having an unswept fin and rounded profile rudder and elevator.

Two thousand of the total production have been built in France by Reims Aircraft with the French built Cessnas prefixed with an 'F'.

It is also supplied to the US armed forces, fitted with a 210 hp Continental, as the T-41 Mescalero trainer and to various South American air forces for a range of duties.

The wing with its tapered outer panels and single strut brace, low set tailplane, all round view cabin and swept fin with dorsal extension are all distinctive features of this all metal aeroplane.

About 400 are on the UK Register.

# CESSNA
# 172 SKYHAWK

LIGHT PLANE
Continental, 165 hp

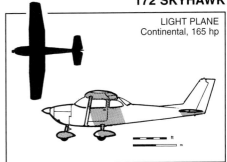

| DATA | IMPERIAL | | METRIC | |
|---|---|---|---|---|
| Span | 36.16 | ft | 11.1 | m |
| Wing area | 174 | sq ft | 16.3 | sq m |
| Aspect ratio | 7.5 | | 7.5 | |
| Empty Weight | 1260 | lb | 572 | kg |
| Loaded weight | 2300 | lb | 1044 | kg |
| Wing loading | 13.2 | lb/sq ft | 64.4 | kg/sq m |
| Max speed | 138 | mph | 220 | kmh |
| Cruise speed | 130 | mph | 208 | kmh |
| Stalling speed | 57 | mph | 91 | kmh |
| Climb rate | 645 | ft/min | 198 | m/min |
| Range | 720 | mls | 1152 | km |

Developed from the Cessna 180 tail dragger the 182, with nose wheel undercarriage, initially retained the 180's unswept fin and rudder and first flew in 1955.

An ongoing period of resulted in the swept fin version of 1960, and in 1962, the stepped rear fuselage with the 'Omnivision' rear window.

The aircraft is all metal and has the typical Cessna wing braced by a single strut.

In appearance, the 182 is almost identical to the 172 but has a more swept fin and rudder and is a foot (0.3 m) longer than the '172, which, strangely, came after the 182, chronologically.

The 182 has a more powerful engine, a six cylinder Continental of 230 hp, and can seat up to six people.

Built in France by Reims Aviation as the Skyrocket this version is, in fact, a six cylindered 172. Reims have, quite recently, considered re-starting 182 production.

Around 100 182s are on the UK Register, including the 182 R which is the retractable gear version.

Some 18,000 were built.

# CESSNA
# 182 SKYLANE

LIGHT PLANE
Continental, 230 hp

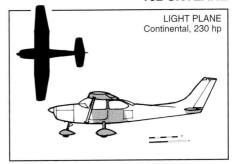

| DATA | IMPERIAL | | METRIC | |
|---|---|---|---|---|
| Span | 36 | ft | 11.1 | m |
| Wing area | 174 | sq ft | 16.3 | sq m |
| Aspect ratio | 7.4 | | 7.4 | |
| Empty Weight | 1550 | lb | 703 | kg |
| Loaded weight | 2800 | lb | 1271 | kg |
| Wing loading | 16.1 | lb/sq ft | 78.6 | kg/sq m |
| Max speed | 167 | mph | 267 | kmh |
| Cruise speed | 155 | mph | 248 | kmh |
| Stalling speed | 59 | mph | 94 | kmh |
| Climb rate | 905 | ft/min | 1448 | m/min |
| Range | 925 | mls | 1480 | km |

When first flown in 1957 the Model 150 had a vertical fin and rudder and a full depth rear fuselage, by the time the 150F arrived the fin was swept and the rear fuselage slimmed to allow for the wrap around rear window. A all metal side-by-side two seater, a reliable Continental engine, tricycle landing gear and electrically operated flaps make the Models 150 and 152 the all time most popular trainer, with a total production of 24,000.

The Reims Aviation built aircraft are prefixed with an 'F', ie F150.

The Model 152 has a 110 hp Lycoming, 28-volt electrics, new fuel tanks and a thirty degree flap setting. Both Models 150 and 152 are produced as Aerobats. The derisory 'Spam Can' tag is ill deserved for one of the worlds most successful aeroplanes.

# CESSNA
# MODEL 150/152

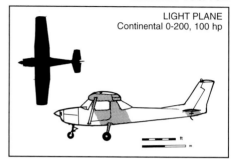

LIGHT PLANE
Continental 0-200, 100 hp

| DATA | IMPERIAL | | METRIC | |
|---|---|---|---|---|
| Span | 32.6 | ft | 10 | m |
| Wing area | 157 | sq ft | 14.7 | sq m |
| Aspect ratio | 6.8 | | 6.8 | |
| Empty Weight | 975 | lb | 442 | kg |
| Loaded weight | 1600 | lb | 726 | kg |
| Wing loading | 10.2 | lb/sq ft | 50 | kg/sq m |
| Max speed | 123 | mph | 197 | kmh |
| Cruise speed | 98 | mph | 157 | kmh |
| Stalling speed | 50 | mph | 80 | kmh |
| Climb rate | 670 | ft/min | 200 | m/min |
| Range | 300 | mls | 480 | km |

When Beagle took on the Auster concern they designed the four seat Airedale as a competitor to the prolific Cessnas then beginning to flood the country.

Though considerably improved, the Airedale was essentially an old 'low tech' Auster and was not enough to check the American invasion.

The improvements embodied in the new aeroplane included, a swept back fin and rudder, an all metal wing structure, though still partly fabric covered, improved interior (to 'car standards'), front and rear doors, slotted flaps, disc brakes and steerable nose wheel undercarriage and improved instrumentation.

The prototype first flew in 1961 and production petered out in 1964 when forty-three had been made, seventeen remain on the UK Register.

Variants included a 175 hp Continental version, the A111 and a lighter less comprehensively equipped version for club use.

Beagle built their aeroplanes to last and owners to cherish them, the Airedale (and the rest of the Beagle 'litter') will be around for some time yet!

# BEAGLE
# A109 AIREDALE

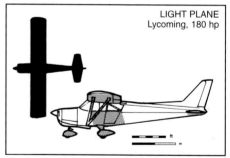

LIGHT PLANE
Lycoming, 180 hp

| DATA | IMPERIAL | | METRIC | |
|---|---|---|---|---|
| Span | 36.3 | ft | 11.2 | m |
| Wing area | 190 | sq ft | 17.8 | sq m |
| Aspect ratio | 7 | | 7 | |
| Empty Weight | 1700 | lb | 772 | kg |
| Loaded weight | 2750 | lb | 1248 | kg |
| Wing loading | 14.5 | lb/sq ft | 70.6 | kg/sq m |
| Max speed | 141 | mph | 226 | kmh |
| Cruise speed | 133 | mph | 213 | kmh |
| Stalling speed | 50 | mph | 80 | kmh |
| Climb rate | 650 | ft/min | 200 | m/min |
| Range | 560 | mls | 896 | km |

The five seat Model 206 first flew in 1962 and deliveries commenced in 1964. It was a development of the Model 205 as was the retractable gear Model 210 which illogically flew before the 206 in 1950. The Model 206 is the fixed gear version of the 210 and 7,500 variants have been built. Amongst the variant types are the P206 Super Skylane six seater, TP206 Super Skylane with a turbo-supercharged engine, U206 Super Skywagon, Stationair and Stationair 6 (1978), to name but a few of the fifteen models.these are all comfortable, fast cruising metal aircraft with a useful range.

Distinguishing features are down turned wing tips and three full cabin windows per side, going well beyond the wing training edge.

The Model 207 is even longer with four cabin windows per side but retaining the same wing and tail. There are twenty-seven Model 206s on the UK Register.

# CESSNA
# MODEL 206

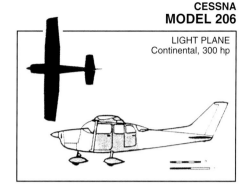

LIGHT PLANE
Continental, 300 hp

| DATA | IMPERIAL | | METRIC | |
|---|---|---|---|---|
| Span | 36.3 | ft | 11.2 | m |
| Wing area | 176 | sq ft | 16.5 | sq m |
| Aspect ratio | 7.6 | | 7.6 | |
| Empty Weight | 1265 | lb | 801 | kg |
| Loaded weight | 3600 | lb | 1634 | kg |
| Wing loading | 10 | lb/sq ft | 48.8 | kg/sq m |
| Max speed | 174 | mph | 278 | kmh |
| Cruise speed | 164 | mph | 262 | kmh |
| Stalling speed | 50 | mph | 80 | kmh |
| Climb rate | 920 | ft/min | 283 | m/min |
| Range | 800 | mls | 1280 | km |

Intended for ease of construction without complicated jigs and using only hand tools, the BN-3 was an ingenious design allowing licence building anywhere in the world.

First flown in 1969 the all-metal two-seat prototype, subsequent versions seating up to four were to have 130 and 160 hp engines.

Clearly a rival to the omnipresent Cessna tribe the brilliant and competitively price BN-3 inexplicably never sold and is little known today.

The two spar high aspect ratio wings carried electrically operated plain flaps and were foldable for ease of hangarage, a big plus over its rivals.

After its debut at the 1969 Paris Air Show and talk of an Australian order for 100, the Nymph faded away.

In 1981 the ten years stored BN-3 was sold in Scotland, bought back by Desmond Norman later rebuilt and modified as the NAC-1 Freelance (G-NAC1) and flown again in 1984. A second Freelance (G-NACA) has been built and is stored.

# BRITTEN-NORMAN
# BN-3 NYMPH

LIGHT PLANE
Lycoming, 115 hp

| DATA | IMPERIAL | | METRIC | |
|---|---|---|---|---|
| Span | 39 | ft | 12 | m |
| Wing area | 169 | sq ft | 16 | sq m |
| Aspect ratio | 9 | | | |
| Empty Weight | 1140 | lb | 517 | kg |
| Loaded weight | 1925 | lb | 874 | kg |
| Wing loading | 28 | lb/sq ft | 136 | kg/sq m |
| Max speed | 117 | mph | 187 | kmh |
| Cruise speed | 113 | mph | 181 | kmh |
| Stalling speed | 65 | mph | 104 | kmh |
| Climb rate | 580 | ft/min | 178 | m/min |
| Range | 500 | mls | 800 | km |

The MW-5 Scorcerer was designed by Mike Whittaker in 1983, based on the MW 4 which first flew in 1982, and is a single seat microlight under whose extremely simple lines lies a very well engineered airframe.

The MW 5 is sold as a 'plans only' and over forty are currently on the British Register, a fair proportion of which can be seen at the annual MW rally held at Charterhouse.

The tail boom and main spar are of light alloy tube the wing having plywood ribs and leading edge with fabric covering. The main boom carries an all moving rudder and elevator at one end and the Rotax 447 at the other. Other Rotax and Robin engines may be fitted.

The main wheels are mounted on leaf springs and may be fitted with spats and brakes. The nose wheel is steerable.

A batch of eighteen were built by Aerotech with tapered wings.

This is an enduring little aeroplane with a good safety record, very satisfied owners and PFA approved.

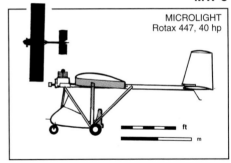

## WHITTAKER
## MW 5

MICROLIGHT
Rotax 447, 40 hp

| DATA | IMPERIAL | | METRIC | |
|---|---|---|---|---|
| Span | 28 | ft | 8.62 | m |
| Wing area | 140 | sq ft | 13.16 | sq m |
| Aspect ratio | 5.6 | | 5.6 | |
| Empty Weight | *300* | lb | *136* | kg |
| Loaded weight | 625 | lb | 284 | kg |
| Wing loading | 4.46 | lb/sq ft | 21.8 | kg/sq m |
| Max speed | 92 | mph | 147 | kmh |
| Cruise speed | 63 | mph | 101 | kmh |
| Stalling speed | 34 | mph | 54 | kmh |
| Climb rate | 600 | ft/min | 185 | m/min |
| Range | 200 | mls | 320 | km |

The Cyclone design originated in the USA and has been produced in France since 1982 by Ultralair where it has proved hugely popular with over 5,000 being sold worldwide, making it the most numerous microlight?

Produced in this country by Cyclone Airsports near Oxford, the AX3 is being flown by a RAF flying club, quite a feather in its cap!

The structure is of light alloy tubing with Dacron covering, the cockpit pod being of GRP with an optional side door. Lateral control is by flaperons the other axis being looked after by a conventional tailplane, elevator, fin and rudder. The tricycle gear is sprung and braked with a steerable nose-wheel.

It is available as a kit and is PFA approved.

A development, the AX2000 marketed by Pegasus Aviation has a water cooled Rotax.

There are thirty-nine AX3s and thirty-two AX2000s on the UK Register.

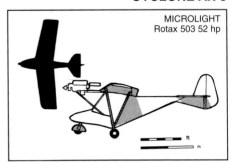

## CYCLONE AIRSPORTS
## CYCLONE AX 3

MICROLIGHT
Rotax 503 52 hp

| DATA | IMPERIAL | | METRIC | |
|---|---|---|---|---|
| Span | 32 | ft | 19.8 | m |
| Wing area | 175 | sq ft | 16.5 | sq m |
| Aspect ratio | 5.8 | | 5.8 | |
| Empty Weight | 429 | lb | 195 | kg |
| Loaded weight | 858 | lb | 390 | kg |
| Wing loading | 4.9 | lb/sq ft | 23.9 | kg/sq m |
| Max speed | 75 | mph | 120 | kmh |
| Cruise speed | 60 | mph | 96 | kmh |
| Stalling speed | 34 | mph | 54 | kmh |
| Climb rate | 433 | ft/min | 133 | m/min |
| Range | 200 | mls | 320 | km |

The British designed and built microlight two seater was the brainchild of Richard Noble, not the ARV designer, in 1962 and launched as the Noble-Hardman Snowbird. In 1984 it was marketed by the Snowbird Aeroplane Company in Cowbridge, South Glamorgan.

This is a factory built aeroplane (no kits yet) with a fully enclosed fuselage constructed of light alloy tubes and covered in Dacron. The two spar wing has, unusually, spoilers on the top surface instead of ailerons. The tricycle undercarriage has a steerable nose wheel and cable operated main wheel brakes, the cable being situated in the cabin roof!

There are over seventeen Snowbirds currently on the British Register, a proportion are airworthy and one, G-MVIM is in the Yorkshire Air Museum.

## NOBLE-HARDMAN
# SNOWBIRD

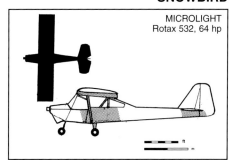

MICROLIGHT
Rotax 532, 64 hp

| DATA | IMPERIAL | | METRIC | |
|------|----------|--|--------|--|
| Span | 31 | ft | 9.5 | m |
| Wing area | 186 | sq ft | 17.4 | sq m |
| Aspect ratio | 5.2 | | 5.2 | |
| Empty Weight | 399 | lb | 181 | kg |
| Loaded weight | 848 | lb | 385 | kg |
| Wing loading | 4.6 | lb/sq ft | 22.4 | kg/sq m |
| Max speed | 75 | mph | 120 | kmh |
| Cruise speed | 60 | mph | 96 | kmh |
| Stalling speed | 38 | mph | 61 | kmh |
| Climb rate | 900 | ft/min | 277 | m/min |
| Range | 180 | mls | 288 | km |

Designed by Mike Whittaker, as are all the MW range, the MW6 is the two seater of the family, either in tandem MW6, or side-by-side MW6S the prototype MW6S being nick-named Fat Boy Flyer.

It is a microlight of simple but soundly engineered construction with large diameter light alloy tubes taking the principle loads in single spar wings and tail boom. The wing has plywood ribs, fabric covering half span ailerons and is braced to the cockpit 'pod' basically the same as the well-proved MW4 and MW5. The tricycle undercarriage main wheels are mounted on leaf springs.

This two seat MW has proved popular, there being forty-nine or more on the British Register and is PFA approved.

## WHITTAKER
# MW6

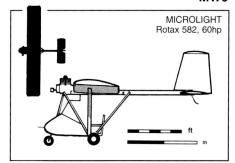

MICROLIGHT
Rotax 582, 60hp

| DATA | IMPERIAL | | METRIC | |
|------|----------|--|--------|--|
| Span | 32.7 | ft | 10.1 | m |
| Wing area | 164 | sq ft | 15.4 | sq m |
| Aspect ratio | 6.5 | | 6.5 | |
| Empty Weight | *400* | lb | 182 | kg |
| Loaded weight | 858 | lb | 389 | kg |
| Wing loading | 5.2 | lb/sq ft | 25.4 | kg/sq m |
| Max speed | 86 | mph | 138 | kmh |
| Cruise speed | 63 | mph | 101 | kmh |
| Stalling speed | 34 | mph | 54 | kmh |
| Climb rate | 1000 | ft/min | 308 | m/min |
| Range | 150 | mls | 240 | km |

This attractive two seat Canadian design has been demonstrated around Europe by various agents and sales now include two, which are on the UK Register. over 75 have been built in the USA and Canada.

The prototype first flew in 1984 and current models offer a range of wing spans and engines. Designed to be assembled from a kit of parts, the Pelican's fuselage is of moulded GRP/Epoxy foam sandwich and the single strut braced wing is all metal (Early models had fabric covered wings).

Both nose wheel and tail-dragger undercarriages are available.

Rotax, Continental and Hapi engines ranging in power from 52 to 115 hp are also options. (Figures below are for the PL version with Rotax 912, 80 hp).

The Pelican, with its high aspect ratio wing has a good cruise speed on modest power using only four gallons of fuel per hour. The roomy cockpit is well appointed and has comprehensive instrumentation.

## ULTRAVIA PELICAN

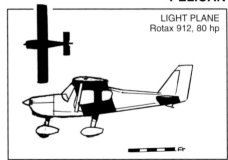

LIGHT PLANE
Rotax 912, 80 hp

| DATA | IMPERIAL | | METRIC | |
|---|---|---|---|---|
| Span | 29.5 | ft | 9.1 | m |
| Wing area | 108 | sq ft | 10.1 | sq m |
| Aspect ratio | 8 | | 0 | |
| Empty Weight | 700 | lb | 318 | kg |
| Loaded weight | 1250 | lb | 567 | kg |
| Wing loading | 11.5 | lb/sq ft | 56 | kg/sq m |
| Max speed | 135 | mph | 216 | kmh |
| Cruise speed | 123 | mph | 197 | kmh |
| Stalling speed | 48 | mph | 77 | kmh |
| Climb rate | 950 | ft/min | 293 | m/min |
| Range | 600 | mls | 960 | km |

The Canadian, Chris Heintz designed, CH701 STOL first flew in 1986 and is now produced by Zenair in Mexico, Missouri, as an all metal kit plane. Available as a tail-dragger or a nose wheel trike the CH701 is an ultra light two seater with a genuine STOL performance. The wing has full span, Fowler type flaperons plus full span fixed leading edge slats; giving it a single seat stall of 23 mph, a claimed Lift Coefficient of 3.1.

Power may be supplied by Rotax 503, 532, 912 or other units up to 100 hp.

The CH701 is an approved design in many countries and over 400 have been built worldwide, including thirteen on the UK Register.

PFA approved, the '701 is an ultralight that has a 'real' aeroplane feel about it. The metal structure is stressed for +6 to –3g and is devoid of double curvature panels and is mainly secured by blind rivets (Pop rivets). The main gear is on a leaf spring and the steerable nose wheel is bungee sprung, or as a tail-dragger, a sprung tail wheel.

Zenair and the Czech Aircraft Works have co-operated to build an economic crop duster version.

Data for 52 hp Rotax 503 model.

## ZENAIR CH701 STOL

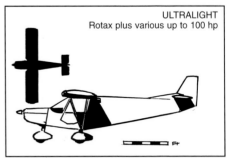

ULTRALIGHT
Rotax plus various up to 100 hp

| DATA | IMPERIAL | | METRIC | |
|---|---|---|---|---|
| Span | 27 | ft | 8.3 | m |
| Wing area | 122 | sq ft | 11.5 | sq m |
| Aspect ratio | 6 | | 6 | |
| Empty Weight | 430 | lb | 195 | kg |
| Loaded weight | 880 | lb | 400 | kg |
| Wing loading | 7.2 | lb/sq ft | 35 | kg/sq m |
| Max speed | 82 | mph | 131 | kmh |
| Cruise speed | 74 | mph | 118 | kmh |
| Stalling speed | 26 | mph | 42 | kmh |
| Climb rate | 820 | ft/min | 253 | m/min |
| Range | 200 | mls | 320 | km |

A gem from Australia! The two seater Jabiru first flew in 1989, was certificated in 1991 and is now well established in the UK. An all composites kit, or factory built plane powered by the company's own engine.

This is the first aero engine to be designed and approved in Australia; the Jabiru is a four cylinder, horizontally opposed four stroke with direct drive to the prop via a six bearing crankshaft. In two models, 1600 cc/60 hp and 2200 cc/80 both quiet and efficient, they are increasingly sought after.

The wing, braced by a single steel strut, has a 'glass skin over a foam core and composites spar and has generous plain flaps and inset ailerons. The fuselage is built in two halves, top and bottom, and houses the side by side dual control seating, fuel tank (behind seats) and the hydraulically braked tricycle undercarriage.

There are over one hundred on the UK Register and others are being built with PFA approval.

## JABIRU AIRCRAFT
## JABIRU ST

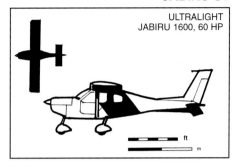

ULTRALIGHT
JABIRU 1600, 60 HP

| DATA | IMPERIAL | | METRIC | |
|---|---|---|---|---|
| Span | 26.3 | ft | 8 | m |
| Wing area | 85 | sq ft | 7.9 | sq m |
| Aspect ratio | 8.1 | | 8.1 | |
| Empty Weight | 517 | lb | 275 | kg |
| Loaded weight | 990 | lb | 450 | kg |
| Wing loading | 11.6 | lb/sq ft | 56.6 | kg/sq m |
| Max speed | 134 | mph | 214 | kmh |
| Cruise speed | 120 | mph | 192 | kmh |
| Stalling speed | 46 | mph | 73 | kmh |
| Climb rate | 800 | ft/min | 244 | m/min |
| Range | 575 | mls | 920 | km |

Developed from the single seat Sparrow Sport Special the two seat, side-by-side Sparrow 2 is a product of Carlson Aircraft Inc. of East Palestine, Ohio.

This neat microlight/ultralight comes in kit form, factory built models are under consideration, and has a welded steel tube fuselage and tail unit. The wing spars are of extruded light alloy with built up light alloy ribs, all covered in Dacron.

The tricycle undercarriage is bungee sprung and has hydraulic disc brakes on the main wheels.

Dual controls are standard and its short field performance is very good with an initial climb rate of 1000 ft/min.

There are only two on the UK Register currently, the pilots of which report 'excellent handling characteristics with no bad habits'.

## CARLSON
## SPARROW 2

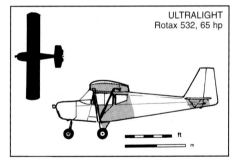

ULTRALIGHT
Rotax 532, 65 hp

| DATA | IMPERIAL | | METRIC | |
|---|---|---|---|---|
| Span | 32 | ft | 9.8 | m |
| Wing area | 144 | sq ft | 13.5 | sq m |
| Aspect ratio | 7.1 | | 7.1 | |
| Empty Weight | 390 | lb | 177 | kg |
| Loaded weight | 945 | lb | 429 | kg |
| Wing loading | 6.5 | lb/sq ft | 32 | kg/sq m |
| Max speed | 90 | mph | 144 | kmh |
| Cruise speed | 70 | mph | 112 | kmh |
| Stalling speed | 30 | mph | 48 | kmh |
| Climb rate | 1000 | ft/min | 308 | m/min |
| Range | 300 | mls | 480 | km |

The two seat Rans S6 Coyote, developed from the single seat S4/S5 went into production in 1990 at the Rans Hays factory in Kansas and is available with three motor and three wing options covering its categorisation from microlight to 1100 lb light aircraft with a 120 mph cruise, shortly to be adapted to the 450 kg microlight category with a Rotax 582.

The kit comprises a welded tube cabin module and bolt together light alloy tubes for the rear fuselage. The wing has two tubular spars and a slip-on Dacron covering with light alloy riblets in sewn pockets. It has ailerons and flaps, not flaperons.

Other options are trike or tail-dragger, with or without spats, and disc or drum brakes. A unusual option is a rocket deployed total aircraft recovery ballistic parachute.

The Coyote is a PFA approved design, with 165 on the Register and flying, plus approximately forty being built.

Date below is for the 450 kg microlight.

## RANS
## S6 COYOTE

MICROLIGHT/ULTRALIGHT
Rotax, 47 to 78 hp

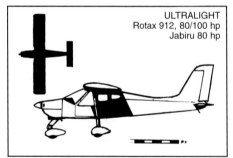

| DATA | IMPERIAL | | METRIC | |
|---|---|---|---|---|
| Span | 34.5 | ft | 10.6 | m |
| Wing area | 155 | sq ft | 15.1 | sq m |
| Aspect ratio | 7.6 | | 7.6 | |
| Empty Weight | 499 | lb | 227 | kg |
| Loaded weight | 990 | lb | 450 | kg |
| Wing loading | 6.4 | lb/sq ft | 31.2 | kg/sq m |
| Max speed | 100 | mph | 160 | kmh |
| Cruise speed | 80 | mph | 128 | kmh |
| Stalling speed | 34 | mph | 54 | kmh |
| Climb rate | 1000 | ft/min | 308 | m/min |
| Range | 350 | mls | 560 | km |

Initially badged as the Partenavia P92 Echo this Pascalle brothers design is now produced by Tecnam at their plant near Naples as either a kit or a factory built aircraft.

The two seat Echo first flown in 1992 is an all metal aeroplane which, depending on fit and equipment can be in the SLA or VLA class – only VLAs are allowed the weight/luxury of wheel spats and cabin trim.

The wing has metal spars and ribs and is metal skinned, the metal tailplane is fabric covered but fin and rudder have metal skins. The fuselage has a welded steel tube safety cage, a light alloy rear section with composites fairings. The main gear is sprung on a cantilever composites leg with powerful hydraulic disc brakes. The all moving tail plane's trim tab is electrically operated as are the wing flaps which, like the Frise type ailerons, are metal framed with fabric covering. As a kit plane the Echo comes with many major assemblies complete and all holes pre-drilled. The UK agent is Mike Rudd of Dorchester, Dorset who has provided fifteen for the UK Register with others being built. World sales are over 500. The Echo SLA has a Jabiru engine of 80 hp and the Rotax 912 engined versions are in the VLA category.

## TECNAM
## P92 ECHO SLA/VLA

ULTRALIGHT
Rotax 912, 80/100 hp
Jabiru 80 hp

| DATA | IMPERIAL | | METRIC | |
|---|---|---|---|---|
| Span | 30.6 | ft | 9.3 | m |
| Wing area | 142 | sq ft | 13.2 | sq m |
| Aspect ratio | 6.6 | | 6.6 | |
| Empty Weight | 619 | lb | 281 | kg |
| Loaded weight | 1212 | lb | 550 | kg |
| Wing loading | 8.53 | lb/sq ft | 41.6 | kg/sq m |
| Max speed | 135 | mph | 216 | kmh |
| Cruise speed | 117 | mph | 187 | kmh |
| Stalling speed | 37 | mph | 59 | kmh |
| Climb rate | 1260 | ft/min | 388 | m/min |
| Range | 448 | mls | 717 | km |

A Czechoslovakian designed microlight that arrived in the UK in 1993. The Sluka is a single seater though a two seat version, of almost identical appearance, the ST-4 Aztek has been introduced recently.

Of standard microlight construction, light alloy tubes and Dacron covering - the Sluka has a neat GRP nacelle with an integral semi-reclining seat.

This is a three axis control aircraft that comes in a very comprehensive kit, complete with engine and all instruments - but the wheel spats are part of a 'speed modification' kit!

A handy feature is the folding wing arrangement making for ease of towing and storage.

Lateral control is by flaperons and the other axes being looked after by the conventional fin/rudder and tailplane/elevator.

The main 'gear wheels are sprung on a carbon fibre semi-elliptic beam and the nose wheel is steerable.

There are eighteen Slukas currently on the Register, but the attractive price and comprehensive kitting should ensure that many more will be added.

## LETOV
## LK-2M SLUKA

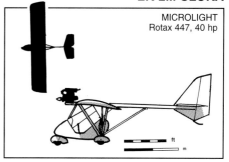

MICROLIGHT
Rotax 447, 40 hp

| DATA | IMPERIAL | | METRIC | |
|---|---|---|---|---|
| Span | 30.6 | ft | 9.3 | m |
| Wing area | 142 | sq ft | 13.2 | sq m |
| Aspect ratio | 6.6 | | | |
| Empty Weight | 619 | lb | 281 | kg |
| Loaded weight | 1212 | lb | 550 | kg |
| Wing loading | 8.53 | lb/sq ft | 41.6 | kg/sq m |
| Max speed | 135 | mph | 216 | kmh |
| Cruise speed | 117 | mph | 187 | kmh |
| Stalling speed | 37 | mph | 59 | kmh |
| Climb rate | 1260 | ft/min | 388 | m/min |
| Range | 448 | mls | 717 | km |

An Australian success story. Jabiru Aircraft founded in 1988 by Rodney Stiff and Phil Ainsworth to manufacture the two seat Jabiru, soon branched out into engine manufacture, producing flat four and flat six engines. The J400 is a four seat development of the original two-seat Jabiru UL and first flew in 2001. All the Jabirus come mainly as kit planes though a minority are factory built. The constructing is almost entirely composites, including the undercarriage spring legs; the wing is braced with a single steel strut and has wide span slotted flaps. the J400 with two people aboard conforms to the UK ultralight rules – but with four up is amongst the big boys!

Powered by Jabirus own 3300 flat six cylinder engine which drives a fixed pitch propeller, the fuel comes from wing tanks of 100 litre/22 imperial gallon capacity. The UL Jabiru has a fuselage tank. Jabiru 400s are starting to arrive in the UK the importer/agent ST Aviation, Horsham, West Sussex. Six are being built under pending PFA approval.

## JABIRU
## J400

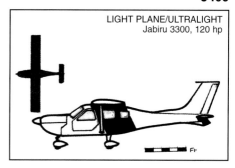

LIGHT PLANE/ULTRALIGHT
Jabiru 3300, 120 hp

| DATA | IMPERIAL | | METRIC | |
|---|---|---|---|---|
| Span | 26.6 | ft | 8.1 | m |
| Wing area | 86.1 | sq ft | 8 | sq m |
| Aspect ratio | 8.2 | | | |
| Empty Weight | 683 | lb | 310 | kg |
| Loaded weight | 1200 | lb | 544 | kg |
| Wing loading | 13.9 | lb/sq ft | 68 | kg/sq m |
| Max speed | 150 | mph | 420 | kmh |
| Cruise speed | 138 | mph | 222 | kmh |
| Stalling speed | 69 | mph | 111 | kmh |
| Climb rate | 1500 | ft/min | 457 | m/min |
| Range | 598 | mls | 963 | km |

Designed in Germany by Flugsport and built in the Ukraine, the CT is marketed in the UK by Pegasus Aviation who assemble the aircraft for sale as ready-to-fly.

Of mainly composites/carbon fibre construction the CT has a cantilever wring with electrically operated flaps giving 9-12°/+40° range. The tricycle undercarriage has aluminium legs and hydraulically braked main wheels. The side by side seating is comfortable within a 48ins wide cockpit with excellent visibility through the generous glazing.

The original CT was certificated in 1997 and the current CT2K model differs in having a lighter airframe and downturned wing tips. Amongst the optional extras offered are Junkers High Speed or BRS UL1050 ballistic recovery parachutes.

With its slippery shape and good performance plus its factory-built cache the CT has a lot going for it. So far thirty are on the UK Register.

# FLIGHT DESIGN
## CT

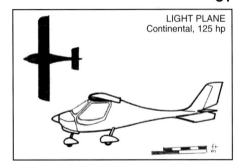

LIGHT PLANE
Continental, 125 hp

| DATA | IMPERIAL | | METRIC | |
|---|---|---|---|---|
| Span | 30.5 | ft | 9.3 | m |
| Wing area | 110 | sq ft | 10.8 | sq m |
| Aspect ratio | 8.5 | | | |
| Empty Weight | 583 | lb | 265 | kg |
| Loaded weight | 991 | lb | 450 | kg |
| Wing loading | 9 | lb/sq ft | 44 | kg/sq m |
| Max speed | 155 | mph | 248 | kmh |
| Cruise speed | 132 | mph | 211 | kmh |
| Stalling speed | 46 | mph | 73 | kmh |
| Climb rate | 1054 | ft/min | 1686 | m/min |
| Range | 1040 | mls | 1664 | km |

From the same stable as the sleek and fast Glasair the high wing, side by side two seat GlaStar is not, in spite of its swoopy lines an all composites aeroplane like its sister. Construction is mixed, GRP panels cover a welded steel tube forward fuselage, aft of the cabin it is composite, trike or tail-dragger gear can be easily fitted. All flying surfaces are metal and of simple construction - the high aspect ratio wing has only four full chord ribs per side - and is 'Fowler' flapped.

During 1995-96 the GlaStar demonstrator has been 'strutting its stuff' around Europe and the company have reported much interest and over 200 orders - including, we believe, some from the UK.

The GlaStar is much compared with the, now venerable, Cessna 150/152, which it out performs in both range and speed. It is roomier and has wings designed to fold alongside the fuselage. PFA aeroplanes (home built) cannot be used as trainers.

Wing vortex generators and tailplane cuffs are fitted to later models, making a nice handling aeroplane even nicer.

Sixteen on the UK Register and ten in construction.

# STODDARD HAMILTON
## GLASTAR

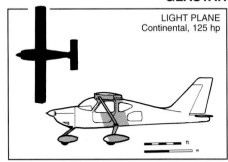

LIGHT PLANE
Continental, 125 hp

| DATA | IMPERIAL | | METRIC | |
|---|---|---|---|---|
| Span | 35 | ft | 10.8 | m |
| Wing area | 116 | sq ft | 10.9 | sq m |
| Aspect ratio | 10.5 | | 10.5 | |
| Empty Weight | 1100 | lb | 500 | kg |
| Loaded weight | 1900 | lb | 862 | kg |
| Wing loading | 16.4 | lb/sq ft | 80 | kg/sq m |
| Max speed | 156 | mph | 250 | kmh |
| Cruise speed | 140 | mph | 141 | kmh |
| Stalling speed | 45 | mph | 72 | kmh |
| Climb rate | 800 | ft/min | 308 | m/min |
| Range | 797 | mls | 1275 | km |

The Ukranian Aeroprakt A22 Foxbat is, at the time of writing, being assessed by the PFA for BCAR-S approval. In the 450kg SLA category, the design was originally called the Shark and its designer carries the famous name of Yuri Yakovlev.

The A22 is already approved in Germany, where it has a control wheel instead of a stick, and is marketed in the USA by Spectrum Aircraft Corp as the Valor.

The airframe kit is composed of rivetted metal sheet and tube with fabric covering plus GRP panels and fairings. the wings come completely assembled less covering.

Fitted with a Rotax 912-S engine the Foxbat has a real STOL performance, the full span flaperons getting its stall down to 34 mph and the initial climb is a respectable 1200 fpm.

Identification features include the large glazed area aft of the cabin, the large fin and rudder and the swept forward wings.

Marketed in the UK by the Small Light Aeroplane Co. Ltd at Otherton Airfield. Nine are on the UK Register.

## AEROPRAKT
## A22 FOXBAT

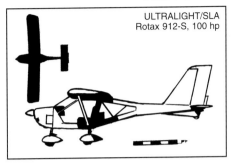

ULTRALIGHT/SLA
Rotax 912-S, 100 hp

| DATA | IMPERIAL | | METRIC | |
|---|---|---|---|---|
| Span | 32.4 | ft | 10 | m |
| Wing area | 145 | sq ft | 13.7 | sq m |
| Aspect ratio | 7.1 | | | |
| Empty Weight | 566 | lb | 255 | kg |
| Loaded weight | 991 | lb | 450 | kg |
| Wing loading | 6.8 | lb/sq ft | 33 | kg/sq m |
| Max speed | 100 | mph | 160 | kmh |
| Cruise speed | 85 | mph | 136 | kmh |
| Stalling speed | 34 | mph | 54 | kmh |
| Climb rate | 1200 | ft/min | 370 | m/min |
| Range | 600 | mls | 960 | km |

Joel Koechlin of Raj Hamsa Ultralights, Bangalore, have developed the US Weedhopper design into the X-Air which was launched in 1993 as a kit built ultralight of simple and rugged construction. The part assembled kits began to arrive in the UK is the mid 90s and now in 2004 there are 100 on the UK Register. X-Air Australia are the local agents and some 200 are now current worldwide. Worldwide there are 500 sales.

The X-Air is a conventional three axis control microlight with side by side seating. The airframe is of bolted together aluminium tube with Dacron fabric covering, making for ease of assembly and repair. The differential braked tricycle undercarriage has, thanks to generous gas/oil shock struts, excellent energy absorbing qualities; the nose wheel is a steerable light alloy unit. the standard X-Air is powered by Rotax 503, 582 or 618 and the X-Air Falcon has an 80 hp Rotax 912 four-stroke up front with a subsequent hike in performance. The X-Airs are rugged, reasonably priced and here to stay.

## RAJ HAMSA
## X-AIR FALCON

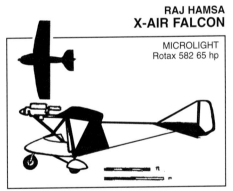

MICROLIGHT
Rotax 582 65 hp

| DATA | IMPERIAL | | METRIC | |
|---|---|---|---|---|
| Span | 32.1 | ft | 9.8 | m |
| Wing area | 172 | sq ft | 16 | sq m |
| Aspect ratio | 6 | | | |
| Empty Weight | 507 | lb | 230 | kg |
| Loaded weight | 903 | lb | 410 | kg |
| Wing loading | 5.25 | lb/sq ft | 25.6 | kg/sq m |
| Max speed | 75 | mph | 120 | kmh |
| Cruise speed | 56 | mph | 90 | kmh |
| Stalling speed | 29 | mph | 46 | kmh |
| Climb rate | 591 | ft/min | 180 | m/min |
| Range | 150 | mls | 240 | km |

The latest design from German firm Ikarus Comco, producers of the popular tube and fabric C22 microlight, is the C42, of more traditional layout with a sleek composites fuselage and tube and fabric wings.

First deliveries of the C42 began in 1997 and in the 'States, 1998 as the C42 Cyclone, marketed by Flightstar Sportplanes.

The strut braced wings fold for economic hangarage and the tube and fabric 'tail feathers' are also strut braced. The 50% span flaps are electrically operated.

Unusually for a new type the undercarriage is of the three strut split axle type rather than the fashionable cantilever spring leg. 'Speed fairings' are standard on the hydraulically braked wheels.

It is claimed that a ballistic recovery parachute is fitted as standard – a brilliant 'non-extra' safety feature.

The side by side seats are reached under upward hinging doors on each side.

Microlight and ULA versions are available ready built or as PFA approved kit. C42 is marketed by Fly Buy Ultralights.

# IKARUS COMCO C42

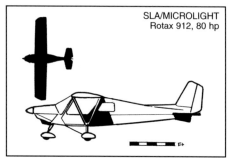

SLA/MICROLIGHT
Rotax 912, 80 hp

| DATA | IMPERIAL | | METRIC | |
|------|----------|---|--------|---|
| Span | 31 | ft | 9.45 | m |
| Wing area | 134 | sq ft | 12.5 | sq m |
| Aspect ratio | 7.2 | | | |
| Empty Weight | 551 | lb | 250 | kg |
| Loaded weight | 992 | lb | 450 | kg |
| Wing loading | 7.4 | lb/sq ft | 36 | kg/sq m |
| Max speed | 120 | mph | 192 | kmh |
| Cruise speed | 109 | mph | 175 | kmh |
| Stalling speed | 40 | mph | 63 | kmh |
| Climb rate | 1000 | ft/min | 308 | m/min |
| Range | 497 | mls | 800 | km |

When first flown in 1957 the 210 was a four seater based on the Model 182, with a strut braced wing, but having a retractable tricycle undercarriage and a 260 hp Continental engine. Various modifications, mainly to windows and cabin rear roof line took the model number up to 210D, when it also became Centurion and acquired two child seats, making it 4+2. (1500 of the 210 to 210D were built).

With the 210G the cantilever wing was introduced and later the 210K became a full adult six seater at an AUW of 3800 lb. Wing tip and stabiliser changes plus nose lights, turbo engines and finally, pressurisation took the type to 210R (325 hp. Continental). Over 7000 of the cantilever 210s were built, the most numerous being the 210L Centurion, with 6 seats nose light and tubular legs instead of spring steel, 2,070 of these being built.

The construction is standard Cessna all metal with large cabin doors either side.(The complicated doors fully covering the retracted wheels were dropped in '79)

Though weighing in at around two tons, its owners say it handles like a 172, and furthermore, they are hanging on to them! There are fifteen on the UK Register. Figs. for 210N (310 hp).

# CESSNA 210 CENTURION

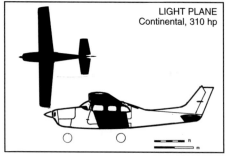

LIGHT PLANE
Continental, 310 hp

| DATA | IMPERIAL | | METRIC | |
|------|----------|---|--------|---|
| Span | 36.7 | ft | 11.3 | m |
| Wing area | 175.5 | sq ft | 16.4 | sq m |
| Aspect ratio | 7.6 | | 7.6 | |
| Empty Weight | 2303 | lb | 1045 | kg |
| Loaded weight | 4000 | lb | 1816 | kg |
| Wing loading | 22.8 | lb/sq ft | 111 | kg/sq m |
| Max speed | 235 | mph | 376 | kmh |
| Cruise speed | 221 | mph | 353 | kmh |
| Stalling speed | 67 | mph | 107 | kmh |
| Climb rate | 930 | ft/min | 286 | m/min |
| Range | 1800 | mls | 2880 | km |

Introduced in 1967, the Cessna Cardinal, a roomy four seater, had a cantilever wing; though somewhat unusual for the range, this configuration was always a favourite with Clyde Cessna - his first series production 'plane, the Model A of 1927 was, in fact, a high wing cantilever monoplane! First models of the '177 had 150 hp. Lycomings which were replaced by 180 hp. units in the 177A.

The 177B or Cardinal 2 had a fifth (child's) seat, a constant speed prop and curved down wing tips. The 1978 Cardinal Classic was a de Luxe version of the 177B.

The big step of retracting the undercarriage came in 1970 with the Cardinal RG (Retractable Gear) which also incorporated a 200 hp. Lycoming, the combination adding about 40 mph to the top speed.

The sleek and slippery RG has a straight tapered wing (like the other cantilever Cessna, the Centurion) electric flaps and an all moving stabilator.

There are twenty-seven Cardinals on the UK Register. twenty of them RGs. Total production is 4000.

## CESSNA
## 177 CARDINAL RG

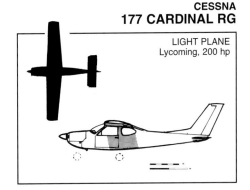

LIGHT PLANE
Lycoming, 200 hp

| DATA | IMPERIAL | | METRIC | |
|---|---|---|---|---|
| Span | 35.5 | ft | 11 | m |
| Wing area | 174 | sq ft | 16.3 | sq m |
| Aspect ratio | 7 | | 7 | |
| Empty Weight | 1707 | lb | 775 | kg |
| Loaded weight | 2800 | lb | 1271 | kg |
| Wing loading | 16.1 | lb/sq ft | 78.6 | kg/sq m |
| Max speed | 180 | mph | 290 | kmh |
| Cruise speed | 170 | mph | 273 | kmh |
| Stalling speed | 57 | mph | 92 | kmh |
| Climb rate | 925 | ft/min | 282 | m/min |
| Range | 1005 | mls | 1608 | km |

American Airlines pilot Tom Cassutt designed and built the first Cassutt Special 1 in 1954 as a small fast and practical aeroplane suitable for home building.

After winning its class at the National Air Races in 1958 a Cassutt Special 2 was built, smaller and faster with the pilot 'shoe horned' into a very narrow cockpit, an out and out racer. After twenty-five years from the first flight Cassutt Specials finished first, second and third in the Cleveland Nationals.

2000 plans have been sold world wide and in 1985 at least 125 were flying. Thirteen are on the UK Register.

The wooden wing has no incidence, no dihedral and no flaps, and the spring steel legs carry braked wheels. The Cassutt is a PFA approved design, two are being built.

## CASSUTT
## SPECIAL

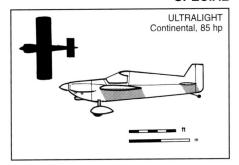

ULTRALIGHT
Continental, 85 hp

| DATA | IMPERIAL | | METRIC | |
|---|---|---|---|---|
| Span | 17 | ft | 5.18 | m |
| Wing area | 76.5 | sq ft | 7.11 | sq m |
| Aspect ratio | 3.75 | | 3.75 | |
| Empty Weight | 500 | lb | 277 | kg |
| Loaded weight | 800 | lb | 363 | kg |
| Wing loading | 10.5 | lb/sq ft | 51.24 | kg/sq m |
| Max speed | 200 | mph | 322 | kmh |
| Cruise speed | 180 | mph | 290 | kmh |
| Stalling speed | 50 | mph | 80 | kmh |
| Climb rate | 3000 | ft/min | 914 | m/min |
| Range | 490 | mls | 788 | km |

A plans homebuilt aerobatic single seater, the Akro won the US Championships in 1975 and competed at world level in the mid 70s.

The design is PFA approved and several have been built in the UK, six are on the UK Register, three airworthy.

The prototype first flew in 1967 and a bigger wing version, the Model B, in 1969. Like most modern aerobats the Akro is without dihedral or incidence and the wooden two-spar wing is built in one piece. The ailerons are fabric covered and have ground adjustable tabs. The fuselage is of welded steel tube construction with Ceconite covering as is the tail unit, which is wire braced. The tailplane and rudder and elevator tabs are ground adjustable.

The cantilever, spring steel tail dragger undercarriage has disc brakes and the steerable tail-wheel is by Maule. Some early models had a floor window

Fixed pitch or constant speed propellers may be fitted and special fuel tanks for prolonged inverted flying may be fitted.

The Akro has had many variant designs based on it inc. the Extra 230 (Akro Laser) and the Pace Spirit.

## STEPHENS AKRO

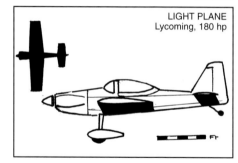

LIGHT PLANE
Lycoming, 180 hp

| DATA | IMPERIAL | | METRIC | |
|---|---|---|---|---|
| Span | 24.5 | ft | 7.5 | m |
| Wing area | 94 | sq ft | 8.7 | sq m |
| Aspect ratio | 6.4 | | | |
| Empty Weight | 950 | lb | 430 | kg |
| Loaded weight | 1300 | lb | 589 | kg |
| Wing loading | 13.8 | lb/sq ft | 67 | kg/sq m |
| Max speed | 170 | mph | 274 | kmh |
| Cruise speed | 160 | mph | 257 | kmh |
| Stalling speed | 55 | mph | 89 | kmh |
| Climb rate | 4000 | ft/min | 1220 | m/min |
| Range | 350 | mls | 563 | km |

The small, sleek, Sonerai, first flown in 1973, comes in single and two seat versions, Sonerai 1 and 2 respectively.

An American design, the Sonerai is constructed in the American way with a welded steel tube fuselage but has metal cantilever wings, in mid or low wing configuration, which carry full span ailerons.

The standard power unit is the reliable 2200cc VW of 82 hp hiving the Sonerai 2 a top speed of 165 mph.

Marketed ready made or in kit form by Mosler of Hendersonville, USA, over 500 have been built stateside and sixteen are registered in this country, one being built.

It is a PFA approved design which is also available with tricycle landing gear.

The figures below are for the Sonerai 2.

## MONNETT SONERAI

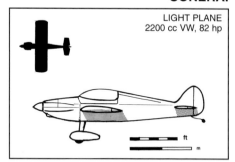

LIGHT PLANE
2200 cc VW, 82 hp

| DATA | IMPERIAL | | METRIC | |
|---|---|---|---|---|
| Span | 18.8 | ft | 5.69 | m |
| Wing area | 84 | sq ft | 7.5 | sq m |
| Aspect ratio | 4.15 | | 4.15 | |
| Empty Weight | 500 | lb | 227 | kg |
| Loaded weight | 1150 | lb | 521 | kg |
| Wing loading | 13.7 | lb/sq ft | 68.8 | kg/sq m |
| Max speed | 160 | mph | 257 | kmh |
| Cruise speed | 130 | mph | 209 | kmh |
| Stalling speed | 44 | mph | 71 | kmh |
| Climb rate | 500 | ft/min | 152 | m/min |
| Range | 350 | mls | 563 | km |

The Cygnet, designed and built by ex Boeing 747 captain, Bert Sisler, has had a checkered background. known first as the Sisler Cygnet, the rights and prototype were sold to HAPI (Homebuilt Aircraft Plans Inc) in 1983, hence the HAPI Cygnet, only to merge with Mosler in 1992 so sometimes known as the Mosler Cygnet.

This sturdy, side-by-side, two seater has, like the ARV2, a shoulder mounted swept forward wing giving excellent visibility from the high set cockpit.

The all wooden wing, designed to fold for storage is multi sparred with plywood ribs, the whole being encased in a geodetic like matrix of spruce laths, giving it great strength in torsion and shear.

The fuselage is built up with welded steel tube with a few wooden formers under the fabric covering.

Rotax Mosler and VW engines have been fitted, the data below is for the 62hp VW model.

The first UK example flew at the 1995 PFA rally. There are now five on the UK Register and two are being built. It is PFA approved.

# HAPI
# CYGNET

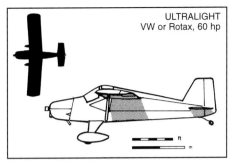

ULTRALIGHT
VW or Rotax, 60 hp

| DATA | IMPERIAL | | METRIC | |
|---|---|---|---|---|
| Span | 30 | ft | 9.2 | m |
| Wing area | 120 | sq ft | 11.3 | sq m |
| Aspect ratio | 7 | | 7 | |
| Empty Weight | 585 | lb | 266 | kg |
| Loaded weight | 1100 | lb | 500 | kg |
| Wing loading | 9.1 | lb/sq ft | 44 | kg/sq m |
| Max speed | 100 | mph | 160 | kmh |
| Cruise speed | 90 | mph | 144 | kmh |
| Stalling speed | 41 | mph | 66 | kmh |
| Climb rate | 600 | ft/min | 185 | m/min |
| Range | 300 | mls | 480 | km |

Bearing a Yakovlev family resemblance to the late Model YAK 18, the Model 55, which first flew in 1984 is a smaller aeroplane designed from the start as an aerobat and developed from the YAK 50 of 1975 vintage.

The Model 55 differs from its predecessor in having a mid wing of symmetrical section with zero dihedral as a opposed to a low wing and a fixed rather than retractable undercarriage giving it a seriously aerobatic look!

Such is the pace of aerobatic aircraft design at World' level that the Model 55 was never quite as successful as the Model 50 and subsequently was released on to the open market.

The all metal construction makes for a heavier aeroplane than most of its competitors - hence the lighter weight YAK 55M. With its full span ailerons and big radial engine the YAK 55 is still very competitive and a delight to fly.

One is currently on the UK Register.

# YAKOLEV
# YAK 55

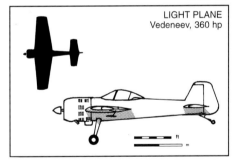

LIGHT PLANE
Vedeneev, 360 hp

| DATA | IMPERIAL | | METRIC | |
|---|---|---|---|---|
| Span | 26.5 | ft | 8.16 | m |
| Wing area | 138 | sq ft | 13 | sq m |
| Aspect ratio | 5.1 | | 5.1 | |
| Empty Weight | 1594 | lb | 724 | kg |
| Loaded weight | 1894 | lb | 860 | kg |
| Wing loading | 13.8 | lb/sq ft | 67 | kg/sq m |
| Max speed | 136 | mph | 218 | kmh |
| Cruise speed | 108 | mph | 172 | kmh |
| Stalling speed | 51 | mph | 82 | kmh |
| Climb rate | 3050 | ft/min | 939 | m/min |
| Range | 430 | mls | 690 | km |

Built in the USA by Rans Co. and marketed in the UK by Sport Air of Thirsk. Yorkshire, the S10 is available as a kit plane. The kit is PFA approved as non-aerobatic but is cleared for aerobatics in the USA. British agents can check individual aircraft during construction for aerobatic clearance.

The two seat, side-by-side accommodation is within a welded steel tube fuselage with a two door centre hinged canopy. The wings have alloy tube spars and ribs and are fabric covered, flaperons run full span and two struts brace the wing to the lower longerons.

The performance with it is fairly high wing loading, is lively and is not for the tyro. Its Rotax 65 hp, engine gives it a cruising speed of 100 mph and a climb of 500 fpm.

200 have been built in the USA twenty-five are on the UK Register and six are being built, PFA approved.

# RANS
# S10 SAKOTA

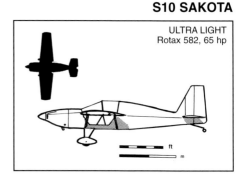

ULTRA LIGHT
Rotax 582, 65 hp

| DATA | IMPERIAL | | METRIC | |
|---|---|---|---|---|
| Span | 24 | ft | 7.4 | m |
| Wing area | 98 | sq ft | 9.1 | sq m |
| Aspect ratio | 5.4 | | 5.4 | |
| Empty Weight | 420 | lb | 191 | kg |
| Loaded weight | 895 | lb | 406 | kg |
| Wing loading | 9.1 | lb/sq ft | 44.5 | kg/sq m |
| Max speed | 120 | mph | 192 | kmh |
| Cruise speed | 45 | mph | 72 | kmh |
| Stalling speed | 26 | mph | 72 | kmh |
| Climb rate | 500 | ft/min | 152 | m/min |
| Range | 341 | mls | 545 | km |

The TEAM bit of Minimax stands for its patent company Tennessee Engineering and Manufacturing Inc. In the UK it was factored by UFM (Ultralight Flying Machines) of Gloucestershire until recently.

First flown in the USA in 1985 and sold as a kit, component built, or plans, the Minimax has sold well, and over 500 plans have been purchased to date. Most Minimax have the Rotax 447 engine, an alternative fit is the 40hp Mosler (VW based). Data below is for the Rotax version.

Of all wood construction with mainly fabric covering the Minimax has its mainplane strut braced to the unsprung landing gear and full span flaperons, which when doing duty as flaps, help achieve its landing speed of 34mph. As there is no agent or distributor for the aircraft in the UK the Minimax Owners Club does a very good job of keeping owners happy.

There are fifty-three on the UK Register and ten are being built.

# TEAM
# MINIMAX

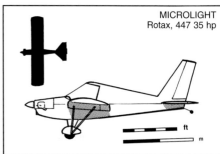

MICROLIGHT
Rotax, 447 35 hp

| DATA | IMPERIAL | | METRIC | |
|---|---|---|---|---|
| Span | 25 | ft | 7.7 | m |
| Wing area | 118 | sq ft | 11.6 | sq m |
| Aspect ratio | 5.3 | | 5.3 | |
| Empty Weight | 300 | lb | 136 | kg |
| Loaded weight | 560 | lb | 254 | kg |
| Wing loading | 4.75 | lb/sq ft | 23 | kg/sq m |
| Max speed | 82 | mph | 131 | kmh |
| Cruise speed | 70 | mph | 112 | kmh |
| Stalling speed | 34 | mph | 54 | kmh |
| Climb rate | 1000 | ft/min | 308 | m/min |
| Range | 120 | mls | 192 | km |

The Sukhoi SU 26 marked a departure from the strictly all sheet metal structures of the preceding Soviet aerobatic aircraft. The SU 26 has a welded steel tube fuselage and 'plastic' wings ie. GRP and foam skins over a ribless aerofoil with a carbon fibre spar. The airframe is incredibly strong +12 -11g, plus a factor of x2! (24g ultimate!).

The SU 26 first flew in 1984 and compared with its compatriot, and rival, the YAK 55, is smaller, lighter, faster and quicker in the climb.

The SU 31 is the export version of the Model 26 and is generally better finished; the SU 29 is a two seat version of the Model 26.

The pilots seat is set at approximately 45 degrees, putting the rudder pedals at about shoulder height, this position enabling high g's to be sustained without early black/red out.

Looking rather similar to the YAK 55, the little waist level windows of the Sukhoi are a give away.

There is only one SU26 on the UK Register.

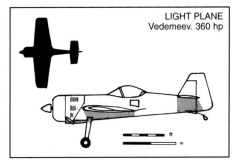

LIGHT PLANE
Vedemeev. 360 hp

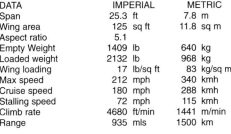

| DATA | IMPERIAL | | METRIC | |
|---|---|---|---|---|
| Span | 25.3 | ft | 7.8 | m |
| Wing area | 125 | sq ft | 11.8 | sq m |
| Aspect ratio | 5.1 | | | |
| Empty Weight | 1409 | lb | 640 | kg |
| Loaded weight | 2132 | lb | 968 | kg |
| Wing loading | 17 | lb/sq ft | 83 | kg/sq m |
| Max speed | 212 | mph | 340 | kmh |
| Cruise speed | 180 | mph | 288 | kmh |
| Stalling speed | 72 | mph | 115 | kmh |
| Climb rate | 4680 | ft/min | 1441 | m/min |
| Range | 935 | mls | 1500 | km |

Walter Extra the German designer has created a range of superlative aerobatic monoplanes, both single and two seater. The Extra 300 is the latest model, the suffix indicates the horse power - essentially an aerobat, it is well suited to training and fast touring.

Earlier Extras of similar layout were the single seat Extra 230 and the Extra 260, all acclaimed in the aerobatic world. These earlier models have wooden wings whereas the '300 has a one piece composites wing with carbon fibre spars - the tailplane is of similar construction. The fuselage is of welded steel tube with part fabric and part metal covering - an unusual feature being the windows in the fuselage belly.

This is a factory built aeroplane and at the time of writing twenty are on the UK Register. This is the top UK aerobatic display aircraft.

LIGHT PLANE
Lycoming, 300 hp

| DATA | IMPERIAL | | METRIC | |
|---|---|---|---|---|
| Span | 26.25 | ft | 8.08 | m |
| Wing area | 115 | sq ft | 10.8 | sq m |
| Aspect ratio | 6 | | 6 | |
| Empty Weight | 1500 | lb | 681 | kg |
| Loaded weight | 2095 | lb | 968 | kg |
| Wing loading | 17.3 | lb/sq ft | 84 | kg/sq m |
| Max speed | 220 | mph | 352 | kmh |
| Cruise speed | 181 | mph | 288 | kmh |
| Stalling speed | 64 | mph | 102 | kmh |
| Climb rate | 2600 | ft/min | 800 | m/min |
| Range | 517 | mls | 827 | km |

Scooping three trophies at the 1995 PFA Rally at Cranfield, Barry Smith's sleek little Acro Advanced aerobatic mid winger was the outcome of his quest for a simple, light weight (actually in the microlight weight category!) - aerobat powered by the cheap and reliable Volkswagen engine, thus putting serious aeros within the reach of many more.

The fuselage is of welded steel tube and the wings are wooden with fabric covering and no flaps. The powerful push rod operated balanced ailerons are 60% of the span.

The VW engine modified by Barry Smith for aerobatics - and renamed the Acro Aerobatic - is fuel injected and will run in all attitudes and with negative 'g'.

The cantilever spring legs carry disc braked wheels (of Barry Smith design) - spats, and a castoring tail wheel.

Only one Acro Advanced exists at the time of writing but production is under consideration. It is PFA approved.

# SMITH
# ACRO ADVANCED

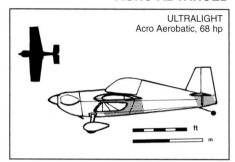

ULTRALIGHT
Acro Aerobatic, 68 hp

| DATA | IMPERIAL | | METRIC | |
|---|---|---|---|---|
| Span | 19.8 | ft | 6.1 | m |
| Wing area | 76 | sq ft | 7.1 | sq m |
| Aspect ratio | 5.1 | | 5.1 | |
| Empty Weight | 480 | lb | 218 | kg |
| Loaded weight | 750 | lb | 340 | kg |
| Wing loading | 9.8 | lb/sq ft | 48 | kg/sq m |
| Max speed | 170 | mph | 272 | kmh |
| Cruise speed | 140 | mph | 224 | kmh |
| Stalling speed | 48 | mph | 77 | kmh |
| Climb rate | 1500 | ft/min | 462 | m/min |
| Range | 479 | mls | 766 | km |

The original Tipsy Nipper, first flew in 1957 and was designed by E.O. Tips who worked for the Belgian arm of Fairey Aviation. Marks 1 and 2 were produced in Belgium, as ready built or part kitted, up to 1966 when the manufacturing rights were sold off to various companies, amongst them being Slingsby who produced the Mark 3, to suit British Airworthiness requirements.

The wing is a single spar, all wood, cantilever structure with a plywood leading edge and fabric covering aft. there are no flaps and wing removal for storage is simple. The fuselage employs a light but strong, +6-3g, welded steel tube framework with a GRP undertray and fabric covered rear end. The empennage consists of braced wood and fabric horizontal surfaces and a welded tube, fabric covered finless rudder. The rubber sprung legs have disc braked wheels and the nose wheel is steerable, making it very ground friendly.

The Nipper is a PFA approved design and there are thirty-five on the UK Register.

# TIPSY
# NIPPER

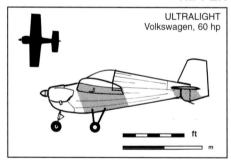

ULTRALIGHT
Volkswagen, 60 hp

| DATA | IMPERIAL | | METRIC | |
|---|---|---|---|---|
| Span | 19.6 | ft | 6.04 | m |
| Wing area | 80.7 | sq ft | 7.6 | sq m |
| Aspect ratio | 4.8 | | 4.8 | |
| Empty Weight | 465 | lb | 211 | kg |
| Loaded weight | 750 | lb | 340 | kg |
| Wing loading | 9.3 | lb/sq ft | 45.3 | kg/sq m |
| Max speed | 115 | mph | 184 | kmh |
| Cruise speed | 90 | mph | 144 | kmh |
| Stalling speed | 39 | mph | 62 | kmh |
| Climb rate | 650 | ft/min | 200 | m/min |
| Range | 184 | mls | 294 | km |

Built in the USA to the designs of Bjorn Andreasson, and first flown in 1958 as the MFI 9B, the design was taken up by Bolkow in West Germany in 1962 and produced as the Bo 208 Junior, 200 being built in the first seven years.

The Junior seats two, side by side, and is fully aerobatic, its swept forward wing braced by a single strut is a distinguishing feature. Its airframe is all light alloy, the wing having the minimum ribs under a heavy gauge skin and the fuselage has unusual external stringers.

Power is supplied by a Rolls Royce Continental four cylinder engine of 100 hp. giving it a useful cruising speed of 125 mph. and a range of nearly 500 miles.

The Junior has a lot of 'modern' features for a thirty-five year old design, like cantilever spring legs and steerable nose wheel, and still looks good.

There are seventeen on the UK Register.

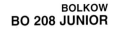

LIGHT PLANE
RR Continental, 100 hp

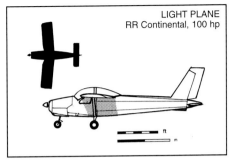

| DATA | IMPERIAL | METRIC |
|---|---|---|
| Span | 24.3 ft | 7.4 m |
| Wing area | 93.1 sq ft | 8.65 sq m |
| Aspect ratio | 6.4 | 6.4 |
| Empty Weight | 740 lb | 335 kg |
| Loaded weight | 1256 lb | 570 kg |
| Wing loading | 13.5 lb/sq ft | 66 kg/sq m |
| Max speed | 140 mph | 224 kmh |
| Cruise speed | 125 mph | 200 kmh |
| Stalling speed | 45 mph | 72 kmh |
| Climb rate | 790 ft/min | 240 m/min |
| Range | 510 mls | 816 km |

A two seat side-by-side microlight motor glider, the Chevvron in it's first form was a wooden aeroplane that first flew in 1980. Three years later it re-appeared as an all composites materials constructed aeroplane.

The Chevvron is not marketed as a kit plane and is manufactured by AMF Microlight Ltd at Membury who also make glider trailer, and Chevvron trailers!

At the time of writing twenty Chevvrons are flying and a squadron of enthusiastic owners has been formed.

Due to it's low wing loading and large span (44 ft), good for motor off performance, extended landing float can occur, and to counter this a version fitted with spoilers is available.

A well built modern 'plane of original lines with a quiet motor needing only two galls fuel per hour.

MICROLIGHT
Konig, 32 hp

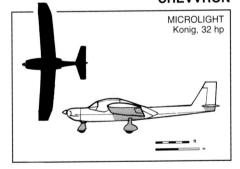

| DATA | IMPERIAL | METRIC |
|---|---|---|
| Span | 44 ft | 13.5 m |
| Wing area | 189 sq ft | 17.7 sq m |
| Aspect ratio | 10 | 10 |
| Empty Weight | 370 lb | 167 kg |
| Loaded weight | 842 lb | 382 kg |
| Wing loading | 4.32 lb/sq ft | 21 kg/sq m |
| Max speed | 92 mph | 142 kmh |
| Cruise speed | 64 mph | 102 kmh |
| Stalling speed | 31 mph | 49 kmh |
| Climb rate | 300 ft/min | 92 m/min |
| Range | 232 mls | 370 km |

This all metal two seater was the brain child of World Land Speed record holder, Richard Noble. It was originally produced on the Isle of Wight in 1986. Powered by a Hewland three cylinder, in-line, two stroke engine, specially developed for the ARV. This engine ran into trouble, causing the aircraft to be grounded and the company made bankrupt. Several attempts at reviving the ARV have been made in England, Scotland and Sweden (Opus 2).

Successful engine installations have been, the Rotax 912, the 90 hp AE 100 Rotary, and the modified Hewland, fitted to the majority still flying.

Sturdily built with a swept forward wing which has a highish loading of 12.6lb/ft the ARV will cruise at over 100 mph with excellent visibility and a well mannered stall.

Thirty have been built, twenty-seven still on the UK Register, nineteen are flying and it is listed as a PFA approved kit.

# NOBLE
# ARV SUPER 2

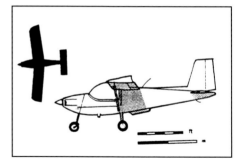

| DATA | IMPERIAL | | METRIC | |
|---|---|---|---|---|
| Span | 29.5 | ft | 9.1 | m |
| Wing area | 92.5 | sq ft | 8.7 | sq m |
| Aspect ratio | 9.4 | | 9.4 | |
| Empty Weight | 715 | lb | 321 | kg |
| Loaded weight | 1100 | lb | 500 | kg |
| Wing loading | 11.9 | lb/sq ft | 58 | kg/sq m |
| Max speed | 107 | mph | 171 | kmh |
| Cruise speed | 92 | mph | 147 | kmh |
| Stalling speed | 48 | mph | 77 | kmh |
| Climb rate | 750 | ft/min | 231 | m/min |
| Range | 350 | mls | 560 | km |

The all composites shoulder wing Lambada is a product of the Czech company Urban Air and when fitted with a Rotax 447 comes within the 450 kg microlight category. None in UK at this time but could become a popular Euro-microlight. One in Irish ownership Jabiru powered.

The two versions UFM13 and UFM11 have wing spans of the suffix approximately, the larger span version with a Rotax 447 is essentially a motor glider whilst the UFM11 with a HKS700E engine 65 hp is niftier but too heavy for the microlight limit. A Rotax 912, four stroke, four cylinder engine of 80 hp can also be fitted.

The composite wing structure, though beautifully slender, has been tested to +12.5-10.5g.

Views from the side-by-side cockpit are excellent, positioned as it is ahead of the eye level wing and behind a short and not too bulbous nose.

Handling in the air is described as 'easy and forgiving'. The wings quickly detach for ease of storage and a kit version is also available.

Data below is for the UFM13 with a Rotax 447.

# URBAN
# LAMBADA

MICRO/ULTRALIGHT
Rotax 447/912, 40/80 hp

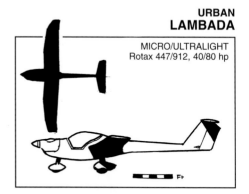

| DATA | IMPERIAL | | METRIC | |
|---|---|---|---|---|
| Span | 39 | ft | 12.2 | m |
| Wing area | 126 | sq ft | 11.1 | sq m |
| Aspect ratio | 12 | | | |
| Empty Weight | 601 | lb | 225 | kg |
| Loaded weight | 991 | lb | 450 | kg |
| Wing loading | 7.8 | lb/sq ft | 38 | kg/sq m |
| Max speed | 120 | mph | 192 | kmh |
| Cruise speed | 85 | mph | 136 | kmh |
| Stalling speed | 40 | mph | 64 | kmh |
| Climb rate | 470 | ft/min | 144 | m/min |
| Range | 280 | mls | 448 | km |

The bruiser is a WW2 advanced trainer manufactured by North American aircraft and powered by a huge 550 hp Pratt and Whitney single row radial engine.

The prototype, designated NA-26, first flew in 1937 and subsequent production ran to an incredible 15,000 aircraft. It was operated by thirty air forces throughout the world, including both the Luftwaffe and the RAF!

The USAAF designated was AT-6 (becoming T6, post war), and Harvard in the Allied air forces. Production continued up to 1954 including 2000 wartime AT-6s being 're-manufactured' as T-6G Texans.

An all metal heavy-weight with an inward retracting undercarriage, split trailing edge flaps, a swept back mean chord and a long glass house canopy over the tandem cockpits.

The un-geared radial engine and the fast spinning CS prop produces a very distinctive rasp!

There are twenty-eight on the UK Register.

## NORTH AMERICAN
# HARVARD

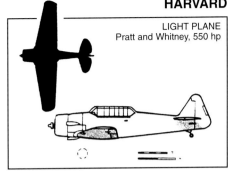

LIGHT PLANE
Pratt and Whitney, 550 hp

| DATA | IMPERIAL | | METRIC | |
|---|---|---|---|---|
| Span | 42 | ft | 13 | m |
| Wing area | 254 | sq ft | 24 | sq m |
| Aspect ratio | 7 | | 7 | |
| Empty Weight | 4271 | lb | 1939 | kg |
| Loaded weight | 5617 | lb | 2550 | kg |
| Wing loading | 23 | lb/sq ft | 112 | kg/sq m |
| Max speed | 212 | mph | 339 | kmh |
| Cruise speed | 170 | mph | 272 | kmh |
| Stalling speed | 60 | mph | 96 | kmh |
| Climb rate | 1643 | ft/min | 502 | m/min |
| Range | 870 | mls | 1392 | km |

With an original Albert Mooney design K. K. Culver formed the Dart Aircraft Co. in the early Model 30s to produce the two seat Dart Dart. Dart became Culver Aircraft in Model 39 and the Dart became the Culver Dart.

The many variants all looked, pretty much, the same and were renowned for their good performance on low power (140 mph on 80 hp is a pretty good two seater).

The Cadet has a wooden semi monocoque fuselage, elliptical wooden cantilever wings with 'letter box' type slots at the tips. The manually retractable gear' folds inwards, with only two turns of the crank!

Civil Cadet production was curtailed by WW2 but over 400 of these pretty aeroplanes were fitted with R/C and trike gear and became target drones!

368 Cadets were built between Model 39 and Model 42, 100 of which are still flying. There is one on the UK Register and a 'new' homebuilt version has flown in Kansas.

Various attempts were made to bring the Cadet back 'on stream', including, Lark Aviation's Lark 95 and the Helton Lark from Arizona (one on the UK Register).

We can learn a thing or two from this 60 year old design.

## CULVER
# CADET

LIGHT PLANE
Franklin, 80 hp/ Continental 75 hp

| DATA | IMPERIAL | | METRIC | |
|---|---|---|---|---|
| Span | 27 | ft | 8.1 | m |
| Wing area | 120 | sq ft | 11.1 | sq m |
| Aspect ratio | 6 | | | |
| Empty Weight | 720 | lb | 327 | kg |
| Loaded weight | 1305 | lb | 592 | kg |
| Wing loading | 10.9 | lb/sq ft | 42.2 | kg/sq m |
| Max speed | 140 | mph | 224 | kmh |
| Cruise speed | 120 | mph | 193 | kmh |
| Stalling speed | 45 | mph | 72 | kmh |
| Climb rate | 800 | ft/min | 244 | m/min |
| Range | 600 | mls | 965 | km |

An advanced concept, for its time, it first flew in 1941 as GC-1, and was a fast two seater with side-by-side seating and a retractable undercarriage.

The prototype had wooden wings and a welded tube fuselage but appeared in 1945 as an all metal aeroplane manufactured by the Glove Aircraft Co. Later, to speed up production, Temco came into the picture until production ceased in 1951 when over 1000 Swifts had been made.

As recently as 1999 plans were being made to re-start production of the Swift by Aviat Inc.

A keen owners club exists in the USA, where several hundred are still flying, and a variety of engines have been fitted, including a turbo-prop.

The undercarriage and flaps are operated by an electro Hydraulic power pack and later model have disc braked main wheels in place of the rather poor drums.

The Swift, being a small aeroplane with a big engine, is fairly fast with fighter like handling, though the range is rather limited.

There is only one Swift on the UK Register.

## GLOBE SWIFT

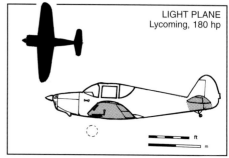

LIGHT PLANE
Lycoming, 180 hp

| DATA | IMPERIAL | | METRIC | |
|---|---|---|---|---|
| Span | 29.3 | ft | 9 | m |
| Wing area | 131.2 | sq ft | 12.3 | sq m |
| Aspect ratio | 6.5 | | 6.5 | |
| Empty Weight | 1110 | lb | 503 | kg |
| Loaded weight | 1710 | lb | 776 | kg |
| Wing loading | 13 | lb/sq ft | 63.4 | kg/sq m |
| Max speed | 185 | mph | 296 | kmh |
| Cruise speed | 156 | mph | 250 | kmh |
| Stalling speed | 60 | mph | 96 | kmh |
| Climb rate | 1000 | ft/min | 308 | m/min |
| Range | 320 | mls | 512 | km |

This Swiss 'fighter trainer' first flew in 1945 and only fifty-seven were produced, they served in the Swiss Air Force up to 1981 when they were sold on to the civilian market, four being UK registered.

Messerschmitt Bf 109 main gear and tailplane and elevator are incorporated in the design which is of mixed wood and metal construction The wings are all wood with two box spars, plywood ribs and skinning. The fuselage is a metal semi monocoque with a long sliding canopy over the tandem seats and fronted by the long, slim, inverted V12 air cooled Argus engine. An interesting feature is the constant speed prop which is actuated by a vaned spinner.

All the control surfaces and flaps are fabric covered.

Pilatus produce the more famous Porter. The P2 is popular for film work disguised as a Luftwaffe type.

## PILATUS P2

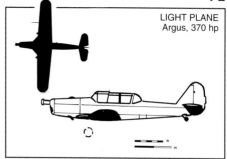

LIGHT PLANE
Argus, 370 hp

| DATA | IMPERIAL | | METRIC | |
|---|---|---|---|---|
| Span | 36.1 | ft | 11.1 | m |
| Wing area | 183 | sq ft | 17.2 | sq m |
| Aspect ratio | 7 | | 7 | |
| Empty Weight | 3345 | lb | 1518 | kg |
| Loaded weight | 4335 | lb | 1968 | kg |
| Wing loading | 23.7 | lb/sq ft | 116 | kg/sq m |
| Max speed | 211 | mph | 337 | kmh |
| Cruise speed | 206 | mph | 329 | kmh |
| Stalling speed | 63 | mph | 101 | kmh |
| Climb rate | 1280 | ft/min | 394 | m/min |
| Range | 350 | mls | 560 | km |

Rene Fournier called his 'motor glider' an Avions Planeur and worked initially with Pierre Robin.

An all wood glider type aeroplane which first flew in 1960 and RF-1 to be followed by the developments RF-2 and RF-3 which flew in 1963 to become in production the RF-4, an aerobatic single seater.

Alpavia in France, produced the first RF3/4s, eighty-nine of them before the German company Sportavia began building the RF-4 as the RF-4D and the two seat tandem, RF-5, which first flew in 1968.

The engines for both models are VW based units including the RF-5s 68 hp Limbach. An exception being the RF-55 which has the 60 hp Franklin.

The CFI (Club Fournier International) is the Fournier owners club, active both sides of the Channel. A total of thirty-nine RF-3s, RF-4s and RF-5s are on the UK Register.

Details below are for the single seat RF-4.

## SPORTAVIA/FOURNIER
## RF-4 AND RF-5

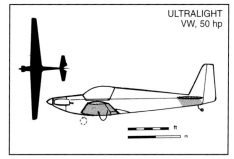

ULTRALIGHT
VW, 50 hp

| DATA | IMPERIAL | | METRIC | |
|---|---|---|---|---|
| Span | 37 | ft | 11.26 | m |
| Wing area | 121.7 | sq ft | 11.3 | sq m |
| Aspect ratio | 11.24 | | 11.24 | |
| Empty Weight | 584 | lb | 265 | kg |
| Loaded weight | 859 | lb | 390 | kg |
| Wing loading | 7 | lb/sq ft | 34 | kg/sq m |
| Max speed | 112 | mph | 180 | kmh |
| Cruise speed | 100 | mph | 160 | kmh |
| Stalling speed | 40 | mph | 64 | kmh |
| Climb rate | 690 | ft/min | 212 | m/min |
| Range | 422 | mls | 680 | km |

A handsome low winged motor glider from Germany, the two seat, side-by-side AS-K16 first flew in 1971 and was placed third in the First International Motor Glider Competition in 1974.

No longer in production, there are two on the UK register.

Of mixed construction the AS-K16 has a welded steel tube fuselage frame with plywood and GRP fairings. The wings, which are swept forward one degree, have a single wooden spar with a plywood 'D box' nose and fabric covering behind the spar. The ailerons are operated by push rods, no flaps are fitted but upper surface spoilers are. The main undercarriage, with its trouser-like doors, retracts very smartly inwards and has drum braked wheels.

The Limbach (VW conversion) engine drives a VP prop and has an electric starter.

The 52 ft span wing has detachable outer panels as an option.

In many ways similar to the Fournier RF-9, the AS-K16 with its lower aspect ratio wing (13.5 to the RF-9s 16) has a slightly higher gliding angle.

## SCHLEICHER
## ASK16

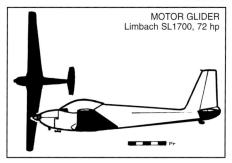

MOTOR GLIDER
Limbach SL1700, 72 hp

| DATA | IMPERIAL | | METRIC | |
|---|---|---|---|---|
| Span | 52.5 | ft | 16 | m |
| Wing area | 204 | sq ft | 19 | sq m |
| Aspect ratio | 13.5 | | | |
| Empty Weight | 1036 | lb | 470 | kg |
| Loaded weight | 1543 | lb | 700 | kg |
| Wing loading | 7.5 | lb/sq ft | 37 | kg/sq m |
| Max speed | 120 | mph | 200 | kmh |
| Cruise speed | 100 | mph | 160 | kmh |
| Stalling speed | 41 | mph | 69 | kmh |
| Climb rate | 200 | ft/min | 61 | m/min |
| Range | - | mls | - | km |

Californians Ken Rand and Stuart Robinson designed and built the single seat KR-1 which first flew in 1972 and had a top speed of 200 mph powered by a 1700cc VW engine.

Kitted in 1974, it proved to be popular with homebuilders and around 200 were built and flying mainly in he USA.

The KR-1 was followed up by a side-by-side two seat version, the KR-2 which was also snapped up by the DIY boys and over 300 are now in the air.

Of pioneering mixed wood and plastics construction the KR-2 has wooden spar wings with foam ribs and infill covered with Dynel reinforced epoxy. The fuselage and tail unit are of similar construction.

Continental 65 hp and VW 1600-2000 cc are fitted giving the tiny plane a very nifty performance. The retractable undercarriage version is standard but tail-dragger and nose wheel versions have been devised.

Thirty-one are on the Register and it is PFA approved.

# RAND ROBINSON
## KR-2

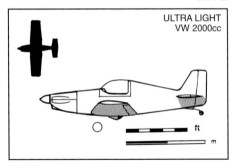

ULTRA LIGHT
VW 2000cc

| DATA | IMPERIAL | | METRIC | |
|---|---|---|---|---|
| Span | 20.6 | ft | 6.34 | m |
| Wing area | 80 | sq ft | 7.5 | sq m |
| Aspect ratio | 5.3 | | 5.3 | |
| Empty Weight | 440 | lb | 200 | kg |
| Loaded weight | 800 | lb | 363 | kg |
| Wing loading | 10 | lb/sq ft | 48.8 | kg/sq m |
| Max speed | 180 | mph | 288 | kmh |
| Cruise speed | 170 | mph | 272 | kmh |
| Stalling speed | 45 | mph | 72 | kmh |
| Climb rate | 800 | ft/min | 246 | m/min |
| Range | 2000 | mls | 3200 | km |

WAR, War Aircraft Replicas, of Santa Paula, California, have produced a range of realistic war bird look-a-likes; starting with the Peter Nieber designed FW190, which first flew in 1973.

The realistic contours are obtained by carving to shape blocks of urethane foam that have been attached to a basic wooden core airframe before the final 'glassing over. The wings have two wooden spars and the foam and plywood sandwich ribs give it the correct plan shape.

Just like the real thing, the undercarriage retracts inwards and is electrically operated.

Approximately 2/3 scale, the 'FW190, in its authentic camouflage and markings looks just like its famous 'role model' and it is only when close up that it is seen to be a very small aeroplane, 20 ft wing span!

The range includes, Sea Fury, Corsair, Thunderbolt, Mustang and Zero; they are supplied as kits or sets of plans. The type is PFA approved and there are four on the UK Register.

# WAR
## FW-190

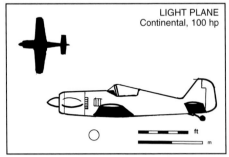

LIGHT PLANE
Continental, 100 hp

| DATA | IMPERIAL | | METRIC | |
|---|---|---|---|---|
| Span | 20.5 | ft | 6.1 | m |
| Wing area | 79 | sq ft | 7.4 | sq m |
| Aspect ratio | 5.3 | | 5.3 | |
| Empty Weight | 650 | lb | 292 | kg |
| Loaded weight | 950 | lb | 427 | kg |
| Wing loading | 12 | lb/sq ft | 57 | kg/sq m |
| Max speed | 195 | mph | 314 | kmh |
| Cruise speed | 125 | mph | 201 | kmh |
| Stalling speed | 55 | mph | 89 | kmh |
| Climb rate | 1000 | ft/min | 305 | m/min |
| Range | 400 | mls | 643 | km |

Czechoslovakia, as it was known, designed and built, like many mid European aeroplane makers, their 'planes to suit many tasks. The Trener is well known in its single seat aerobatic role, a big winner in its day, and as a tourer/ trainer with tandem seating; it also does duty as a glider tug.

The Trener nomenclature ranges from Z26, the wooden prototype ranging to the Z726K, first flown in 1973, is all metal and has a 210 hp. supercharged Avia.

The Z326 was the first in the range to have a retractable undercarriage and the aerobatic versions, Z226, Z326, Z526, are all named Akrobat.

In production since 1947 the Trener range has run to over 1400 units. All are distinguished by their swept back main plane leading edge, narrow in-line six cylinder engine and a long 'glass house' canopy (two seaters).

There are thirteen of the Z-26 range on the UK Register. The data below is for the Z526, 180 hp. Avia.

## ZLIN
## Z526 TRENER

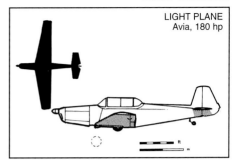

LIGHT PLANE
Avia, 180 hp

| DATA | IMPERIAL | | METRIC | |
|---|---|---|---|---|
| Span | 32.5 | ft | 10 | m |
| Wing area | 155 | sq ft | 14.6 | sq m |
| Aspect ratio | 6.8 | | 6.8 | |
| Empty Weight | 1465 | lb | 665 | kg |
| Loaded weight | 2072 | lb | 940 | kg |
| Wing loading | 13.4 | lb/sq ft | 65.2 | kg/sq m |
| Max speed | *145* | mph | *232* | kmh |
| Cruise speed | 130 | mph | 210 | kmh |
| Stalling speed | *55* | mph | *88* | kmh |
| Climb rate | 1181 | ft/min | 360 | m/min |
| Range | 295 | mls | 480 | km |

Strikingly similar to the WW2 fighter it is modelled on the Loehle 5151 Mustang is a three-quarter scale light plane powered by a Rotax 582 engine.

Designed in 1985 and produced in kit form in the USA by Mike Loehle the Mustang, is of all wood construction. The rear fuselage and empennage are of semi-geodetic construction and the two spar wing is fabric covered and devoid of flaps.

Fixed gear or manually retractable models are available, the drag reduction with the latter is minimal at a cruise of 80 mph, but it looks much nicer!

Over 200 kits have been sold in the USA, over thirty are flying and one, with PFA approval appears on the UK Register.

Though looking like a really 'hot ship' the 5151 Mustang with its 65 hp engine and 80 mph cruise is a 'pussy cat', and almost in the microlight category.

The one example of this attractive and interesting aeroplane was in storage at the time of writing.

## LOEHLE
## 5151 MUSTANG

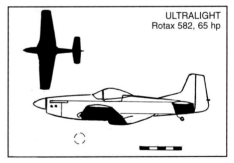

ULTRALIGHT
Rotax 582, 65 hp

| DATA | IMPERIAL | | METRIC | |
|---|---|---|---|---|
| Span | 27.4 | ft | 8.43 | m |
| Wing area | 130 | sq ft | 12.2 | sq m |
| Aspect ratio | 5.8 | | 6.8 | |
| Empty Weight | 513 | lb | 232 | kg |
| Loaded weight | 885 | lb | 401 | kg |
| Wing loading | 6.8 | lb/sq ft | 33 | kg/sq m |
| Max speed | 100 | mph | 160 | kmh |
| Cruise speed | 80 | mph | 128 | kmh |
| Stalling speed | 30 | mph | 48 | kmh |
| Climb rate | 1200 | ft/min | 370 | m/min |
| Range | 250 | mls | 400 | km |

A Rene Fournier design built under licence by Aeromot in Brazil the Super Ximango is the twin of Fourniers RF 10 an all composites high performance motor glider. The AMT100 Ximango which preceded it was Limbach powered whereas the Super' has a Rotax 912 with a three pitch Hoffman prop.

An exceedingly elegant aeroplane with side by side seating under a huge bubble canopy, folding wings (Navy style) and a wide track retractable undercarriage.

The AMT200 Super Ximango is an efficient glider and an even more efficient powered aircraft – 152 mph on 80 hp is remarkable! Its low drag profile is enhanced by the clean cowling lines afforded by the water cooled engine,

At the time of writing six Super Ximango are on the UK Register. Supers' are only just coming on stream but 50 or more plain Ximangos have been made.

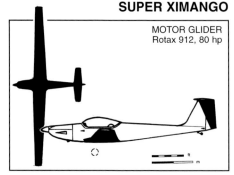

MOTOR GLIDER
Rotax 912, 80 hp

| DATA | IMPERIAL | | METRIC | |
|---|---|---|---|---|
| Span | 57.5 | ft | 17.7 | m |
| Wing area | 201 | sq ft | 18.9 | sq m |
| Aspect ratio | 16.3 | | 16.3 | |
| Empty Weight | 1334 | lb | 605 | kg |
| Loaded weight | 1874 | lb | 851 | kg |
| Wing loading | 9.3 | lb/sq ft | 45 | kg/sq m |
| Max speed | 152 | mph | 243 | kmh |
| Cruise speed | 126 | mph | 201 | kmh |
| Stalling speed | 44 | mph | 70 | kmh |
| Climb rate | 600 | ft/min | 185 | m/min |
| Range | 800 | mls | 1280 | km |

Designed and built by Ivan Shaw and Don Dykins the Europa first flew in 1992. The aim was to come up with a fast cruising two seater with STOL capabilities suitable for home construction. The kits of pre moulded GRP, foam and carbon fibre are marketed by Europa Aviation at Kirkbymoorside. The de-rigged size enables the completed aeroplane to fit into a domestic garage and be trailered to the air strip,where it is quite happy to operate from grass and will take off in 100 metres and land in 200m!

The single semi retracting main wheel and wing outriggers are simple, light weight and low drag. Flaps, an all flying tailplane, dual control and a very quiet Rotax 912 double silenced engine are all features of this little beauty.

The Europa must be the most successful UK homebuilt light plane ever, with over 1,000 sold in thirty-two countries, and 189 on the UK Register, including the tri gear version (page 126) and the new Liberty XL-2 factory-built.

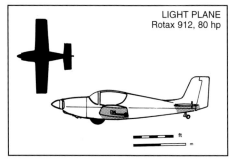

LIGHT PLANE
Rotax 912, 80 hp

| DATA | IMPERIAL | | METRIC | |
|---|---|---|---|---|
| Span | 26 | ft | 8 | m |
| Wing area | 95 | sq ft | 8.9 | sq m |
| Aspect ratio | 6.58 | | 6.58 | |
| Empty Weight | 680 | lb | 308 | kg |
| Loaded weight | 1300 | lb | 590 | kg |
| Wing loading | 13.7 | lb/sq ft | 66 | kg/sq m |
| Max speed | 166 | mph | 267 | kmh |
| Cruise speed | 115 | mph | 184 | kmh |
| Stalling speed | 56 | mph | 90 | kmh |
| Climb rate | 800 | ft/min | 246 | m/min |
| Range | 500 | mls | 800 | km |

The T61 Venture is a motor glider originally designed and built, in some numbers, in Germany by Scheibe as the SF25 Falke, which first flew in 1963. Slingsby built 75 T61s before 'moving up a gear' to the T67 Firefly.

The wing is all wood, though late models have a GRP spar, with about thirty percent fabric covering, the rest being plywood. Welded steel tubes form the fuselage basic frame with plywood formers and stringers under a fabric skin. the mono-wheel undercarriage is braked, the tail-wheel is steerable and there are lift spoilers.

At one time the main ATC trainer but decommissioned in 1991 and many sold onto the civil market.

A pleasant, docile and cheap aeroplane to operate, 2 galls/hr.

Ninety-six T61s are on the UK Register and thirty-six SF25s.

**SLINGSBY**
# T61 VENTURE

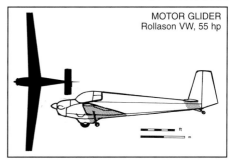

MOTOR GLIDER
Rollason VW, 55 hp

| DATA | IMPERIAL | | METRIC | |
|------|---------|---|--------|---|
| Span | 50 | ft | 15.2 | m |
| Wing area | 188 | sq ft | 17.5 | sq m |
| Aspect ratio | 13.3 | | 13.3 | |
| Empty Weight | 739 | lb | 335 | kg |
| Loaded weight | 1168 | lb | 530 | kg |
| Wing loading | 6.2 | lb/sq ft | 30.3 | kg/sq m |
| Max speed | 103 | mph | 165 | kmh |
| Cruise speed | 86 | mph | 138 | kmh |
| Stalling speed | 46 | mph | 73 | kmh |
| Climb rate | 350 | ft/min | 107 | m/min |
| Range | 276 | mls | 442 | km |

Monnett are based at the epi-centre of home-building Oshkosh. After building sailplanes for many years, Monnett turned in 1980 to the Moni power-glider, Monnett call it an Air Recreation Vehicle and it first flew in 1981.

Construction is all metal and several hundred sets of plans and kits have been sold, it is a PFA approved design, though currently, new sets of plans are not available.

The distinctive Moni, which in spite of being all metal only just misses out on Microlight classification on wing load, is powered by a KFM engine of 30 hp. The prototype had a 22 hp KFM.

A variety of undercarriages may be fitted, the classic glider mono-wheel with small tip wheels tail dragger with cantilever spring legs of these legs plus a nose wheel. A number of span options are also apparent, the parallel chord wing being eminently suitable for chopping off to suit.

There are five Monis on the UK Register, one being built by a school in Sheffield.

**MONNETT**
# MONI

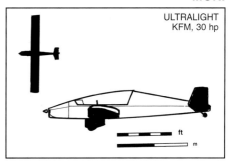

ULTRALIGHT
KFM, 30 hp

| DATA | IMPERIAL | | METRIC | |
|------|---------|---|--------|---|
| Span | 50 | ft | 15.2 | m |
| Wing area | 188 | sq ft | 17.5 | sq m |
| Aspect ratio | 13.3 | | 13.3 | |
| Empty Weight | 739 | lb | 335 | kg |
| Loaded weight | 1168 | lb | 530 | kg |
| Wing loading | 6.2 | lb/sq ft | 30.3 | kg/sq m |
| Max speed | 103 | mph | 165 | kmh |
| Cruise speed | 86 | mph | 138 | kmh |
| Stalling speed | 46 | mph | 73 | kmh |
| Climb rate | 350 | ft/min | 107 | m/min |
| Range | 276 | mls | 442 | km |

The Humming Bird was built for the Daily Mail Light Aeroplane Trials of 1923 held at Lympne. De Haviland entered two of the little strut braced low wing monoplanes powered by 750 cc Douglas motor cycle engines, approximately 15 hp and though they won no prizes they were considered the best all round performers.

Of all wood construction with a plywood covered fuselage and fabric covered wings and tail G-EBHX was soon re-engined with a Blackburn Tomtit of 26 hp and so powered flew non stop to Brussels on ten shillings worth of petrol (50p), at that time about three gallons.

Surprisingly, no civil orders were forthcoming but the RAF ordered ten for communication duties and five were sold abroad, three Australia, one Russia and one Czech.

In October 1925 a Humming Bird with a hook above the cockpit was dropped from the airship R33 and successfully re attached itself back to the mother ship.

The prototype G-EBHX still flies at Old Warden and Continental powered replica is flying in Canada.

# DE HAVILAND
# HUMMING BIRD

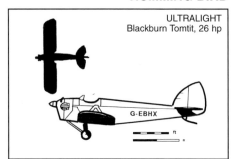

ULTRALIGHT
Blackburn Tomtit, 26 hp

| DATA | IMPERIAL | | METRIC | |
| --- | --- | --- | --- | --- |
| Span | 30 | ft | 9.2 | m |
| Wing area | 125 | sq ft | 6 | sq m |
| Aspect ratio | 7 | | 7 | |
| Empty Weight | 326 | lb | 148 | kg |
| Loaded weight | 565 | lb | 256 | kg |
| Wing loading | 4.5 | lb/sq ft | 22 | kg/sq m |
| Max speed | 73 | mph | 117 | kmh |
| Cruise speed | 50 | mph | 80 | kmh |
| Stalling speed | 33 | mph | 53 | kmh |
| Climb rate | 225 | ft/min | 70 | m/min |
| Range | 200 | mls | 320 | km |

The BA (British Aircraft Manufacturing Co.Ltd) Swallow is, essentially, the 1927 German Klemm L25 which was distributed in this country in the 1930s powered by a 75 hp Salmson radial engine. The type proved so popular that the British Klemm Aeroplane Company Ltd was formed to build them at Hanworth with the Pobjoy radial as an alternative power unit. In 1934 FAM was formed, and the Swallow 2, illustrated, appeared with a square cut tail and wing tips, as opposed to the rounded original Klemms, and the engine options included the Cirrus Minor of 90 hp.

Of all wood construction, plywood covered, the Swallow had one of the earliest production light plane cantilever wings.

About 150 were built and were very well liked by their pilots. Thirty-seven survived WW2 and there are still four on the UK Register plus a recently built Klemm L25 and the well-known Shuttleworth Swallow.

# BRITISH AIRCRAFT
# BA SWALLOW

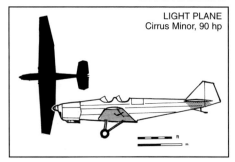

LIGHT PLANE
Cirrus Minor, 90 hp

| DATA | IMPERIAL | | METRIC | |
| --- | --- | --- | --- | --- |
| Span | 46.2 | ft | 13.1 | m |
| Wing area | 219 | sq ft | 20.6 | sq m |
| Aspect ratio | 8.3 | | 8.3 | |
| Empty Weight | 990 | lb | 450 | kg |
| Loaded weight | 1500 | lb | 681 | kg |
| Wing loading | 6.8 | lb/sq ft | 33.2 | kg/sq m |
| Max speed | 104 | mph | 166 | kmh |
| Cruise speed | 90 | mph | 144 | kmh |
| Stalling speed | 40 | mph | 64 | kmh |
| Climb rate | 800 | ft/min | 246 | m/min |
| Range | 420 | mls | 672 | km |

This remarkable little aeroplane was built and first flown in 1927 to further the cause of the monoplane and the Cirrus engine. Faster than many fighters of its day, a short span DH 71, with a 135 hp Gipsy, was capable of nearly 200 mph. and set an official world 100km closed circuit speed record for Class 2 Light Aeroplanes at 186 mph.

Built entirely of wood with fabric covered wings and plywood skinned fuselage, the wings were totally wire braced as was the undercarriage, which had internally sprung wheel hubs.

Though entered for several air races the DH 71, or Tiger Moth, its official name, never carried of any prizes.

Only two were built, one going to Australia, where it crashed and the other, after its 'days in the sun', went into storage at Hatfield and eventually was destroyed by a German bomb in 1940.

Two replicas have been built in the UK, one static, one to fly; but a USA example is flying and alleged to be 'a bit of a handful'! (Though Hubert Broad, the DH test pilot, around whom the aircraft was built, had no complaints). Data below for 'tourer'.

# DE HAVILAND
## DH 71 TIGER MOTH

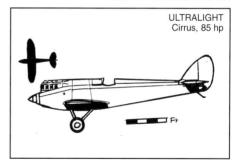

ULTRALIGHT
Cirrus, 85 hp

| DATA | IMPERIAL | | METRIC | |
|---|---|---|---|---|
| Span | 22.5 | ft | 7 | m |
| Wing area | 76.5 | sq ft | 7.2 | sq m |
| Aspect ratio | 6.6 | | | |
| Empty Weight | 618 | lb | 308 | kg |
| Loaded weight | 905 | lb | 411 | kg |
| Wing loading | 11.5 | lb/sq ft | 57.6 | kg/sq m |
| Max speed | 166 | mph | 265 | kmh |
| Cruise speed | 150 | mph | 240 | kmh |
| Stalling speed | 60 | mph | 96 | kmh |
| Climb rate | 1500 | ft/min | 462 | m/min |
| Range | 200 | mls | 320 | km |

Originally the British Klemm BK1 Eagle, this attractive three seater, became, on the change of company name, the British Aircraft BA Eagle. Klemm, a German company, produced a similar type, the L32, but the BA Eagle was an entirely new design from the 'board of G.H. Handasyde.

First flown in 1934, the Eagle with the pilot in the front seat and the two passengers behind, was ahead of its time in having a retractable undercarriage, albeit manually operated. (and strangely, no flaps!)

The first production model was powered by a 200 hp. Gipsy Six engine and flew in the 1934 Kings Cup air race; subsequent models were 130 hp. Gipsy Major powered.

Much raced and given to breaking point to point records - including a record crossing of the South Atlantic on a delivery flight! The Eagles boasted many famous pilots, including, Amy Johnson, Tommy Rose and A. E Clouston.

The sole remaining Eagle, G-AFAX, is the only one produced with a fixed undercarriage - and it is still flying.

# BRITISH AIRCRAFT
## EAGLE

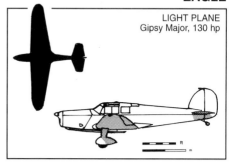

LIGHT PLANE
Gipsy Major, 130 hp

| DATA | IMPERIAL | | METRIC | |
|---|---|---|---|---|
| Span | 39.2 | ft | 12.1 | m |
| Wing area | 200 | sq ft | 18.8 | sq m |
| Aspect ratio | 7.7 | | 7.7 | |
| Empty Weight | 1450 | lb | 658 | kg |
| Loaded weight | 2400 | lb | 1090 | kg |
| Wing loading | 12 | lb/sq ft | 58.5 | kg/sq m |
| Max speed | 148 | mph | 237 | kmh |
| Cruise speed | 130 | mph | 208 | kmh |
| Stalling speed | 55 | mph | 88 | kmh |
| Climb rate | 700 | ft/min | 215 | m/min |
| Range | 650 | mls | 1040 | km |

67

The Percival Mew Gull, probably the most charismatic British light plane of the pre-war era.

First flown in 1934 the small single seater with the big engine was all wood and initially powered by a Napier Javelin engine of 165 hp. With a Gipsy Six, 200 hp fitted it flew in the Kings Cup air race, lapping at 191 mph but was handicapped out of prize.

In 1935 the Mew Gull 2 with single leg gear and flaps won many races including Deauville, Cannes and Heston, Cardiff at 218 mph. A Model 2A Mew won the 1937 Kings Cup another coming third and in 1938 G-AEXF won the race at an incredible 236 mph.

In 1939 Alex Henshaw, in XF made a record dash to Cape Town and back in a gruelling four days, ten hours.

This aircraft was sold to France where it was stored during the war, it was later repatriated and restored in the UK to fly again in 1950.

Six Mews were built, two were destroyed by enemy bombing, one sold to SA crashed and two were scrapped.

G-AEXF still flies at Breighton, a joy to behold.

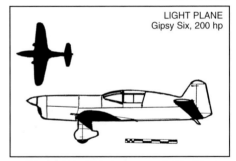

LIGHT PLANE
Gipsy Six, 200 hp

| DATA | IMPERIAL | | METRIC | |
|---|---|---|---|---|
| Span | 22.7 | ft | 7 | m |
| Wing area | 75 | sq ft | 7 | sq m |
| Aspect ratio | 6.8 | | | |
| Empty Weight | 1150 | lb | 522 | kg |
| Loaded weight | 2125 | lb | 963 | kg |
| Wing loading | 28.3 | lb/sq ft | 138 | kg/sq m |
| Max speed | 235 | mph | 376 | kmh |
| Cruise speed | 232 | mph | 371 | kmh |
| Stalling speed | 70 | mph | 112 | kmh |
| Climb rate | 1800 | ft/min | 554 | m/min |
| Range | 875 | mls | 1320 | km |

E.O. Tips of Avion Fairey, Belgium, designed the pretty little single seat S2 in 1935 which led to the side-by-side two seat Tipsy B a year later.

An all wooden aeroplane, it was built by Tipsy Aircraft Ltd and was powered by the Czech-built Walter Mikron engine. It came at a time when the Civil Air Guard needed trainers and a third of the pre war production of fifteen were upgraded to and named Trainer.

Ten survived the war, three of which were soon sold overseas and when production was resumed after the war only three were completed, one having a long and useful life teaching Fairey employees to fly.

The aircraft's apparently elliptical wing is composed of three straight lines at the trailing edge.

Fairey Avions Belge built a cabin version in 1939 which served with distinction throughout the conflict, and a further seven in 1947 named Belfair.

The specification of all three types are similar, the Trainer and Belfair being heavier.

There are ten on the UK Register.

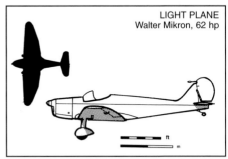

LIGHT PLANE
Walter Mikron, 62 hp

| DATA | IMPERIAL | | METRIC | |
|---|---|---|---|---|
| Span | 31.2 | ft | 9.6 | m |
| Wing area | 129 | sq ft | 12.1 | sq m |
| Aspect ratio | 7.5 | | 7.5 | |
| Empty Weight | 496 | lb | 225 | kg |
| Loaded weight | 992 | lb | 450 | kg |
| Wing loading | 7.7 | lb/sq ft | 37.5 | kg/sq m |
| Max speed | 124 | mph | 198 | kmh |
| Cruise speed | 100 | mph | 160 | kmh |
| Stalling speed | 42 | mph | 67 | kmh |
| Climb rate | 450 | ft/min | 139 | m/min |
| Range | 450 | mls | 720 | km |

The first DW-1 was designed and built by two ex de Haviland Technical School students, A. Dalrymple and A.R. Ward in 1937 at Hungerford in Berkshire.

Intended as a cheap easy-build single seater with a good performance on low power. The all wood cantilever monoplane achieved remarkable figures, 112 mph on 32 hp. This was with a Carden Ford engine, modified water cooled car engine, later to be replaced by a 44 hp Train engine of French manufacture.

Four aircraft were built before the outbreak of WW2, and all survived to be resurrected and flown again. In the 1950s the DW1 was popular in the big air races, with various clean up modifications, G-AFSV, in fact it lapped the Kings Cup course in 1957 at 144 mph with a Walter Mikron 62 hp.

A pretty little aeroplane with eight on the UK Register, four originals, plus one original completed post war and three new PFA builds.

# CHILTON
## DW-1 MONOPLANE

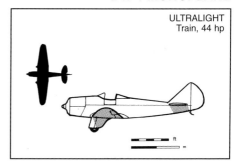

ULTRALIGHT
Train, 44 hp

| DATA | IMPERIAL | | METRIC | |
|---|---|---|---|---|
| Span | 24 | ft | 7.32 | m |
| Wing area | 78 | sq ft | 7.24 | sq m |
| Aspect ratio | 7.4 | | 7.4 | |
| Empty Weight | 370 | lb | 168 | kg |
| Loaded weight | 650 | lb | 295 | kg |
| Wing loading | 8.4 | lb/sq ft | 41 | kg/sq m |
| Max speed | 112 | mph | 179 | kmh |
| Cruise speed | 100 | mph | 160 | kmh |
| Stalling speed | 35 | mph | 56 | kmh |
| Climb rate | 300 | ft/min | 198 | m/min |
| Range | 500 | mls | 800 | km |

The last model produced by Phillips and Powis (later Miles Aircraft) before WW2, it first flew in 1938 and was the first design to be entrusted to F G Miles brother George. Based on the two seat Whitney Straight of 1936 the Monarch was a three seater of similar all wood construction without the 'Straight's folding wing facility but incorporating a unique 'glide control' - a system linking the throttle with the vacuum operated flaps.

Only eleven were built, eight carrying UK registrations (though three of these were soon sold abroad).

Six were impressed for communications duties during the war and G-AFLW was a camouflaged hack for Rolls Royce. Five returned to 'civvie street' in '46 and three are still on the 'Register. G-AFRZ was registered for a while as G-AIDE and in this guise won the 1956 Goodyear Trophy at an av. 131 mph.(now in storage in Birmingham). G-AFJU is in the Museum of flight at East Fortune.

A desirable aeroplane of its day, fast, comfortable and economical and much praised by the aviation press.

# MILES
## MONARCH

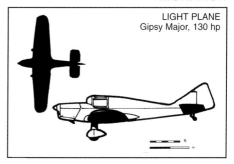

LIGHT PLANE
Gipsy Major, 130 hp

| DATA | IMPERIAL | | METRIC | |
|---|---|---|---|---|
| Span | 35.5 | ft | 11 | m |
| Wing area | 180 | sq ft | 17 | sq m |
| Aspect ratio | 74 | | 7 | |
| Empty Weight | 1390 | lb | 631 | kg |
| Loaded weight | 2200 | lb | 998 | kg |
| Wing loading | 12.2 | lb/sq ft | 58 | kg/sq m |
| Max speed | 145 | mph | 232 | kmh |
| Cruise speed | 130 | mph | 208 | kmh |
| Stalling speed | 55 | mph | 88 | kmh |
| Climb rate | 850 | ft/min | 261 | m/min |
| Range | 600 | mls | 960 | km |

Miles Aircraft came to prominence with the Hawk range of wooden low wing cantilever monoplanes in the mid thirties. Being fairly nifty for their time, they were very popular air racers – in the 1935 Kings cup no less than seven were entered, a Gipsy six engined single seat version, the Hawk Speed Six, finished thirteenth at an average of 177mph – but in the following year came second in the hands of the colourful Miles test pilot Tommy Rose. Three Speed Sixes were built only one of which survives today G-ADGP, currently owned and regularly flown by Roy Mills. It's crackling exhaust roar as it flashes fast and low across an air show crowd is truly memorable – and not bad for a seventy-year-old. The look-a-like Miles M5 Sparrowhawk had a smaller span and a Gipsy Major engine – six were built, none now flying, but one is being rebuilt.

## MILES HAWK SPEED SIX

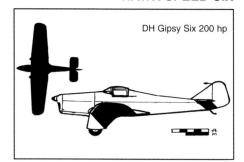

DH Gipsy Six 200 hp

| DATA | IMPERIAL | | METRIC | |
|---|---|---|---|---|
| Span | 33 | ft | 10 | m |
| Wing area | 169 | sq ft | 15.8 | sq m |
| Aspect ratio | 6.4 | | 6.4 | |
| Empty Weight | 1355 | lb | 615 | kg |
| Loaded weight | 1900 | lb | 862 | kg |
| Wing loading | 11.2 | lb/sq ft | 54.6 | kg/sq m |
| Max speed | 185 | mph | 296 | kmh |
| Cruise speed | 160 | mph | 856 | kmh |
| Stalling speed | 50 | mph | 31 | kmh |
| Climb rate | 1450 | ft/min | 442 | m/min |
| Range | 500 | mls | 800 | km |

Following the success of Miles first production aircraft, the tandem two seat Hawk, the first Falcon was a three seat cabin tourer (pilot in the front and two passengers behind) of very clean lines with a Gypsy Major, 130 hp. engine. Hardly out of the workshop this 'plane made a record breaking Australia - England flight in 1935.

Subsequent models (M3A) had four seats within a wider cabin and the M3B, Falcon Six, with three seats and a Gipsy Six engine of 200 hp., won the Kings Cup Race the same year with Tommy Rose at the controls; later in the same aircraft he broke the England - Cape town record.

The M3C Falcons were full four seaters with dual controls and the Gipsy Six engine.

Of the twenty or so Falcons built pre war only six survived the conflict and four of these, not for long. Of the two remaining, one is flying and the other is being restored at Booker.

An advanced design, for its day, cantilever wing, all wood stressed skin structure, split flaps and no sluggard at 180 mph!

The figures below are for the Falcon Six, a rare and beautiful bird, long may it enthral us.

## MILES M3 FALCON

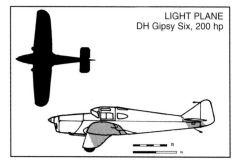

LIGHT PLANE
DH Gipsy Six, 200 hp

| DATA | IMPERIAL | | METRIC | |
|---|---|---|---|---|
| Span | 35 | ft | 10.7 | m |
| Wing area | 174 | sq ft | 16.3 | sq m |
| Aspect ratio | 7 | | 7 | |
| Empty Weight | 1550 | lb | 703 | kg |
| Loaded weight | 2350 | lb | 1066 | kg |
| Wing loading | 13.5 | lb/sq ft | 65 | kg/sq m |
| Max speed | 180 | mph | 288 | kmh |
| Cruise speed | 160 | mph | 256 | kmh |
| Stalling speed | 55 | mph | 88 | kmh |
| Climb rate | 1000 | ft/min | 307 | m/min |
| Range | 560 | mls | 896 | km |

Built by Dart Aircraft Ltd at Dunstable and first flown in 1936, the pretty little Dart single seater was designed by Alfred Weyl and was originally powered by a French Ava two stroke engine of 27 hp.

Of all wood construction with a cantilever wing and single leg undercarriage struts, the prototype was built in four months. The Mk 2 Kitten appeared a year later with revised top decking, stub axles, instead of forks, and the more powerful JAP engine.

The Mk 2 Kitten took part in several pre war air races for which it wore spats. Both Kittens were stored during WW2 and flew again after the war, the Mk 1, up to 1952 when it was written off in a crash at Broxbourne.

The Mk 2s wings went missing during storage but a rebuild was completed, followed by another crash in1964. The wreck lay in a barn until 1976 when restoration started, it flew again in 1985, and is one of the oldest UK Registered aircraft in private hands, still flying.

# DART
# KITTEN

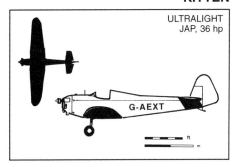

ULTRALIGHT
JAP, 36 hp

G-AEXT

| DATA | IMPERIAL | | METRIC | |
|---|---|---|---|---|
| Span | 31.7 | ft | 9.7 | m |
| Wing area | 129 | sq ft | 12.1 | sq m |
| Aspect ratio | 7.8 | | 7.8 | |
| Empty Weight | 510 | lb | 231 | kg |
| Loaded weight | 752 | lb | 341 | kg |
| Wing loading | 5.83 | lb/sq ft | 28 | kg/sq m |
| Max speed | 95 | mph | 152 | kmh |
| Cruise speed | 83 | mph | 133 | kmh |
| Stalling speed | 38 | mph | 61 | kmh |
| Climb rate | 600 | ft/min | 185 | m/min |
| Range | 340 | mls | 544 | km |

The main primary trainer of the US Air Forces during WW2 the Fairchild M-62 first flew in 1939 and subsequent production ran to 8000 aircraft. The M-62 was in service with many foreign air forces long after the war, including Paraguay, Haiti, Nicaragua and Honduras.

A tandem two seater with open cockpits or, in the Canadian built version, a long greenhouse enclosing both. The fuselage is of welded steel tube with fabric covering and the wings are wooden. Both Canada and Brazil built M-62s and the Canadian version PT-26 was named Cornell.

Designated PT-19 and PT-26 when fitted with the 200 hp Ranger engine and PT-23 when powered by the Continental R-640 radial engine of 220 hp. Many are still in existence, over 1000 still on the registers, mainly in the USA where there are about 150 still flying. There are none on the UK Register today.

# FAIRCHILD
# PT-19 CORNELL

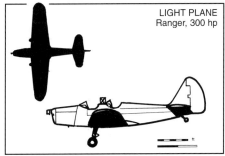

LIGHT PLANE
Ranger, 300 hp

| DATA | IMPERIAL | | METRIC | |
|---|---|---|---|---|
| Span | 36 | ft | 11.1 | m |
| Wing area | 200 | sq ft | 18.8 | sq m |
| Aspect ratio | 6.5 | | 6.5 | |
| Empty Weight | 2000 | lb | 908 | kg |
| Loaded weight | 2702 | lb | 1227 | kg |
| Wing loading | 13.5 | lb/sq ft | 66 | kg/sq m |
| Max speed | 126 | mph | 202 | kmh |
| Cruise speed | 110 | mph | 176 | kmh |
| Stalling speed | 58 | mph | 93 | kmh |
| Climb rate | 690 | ft/min | 212 | m/min |
| Range | 450 | mls | 720 | km |

A pre-war Bucker design, adopted as a trainer by the Luftwaffe and produced in considerable numbers, Fokker made 700 of them. After the war Zlin took over manufacture for delivery to the Czech Air Force and the civil market. Over 1000 181s were made and forty or more are still flying, mainly on the Continent especially Germany, others are static in private collections and museums.

In 1947 a Bestmann was registered G-AKAX, and stored at Denham, but was never flown, and finally broken up in 1950.

The fuselage consisted of steel tubes forward and plywood monocoque aft, the wooden wings covered in ply and fabric carried trailing edge flaps. A variety of engines were fitted including, Toma and Walter Mikron; the UK example had a 105 hp Hirth which was standard Zlin fit.

This charming little pre-war side by side two seater is much prized on the Continent and is said to be the 'inspiration' for the SAAB Safir. The one remaining Bestmann in the UK has recently been sold to the USA.

# BUCKER
# BU 181 BESTMANN

LIGHT PLANE
Hirth, 105 hp

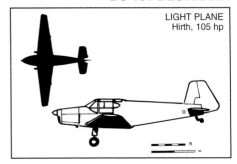

| DATA | IMPERIAL | | METRIC | |
|---|---|---|---|---|
| Span | 34.7 | ft | 10.7 | m |
| Wing area | 145.3 | sq ft | 13.6 | sq m |
| Aspect ratio | 8.3 | | 8.3 | |
| Empty Weight | 1056 | lb | 479 | kg |
| Loaded weight | 1650 | lb | 742 | kg |
| Wing loading | 11.3 | lb/sq ft | 55 | kg/sq m |
| Max speed | 133 | mph | 213 | kmh |
| Cruise speed | 121 | mph | 193 | kmh |
| Stalling speed | 60 | mph | 96 | kmh |
| Climb rate | 700 | ft/min | 215 | m/min |
| Range | 497 | mls | 795 | km |

As if loathe to give up the trappings of the biplane the Ryan trainers, the USAAC's first monoplane trainer, had wires, struts, exposed cylinder heads, fixed gear and open cockpits.

First flown in 1939 the PT-22 was developed from the earlier Menasco powered STA and had the more powerful five cylinder 160 hp Kinner R440 radial engine.

Of mixed construction the PT-22 has a light alloy monocoque fuselage, metal wing ribs and nose skinning – but wooden spars. Manually operated flaps were fitted, rare for the 1930s, and the long stroke undercarriage, usually faired, is a wonder to behold when un-faired!

Over 1000 were ordered by the Air Corps, 125 by the USN and an order was received from the Netherlands A.F.

Retired at the end of WW2, 500 were sold on to the civil market. Many are still flying in the USA, Australia and the UK – where two are airworthy and three are in collections.

# RYAN
# PT-22 RECRUIT

LIGHT PLANE
Kinner R440, 160 hp

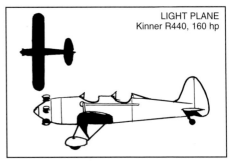

| DATA | IMPERIAL | | METRIC | |
|---|---|---|---|---|
| Span | 30.1 | ft | 9.2 | m |
| Wing area | 134 | sq ft | 12.5 | sq m |
| Aspect ratio | 6.7 | | | |
| Empty Weight | 1313 | lb | 596 | kg |
| Loaded weight | 1860 | lb | 844 | kg |
| Wing loading | 13.6 | lb/sq ft | 66 | kg/sq m |
| Max speed | 115 | mph | 184 | kmh |
| Cruise speed | 100 | mph | 160 | kmh |
| Stalling speed | 60 | mph | 96 | kmh |
| Climb rate | 1000 | ft/min | 308 | m/min |
| Range | 352 | mls | 766 | km |

First flown in 1937 and in production by 1939, the all wooden DH94 Moth Minor was intended as a modern low wing replacement for the famous 'Moth biplane series. Owing something to the DH81 Swallow Moth of 1931, the dainty Minor had an open cockpit tandem seating, though a few tandem enclosed cockpit versions were made. Its elegant, plywood skinned, high aspect ratio wings folded backwards to save hangar space.

With order books full, seventy-three were built at Hatfield before production ceased due to the war when all jigs and fixtures were sent to De Haviland Australia and a further forty-two were made there.

A dozen, or so, went for export before all civil aircraft were impressed, approximately thirty-five, about half of which returned to civil status in 1946. There are five currently on the UK Register, all airworthy, whilst in Australia, ten have survived.

### DE HAVILAND
# MOTH MINOR

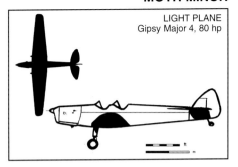

LIGHT PLANE
Gipsy Major 4, 80 hp

| DATA | IMPERIAL | | METRIC | |
|---|---|---|---|---|
| Span | 36.5 | ft | 11.2 | m |
| Wing area | 162 | sq ft | 15.2 | sq m |
| Aspect ratio | 8 | | 8 | |
| Empty Weight | 983 | lb | 446 | kg |
| Loaded weight | 1550 | lb | 70.4 | kg |
| Wing loading | 9.5 | lb/sq ft | 46.7 | kg/sq m |
| Max speed | 118 | mph | 188 | kmh |
| Cruise speed | 100 | mph | 160 | kmh |
| Stalling speed | 47 | mph | 75 | kmh |
| Climb rate | 620 | ft/min | 191 | m/min |
| Range | 300 | mls | 450 | km |

Where did they all go? Twelve hundred Magisters were produced for the RAF during WW2 and most of those still serving were released on to the civil market, only two are still flying. Several non-flying examples are dotted about, three in UK museums, some of which may one day become airworthy. (Ed. three now flying).

The all wood Magister was, in its brief civilian role, known as the Hawk Trainer 3, produced at Woodley by the prolific Miles brothers, Fred and George. Mass production of the Magister as the RAFs monoplane *ab initio* trainer and the equally numerous Master boosted the Miles fortunes during the war years.

First flown as the Hawk Trainer in 1937, it presented quite an advanced design concept with its cantilever wing, split trailing edge flaps and single leg undercarriage.

### MILES
# MAGISTER

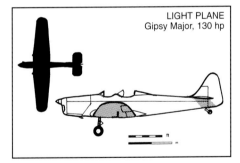

LIGHT PLANE
Gipsy Major, 130 hp

| DATA | IMPERIAL | | METRIC | |
|---|---|---|---|---|
| Span | 33.8 | ft | 10.4 | m |
| Wing area | 172 | sq ft | 16.2 | sq m |
| Aspect ratio | 6.6 | | 6.6 | |
| Empty Weight | 1286 | lb | 584 | kg |
| Loaded weight | 1900 | lb | 863 | kg |
| Wing loading | 11 | lb/sq ft | 54 | kg/sq m |
| Max speed | 132 | mph | 211 | kmh |
| Cruise speed | 123 | mph | 197 | kmh |
| Stalling speed | 50 | mph | 80 | kmh |
| Climb rate | 850 | ft/min | 262 | m/min |
| Range | 380 | mls | 608 | km |

A militarised version of the, then four year old, P10 Vega Gull, the Proctor, otherwise identical, had revised cabin framing with a four piece blown windscreen. Due to the more comprehensive equipment specification the Proctor 1,2 and 3 carried only three people whilst its civil sister was a four seater.

First flown in 1939 the Proctors structure was all wood, with plywood covering; there were split trailing edge flaps, folding wings and neatly spatted main wheels.

Its performance, 150 mph cruise and 1000 ft/min climb was outstanding for its day.

Mks 4 and 5 appeared in 1943 with a plumper fuselage and four seats.

After the war 225 were civilianised, many being sold abroad - some making the trip under their own power as far as Australia.

Seven are on the UK Register, two airworthy, three stored and two in museums.

# PERCIVAL PROCTOR

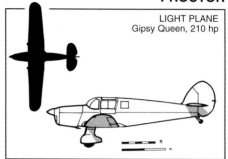

LIGHT PLANE
Gipsy Queen, 210 hp

| DATA | IMPERIAL | | METRIC | |
|---|---|---|---|---|
| Span | 39.4 | ft | 12 | m |
| Wing area | 197 | sq ft | 18.5 | sq m |
| Aspect ratio | 7.9 | | 7.9 | |
| Empty Weight | 1875 | lb | 851 | kg |
| Loaded weight | 3250 | lb | 1475 | kg |
| Wing loading | 16.5 | lb/sq ft | 80.5 | kg/sq m |
| Max speed | 165 | mph | 264 | kmh |
| Cruise speed | 150 | mph | 241 | kmh |
| Stalling speed | 60 | mph | 96 | kmh |
| Climb rate | 1020 | ft/min | 314 | m/min |
| Range | 660 | mls | 1056 | km |

The all wooden M38 Messenger was designed for small field liaison duties and first flew in 1942. About 25 were delivered to the armed forces - one being General Montgomery's hack - and with the cessation of hostilities production was geared to the civil market, bringing total production figures up to 80. Ex army Messengers also came onto the civil market.

A clean, capacious fuselage, long stroke trailing link undercarriage and fixed Miles trailing edge flaps were all features of this four seat STOL aeroplane.

A Messenger made aviation history in 1947 when, after its engine detached itself from the fuselage (due to prop. failure) it made a safe landing, almost undamaged!

There are currently twelve Messengers on the UK Register, five flying and three under resotration.

# MILES M38 MESSENGER

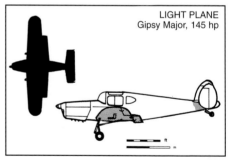

LIGHT PLANE
Gipsy Major, 145 hp

| DATA | IMPERIAL | | METRIC | |
|---|---|---|---|---|
| Span | 36.2 | ft | 11.1 | m |
| Wing area | 191 | sq ft | 18 | sq m |
| Aspect ratio | 6.8 | | 6.8 | |
| Empty Weight | 1360 | lb | 617 | kg |
| Loaded weight | 2400 | lb | 1089 | kg |
| Wing loading | 12.5 | lb/sq ft | 61.3 | kg/sq m |
| Max speed | 115 | mph | 184 | kmh |
| Cruise speed | 100 | mph | 160 | kmh |
| Stalling speed | 45 | mph | 72 | kmh |
| Climb rate | 1100 | ft/min | 338 | m/min |
| Range | 460 | mls | 736 | km |

Designed by E. O. Tips of Fairey Avions Belge and first flying in 1948, the single seat Junior was one of the first new, post WW2, ultralights.

Two prototypes were built; one powered by a 36 hp JAP J99 and the other a Walter Mikron of 60 hp. Both aircraft were demonstrated in this country and assessed at Boscombe Down in 1950. The report of this assessment was highly favourable; but no orders were forthcoming.

The Mikron powered Belgian registered aircraft, OO-ULA was re-registered to Fairey UK as G-AMVP and later passed into private ownership. It was seen at the '1993 PFA Rally in camouflage and is currently undergoing repairs to a damaged undercarriage on the Isle of Wight.

With an all wooden airframe, part plywood and part fabric covered, the Junior, strong and well built, was never offered as a kit, though Tips must have had a sense of 'humour' as the apparently parallel chord wing tapers just three inches, about half an inch in length per rib!

The late 1940s were lean years for light aviation and the Junior, sadly, 'withered on the vine'.

### FAIREY JUNIOR

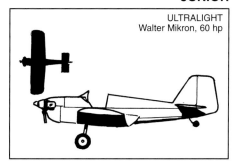

ULTRALIGHT
Walter Mikron, 60 hp

| DATA | IMPERIAL | | METRIC | |
|---|---|---|---|---|
| Span | 22.6 | ft | 7 | m |
| Wing area | 111 | sq ft | 10.4 | sq m |
| Aspect ratio | 4.6 | | | |
| Empty Weight | 486 | lb | 220 | kg |
| Loaded weight | 770 | lb | 350 | kg |
| Wing loading | 7 | lb/sq ft | 34 | kg/sq m |
| Max speed | 108 | mph | 173 | kmh |
| Cruise speed | 98 | mph | 157 | kmh |
| Stalling speed | 32 | mph | 51 | kmh |
| Climb rate | 800 | ft/min | 246 | m/min |
| Range | 300 | mls | 480 | km |

A design competition organised by the Service de l'Aviation Legere et Sportive in 1946, to promote sport flying in France, produced winners in several classes, SIPA one of which was the two seat SIPA S90. S 903.

Designed by Yves Gardan, the SIPA S90 was powered by a 75 hp Mathis engine. Many variants followed, almost identical, but with different engines, i.e. S91, 85 hp Continental; S93, 75 hp Salmson; S94, 90 hp Continental; S901 75 hp Minie. The S903 with the 90 hp Continental is the most popular version.

All wooden structure with part fabric covering, rakishly spatted main wheels and steerable tail wheel, the S903 has tapered wings with rounded tips and a similar tailplane. (Its plan silhouette is rather like a Zero!)

Over 100 of the SIPA S903 range were produced of which 9 are on the UK Register.

### SIPA S 903

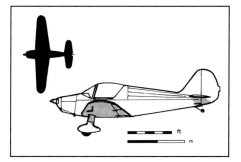

| DATA | IMPERIAL | | METRIC | |
|---|---|---|---|---|
| Span | 28.6 | ft | 8.8 | m |
| Wing area | 120.5 | sq ft | 11.3 | sq m |
| Aspect ratio | 6.8 | | 6.8 | |
| Empty Weight | 895 | lb | 406 | kg |
| Loaded weight | 1390 | lb | 631 | kg |
| Wing loading | 11.5 | lb/sq ft | 56.3 | kg/sq m |
| Max speed | 124 | mph | 198 | kmh |
| Cruise speed | 96 | mph | 153 | kmh |
| Stalling speed | 52 | mph | 83 | kmh |
| Climb rate | 492 | ft/min | 151 | m/min |
| Range | 280 | mls | 448 | km |

Designed and built by De Haviland Canada Ltd and first flown in 1946, the first Chipmunks were built in Canada, 217 off, and subsequently in the UK, 1014 off, and by OGMA in Portugal.

Built either as a civilian or RAF tandem two seat trainer, 740 for military use. The Chipmunk is of all metal construction and of the 1200 plus built, 135 are still on the British Register, and most of them still working for a living, not bad for forty-eight year old aeroplane.

The Gipsy Major 10 is the most common power plant and the long greenhouse canopy is replaced by a one piece blown perspex hood in the Canadian versions. Wheel spats are occasionally fitted.

The slim fully tapered wing, elliptical fin and rudder and the long glazed cockpit cover are all distinctive features.

A few single seat agricultural versions were also built.

# DE HAVILAND
# CHIPMUNK

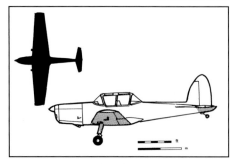

| DATA | IMPERIAL | | METRIC | |
|---|---|---|---|---|
| Span | 34.3 | ft | 10.6 | m |
| Wing area | 172.5 | sq ft | 16.2 | sq m |
| Aspect ratio | 6.8 | | 6.8 | |
| Empty Weight | 1425 | lb | 647 | kg |
| Loaded weight | 2014 | lb | 914 | kg |
| Wing loading | 11.7 | lb/sq ft | 55.6 | kg/sq m |
| Max speed | 138 | mph | 221 | kmh |
| Cruise speed | 102 | mph | 163 | kmh |
| Stalling speed | 50 | mph | 80 | kmh |
| Climb rate | 840 | ft/min | 159 | m/min |
| Range | 280 | mls | 448 | km |

An early post war French design from the drawing board of Roger Druine. It was the first really popular and successful ultralight for the homebuilder to emerge after the dark years of WW2. Many have been built over the last forty years all over the world and are still being built.

From 1958 Rollason Aircraft of Croydon produced twenty-nine Turbulents and supplied components to home constructors to the PFA drawings.

The Turbulent is of all wood construction, the cantilever wing being ply skinned up to the main spar and fabric aft. The fuselage is ply all over, as are the tailplane and fin, with the control surfaces all fabric covered.

The landing gear has a spring strut and may be braked plus a steerable tailwheel or unbraked with a skid.

This rather cheeky little aeroplane is invariably powered by a VW engine of 36 hp. There are forty-one on the UK Register and others being built.

# DRUINE
# TURBULENT

ULTRALIGHT
VW 36hp

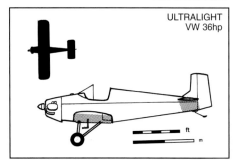

| DATA | IMPERIAL | | METRIC | |
|---|---|---|---|---|
| Span | 21.4 | ft | 6.5 | m |
| Wing area | 80.7 | sq ft | 7.5 | sq m |
| Aspect ratio | 5.4 | | 5.4 | |
| Empty Weight | 350 | lb | 159 | kg |
| Loaded weight | 607 | lb | 275 | kg |
| Wing loading | 7.5 | lb/sq ft | 36.7 | kg/sq m |
| Max speed | 87 | mph | 140 | kmh |
| Cruise speed | 75 | mph | 121 | kmh |
| Stalling speed | 25 | mph | 40 | kmh |
| Climb rate | 492 | ft/min | 150 | m/min |
| Range | 180 | mls | 288 | km |

One of Fokker's first products after WW2 the side by side S11 was designed as a military trainer, powered by a 190 hp Lycoming 0-435-A, the S11 first flew in 1947. The Netherlands Air Force took delivery of 40, 41 went to the Israeli Defence Force and 150 were built under licence in Italy as the Macchi M416. A further 100 were built in Brazil.

A nose wheel version, the S12, was prototyped in Holland but all production took place in Brazil, where 70 were built.

When the S11 was de-militarised many came on to the civil market – most of them going to Italian clubs – though two are shown on the UK Register – one is stored at Spanhoe but permit expired in 1933 and the other, G-BIYU, is airworthy.

The S11's fuselage is of welded steel tube with fabric covering and the wings are all metal with fabric covered ailerons and manually operated flaps. The tail surfaces have a fabric covered metal structure and the tailplane is strut braced.

The cranked undercarriage legs are distinctive and terminate in hydraulically braked wheels.

This interesting 50 year old aeroplane may yet be seen!

## FOKKER
## S11 INSTRUCTOR

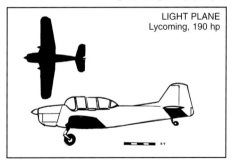

LIGHT PLANE
Lycoming, 190 hp

| DATA | IMPERIAL | | METRIC | |
|---|---|---|---|---|
| Span | 36 | ft | 11 | m |
| Wing area | 199 | sq ft | 18.7 | sq m |
| Aspect ratio | 6.5 | | | |
| Empty Weight | 1784 | lb | 810 | kg |
| Loaded weight | 2426 | lb | 1100 | kg |
| Wing loading | 12.2 | lb/sq ft | 59.5 | kg/sq m |
| Max speed | 130 | mph | 209 | kmh |
| Cruise speed | 102 | mph | 164 | kmh |
| Stalling speed | 55 | mph | 88 | kmh |
| Climb rate | 650 | ft/min | 200 | m/min |
| Range | 400 | mls | 640 | km |

Designed and built by Edouard Joly and Jean Delamontez just after WW2 and first flown in 1948, the D9 is the progenitor of the whole family crank wing Jodels and Robins.

A brilliantly simple design in all wood ideal for the amateur constructor. This little aeroplane, in the microlight weight class, has been built in the hundreds in France and elsewhere, with eleven on the UK Register, plus two being built.

The original D9 had a Poinsard engine, all subsequent D9s had a suffix that denoted the engine type, and the D92 with the VW being the most popular.

The wing, which is stressed for 9g, has a unique main spar, a four longeron plywood covered box which takes all the lift, drag and torque loads. The wide parallel chord centre section and tapered, unswept outer panels from a famously efficient wing.

The rudder is aerodynamically balanced and may or may not have a minuscule, fixed fin atop the tail plane.

## JODEL
## D9 BEBE

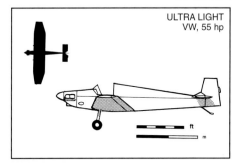

ULTRA LIGHT
VW, 55 hp

| DATA | IMPERIAL | | METRIC | |
|---|---|---|---|---|
| Span | 23 | ft | 7.1 | m |
| Wing area | 97 | sq ft | 9.1 | sq m |
| Aspect ratio | 5.45 | | 5.45 | |
| Empty Weight | 435 | lb | 197 | kg |
| Loaded weight | 715 | lb | 325 | kg |
| Wing loading | 7.37 | lb/sq ft | 36 | kg/sq m |
| Max speed | 103 | mph | 165 | kmh |
| Cruise speed | 85 | mph | 136 | kmh |
| Stalling speed | 50 | mph | 58 | kmh |
| Climb rate | 36 | ft/min | 200 | m/min |
| Range | 300 | mls | 480 | km |

Roger Druine's single seat Turbulent was a pioneering plane in the homebuilt movement. He followed it with the two seat, in tandem. Turbi in the late 1940s. Though not as numerous as the Turbulent, three were built in the UK.

The prototype was powered by a Beaussier engine of 45 hp most subsequent models, however, were Walter Mikron, 62 hp, powered. other engines fitted have been, Gipsy Minor, Cirrus Minor, Coventry Victor and Continental A75.

An all wooden aeroplane of simple construction it is PFA approved and is a 'plans only' build. the flapless wing has two box spars and is fabric covered aft of the main spar, as are the tail surfaces. The undercarriage has rubber block sprung legs and braked wheels with a steerable tail wheel, unbraked models have a steerable tail skid. both open cockpit and coupe versions have been built and the wings have letterbox lead edge slots.

Two of the three UK Turbis are airworthy.

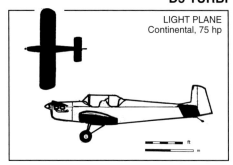

LIGHT PLANE
Continental, 75 hp

| DATA | IMPERIAL | | METRIC | |
|---|---|---|---|---|
| Span | 28.7 | ft | 8.76 | m |
| Wing area | 130 | sq ft | 12.9 | sq m |
| Aspect ratio | 6.3 | | 6.3 | |
| Empty Weight | 725 | lb | 330 | kg |
| Loaded weight | 1240 | lb | 562 | kg |
| Wing loading | 9.5 | lb/sq ft | 46 | kg/sq m |
| Max speed | 94 | mph | 150 | kmh |
| Cruise speed | 74 | mph | 119 | kmh |
| Stalling speed | 32 | mph | 51 | kmh |
| Climb rate | 500 | ft/min | 152 | m/min |
| Range | 250 | mls | 400 | km |

A French design from the drawing board of Yves Gardan, a lightweight version of the SIPA 90, built by Constructions Aeronautique du Bearn and first flown in 1949. CAB built only a few of the neat little all wood two seater before the drawings and production rights were acquired by A. Order-Hume who re-designed it to meet UK Airworthiness Requirements and to enable it to be easily to 'home build'.

Sets of plans have been sold world-wide including USA and Australia, where it was the first post war DCA approved plane to fly. It is also approved by the PFA and eighteen are currently on the UK Register. Various motors (65-120hp) have been fitted, the figures in our table are for the 65 hp Continental model.

A retractable undercarriage version is known as the Gardan GY30 Supercab which has plywood covered wings.

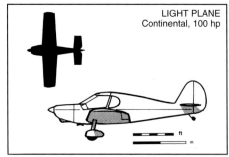

LIGHT PLANE
Continental, 100 hp

| DATA | IMPERIAL | | METRIC | |
|---|---|---|---|---|
| Span | 25 | ft | 17.62 | m |
| Wing area | 107.6 | sq ft | 10 | sq m |
| Aspect ratio | 5.8 | | 5.8 | |
| Empty Weight | 595 | lb | 270 | kg |
| Loaded weight | 1235 | lb | 560 | kg |
| Wing loading | 11.47 | lb/sq ft | 56 | kg/sq m |
| Max speed | 124 | mph | 200 | kmh |
| Cruise speed | 112 | mph | 180 | kmh |
| Stalling speed | 47 | mph | 76 | kmh |
| Climb rate | 680 | ft/min | 207 | m/min |
| Range | 466 | mls | 750 | km |

David Long, one time Piper Chief Engineer, designed and built the Midget Mustang, an all metal singe seater for air racing. In 1949 it came fourth in the Continental Trophy. Afterwards it languished as a one off homebuilt racer, and David Long died before any further development could take place.

In the early 1950s Robert Bushby set about production on the Midget Mustang parts for kit assembly and by 1959 the re-engineered plane took to the air as the MM-1-85 with a 85 hp Continental.

The MM-1-125 followed in 1963 with a 125 hp Continental and then a two seat version, Mustang 2, with a 160 hp Lycoming. Over 900 sets of plans and kits have been sold.

This pioneering all metal kit plane is PFA approved and there are three on the British Register.

The data below is for the MM-1-125.

## BUSHBY
# MIDGET MUSTANG

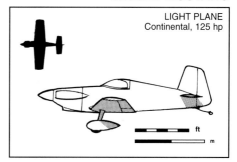

LIGHT PLANE
Continental, 125 hp

| DATA | IMPERIAL | | METRIC | |
|---|---|---|---|---|
| Span | 18.5 | ft | 5.7 | m |
| Wing area | 68 | sq ft | 6.4 | sq m |
| Aspect ratio | 5 | | 5 | |
| Empty Weight | 575 | lb | 261 | kg |
| Loaded weight | 875 | lb | 397 | kg |
| Wing loading | 12.8 | lb/sq ft | 63 | kg/sq m |
| Max speed | 190 | mph | 304 | kmh |
| Cruise speed | 175 | mph | 280 | kmh |
| Stalling speed | 57 | mph | 91 | kmh |
| Climb rate | 1750 | ft/min | 540 | m/min |
| Range | 400 | mls | 640 | km |

Designed to AM specification T16/48, the prototype Provost first flew in 1950 with an AS Cheetah 17 engine. Subsequent production aircraft all had the Leonides 126.

Of all metal construction, the Provost, an ab initio to advanced trainer was capable of carrying machine guns and under-wing bombs and was in production for ten years, during which time 461 aircraft were built. These sturdy trainers were supplied to many foreign air forces including Eire, Burma, Rhodesia, Iraq, Muscat and Sudan. Finally being succeeded by the Jet Provost, though prop and jet models overlapped for two years.

Flaps, brakes and windscreen wipers were operated pneumatically from an engine driven compressor.

Fully aerobatic, a Percival owned and civil registered provost (G-AMZM) was entered for the 1956 Lockhead aerobatic Contest, however, it failed to gain a place against the specialist stunters.

On 'de-mobilisation' the Provosts were overhauled stripped of AM gear and sold on to the civil market and to foreign buyers.

Nine are currently on the UK Register, five of which appear to be airworthy, eight are static in various UK museums.

## HUNTING-PERCIVAL
# PROVOST

EX RAF TRAINER
Alvis Leonides 126, 550 hp

| DATA | IMPERIAL | | METRIC | |
|---|---|---|---|---|
| Span | 35.16 | ft | 10.8 | m |
| Wing area | 214 | sq ft | 20.1 | sq m |
| Aspect ratio | 5.8 | | | |
| Empty Weight | 3350 | lb | 1520 | kg |
| Loaded weight | 4400 | lb | 1997 | kg |
| Wing loading | 20.5 | lb/sq ft | 100 | kg/sq m |
| Max speed | 195 | mph | 312 | kmh |
| Cruise speed | 177 | mph | 283 | kmh |
| Stalling speed | 64 | mph | 102 | kmh |
| Climb rate | 2200 | ft/min | 677 | m/min |
| Range | 450 | mls | 720 | km |

Percival's first all metal aeroplane the Prentice replaced the Tiger Moth as the RAF's *ab initio* trainer after WW2. With a variable pitch airscrew, flaps, more comprehensive instrumentation, side-by-side seating and a more powerful engine the Prentice brought training more up to date.

About 400 were delivered between 1948-1949, many of them built under contract by Blackburn Aircraft Ltd. Replaced by the Provost in 1955 a batch of 250 were sold to Aviation Traders Ltd for conversion to civil use and dispersed at airfields up and down the country. The conversion and subsequent obtaining of C of A took a couple of years and eventually twenty or more made it on to the UK Register. Devoid of military kit, four or five seats could be fitted. Some were sold abroad the rest were scrapped!

The sturdy Prentice (stressed for 10g) was, in its early days, a 'spinner' and various tail forms were tried before it was cured.

Ten are still on the UK Register, four are flying (one with the Shuttleworth Trust), six are in UK museums and about the same number in museums abroad. A flying example exists in the USA.

## PERCIVAL PRENTICE

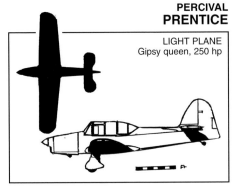

LIGHT PLANE
Gipsy queen, 250 hp

| DATA | IMPERIAL | | METRIC | |
|------|---------|---|--------|---|
| Span | 46 | ft | 14.2 | m |
| Wing area | 305 | sq ft | 28.7 | sq m |
| Aspect ratio | 7 | | | |
| Empty Weight | 3232 | lb | 1055 | kg |
| Loaded weight | 4350 | lb | 1975 | kg |
| Wing loading | 14.3 | lb/sq ft | 70 | kg/sq m |
| Max speed | 143 | mph | 229 | kmh |
| Cruise speed | 126 | mph | 202 | kmh |
| Stalling speed | *55* | mph | *88* | kmh |
| Climb rate | 650 | ft/min | 200 | m/min |
| Range | 350 | mls | 560 | km |

The Jodel D11 of 1950 has spawned a shoal of variants and, logically, if the first two digits are 11 it is of D11 parentage, ie D117, D119, even D1190, plus the D127 and D128 built by EAC with sliding canopies. More than a little confusing!

The main Jodel trade mark, common to all, is its wing, a large parallel chord centre-section with no dihedral and tapered outer planes with pronounced dihedral and considerable wash-out. The Aerodynamic efficiency of this wing is legendary.

This side-by-side, all wood, two seater was developed from the pioneering single seat D9 of 1948 by the Designers E. Joly and J. Delemontez.

Jodels are still being built at Dijon and remain popular with homebuilders.

Over 100 of the D11 tribe are on the UK Register.

## JODEL D112 CLUB

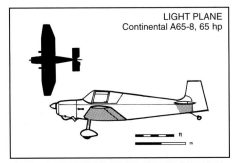

LIGHT PLANE
Continental A65-8, 65 hp

| DATA | IMPERIAL | | METRIC | |
|------|---------|---|--------|---|
| Span | 26.8 | ft | 8.25 | m |
| Wing area | 136.7 | sq ft | 12.8 | sq m |
| Aspect ratio | 5.25 | | 5.25 | |
| Empty Weight | 600 | lb | 272 | kg |
| Loaded weight | 1145 | lb | 520 | kg |
| Wing loading | 8.4 | lb/sq ft | 41 | kg/sq m |
| Max speed | 118 | mph | 189 | kmh |
| Cruise speed | 93 | mph | 149 | kmh |
| Stalling speed | 45 | mph | 72 | kmh |
| Climb rate | 632 | ft/min | 194 | m/min |
| Range | 373 | mls | 597 | km |

Ray Stits designed a range of light aircraft for home building, one of the first being the single seat Playboy that first flew in 1953. A pioneer of home building, Stits started by supplying kits but went on to plans only.

Well known now for the covering products, Stits Poly-Fiber Aircraft Coatings, the light plane movement has had a doughty champion in Mr Stits.

A low wing, strut braced single seater with fixed tail-dragger undercarriage, the Playboy is to be seen with many minor variations of cockpit, strut arrangement, fin shape and engine model.

The fuselage is of welded steel tube and the wings are all wood with a plywood leading edge, the tail is welded tube and the whole is fabric covered.

A two seat Playboy, the SA-3B, with a two foot span increase has also been built in some numbers.

An enduring 47 year old homebuilt with up to 1000 built in the USA and three currently on the UK Register.

## STITTS
# SA-3A PLAYBOY

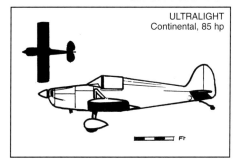

ULTRALIGHT
Continental, 85 hp

| DATA | IMPERIAL | | METRIC | |
|---|---|---|---|---|
| Span | 22.1 | ft | 6.76 | m |
| Wing area | 96 | sq ft | 8.92 | sq m |
| Aspect ratio | 5.15 | | | |
| Empty Weight | 600 | lb | 272 | kg |
| Loaded weight | 902 | lb | 409 | kg |
| Wing loading | 9 | lb/sq ft | 44 | kg/sq m |
| Max speed | 145 | mph | 232 | kmh |
| Cruise speed | 130 | mph | 209 | kmh |
| Stalling speed | 45 | mph | 72 | kmh |
| Climb rate | 1000 | ft/min | 305 | m/min |
| Range | 250 | mls | 400 | km |

First flown in 1954 the Nord 3202, developed from the 3200 and 3201 civilian and military trainers, it's role was basic training, aerobatics and blind flying training.

Production ceased in 1961 by which time 100 machines had been made. Subsequently withdrawn from service during '73/75 they were sold on to the civilian market, many going to the USA.

The power unit is a Potez 4D-32 of 240 hp or - in the last batch of 50, the Potez 4D-34D of 260 hp.

Construction comprises a welded tube fuselage with fabric covering and detachable panels; the wing has a single spar, metal nose sheeting and fabric aft. It is fitted with plain flaps which are fabric covered, as are all the flying control surfaces. The tailplane is braced by a single strut and the trailing link undercarriage legs are a distinctive feature.

Being an ex military type of rather dated construction the '3202 is much prized as a pseudo war bird and there are three on the UK Register.

Nord 3202s were flown in the 1966 World Aerobatic Championships by the French team.

## NORD
# 3202

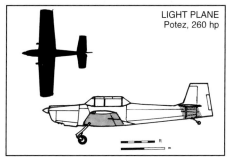

LIGHT PLANE
Potez, 260 hp

| DATA | IMPERIAL | | METRIC | |
|---|---|---|---|---|
| Span | 31.1 | ft | 9.6 | m |
| Wing area | 175 | sq ft | 16.4 | sq m |
| Aspect ratio | 5.5 | | 5.5 | |
| Empty Weight | 1965 | lb | 892 | kg |
| Loaded weight | 2690 | lb | 1221 | kg |
| Wing loading | 15.4 | lb/sq ft | 75.1 | kg/sq m |
| Max speed | 180 | mph | 288 | kmh |
| Cruise speed | 120 | mph | 192 | kmh |
| Stalling speed | 72 | mph | 115 | kmh |
| Climb rate | 1122 | ft/min | 345 | m/min |
| Range | 575 | mls | 920 | km |

French engineer, Claude Piel designed and built the Emeraude in which he and his wife made the first flight in 1954. Since then many variants have appeared with engines ranging from 65 hp to 125 hp.

Manufactured in ready-made or kit form by Scintex in France, in Germany, as Smaragd, by Schempp Hirth and in the UK by Fairtravel and Garland Bianchi as the Linnet.

Of all wood construction with a semi elliptical wing, sometimes with a cropped tip, the construction is conventional with two spars, plywood covering, flaps and insert ailerons (much praised for their effectiveness).

A British built Emeraude won the Best Homebuilt award at the 1990 PFA rally.

The Super Emeraude is identical to look at but is stronger and has a more powerful engine.

A good looking fifty-year-old aeroplane, much cherished by its owners. Forty-six on the UK Register (thirty-five CP301 and ten CP1310).

## PIEL
## CP301 EMERAUDE

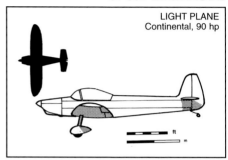

LIGHT PLANE
Continental, 90 hp

| DATA | IMPERIAL | | METRIC | |
|---|---|---|---|---|
| Span | 26.5 | ft | 8.1 | m |
| Wing area | 117 | sq ft | 10.9 | sq m |
| Aspect ratio | 6 | | 6 | |
| Empty Weight | 850 | lb | 386 | kg |
| Loaded weight | 1500 | lb | 6811 | kg |
| Wing loading | 12.8 | lb/sq ft | 62.5 | kg/sq m |
| Max speed | 124 | mph | 198 | kmh |
| Cruise speed | 104 | mph | 166 | kmh |
| Stalling speed | 47 | mph | 75 | kmh |
| Climb rate | 700 | ft/min | 215 | m/min |
| Range | 275 | mls | 440 | km |

The Tempete, a single seat, aerobatic sport plane which first flew in 1956, is from the drawing board of prolific Romanian/French designer Marcel Jurca.

The prototype specially designed for the amateur constructor, was built by a team from the Courevoie Aero Club and has since been copied in many countries and marketed in N. America by Falconair Aircraft in Canada.

Of all wood construction the Tempete's high rear top decking integral with the fin is a distinctive feature as are the truly half round tips to the wings and tailplane.

The single spar, low aspect ratio wing, with no dihedral, is built in three sections and supports a wide track Jodel D112 tail-dragger undercarriage.

Engines ranging from 65 to 125 hp. may be fitted, figures below are for the 110 hp. model.

There are two on the UK Register and several being built, the type being PFA approved.

## JURCA
## MJ-2 TEMPETE

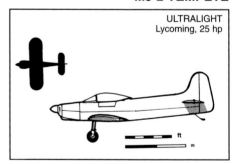

ULTRALIGHT
Lycoming, 25 hp

| DATA | IMPERIAL | | METRIC | |
|---|---|---|---|---|
| Span | 19.6 | ft | 6 | m |
| Wing area | 86 | sq ft | 8 | sq m |
| Aspect ratio | 4.5 | | 4.5 | |
| Empty Weight | 539 | lb | 290 | kg |
| Loaded weight | 948 | lb | 430 | kg |
| Wing loading | 7.4 | lb/sq ft | 36 | kg/sq m |
| Max speed | 120 | mph | 193 | kmh |
| Cruise speed | 102 | mph | 163 | kmh |
| Stalling speed | 45 | mph | 72 | kmh |
| Climb rate | 550 | ft/min | 170 | m/min |
| Range | 320 | mls | 512 | km |

Developed by the Societe Aeronautique Normande, the D140 Mousquetaire (Musketeer) first flew in 1958, a typical 'crank wing' Jodel with very sporty lines and four seats.

The first D140s had an un-Jodel-like triangular fin and horn balanced rudder (as shown on drawing) this soon gave way to a square tipped swept back assembly.

The D140R Abeille (Bee) is a dedicated glider tug version with a bubble canopy.

The structure of both aircraft is all wood with the wings part fabric covered, the D150 has an all moving tail plane.

These Jodels were designed for touring and their generous tankage gives them both a range of about 1000 miles.

There are fourteen on the UK Register. It is a PFA approved design and one, at least, is being built.

# JODEL
# D140 MOUSQUETAIRE

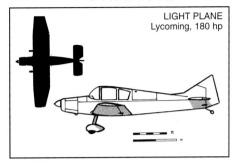

LIGHT PLANE
Lycoming, 180 hp

| DATA | IMPERIAL | | METRIC | |
|---|---|---|---|---|
| Span | 33.6 | ft | 10.3 | m |
| Wing area | 192 | sq ft | 18 | sq m |
| Aspect ratio | 6 | | 6 | |
| Empty Weight | 1367 | lb | 621 | kg |
| Loaded weight | 2645 | lb | 1200 | kg |
| Wing loading | 14 | lb/sq ft | 68.3 | kg/sq m |
| Max speed | 150 | mph | 240 | kmh |
| Cruise speed | 115 | mph | 184 | kmh |
| Stalling speed | 52 | mph | 83 | kmh |
| Climb rate | 750 | ft/min | 231 | m/min |
| Range | 870 | mls | 1393 | km |

Developed from the Jodel D11 two seater, the D1050 was built under licence by SAN a close associate of Jodel, and started out as the DR100A with a 90 hp Continental, first flying in 1958. The DR1050 Ambassadeur, which followed, flew in 1959 and with it's close relative, the DR1051 Sicile, had the Potez E4-20 engine as an option to the 100 hp. Continental.

All these models had straight up rudders - with mini fins, and pitch control by tailplane and elevator.

In 1963 the '1051M variants introduced the swept fin and rudder and the one piece tailplane/stabilator.

This highly regarded four seater has the famous Jodel 'crank wing' and a fixed spatted tail dragger undercarriage.

Access to the 41 in. wide cockpit is via half depth car type doors. Construction is all wood, with ply covered fuselage and part fabric covered wings.

Running costs are claimed to be outstanding for a four seat tourer/trainer - said to be 50% better than average!

There are seventy-three Jodel 1050/1051s on the UK Register.

# JODEL
# DR1050 AMBASSADEUR

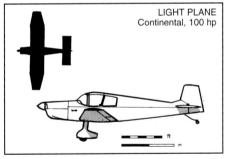

LIGHT PLANE
Continental, 100 hp

| DATA | IMPERIAL | | METRIC | |
|---|---|---|---|---|
| Span | 28.5 | ft | 8.8 | m |
| Wing area | 146.4 | sq ft | 13.7 | sq m |
| Aspect ratio | 5.5 | | 5.5 | |
| Empty Weight | 892 | lb | 405 | kg |
| Loaded weight | 1651 | lb | 750 | kg |
| Wing loading | 11.3 | lb/sq ft | 55 | kg/sq m |
| Max speed | 143 | mph | 229 | kmh |
| Cruise speed | 120 | mph | 192 | kmh |
| Stalling speed | 55 | mph | 88 | kmh |
| Climb rate | 500 | ft/min | 154 | m/min |
| Range | 1000 | mls | 1600 | km |

The Taylor JT1 Monoplane, which first flew in 1959, was one of the first post war British Ultralights and was designed and built by John Taylor at his home in Ilford. This small and sporty monoplane powered, usually, by a 1600 cc VW engine, has a world wide following with 100 sets of plans sold and forty on the UK Register.

The airframe is stressed to +9-9g and is of all wood construction it has a two spar wing with warren girder ribs, plywood leading edge skinning with Dacron aft of the main spar. The fuselage is a four longeron plywood covered box with, depending on builder, an open or bubble hooded cockpit. Coil springs take the loads in the main undercarriage legs and the tail wheel is steerable. Flaps are optional.

The flying qualities of this, now historic, little aeroplane are praised by all who have flown her.

The type is PFA approved and one is being built.

## TAYLOR MONOPLANE

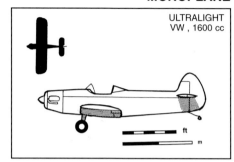

ULTRALIGHT
VW , 1600 cc

| DATA | IMPERIAL | | METRIC | |
|---|---|---|---|---|
| Span | 21 | ft | 6.5 | m |
| Wing area | 76 | sq ft | 7.14 | sq m |
| Aspect ratio | 5.8 | | 5.8 | |
| Empty Weight | 430 | lb | 195 | kg |
| Loaded weight | 660 | lb | 300 | kg |
| Wing loading | 8.7 | lb/sq ft | 42.4 | kg/sq m |
| Max speed | 115 | mph | 184 | kmh |
| Cruise speed | 100 | mph | 160 | kmh |
| Stalling speed | 40 | mph | 64 | kmh |
| Climb rate | 1000 | ft/min | 308 | m/min |
| Range | 290 | mls | 464 | km |

Designed by Fred Weick of Texas A&M as the AG-1 which first flew in 1950 powered by a 150 hp. Lycoming. Piper's took Weick on to develop it and the Piper Pawnee flew in 1959, a dedicated single seat agricultural aeroplane which has proved to be probably the most numerous of its class. (Over 5000 made) Variants are as follows, the Pawnee B, larger hopper and improved spray gear; Pawnee C, (1966) removable rear decking, improved landing gear, cockpit cooling and bigger engine air intake; Pawnee D, wing fuel tanks.

In 1969 a cantilever wing version with square swept fin and rudder appeared as the Pawnee Brave - 938 of these were made, powered by a 285 hp Continental Tiara engine. Later developments had 300 and 375 hp Lycomings and were named Brave 300 and Brave 375.

Though dedicated all metal aircraft builders, Piper reverted back to welded steel tube and fabric for the Pawnee.

There are about forty-one on the UK Register, mainly used for glider tug work. Data below for 235 hp.

## PIPER PA-25 PAWNEE

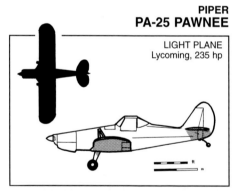

LIGHT PLANE
Lycoming, 235 hp

| DATA | IMPERIAL | | METRIC | |
|---|---|---|---|---|
| Span | 36.1 | ft | 11.1 | m |
| Wing area | 183 | sq ft | 17.2 | sq m |
| Aspect ratio | 7.1 | | 7.1 | |
| Empty Weight | 1488 | lb | 675 | kg |
| Loaded weight | 2900 | lb | 1316 | kg |
| Wing loading | 15.8 | lb/sq ft | 77 | kg/sq m |
| Max speed | 117 | mph | 187 | kmh |
| Cruise speed | 105 | mph | 168 | kmh |
| Stalling speed | 60 | mph | 96 | kmh |
| Climb rate | 630 | ft/min | 194 | m/min |
| Range | 300 | mls | 480 | km |

Designed by Eugene Turner of Oklahoma and first flown in 1961 as a single seater, to be followed in '66 by the two seat version. It is marketed by Turner Aircraft Inc. of Grandview, USA. as a plans built wooden aeroplane of modern appearance.

Variants include, the T40 cabin tail-dragger, the Super T40A with a blister canopy and nose and tail wheel options, the T40B with nose wheel 'gear. G-BRIO, the sole UK aircraft is typed 'Super T40A Modified'; the wing section being drastically modified to cure sharp stall characteristics.

The wooden two spar wing is in three sections the outer panels attaching to a short centre section from which depends the wide track, cantilever legged undercarriage. The wing has plain flaps and pitch control is by elevon.

This neat side by side, fast cruising, two seater has been built in some numbers in its country of origin.

## TURNER T40

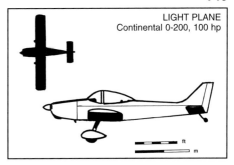

LIGHT PLANE
Continental 0-200, 100 hp

| DATA | IMPERIAL | | METRIC | |
|---|---|---|---|---|
| Span | 29.5 | ft | 9.1 | m |
| Wing area | 109.4 | sq ft | 10.3 | sq m |
| Aspect ratio | 7.9 | | 7.1 | |
| Empty Weight | 1000 | lb | 454 | kg |
| Loaded weight | 1500 | lb | 681 | kg |
| Wing loading | 14.5 | lb/sq ft | 70.7 | kg/sq m |
| Max speed | 170 | mph | 214 | kmh |
| Cruise speed | 115 | mph | 184 | kmh |
| Stalling speed | 61 | mph | 97 | kmh |
| Climb rate | 700 | ft/min | 215 | m/min |
| Range | 400 | mls | 640 | km |

The all wood Sirocco first flew in 1962 is a sturdy tandem two seater designed by Marcel Jurca, a pioneer of the French homebuilding movement. The Sirocco was his seventh design, he has now a total of twenty-eight designs which include many replica war birds. The Sirocco can be fitted with a range of motors – from 90 to 200 hp (the limit for French homebuilts) and may have a fixed or retractable undercarriage.

Developed from the look-a-like single seat Tempete there are several Siroccos flying in the UK and others being built. A side by side version, the Autan is also available like all Jurcas it is a plans homebuilt. The Sirocco is fully aerobatic and PFA approved.

## JURCA SIROCCO

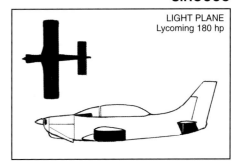

LIGHT PLANE
Lycoming 180 hp

| DATA | IMPERIAL | | METRIC | |
|---|---|---|---|---|
| Span | 23 | ft | 7 | m |
| Wing area | 96 | sq ft | 9.02 | sq m |
| Aspect ratio | 5.5 | | | |
| Empty Weight | 1260 | lb | 572 | kg |
| Loaded weight | 1860 | lb | 844 | kg |
| Wing loading | 19.3 | lb/sq ft | 94 | kg/sq m |
| Max speed | 196 | mph | 313 | kmh |
| Cruise speed | 170 | mph | 272 | kmh |
| Stalling speed | 60 | mph | 96 | kmh |
| Climb rate | 1800 | ft/min | 549 | m/min |
| Range | 477 | mls | 763 | km |

Designed by the husband and wife team Tony and Dorothy Spezio, the Tuholer first flew in 1961. (Tuholer being 'USA speak' for two holes, ie two open cockpits).

Designed with home builders in mind, Tuholer plans are available – though not on the PFA approved list as none as yet built in the UK.

With fold-back wings the aeroplane can be stored in a normal garage and road towed on its own wheels; re-assembly at the 'field takes only ten minutes.

The steel tube fuselage is faired with wooden formers and stringers and fabric covered. The all wood, strut braced, two spar wing is fabric covered aft of the plywood nose skin.

Drum braked and spatted wheels are attached to the bungee sprung undercarriage.

With its 125 hp engine the 24 ft span Tuholer is a lively performer with a top speed of 150 mph and an initial climb rate of 2000 fpm.

Two on the UK Register, although one crashed in France.

## SPEZIO
# DAL-1 TUHOLER

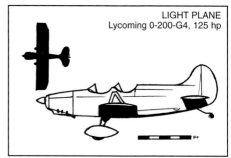

LIGHT PLANE
Lycoming 0-200-G4, 125 hp

| DATA | IMPERIAL | | METRIC | |
| --- | --- | --- | --- | --- |
| Span | 24.7 | ft | 7.55 | m |
| Wing area | 115 | sq ft | 10.7 | sq m |
| Aspect ratio | 5.3 | | | |
| Empty Weight | 810 | lb | 367 | kg |
| Loaded weight | 1400 | lb | 635 | kg |
| Wing loading | 12 | lb/sq ft | 59 | kg/sq m |
| Max speed | 150 | mph | 241 | kmh |
| Cruise speed | 125 | mph | 200 | kmh |
| Stalling speed | 40 | mph | 64 | kmh |
| Climb rate | 2000 | ft/min | 616 | m/min |
| Range | 725 | mls | 1167 | km |

Following up his successful Turbulent, Roger Druine designed the tandem two seat D61 Turbi and the side-by-side D62A followed immediately powered by a Continental 0-200A engine, first flying in 1963 (Flapless, slightly lighter version the D62B was produced in smaller numbers).

Rollasons of Redhill took on the construction of an 'anglicised' version eventually producing about fifty by 1974 when production ceased.

The Condor is an all wood aeroplane with a two spar wing which is fabric covered aft of the main spar as are all the control surfaces. the seating is side by side and the cabin hood hinges on its centre line, opening upwards each side. The tail wheel type undercarriage has cantilever main legs with drum brakes.

Forty Condors are on the British Register and the type is on the PFA approved list.

## DRUINE/ROLLASON
# CONDOR

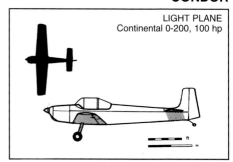

LIGHT PLANE
Continental 0-200, 100 hp

| DATA | IMPERIAL | | METRIC | |
| --- | --- | --- | --- | --- |
| Span | 27.5 | ft | 8.35 | m |
| Wing area | 119 | sq ft | 11.3 | sq m |
| Aspect ratio | 6.3 | | 6.3 | |
| Empty Weight | 950 | lb | 431 | kg |
| Loaded weight | 1475 | lb | 670 | kg |
| Wing loading | 14.62 | lb/sq ft | 71.3 | kg/sq m |
| Max speed | 115 | mph | 185 | kmh |
| Cruise speed | 107 | mph | 172 | kmh |
| Stalling speed | 46 | mph | 74 | kmh |
| Climb rate | 610 | ft/min | 185 | m/min |
| Range | 350 | mls | 560 | km |

Peter Bowers of Boeing, an authority on vintage aeroplanes, designed the Fly Baby with the home builder in mind, made it all wood and very simple.

First flown in 1960, the design was also aimed at the EAA homebuilt competition, which it won in 1962.

Over 3000 sets of plans have been sold by Bowers plus those serialised in Sport Aviation magazine.

Its rather retro looks and wire braced wing belie the design's age and its present day popularity, flocks of them in the USA!

A biplane version, the Fly Baby Bi, was designed and built in 1968, one, at least, modified from the monoplane, is flying in the UK.

The monoplane's wings are hinged to fold alongside the fuselage for easy parking.

The Fly Baby is a PFA approved design, there are three on the Register, plus one being built.

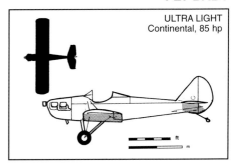

# BOWERS
# FLY BABY

ULTRA LIGHT
Continental, 85 hp

| DATA | IMPERIAL | | METRIC | |
|---|---|---|---|---|
| Span | 28 | ft | 8.6 | m |
| Wing area | 120 | sq ft | 11.3 | sq m |
| Aspect ratio | 6.5 | | 6.5 | |
| Empty Weight | 605 | lb | 274 | kg |
| Loaded weight | 924 | lb | 419 | kg |
| Wing loading | 7.7 | lb/sq ft | 37.6 | kg/sq m |
| Max speed | 120 | mph | 192 | kmh |
| Cruise speed | 105 | mph | 168 | kmh |
| Stalling speed | 45 | mph | 72 | kmh |
| Climb rate | 1100 | ft/min | 338 | m/min |
| Range | 320 | mls | 512 | km |

The sporty Colibri is the brainchild on the Swiss, Max Brugger, who took the fuselage of a Jodel D9 and wings of a Turbulent as the basis of this neat single seater.

First flown in 1965, the Colibri is of all wood construction with some fabric covering and is stressed for aerobatics.

The preferred engine is the 65 hp Volkswagen. Wheel spats may or may not be worn and some models have a finless aerodynamically balanced rudder.

It is popular with homebuilders and an example won the Best Plan Built Aircraft award at the 1993 PFA rally.

There are fifteen on the UK Register and the design is PFA approved.

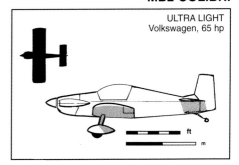

# BRUGGER
# MB2 COLIBRI

ULTRA LIGHT
Volkswagen, 65 hp

| DATA | IMPERIAL | | METRIC | |
|---|---|---|---|---|
| Span | 19.5 | ft | 6 | m |
| Wing area | 89 | sq ft | 8.3 | sq m |
| Aspect ratio | 4.3 | | 4.3 | |
| Empty Weight | 474 | lb | 215 | kg |
| Loaded weight | 727 | lb | 330 | kg |
| Wing loading | 8.1 | lb/sq ft | 39.8 | kg/sq m |
| Max speed | 111 | mph | 177 | kmh |
| Cruise speed | 99 | mph | 159 | kmh |
| Stalling speed | 38 | mph | 61 | kmh |
| Climb rate | 590 | ft/min | 180 | m/min |
| Range | 310 | mls | 497 | km |

An American kit plane par excellence the T18 took on the factory built all metal light planes and showed them a clean pair of heels!

Designed by John Thorp, one time employee of Boeing and Lockhead and designer of the Piper Cherokee. The T18 took to the air for the first time in 1966 and was initially a 'plane only' home built. From 1970 kits were available for the all metal plane with its Jodel type 'crank wing' spanning only 21 ft and a cruising speed of 170 mph.

1500 plans and kits have been sold world-wide with, 400 of them now flying.

Several record breaking flights have been mode by T18s including, round the world, Australia, England and the North Pole and back non stop.the 1976 round the world plane is now in the EAA museum, it being the first homebuilt to circumnavigate.

PFA approved, four on the UK Register and two being built.

## THORP
## T18

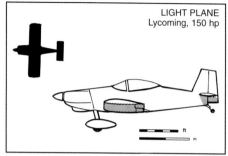

LIGHT PLANE
Lycoming, 150 hp

| DATA | IMPERIAL | | METRIC | |
|---|---|---|---|---|
| Span | 20.8 | ft | 6.4 | m |
| Wing area | 86 | sq ft | 8.1 | sq m |
| Aspect ratio | 5 | | 5 | |
| Empty Weight | 900 | lb | 390 | kg |
| Loaded weight | 1200 | lb | 521 | kg |
| Wing loading | 14 | lb/sq ft | 68 | kg/sq m |
| Max speed | 209 | mph | 334 | kmh |
| Cruise speed | 165 | mph | 264 | kmh |
| Stalling speed | 40 | mph | 64 | kmh |
| Climb rate | 1200 | ft/min | 370 | m/min |
| Range | 500 | mls | 800 | km |

The Czech LET company's Z-37 Cmelak was designed as an agricultural aircraft and is of tube and fabric construction, in the Eastern block way, strong and simple.

In production from 1966 to 1977 over 700 were made, some fitted with turbo prop engines.

Although basically a single seat Ag-plane it has also been built with dual controls as a trainer an example of which is flying in the UK.

Many countries including Bulgaria, Finland, Germany, Hungary, India operate the Cmelak and Iraq where its rugged construction, big 315 hp nine cylinder engine and large hydraulically operated flaps are ideal for its demanding role.

One of two have found their way on to the UK Register and although many are still flying world-wide it is to be found in several aircraft museums.

Not the prettiest of aeroplanes but a good performer with a spray bar and half a ton of chemical or as a semi aerobatic tandem seat trainer.

## LET
## Z-37 CMELAK

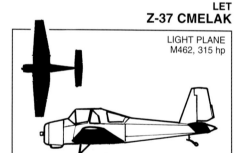

LIGHT PLANE
M462, 315 hp

| DATA | IMPERIAL | | METRIC | |
|---|---|---|---|---|
| Span | 40 | ft | 12.2 | m |
| Wing area | 256 | sq ft | 24 | sq m |
| Aspect ratio | 6.2 | | | |
| Empty Weight | 2138 | lb | 970 | kg |
| Loaded weight | 4080 | lb | 1852 | kg |
| Wing loading | 16 | lb/sq ft | 78 | kg/sq m |
| Max speed | 124 | mph | 198 | kmh |
| Cruise speed | 112 | mph | 179 | kmh |
| Stalling speed | 55 | mph | 88 | kmh |
| Climb rate | 728 | ft/min | 224 | m/min |
| Range | 370 | mls | 592 | km |

John Taylor's first design was the JT-1 Monoplane and was followed by The Titch which first flew in 1967 and had a more powerful engine plus revised easy build structure.

The Titch has proved popular, especially in the USA, its 200 mph, top speed making it a very useful tourer and it is a much admired 'classic' in those parts.

Sixteen are on the UK Register and several are being built, the construction being well thought out for the amateur with limited resources.

A tapered, two spar, wooden wing with part plywood and part fabric covering has optional flaps and broad chord ailerons. The fuselage is a plywood covered semi-monocoque with a bubble canopy and an integral fin.

the main gear legs may be the fuselage mounted leaf spring type or wing mounted coil spring legs, both, nearly always, smartly spatted.

It is PFA approved and plans plus enthusiastic backup are available from Terry Taylor at Leigh on Sea, Essex.

## TAYLOR
# TITCH

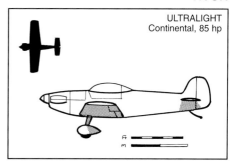

ULTRALIGHT
Continental, 85 hp

| DATA | IMPERIAL | | METRIC | |
|---|---|---|---|---|
| Span | 18.75 | ft | 5.8 | m |
| Wing area | 68 | sq ft | 6.4 | sq m |
| Aspect ratio | 5.2 | | 5.2 | |
| Empty Weight | 505 | lb | 230 | kg |
| Loaded weight | 760 | lb | 345 | kg |
| Wing loading | 11.2 | lb/sq ft | 54.6 | kg/sq m |
| Max speed | 200 | mph | 320 | kmh |
| Cruise speed | 160 | mph | 256 | kmh |
| Stalling speed | 59 | mph | 94 | kmh |
| Climb rate | 1800 | ft/min | 554 | m/min |
| Range | 380 | mls | 608 | km |

The TSR3 Wonderplane was designed and built by Tom Storey in 1968 – closely followed by PFA approval!

Airmark Ltd, of Pulborough, Sussex, was formed in 1969 to build further TSR3s, but in the end only the prototype, G-AWIV, was ever made. (Airmark went on to build, under licence, Cassutts and Rollason-Luton Betas).

Storey was a well-known racing pilot of the late 60s and early 70s and raced the TSR3, with its distinctive union jack colour scheme, as well as the Cassutts and Betas.

The TSR3 is of all wood construction with plywood and fabric covering, fixed tail-dragger gear with main wheel oleos and a tail skid. The wings have no dihedral and the large blister canopy gives excellent vision to the high-seated pilot. Powered, currently by a Continental PC60 GPU (Modified O-200) giving 100 hp plus fine pitch prop gives spectacular rate of climb.

The TSR3 is described by its present owner (who rescued it from ten years storage and restored it over four years), as, 'Great fun to fly'.

## STOREY
# TSR3 WONDERPLANE

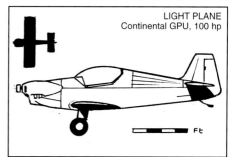

LIGHT PLANE
Continental GPU, 100 hp

| DATA | IMPERIAL | | METRIC | |
|---|---|---|---|---|
| Span | 18.5 | ft | 5.7 | m |
| Wing area | 62 | sq ft | 6.1 | sq m |
| Aspect ratio | 5.5 | | | |
| Empty Weight | 620 | lb | 281 | kg |
| Loaded weight | 926 | lb | 420 | kg |
| Wing loading | 15 | lb/sq ft | 73 | kg/sq m |
| Max speed | 120 | mph | 192 | kmh |
| Cruise speed | 100 | mph | 160 | kmh |
| Stalling speed | 50 | mph | 80 | kmh |
| Climb rate | 1500 | ft/min | 462 | m/min |
| Range | 370 | mls | 582 | km |

First flown in 1968 and type approved two years later the French CAP10 is a development of the Piel Emeraude who's designer Claude Piele was a pioneer of the light plane movement in France and was on the Mudry team.

Development by CAARP the production CAP 10B is more powerful than the Emeraude and is fully aerobatic with dual controls. The Armee de l'air uses them as aerobatic trainers.

Avions Mudry, formed in 1968, build the all wood Cap 10 with its typical Piel semi elliptical wing and neatly faired tailwheel undercarriage.

A single seat version the CAP 20 appeared in 1973 of very similar appearances but with more horse power and a longer nose.

CAARP ceased production in 1981, but SAN at Bernay still make them.

There are twenty-two CAP10s on the British Register.

## MUDRY
## CAP 10B

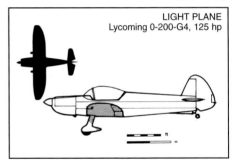

LIGHT PLANE
Lycoming 0-200-G4, 125 hp

| DATA | IMPERIAL | | METRIC | |
|---|---|---|---|---|
| Span | 26.5 | ft | 8.06 | m |
| Wing area | 116.8 | sq ft | 10.85 | sq m |
| Aspect ratio | 6 | | 6 | |
| Empty Weight | 1168 | lb | 530 | kg |
| Loaded weight | 1666 | lb | 756 | kg |
| Wing loading | 14.2 | lb/sq ft | 69.4 | kg/sq m |
| Max speed | 168 | mph | 280 | kmh |
| Cruise speed | 149 | mph | 240 | kmh |
| Stalling speed | 55 | mph | 88 | kmh |
| Climb rate | 1180 | ft/min | 363 | m/min |
| Range | 745 | mls | 1200 | km |

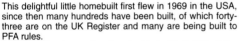

This delightful little homebuilt first flew in 1969 in the USA, since then many hundreds have been built, of which forty-three are on the UK Register and many are being built to PFA rules.

One of the cheapest and easiest to build of all the 'plan planes', the VP1 has been powered by various engines, the 50 hp Volkswagen, however, being the most popular.

The all wood airframe avoids fancy curves and has a strut braced low wing, which is mainly fabric covered, both the tailplane and rudder are 'all moving'.

A cabin or coupe version is available with a higher rear turtle back to blend with a bubble canopy considerably enhancing its rather spartan basic shape.

A side-by-side two-seater model, the VP2 is featured elsewhere in the book.

## EVANS
## VP-1

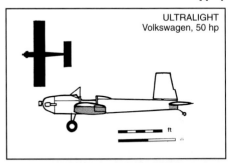

ULTRALIGHT
Volkswagen, 50 hp

| DATA | IMPERIAL | | METRIC | |
|---|---|---|---|---|
| Span | 24 | ft | 7.4 | m |
| Wing area | 82 | sq ft | 7.7 | sq m |
| Aspect ratio | 7 | | 7 | |
| Empty Weight | 475 | lb | 215 | kg |
| Loaded weight | 680 | lb | 308 | kg |
| Wing loading | 8.3 | lb/sq ft | 40 | kg/sq m |
| Max speed | 88 | mph | 140 | kmh |
| Cruise speed | 70 | mph | 112 | kmh |
| Stalling speed | 42 | mph | 67 | kmh |
| Climb rate | 350 | ft/min | 107 | m/min |
| Range | 232 | mls | 370 | km |

The Jodel family are legion and a mass of numbers. Briefly, the single seat D9 spawned the two seat D11 which led to the D111, D112, D113, D114, D115, D117, D118, D119, D120, D121, D122, D123, D124, D125 and D126 - all basically the same airframe with engine and equipment variations and factory or homebuilt status.

The D120 is the D117 built by the French Wassmer company and named the Paris-Nice (the D121 is the homebuilt version of the D120).

An all wooden aeroplane with the famous Jodel crank-wing which is built around a large 'Fokker' type spar which takes all the lift, drag and torsion loads. Fabric covering is employed aft of the main spar.

The, usually spatted, main gear is rubber or oleo sprung and has braked wheels; the tail wheel is steerable.

Wassmer went out of business in 1977, some of their work being taken on by Issoire Aviation.

There are forty-five on the UK Register and many more in its home country.

## JODEL
## D120

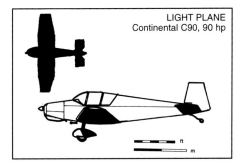

LIGHT PLANE
Continental C90, 90 hp

| DATA | IMPERIAL | | METRIC | |
|---|---|---|---|---|
| Span | 27 | ft | 8.22 | m |
| Wing area | 136 | sq ft | 12.7 | sq m |
| Aspect ratio | 5.4 | | 5.4 | |
| Empty Weight | 827 | lb | 375 | kg |
| Loaded weight | 1433 | lb | 650 | kg |
| Wing loading | 10.5 | lb/sq ft | 51.4 | kg/sq m |
| Max speed | 130 | mph | 210 | kmh |
| Cruise speed | 1180 | mph | 190 | kmh |
| Stalling speed | 45 | mph | 72 | kmh |
| Climb rate | 690 | ft/min | 210 | m/min |
| Range | 680 | mls | 1100 | km |

Designed and built by George Shield in Yorkshire, the Xyla first flew in 1971 at Helmswell. After several years flying the Xyla suffered an accident in 1980 that led to it being grounded and re-sold. The new owner did not finish restorations and it finished up in the roof of a car spray shop. Bought by Ken Snell (ex Concorde and Vimy pilot!) in 1997 who has painstakingly restored it, enabling it to fly in to the PFA Rally in 1999. 1500 hours work and an eye-catching yellow paint job turned many a head.

Xyla is the Greek word for wood – which is the principal constituent of its airframe. The sturdy basic airframe is ply' covered; the main gear legs and outer wing panels are attached to a short centre section and the control surfaces and rear deck are Ceconite covered.

The engine, an ex-wartime Continental of 100 hp. drove a three bladed prop on the original version but is now fitted with a two blader.

The design is PFA approved and took George Shield ten years to build – it's good to see it flying again.

## SHIELD
## XYLA

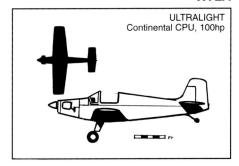

ULTRALIGHT
Continental CPU, 100hp

| DATA | IMPERIAL | | METRIC | |
|---|---|---|---|---|
| Span | 28.2 | ft | 8.7 | m |
| Wing area | 135 | sq ft | 12.7 | sq m |
| Aspect ratio | 6 | | | |
| Empty Weight | 600 | lb | 272 | kg |
| Loaded weight | 100 | lb | 454 | kg |
| Wing loading | 7.4 | lb/sq ft | 36 | kg/sq m |
| Max speed | 120 | mph | 192 | kmh |
| Cruise speed | 97 | mph | 156 | kmh |
| Stalling speed | 35 | mph | 56 | kmh |
| Climb rate | 1200 | ft/min | 370 | m/min |
| Range | 450 | mls | 720 | km |

An all metal sport plane from the drawing board of Ladislao Pazmany of San Diego, the PL-4A which was preceded by the successful PL-1 and PL-2 which were produced in limited numbers by various Eastern air forces.

The PL-4A is a single seater which was first flown in 1972. It has an all moving 'T' mounted tailplane, cantilever spring steel legs for the tail-dragger landing gear and a 1600cc VW engine developing about 50 hp.

The Canadian air Force evaluated the PL-4A in 1973 and ordered 200 for cadet training, the order, in fact, never materialised, but other air forces have shown interest.

Its 'T' tail, large canopy and high ground angle are distinctive features.

PFA approved, the PL-4A is a simple build project and five on the UK Register, two flying.

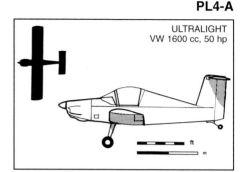

ULTRALIGHT
VW 1600 cc, 50 hp

| DATA | IMPERIAL | | METRIC | |
|---|---|---|---|---|
| Span | 26.6 | ft | 8.1 | m |
| Wing area | 89 | sq ft | 8.28 | sq m |
| Aspect ratio | 8 | | 8 | |
| Empty Weight | 578 | lb | 262 | kg |
| Loaded weight | 850 | lb | 386 | kg |
| Wing loading | 9.5 | lb/sq ft | 46.6 | kg/sq m |
| Max speed | 110 | mph | 173 | kmh |
| Cruise speed | 97 | mph | 156 | kmh |
| Stalling speed | 45 | mph | 72 | kmh |
| Climb rate | 650 | ft/min | 200 | m/min |
| Range | 350 | mls | 560 | km |

This little charmer from Australia was designed by John Corby and first flew in 1972. It is of all wood construction – the wings being part fabric covered - and the main wheels of the fixed tail dragger undercarriage depend on cantilever spring legs.

The Starlet is the most popular Australian homebuilt with an estimated 100 flying and about the same number under construction. In Australia it is essentially a plans built plane, but is also marketed in the USA by CSN of Fort Lauderdale, who kit some parts.

The Starlet is powered by an Aero Conversion VW engine of 60 hp. which propels the little single seater at a highly respectable 160 mph and gives it a climb of 1000 fpm. All this and an airframe stressed for aerobatics - no wonder it's popular!

There are, surprisingly, only three on the UK Register, one flying, and the type is PFA approved.

The drawing shows the enclosed cockpit version, open cockpit models are equally popular.

ULTRALIGHT
VW, 60 hp

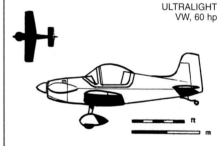

| DATA | IMPERIAL | | METRIC | |
|---|---|---|---|---|
| Span | 18.5 | ft | 5.7 | m |
| Wing area | 68 | sq ft | 6.4 | sq m |
| Aspect ratio | 5 | | 5 | |
| Empty Weight | 450 | lb | 204 | kg |
| Loaded weight | 710 | lb | 322 | kg |
| Wing loading | 10.4 | lb/sq ft | 51 | kg/sq m |
| Max speed | 160 | mph | 257 | kmh |
| Cruise speed | 130 | mph | 209 | kmh |
| Stalling speed | 49 | mph | 79 | kmh |
| Climb rate | 1050 | ft/min | 320 | m/min |
| Range | 266 | mls | 428 | km |

Big brother of the single seat VP-1, one of the simplest plans build planes to construct. The two seat side by side VP-2 is generally similar though it has a bigger wing of greater area and 15% chord/depth ratio (VP-1 has 12%) and a variety of cockpit types including, open, large multi glazed canopy or one piece blown hood (as my drawing, based on G-BMSC).

The VPs were designed by W S Evans, an ex Convair man, the VP-1 first flying in 1969; since then many hundreds of plans have been sold and VP-1s are flying or being built al over the world. (The VP comes from Evans original name for the type, the Volksplane).

VP-2 construction is all wood with fabric covered wings and tail surfaces (which are of the all-moving type). The simple alloy plate undercarriage legs are non shock absorbing (being wire braced) all shocks being taken by the tyres.

The type is PFA approved (though new plans are no longer available) and there are seventeen on the UK Register.

### EVANS
### VP-2

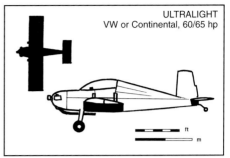

ULTRALIGHT
VW or Continental, 60/65 hp

| DATA | IMPERIAL | | METRIC | |
|---|---|---|---|---|
| Span | 27 | ft | 8.23 | m |
| Wing area | 130 | sq ft | 12.1 | sq m |
| Aspect ratio | 5.6 | | 5.6 | |
| Empty Weight | 640 | lb | 290 | kg |
| Loaded weight | 1040 | lb | 471 | kg |
| Wing loading | 8 | lb/sq ft | 39 | kg/sq m |
| Max speed | 100 | mph | 161 | kmh |
| Cruise speed | 75 | mph | 121 | kmh |
| Stalling speed | 40 | mph | 64 | kmh |
| Climb rate | 400 | ft/min | 122 | m/min |
| Range | 200 | mls | 320 | km |

The RV-6 is a side-by-side two seater designed by Dick van Grunsven and marketed in kit form by Vans Aircraft nc. of North Plains, Oregon. the company has been supplying kits since 1973 and launched the RV-6 in 1985.

Of all metal construction, the fuselage is a monocoque and the wings, identical to the RV-4 have a light alloy skin on alloy ribs and spars. half span ailerons and plain flaps are standard.

Non structural fairings etc are made in GrP and the main wheels are carried on cantilever spring steel legs and have hydraulic brakes.

With a Lycoming engine of 150 or 200 hp the RV-6 is fast, with a top speed of 202 mph.

Approved by the PFA in 1993 (non aerobatic) there are sixty-eight on the UK Register and many being built.

### VANS
### RV-6

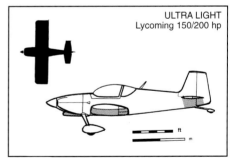

ULTRA LIGHT
Lycoming 150/200 hp

| DATA | IMPERIAL | | METRIC | |
|---|---|---|---|---|
| Span | 23 | ft | 7.1 | m |
| Wing area | 110 | sq ft | 10.3 | sq m |
| Aspect ratio | 4.8 | | 4.8 | |
| Empty Weight | 950 | lb | 431 | kg |
| Loaded weight | 1600 | lb | 726 | kg |
| Wing loading | 14.5 | lb/sq ft | 70.6 | kg/sq m |
| Max speed | 202 | mph | 373 | kmh |
| Cruise speed | 168 | mph | 268 | kmh |
| Stalling speed | 54 | mph | 86 | kmh |
| Climb rate | 1600 | ft/min | 492 | m/min |
| Range | 925 | mls | 1480 | km |

The Vans Aircraft company of North Plains, Oregon launched the all metal side-by-side two seater RV6 in 1985 and it has become the most popular home built design on the market. The earlier RV4 tandem seated model always had an appeal and Dick Van Grunsven its designer decided to tandemise the RV6 and came up with the RV8 in 1995. the RV8 has a wider cockpit than the RV4 and a large bubble canopy on a fuselage with cut down rear decking. Construction is basically similar, but more advanced production methods have improved the kit build. both nose and tail wheel gear versions and available and a range of engines from 150 to 200 hp.

With increased fuel tankage and a top end of the range engine, the RV8 will cruise at 200 mph for 1,000 miles – a very useful tourer. Kits have been available since 1998 and there are about twenty on the UK Register, four flying and others being built.

For the latest RV, the RV9 it's back to side-by-side seating and the RV10 is a four seater.

## VANS
## RV8

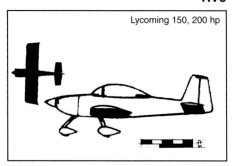

Lycoming 150, 200 hp

| DATA | IMPERIAL | | METRIC | |
|---|---|---|---|---|
| Span | 23 | ft | 7 | m |
| Wing area | 107 | sq ft | 10.1 | sq m |
| Aspect ratio | 4.85 | | 4.85 | |
| Empty Weight | 1066 | lb | 484 | kg |
| Loaded weight | 1820 | lb | 826 | kg |
| Wing loading | 17 | lb/sq ft | 83 | kg/sq m |
| Max speed | 214 | mph | 342 | kmh |
| Cruise speed | 204 | mph | 326 | kmh |
| Stalling speed | 56 | mph | 90 | kmh |
| Climb rate | 1650 | ft/min | 503 | m/min |
| Range | 790 | mls | 1264 | km |

The Isaac's Spitfire, a 6/10 replica of the famous WW2 fighter was the brainchild of John Isaac's, who had built this little 'classic' with its all wood cantilever elliptical wing, no mean feat! the plywood covered wooden fuselage is a semi-monocoque with a neatly faired 100 hp Continental in front.

The Spitfire first flew in 1975 and has a sparkling performance, cruising at 134 mph and climbing at 1100 feet a minute.

The main wheels are disc braked but non retracting. it has no flaps but is fully aerobatic and is a PFA approved design.

Painted in PRU blue with RAF markings this little beauty is a 'show stopper' wherever it goes.

There are two on the UK Register.

## ISAAC'S
## SPITFIRE

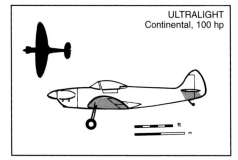

ULTRALIGHT
Continental, 100 hp

| DATA | IMPERIAL | | METRIC | |
|---|---|---|---|---|
| Span | 21.12 | ft | 6.75 | m |
| Wing area | 87 | sq ft | 8.1 | sq m |
| Aspect ratio | 5.6 | | 5.6 | |
| Empty Weight | 805 | lb | 366 | kg |
| Loaded weight | 1100 | lb | 499 | kg |
| Wing loading | 12.6 | lb/sq ft | 61.5 | kg/sq m |
| Max speed | 150 | mph | 240 | kmh |
| Cruise speed | 134 | mph | 215 | kmh |
| Stalling speed | 52 | mph | 84 | kmh |
| Climb rate | 1100 | ft/min | 336 | m/min |
| Range | 200 | mls | 200 | km |

Built by the Cranfield College of Technology as a dedicated aerobatic monoplane, the A1 was built to the specification of the late Neil Williams (UK aeros champion) first flew in 1976. Intended to compete at international level with the French and Eastern bloc aerobatic specialists, the A1 (G-BCIT) never quite 'cut the mustard' and went into storage at Cranfield.

In 1995 the aircraft was re- engineered as a two seater with a new canopy, rudder, paint job, registration (G-COAI) and the name Eagle.

The airframe, designed to withstand +7 to –5g, has a welded steel tube fuselage part plywood and part fabric covered and the one piece wing, which is all metal, has mean chord sweep back and three degrees of dihedral. The fixed tail dragger undercarriage is from a Chipmunk and the two-place hood from a Schliecher ASK 13.

The A1-200 Eagle first flew in September 1998 and development as a joint venture with British Aerospace was undertaken.

# CRANFIELD
# A1-200 EAGLE

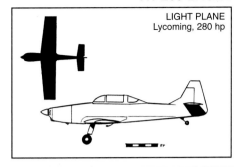

LIGHT PLANE
Lycoming, 280 hp

| DATA | IMPERIAL | | METRIC | |
|---|---|---|---|---|
| Span | 32.9 | ft | 10 | m |
| Wing area | 161.5 | sq ft | 15 | sq m |
| Aspect ratio | 6.7 | | | |
| Empty Weight | 1700 | lb | 772 | kg |
| Loaded weight | 2205 | lb | 1000 | kg |
| Wing loading | 13.7 | lb/sq ft | 67 | kg/sq m |
| Max speed | 170 | mph | 274 | kmh |
| Cruise speed | 150 | mph | 240 | kmh |
| Stalling speed | 561 | mph | 90 | kmh |
| Climb rate | 2255 | ft/min | 688 | m/min |
| Range | 124 | mls | 200 | km |

Designed by Jean Delemontez and Lain Cauchy and first flown in 1984 the D18 (like the D11) is an all wood and fabric kit aeroplane with a VW engine, ancestrally linked to the little D9.

The proof of concept aircraft the DC01 made its first flight in 1979 and was refined into the D18 and has proved very popular with home builders in Britain and France, hundreds being under construction or flying, the traditional wooden structure is preferred by many builders as in the more affordable VW engine. Fourteen on the UK Register and many more on the stocks.

The rubber sprung undercarriage legs may be in either tail or nose-wheel configuration, the latter is typed as the D19. the all flying tailplane/elevator is cable operated and fabric covered.

A neat, tight, light, good looking and efficient aeroplane.

# JODEL
# D18

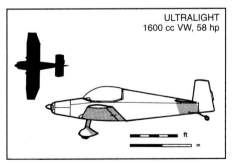

ULTRALIGHT
1600 cc VW, 58 hp

| DATA | IMPERIAL | | METRIC | |
|---|---|---|---|---|
| Span | 24.5 | ft | 7.5 | m |
| Wing area | 105.8 | sq ft | 9.83 | sq m |
| Aspect ratio | 5.7 | | 5.7 | |
| Empty Weight | 551 | lb | 250 | kg |
| Loaded weight | 1014 | lb | 460 | kg |
| Wing loading | 9.6 | lb/sq ft | 46.7 | kg/sq m |
| Max speed | 118 | mph | 190 | kmh |
| Cruise speed | 105 | mph | 170 | kmh |
| Stalling speed | 46 | mph | 75 | kmh |
| Climb rate | 688 | ft/min | 212 | m/min |
| Range | 350 | mls | 560 | km |

This German, side-by-side, two seat motor glider first flew in 1980 and with its all GRP/Composites construction, is a very smooth and handsome aeroplane.

Various motors have been fitted, the later models Havinga single ignition 80 hp Limbach SL2000EJ. (The data below is for this model). A two blade, fully feathering, three position, Hoffman prop is standard.

The canopy opens forwards and the un-flapped wings have air brake/spoilers that are linked to the wheel brakes.

The 109B has a 57ft wing that folds and gull wing cabin doors.

The RAF took delivery of fifty-three 109Bs for Air Cadet training, naming it Vigilant T1.

The performance of the Grob compares with that of the Cessna 150, on less power and fuel.

Over 500 109s have been built of which twenty-eight are on the UK Register.

# GROB G109

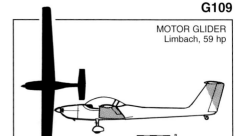

MOTOR GLIDER
Limbach, 59 hp

| DATA | IMPERIAL | | METRIC | |
|---|---|---|---|---|
| Span | 54.5 | ft | 16.6 | m |
| Wing area | 220 | sq ft | 20.7 | sq m |
| Aspect ratio | 13.5 | | | |
| Empty Weight | 1320 | lb | 600 | kg |
| Loaded weight | 1820 | lb | 826 | kg |
| Wing loading | 8.35 | lb/sq ft | 40 | kg/sq m |
| Max speed | 1302 | mph | 208 | kmh |
| Cruise speed | 118 | mph | 189 | kmh |
| Stalling speed | 474 | mph | 75 | kmh |
| Climb rate | 530 | ft/min | 163 | m/min |
| Range | 557 | mls | 892 | km |

The RV-4 is a tandem two seater designed by Dick van Grunsven and sold in kit form by Vans aircraft Inc. of North Plains, Oregon. The company has been in the kit plane business since 1973 and introduced the RV-4, its first two seater in 1981.

Of all metal construction, the fuselage is a monocoque and the wings have light alloy stressed skin over alloy ribs and spars. Half span ailerons and plain flaps are standard. Non structural fairings etc. are moulded in GRP.

The main wheels are carried on spring steel legs and have hydraulic brakes.

With either a 150 or 180 hp Lycoming engine the 23 ft span RV-4 has a slight edge on its sister, RV6 due to its slimmer fuselage.

A PFA approved design, there are twenty-two on the UK Register and several being built.

The RV-8 is a broader, taller version for the taller pilot!

# VANS RV-4

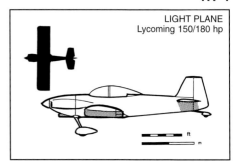

LIGHT PLANE
Lycoming 150/180 hp

| DATA | IMPERIAL | | METRIC | |
|---|---|---|---|---|
| Span | 23 | ft | 7.1 | m |
| Wing area | 110 | sq ft | 10.3 | sq m |
| Aspect ratio | 4.8 | | 4.8 | |
| Empty Weight | 905 | lb | 410 | kg |
| Loaded weight | 1500 | lb | 681 | kg |
| Wing loading | 13.6 | lb/sq ft | 66.4 | kg/sq m |
| Max speed | 205 | mph | 378 | kmh |
| Cruise speed | 170 | mph | 272 | kmh |
| Stalling speed | 54 | mph | 86 | kmh |
| Climb rate | 1650 | ft/min | 508 | m/min |
| Range | 800 | mls | 1280 | km |

A two seat sport plane from France, designed by Henri Nicollier and developed from his single seat HN433, their lines are almost identical, the HN700 first flew in 1989.

Of all wood construction with plywood and fabric covering the Menestrel (Minstrell in English) is usually powered by a 2000cc Limbach engine, distantly related to the VW, and popular in powered gliders, develops 77 hp.

The Menestrels fine lines and semi elliptical wing plan enhance its very useful performance, cruising at 112 mph whilst consuming only 3gph, or forty miles per gallon.

A PFA approved design, with three on the UK Register.

# NICOLLIER
# HN700 MENESTREL

ULTRALIGHT
Limbach, 77 hp

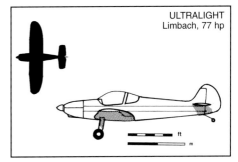

| DATA | IMPERIAL | | METRIC | |
|---|---|---|---|---|
| Span | 25.5 | ft | 7.8 | m |
| Wing area | 105.5 | sq ft | 10 | sq m |
| Aspect ratio | 6.2 | | 6.2 | |
| Empty Weight | 622 | lb | 282 | kg |
| Loaded weight | 1103 | lb | 500 | kg |
| Wing loading | 10.45 | lb/sq ft | 51 | kg/sq m |
| Max speed | 124 | mph | 198 | kmh |
| Cruise speed | 112 | mph | 179 | kmh |
| Stalling speed | 50 | mph | 80 | kmh |
| Climb rate | 1180 | ft/min | 364 | m/min |
| Range | 590 | mls | 944 | km |

The Model 35 Bonanza, which first flew in 1945 and its variants have been in continuous production since 1947, some 18,000 models built and still sought after.

Its continuing popularity and almost cult status is down to its high performance, 200 mph cruise, rugged and superb build, its 4/5 seats and its deserved tag of the Rolls Royce of its class.

The Bonanza is famous (and for a while, infamous) for its 'V' tail, though the later models, still in production, have conventional tails.

The first Bonanzas had 185 hp Continentals and four seats, the specification has crept up to 260 hp and six seats. The Model 33 was originally named the Debonair but became Bonanza in 1967, the current Bonanza, the six seat A36 is essentially a single engined Baron.

Well equipped, with a luxury interior, the Bonanza is not a cheap aeroplane, but one much drooled over! There are thirty on the UK Register, including ten 'V' tails (eleven Model 35, eleven Model 33, eight Model 36).

# BEECH
# BONANZA

LIGHT PLANE
Continental, 285 hp

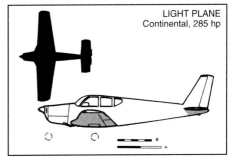

| DATA | IMPERIAL | | METRIC | |
|---|---|---|---|---|
| Span | 33.5 | ft | 15.2 | m |
| Wing area | 181 | sq ft | 17 | sq m |
| Aspect ratio | 6.2 | | 6.2 | |
| Empty Weight | 1885 | lb | 836 | kg |
| Loaded weight | 3300 | lb | 1498 | kg |
| Wing loading | 18.2 | lb/sq ft | 89 | kg/sq m |
| Max speed | 212 | mph | 339 | kmh |
| Cruise speed | 205 | mph | 328 | kmh |
| Stalling speed | 62 | mph | 99 | kmh |
| Climb rate | 1200 | ft/min | 369 | m/min |
| Range | 1145 | mls | 1832 | km |

This Russian plane, well known for its record in top class aerobatics, started life as tandem seat military trainer in 1947. Practically the whole Red Air Force was trained on it - including Yuri Gagarin; and many hundreds were exported to Eastern block countries, even being productionised in China.

In 1960 '18's ' became available on the civil market and it's possibilities as an aerobat were soon realised.

All the early models had rearward retracting under-carriages, with the '18 P came inward retraction and a 260 hp. engine, soon to give way to the 'PM (data below) with less dihedral and a rearward sited cockpit. The lightweight 18 M, though maintaining its metal structure, was largely fabric covered and had upped the power with a 300 hp Ivchenko.

In 1966 YAK 18 PM's took the first four places in the World Aerobatic Championships.

Though based on the YAK 18 series the latest YAK aerobats, the 50 and 55, are totally new, smaller airframes.

There is only one YAK 18 on the UK Register. One 18A just sold to Germany, two are Nanchang CJ-6A, one is 18A (Robs Lamplough).

## YAKOLEV YAK 18

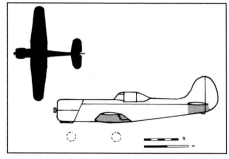

| DATA | IMPERIAL | | METRIC | |
|---|---|---|---|---|
| Span | 35 | ft | 10.6 | m |
| Wing area | 183 | sq ft | 17.2 | sq m |
| Aspect ratio | 6.7 | | 6.7 | |
| Empty Weight | 1819 | lb | 825 | kg |
| Loaded weight | 2425 | lb | 1100 | kg |
| Wing loading | 13.2 | lb/sq ft | 64.6 | kg/sq m |
| Max speed | 196 | mph | 313 | kmh |
| Cruise speed | 175 | mph | 280 | kmh |
| Stalling speed | 58 | mph | 93 | kmh |
| Climb rate | 1368 | ft/min | 606 | m/min |
| Range | 200 | mls | 320 | km |

The Yak 18T is the last in a long line of Yakolev 18s (see elsewhere in book) which go back to 1947. The early trainers were produced in huge numbers - 8000 of the tandem two seater tail dragger with the long 'greenhouse' canopy. With the '18U came a retracting tricycle undercarriage and the '18A, also a trike, had the 260 hp. Ivchenko engine. The '18P was the single seat aerobat and the 'PM had a rear sited cockpit and a 300 hp Ivchenko - the 'PS was the same aircraft with a tail dragger undercarriage

The four seat cabin Yak 18T first flew in 1967 and with its big radial engine, stalky landing gear and substantial cabin framing, has a vaguely vintage look.

Production officially ceased in 1989 when 200 had been made - but limited production re-started in 1993.

Powered by a growling Vedneyev VOKBM M-14P nine cylinder radial of 335 hp the '18T is unique, for a four seater, in being fully aerobatic.

There are eleven in the Register.

## YAKOLEV 18T

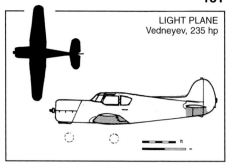

LIGHT PLANE
Vedneyev, 235 hp

| DATA | IMPERIAL | | METRIC | |
|---|---|---|---|---|
| Span | 36.6 | ft | 11.3 | m |
| Wing area | 202 | sq ft | 19 | sq m |
| Aspect ratio | 6.6 | | 6.6 | |
| Empty Weight | 2676 | lb | 1214 | kg |
| Loaded weight | 3637 | lb | 1650 | kg |
| Wing loading | 18 | lb/sq ft | 88 | kg/sq m |
| Max speed | 184 | mph | 294 | kmh |
| Cruise speed | 126 | mph | 202 | kmh |
| Stalling speed | *68* | mph | *108* | kmh |
| Climb rate | 985 | ft/min | 303 | m/min |
| Range | 562 | mls | 900 | km |

The original M20 was of part wooden construction, pressure bonded laminated spruce, and first flew in 1953. it was a four seat touring aeroplane with a retractable tricycle undercarriage, and distinguished from similar low wing cabin types by its raked forward fin (actually vertical), with a tailplane of similar geometry.

In 1961 it was re-engineered as an all metal aeroplane and a year later the M20D flew with fixed undercarriage, one of many variants.

Other models flew with different engines and standard of equipment fit after butler Aviation, and finally Republic Steel corp, took over production. The M20 range continued in production up to 1976 with over 7000 had been produced. Some variants (M20C, M20E) have a small 'acorn' fairing at the top of the fin and a five seat pressurised version, the M22 has three cabin windows.

Latest models, TLS and Ovation have longer fuselages and windows plus turbo charged power.

Forty-five M20s are on the UK Register.

## MOONEY
## M20 CHAPARALL

LIGHT PLANE
Lycoming, 180 hp

| DATA | IMPERIAL | | METRIC | |
|---|---|---|---|---|
| Span | 35 | ft | 10.67 | m |
| Wing area | 167 | sq ft | 15.5 | sq m |
| Aspect ratio | 7.3 | | 7.3 | |
| Empty Weight | 1525 | lb | 691 | kg |
| Loaded weight | 2575 | lb | 1168 | kg |
| Wing loading | 15.4 | lb/sq ft | 75.2 | kg/sq m |
| Max speed | 185 | mph | 296 | kmh |
| Cruise speed | 159 | mph | 254 | kmh |
| Stalling speed | 58 | mph | 93 | kmh |
| Climb rate | 800 | ft/min | 246 | m/min |
| Range | 800 | mls | 1128 | km |

Italian designer, Stelio Frati, a post war light plane pioneer, designed the sleek, two seat Falco which first flew in 1955. Licence built in small numbers by various firms the Falco became available in kit form, from Sequoia, from 1980.

The all wood airframe is stressed for +6-3g, is cleared for basic aerobatics, and carries the PFA 'seal of approval', indeed winning the Best Homebuilt award at the PFA rally in 1989.

The bubble canopy, unswept fin and rudder with long ventral fin, straight tapered wings, are all identifying features as, in the air, are the retractable tricycle wheels.

A fast mover, 212 mph, with faultless flying characteristics the popularity of which is hampered by some weird Anglo-Italian financial hurdles and a fairly long build time.

There are fourteen on the UK Register.

## SEQUOIA/FRATI
## F8L FALCO

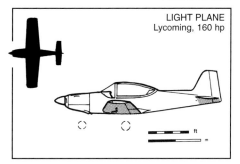

LIGHT PLANE
Lycoming, 160 hp

| DATA | IMPERIAL | | METRIC | |
|---|---|---|---|---|
| Span | 26.25 | ft | 8.1 | m |
| Wing area | 107.5 | sq ft | 10.1 | sq m |
| Aspect ratio | 6.4 | | 6.4 | |
| Empty Weight | 1212 | lb | 550 | kg |
| Loaded weight | 1880 | lb | 853 | kg |
| Wing loading | 17.5 | lb/sq ft | 85.4 | kg/sq m |
| Max speed | 212 | mph | 340 | kmh |
| Cruise speed | 170 | mph | 272 | kmh |
| Stalling speed | 65 | mph | 104 | kmh |
| Climb rate | 1140 | ft/min | 371 | m/min |
| Range | 850 | mls | 1360 | km |

First flown in 1956, powered by a 180 hp. Lycoming, the four seat PA24 Comanche was soon up-engined to a Lycoming of 250 hp, this model the PA 24- 250 soon became the standard production model.

Advanced for its time, this all metal tourer was the predecessor to the Cherokee, which at first it appears to resemble. The Comanche, however, has a retractable tricycle undercarriage, the Cherokee is fixed; the Comanche has tapered chord wings and the Cherokee's are parallel chord, the tailplanes are also tapered and parallel in accord with the mainplanes.

The Comanche with its retracting gear and more hp is the better performer.

Some 5000 Comanches have been built, a great number, but a long way off the 30,000 its best selling brother the Cherokee has clocked up.

The PA 30 Twin Comanche is virtually a PA 24 Comanche with two 160 hp Lycomings; structural interchangeability being kept to a maximum

There are thirty-four PA 24 Comanches on the UK Register.

# PIPER
# PA24 COMANCHE

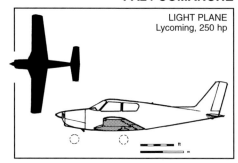

LIGHT PLANE
Lycoming, 250 hp

| DATA | IMPERIAL | | METRIC | |
|---|---|---|---|---|
| Span | 36 | ft | 11.1 | m |
| Wing area | 178 | sq ft | 16.7 | sq m |
| Aspect ratio | 7.3 | | 7.3 | |
| Empty Weight | 1690 | lb | 767 | kg |
| Loaded weight | 2900 | lb | 1316 | kg |
| Wing loading | 16.3 | lb/sq ft | 79.5 | kg/sq m |
| Max speed | 190 | mph | 304 | kmh |
| Cruise speed | 181 | mph | 289 | kmh |
| Stalling speed | 62 | mph | 99 | kmh |
| Climb rate | 1350 | ft/min | 415 | m/min |
| Range | 1650 | mls | 2640 | km |

A French design from the drawing board of Yves Gardan who has been responsible for several light planes including the Minicab.

The Horizon, which first flew in 1960, is a four seater of all metal construction with a retractable tricycle undercarriage.

Design rights were sold in 1962 to Sud Aviation and production continued under the SOCATA banner, 260 or more being built in the sixties. First run models were powered by a 160 hp Lycoming and under SOCATA the 180 Lycoming was offered.

An improved version the Super Horizon or ST 10 Diplomate with a 200 hp Lycoming, longer fuselage, redesigned tail unit and roomier cabin appeared in 1967 but had only a limited production run.

There are nineteen Horizons on the UK Register.

# GARDAN
# GY80 HORIZON

LIGHT PLANE
Lycoming, 160 hp

| DATA | IMPERIAL | | METRIC | |
|---|---|---|---|---|
| Span | 31.8 | ft | 9.7 | m |
| Wing area | 140 | sq ft | 13 | sq m |
| Aspect ratio | 7.2 | | 7.2 | |
| Empty Weight | 1367 | lb | 620 | kg |
| Loaded weight | 2425 | lb | 1100 | kg |
| Wing loading | 17.3 | lb/sq ft | 84.5 | kg/sq m |
| Max speed | 149 | mph | 240 | kmh |
| Cruise speed | 145 | mph | 234 | kmh |
| Stalling speed | 60 | mph | 96 | kmh |
| Climb rate | 690 | ft/min | 212 | m/min |
| Range | 590 | mls | 950 | km |

First flown in 1970 the Commander 112 is powered by a 210 hp. Lycoming, the Commander 114, which followed in 1976 has a Lycoming of 260 hp.

This rakishly good looking all metal aeroplane with a retractable tricycle undercarriage cruises at 175 mph., climbs at 1000 ft/min. and has a range of over 1000 miles - a very useful performance for a comfortable, well equipped four seater.

The tailplane is, unusually mounted half way up the fin and the straight mainplane leading edge can appear to be swept forward due to the swept back root extensions.

Access to the cabin is via car type doors on either side.

Production figures are, Commander 112, 726 off and Commander 114, 429 off.

They are pretty well represented on the UK Register with seventy showing at the last count.

Data below is for the Commander 112.

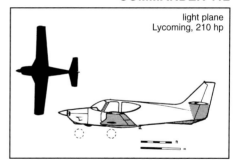

light plane
Lycoming, 210 hp

| DATA | IMPERIAL | | METRIC | |
|---|---|---|---|---|
| Span | 35.5 | ft | 11 | m |
| Wing area | 160 | sq ft | 15 | sq m |
| Aspect ratio | 7.8 | | 7.8 | |
| Empty Weight | 1530 | lb | 694 | kg |
| Loaded weight | 2550 | lb | 1157 | kg |
| Wing loading | 16 | lb/sq ft | 78 | kg/sq m |
| Max speed | 190 | mph | 304 | kmh |
| Cruise speed | 175 | mph | 281 | kmh |
| Stalling speed | 58 | mph | 93 | kmh |
| Climb rate | 1000 | ft/min | 305 | m/min |
| Range | 1130 | mls | 1808 | km |

The HR 100 is one of the all metal Robins, and though similar to the HR 200, it is a bigger aeroplane, carrying up to five people, and unlike the wooden Robins, does not have a crank wing.

First flown in 1972 the HR 100, in the French manner, comes in many variants. The first thirty-one aircraft, designated HR 100/200, were four seaters with a retractable tricycle undercarriage. (The suffix indicates horse power). This was followed by the fixed 'gear version, the HR 100/210, 78 of which were made. In late '72 the Tiara (illustrated) was a retracting 'gear five seater with more horse power, hence HR 100/285. A six seater with extended cabin glazing appeared in 1975 as the HR 100/4+2 (change of nomenclature here!) having a 320 hp Lycoming which booted its cruise up to 168 mph.

On all variants the windscreen has a central glazing bar, divided windscreen.

There are eighteen or more Robin HR 100's on the UK Register.

## ROBIN
## HR 100

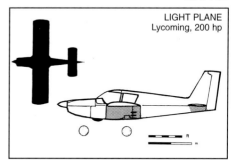

LIGHT PLANE
Lycoming, 200 hp

| DATA | IMPERIAL | | METRIC | |
|---|---|---|---|---|
| Span | 29.8 | ft | 9.08 | m |
| Wing area | 163.6 | sq ft | 15.2 | sq m |
| Aspect ratio | 5.42 | | 5.42 | |
| Empty Weight | 1609 | lb | 730 | kg |
| Loaded weight | 2755 | lb | 1250 | kg |
| Wing loading | 16.8 | lb/sq ft | 82.3 | kg/sq m |
| Max speed | 171 | mph | 275 | kmh |
| Cruise speed | 154 | mph | 248 | kmh |
| Stalling speed | 66 | mph | 106 | kmh |
| Climb rate | 885 | ft/min | 270 | m/min |
| Range | 845 | mls | 1360 | km |

The Russian design philosophy is 'make 'em simple, make 'em strong, and make a lot of them (like the Kalashnikov); so it is with the YAK 18 – 52 series of airframes. Though bearing a family resemblance to the YAK 18, they are structurally different inasmuch that the YAK 50 series have fully monocoque fuselages.

The YAK 50 is a single seat aerobatic aircraft with backward retracting tail-wheel undercarriage (World Champion first in 1976 and '82) and the YAK 52 a tandem two seater with the same airframe and engine (Vedeneyev M-14P) but forward retracting main wheels and rearward nose-wheel retraction. All flying controls are push rod or cable operated and the split trailing edge flaps are pneumatic. Immensely strong (+7, -5g) the YAK 52 is fully aerobatic.

Production of the YAK 52 was taken over by IAv Bacau, the Romanian company in the late '70s - the Bacau built prototype first flying in 1978. In the following ten years over 1500 were built. There are fifty-six in the UK, many with Eastern Bloc markings – inc. in service markings, the R N Flying Clubs.

# YAKOLEV
## YAK 52

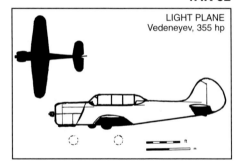

LIGHT PLANE
Vedeneyev, 355 hp

| DATA | IMPERIAL | | METRIC | |
| --- | --- | --- | --- | --- |
| Span | 30.5 | ft | 9.3 | m |
| Wing area | 161.5 | sq ft | 15 | sq m |
| Aspect ratio | 5.8 | | 5.8 | |
| Empty Weight | 2204 | lb | 1000 | kg |
| Loaded weight | 2844 | lb | 1290 | kg |
| Wing loading | 17.6 | lb/sq ft | 86 | kg/sq m |
| Max speed | 186 | mph | 300 | kmh |
| Cruise speed | 160 | mph | 256 | kmh |
| Stalling speed | 56 | mph | 90 | kmh |
| Climb rate | 1476 | ft/min | 450 | m/min |
| Range | 341 | mls | 550 | km |

First flown in 1979, the Malibu, was claimed to be the first cabin class, pressurised piston powered aircraft. Over 700 of these big singles have been sold to date, fifteen are on the UK Register, and the latest variant the Malibu Mirage, is currently in production.

The first Malibu, the PA-46-310P had a straight tapered high aspect ratio wing and a 310 hp turbo charged Continental engine, the following PA-46-350P Malibu Mirage was re-engined with a 350 hp Lycoming.

In 1999 the Malibu Meridian flew with a 400 hp, Pratt and Whitney turbo prop engine and a new wing with swept back inboard 'cuffs'. (Latest Mirages have this wing, without the 'cuffs').

The seating is for five passengers and a pilot in a cabin pressurised to maintain 8,000 ft level up to 25,000 ft.

The inward retracting main wheels and the 90 degree twisting and rearward retracting nose wheel are hydraulically operated, as are the flaps and brakes.

Pneumatic de-icing boots on the wing and tail leading edges are optional.

Details below for the Malibu Mirage.

# PIPER
## PA-46 MALIBU

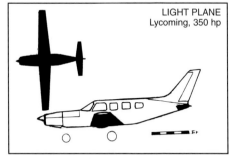

LIGHT PLANE
Lycoming, 350 hp

| DATA | IMPERIAL | | METRIC | |
| --- | --- | --- | --- | --- |
| Span | 43 | ft | 13.1 | m |
| Wing area | 175 | sq ft | 16.3 | sq m |
| Aspect ratio | 10 | | | |
| Empty Weight | 3157 | lb | 1433 | kg |
| Loaded weight | 4340 | lb | 1970 | kg |
| Wing loading | 24.8 | lb/sq ft | 121 | kg/sq m |
| Max speed | 253 | mph | 405 | kmh |
| Cruise speed | 245 | mph | 391 | kmh |
| Stalling speed | 67 | mph | 107 | kmh |
| Climb rate | 1215 | ft/min | 375 | m/min |
| Range | 1213 | mls | 1941 | km |

The two seat Lancair 320 (pronounced Lance-air) is developed from Lancair types 200 and 250, first flown in 1984; the type numbers referring to the model of Continental motor used. the 160 hp Lancair 320 took to the air in 1986 and immediately made a big first impression with its sleek lines and fighter like performance, 250 mph max. level speed.

Constructed of pre moulded and part assembled units of high strength composites giving a very smooth skin finish, which combined with the retractable tricycle undercarriage, electrically operated flaps and constant speed airscrew enhance its remarkable performance figures.

Four seat kit Lancairs are now flying, the Lancair IV and the Columbia.

1600 kits have been sold worldwide, it is PFA approved seven are on the UK Register and three are being built.

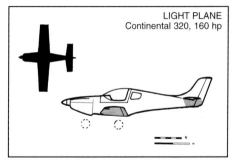

LIGHT PLANE
Continental 320, 160 hp

| DATA | IMPERIAL | | METRIC | |
|---|---|---|---|---|
| Span | 23.5 | ft | 7.2 | m |
| Wing area | 76 | sq ft | 7.1 | sq m |
| Aspect ratio | 7.2 | | 7.2 | |
| Empty Weight | 1000 | lb | 454 | kg |
| Loaded weight | 1685 | lb | 765 | kg |
| Wing loading | 22.2 | lb/sq ft | 108 | kg/sq m |
| Max speed | 250 | mph | 400 | kmh |
| Cruise speed | 241 | mph | 385 | kmh |
| Stalling speed | 61 | mph | 98 | kmh |
| Climb rate | 1650 | ft/min | 508 | m/min |
| Range | 1140 | mls | 1824 | km |

A neat two seater from Switzerland, designed by Max Brandli and first flown in 1982.

The BX-2 is of mixed wood, foam and GRP construction, a basic wooden load bearing structure with GRP covered foam for the curved sections.

In 1885 Max Brandli was awarded the Henri Mignet Diploma by the FAI for his work on the Cherry - praise indeed. Many hours of test flying went into the development of the Cherry and by 1991 the prototype had logged 1100 hours.

Light for a two seater, the BX-2 enjoys the low drag bonus of a retractable tricycle undercarriage as its 125 mph. cruise on 65 hp. reflects - and all on 3 gph. fuel consumption.

Brandli produces no kits but plans are available - over 150 being sold to date. the design is PFA approved, three are under construction and one is already flying.

**BRANDLI**
# BX-2 CHERRY

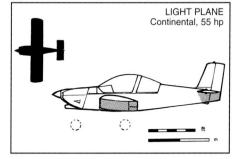

LIGHT PLANE
Continental, 55 hp

| DATA | IMPERIAL | | METRIC | |
|---|---|---|---|---|
| Span | 23 | ft | 7.02 | m |
| Wing area | 90 | sq ft | 8.37 | sq m |
| Aspect ratio | 5.9 | | 5.9 | |
| Empty Weight | 683 | lb | 310 | kg |
| Loaded weight | 1212 | lb | 550 | kg |
| Wing loading | 13.5 | lb/sq ft | 65.7 | kg/sq m |
| Max speed | 140 | mph | 225 | kmh |
| Cruise speed | 125 | mph | 201 | kmh |
| Stalling speed | *55* | mph | *88* | kmh |
| Climb rate | 680 | ft/min | 207 | m/min |
| Range | 575 | mls | 920 | km |

Designed and built by George Periera in Sacramento, California, the GP4 is a sleek two seater first flown in 1984 by Pereira, who later in the same year flew it the 2000 miles to Oshkosh where it won outstanding new design.

With the looks of a state of the art carbon/GRP/foam speedster it is, at first, surprising to find that the GP4 is a wooden aeroplane.

Built for +8 to -6g loads the sleek lines, without double curvature, disguise its orthodox plywood covered fuselage and the one piece wing, again all wood, with its massive main spar taking all the lift loads.

Unusual for a kit plane the GP4 has a retractable tricycle undercarriage with steerable nose wheel. the gear is manually operated though the flaps are electric as are the trimmers.

You will have to hop a 747 if you want to see this stunning 265 mph speedster, none on the UK Register.

## PEREIRA
## GP-4

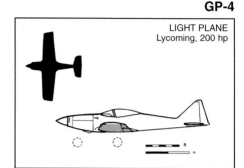

LIGHT PLANE
Lycoming, 200 hp

| DATA | IMPERIAL | | METRIC | |
|---|---|---|---|---|
| Span | 24.6 | ft | 7.6 | m |
| Wing area | 104 | sq ft | 9.8 | sq m |
| Aspect ratio | 5.54 | | 5.54 | |
| Empty Weight | 1248 | lb | 566 | kg |
| Loaded weight | 1985 | lb | 901 | kg |
| Wing loading | 19.1 | lb/sq ft | 93.2 | kg/sq m |
| Max speed | 265 | mph | 424 | kmh |
| Cruise speed | 240 | mph | 384 | kmh |
| Stalling speed | 65 | mph | 104 | kmh |
| Climb rate | 1500 | ft/min | 462 | m/min |
| Range | 1250 | mls | 2000 | km |

An all composites four seater from Germany, the prototype first flew in 1988 and was FAA approved in 1994. Features include gull wing cabin doors, trailing link main gear, four bladed prop and 'wet wing' fuel tanks. Initially powered by a Porsche aero engine of 212 hp., but replaced by a Textron Lycoming 10-540 (230 hp) when the Porsche venture failed.

Production, originally at Melle has moved to Dessau where other variants were being developed; the IO-360 (180 hp) powered fixed undercarriage R90-180FG. There is also a R90 Aerobat and a top of the range, 400 hp. Allison turboprop powered R90-420T – this (the R90 prototype re-engined) first flew in 1993.

An R95 pressurised five seater was on the drawing board but the company is no longer active.

A quiet and comfortable aeroplane that matches up well to its US competitors on less power. Three on the UK Register.

## RUSCHMEYER
## R 90

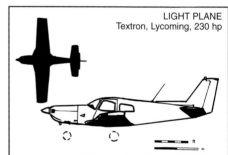

LIGHT PLANE
Textron, Lycoming, 230 hp

| DATA | IMPERIAL | | METRIC | |
|---|---|---|---|---|
| Span | 30.8 | ft | 9.5 | m |
| Wing area | 140 | sq ft | 13 | sq m |
| Aspect ratio | 6.8 | | 6.8 | |
| Empty Weight | 1977 | lb | 898 | kg |
| Loaded weight | 2973 | lb | 1350 | kg |
| Wing loading | 21.3 | lb/sq ft | 104 | kg/sq m |
| Max speed | 202 | mph | 323 | kmh |
| Cruise speed | 190 | mph | 304 | kmh |
| Stalling speed | 70 | mph | 112 | kmh |
| Climb rate | 1140 | ft/min | 351 | m/min |
| Range | 689 | mls | 1103 | km |

The legendary kit plane is manufactured by Stoddard Hamilton of Arlington, Washington; two have sold over 1500 Glasair kits, 100 of which are flying. One winning the Custom Built champion at Oshkosh in 1990.

This aeroplane has fighter like performance and is not for novices, though in the hands of the experts it is said to be impeccable at all speeds.

Earlier versions came with lower powered engines, tail wheel gear, fixed or retracting trikes and long or short fuselages and wings.

The fully retracting undercarriage has a castoring nose wheel and, essentially braked main wheels as it lands at about 90 mph.

The type is PFA approved, two are being built and sixteen are flying in the UK.

**STODDART HAMILTON**
# GLASAIR

LIGHT PLANE
Lycoming 10-540, 300 hp

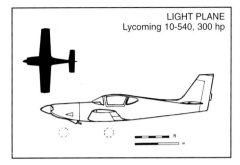

| DATA | IMPERIAL | | METRIC | |
|---|---|---|---|---|
| Span | 23.25 | ft | 7.16 | m |
| Wing area | 90 | sq ft | 8.5 | sq m |
| Aspect ratio | 6 | | 6 | |
| Empty Weight | 1550 | lb | 704 | kg |
| Loaded weight | 2400 | lb | 1089 | kg |
| Wing loading | 26 | lb/sq ft | 127 | kg/sq m |
| Max speed | 335 | mph | 536 | kmh |
| Cruise speed | 284 | mph | 454 | kmh |
| Stalling speed | 74 | mph | 118 | kmh |
| Climb rate | 2400 | ft/min | 740 | m/min |
| Range | 1500 | mls | 2400 | km |

The side by side two seat Cygnet of 1936 was the first all metal stressed skin light aeroplane built in this country. Designed and built initially by C W Aircraft the Cygnet was taken on by General Aircraft Ltd of Hanworth when CWA folded.

GAL fitted the twin fins and rudders, increased the dihedral and, in production aircraft, cantilever undercarriage legs in place of the prototype's strutted ones. The Cygnet 1 had a Gipsy Major, 130 hp and the Cygnet 2 a Cirrus Major 150 hp.

Nine were produced up to 1941, several being exported to S. America and five were impressed for the duration for communications and tricycle u/c training. Four survived the war and became well known in the post war civil scene, taking part in several air races – in one, notably piloted by the famous flyer Jim Mollison.

By 1955 two had crashed, one kept flying until 1969 when it to met its end in France. The sole survivor is on display at East Fortune.

An advanced and good-looking aeroplane that would not look out of place today. They are making Luscombe Silvaires again, how about Cygnets?

**GENERAL AIRCRAFT**
# CYGNET

LIGHT PLANE
Cirrus Major, 150 hp

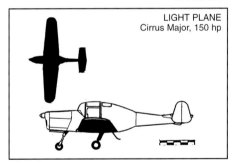

| DATA | IMPERIAL | | METRIC | |
|---|---|---|---|---|
| Span | 34.5 | ft | 10.6 | m |
| Wing area | 179 | sq ft | 16.8 | sq m |
| Aspect ratio | 6.6 | | | |
| Empty Weight | 1475 | lb | 670 | kg |
| Loaded weight | 2200 | lb | 998 | kg |
| Wing loading | 12.3 | lb/sq ft | 60 | kg/sq m |
| Max speed | 135 | mph | 216 | kmh |
| Cruise speed | 115 | mph | 184 | kmh |
| Stalling speed | 55 | mph | 88 | kmh |
| Climb rate | 800 | ft/min | 246 | m/min |
| Range | 445 | mls | 712 | km |

A product of Engineering and Research Corp. the Ercoupe first flew as long ago as 1937. It was in production at ERCO up to 1955 when the design rights were taken up by various other manufacturers including Forney, Alon and Mooney, the latter adding a fin of typical Mooney shape. There are still many hundreds flying in the States.

The all metal Ercoupe has dual controls, side-by-side seating and is one of the first production light planes to have a nose-wheel undercarriage. The ailerons run full span (no flaps) on the much 'dihedralled' wing, which on early models was fabric covered.

Initially a car type wheel was the only control, no rudder pedals, but later models had the more traditional arrangement.

There are fourteen on the UK Register, four are in world museums. Back in 1941 an Ercoupe became the first plane to take-off successfully under rocket power!

# ERCOUPE

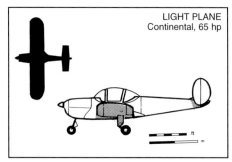

LIGHT PLANE
Continental, 65 hp

| DATA | IMPERIAL | | METRIC | |
|---|---|---|---|---|
| Span | 30 | ft | 9.15 | m |
| Wing area | 142 | sq ft | 13.2 | sq m |
| Aspect ratio | 6.3 | | 6.3 | |
| Empty Weight | 725 | lb | 329 | kg |
| Loaded weight | 1260 | lb | 572 | kg |
| Wing loading | 8.8 | lb/sq ft | 42.9 | kg/sq m |
| Max speed | 117 | mph | 187 | kmh |
| Cruise speed | 105 | mph | 168 | kmh |
| Stalling speed | 42 | mph | 67 | kmh |
| Climb rate | 700 | ft/min | 352 | m/min |
| Range | 526 | mls | 840 | km |

A side by side two seat trainer/tourer from the drawing board of John Thorp, who, amongst other 'planes, designed the Piper Cherokee, the T211 is a simple and robust design that first flew in 1946 as the T11 Sky Scooter. It has been produced by various companies and made several comebacks

The extreme simplicity of the all metal structure has been achieved, in part, by the use of ribbed skinning on the wings, stabilator and rudder, the wing, in fact, having only three ribs!

Economy in maintenance and fuel consumption are big points in the T211s favour and Thorp UK, the UK distributors, are keen to supplant the now ageing Cessna trainer fleets.

The T211 is manufactured in the USA by Thorp T211 Aircraft Inc., but not sold by them (Product liability laws have made things very difficult for 'plane makers over there)

There are five Thorp T211 on our Register at the time of writing.

# THORP
# T211

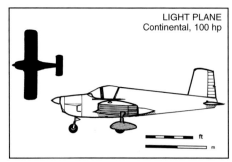

LIGHT PLANE
Continental, 100 hp

| DATA | IMPERIAL | | METRIC | |
|---|---|---|---|---|
| Span | 25 | ft | 7.7 | m |
| Wing area | 104.6 | sq ft | 9.83 | sq m |
| Aspect ratio | 6 | | 6 | |
| Empty Weight | 775 | lb | 352 | kg |
| Loaded weight | 1270 | lb | 576 | kg |
| Wing loading | 12.2 | lb/sq ft | 59.6 | kg/sq m |
| Max speed | 142 | mph | 227 | kmh |
| Cruise speed | 123 | mph | 197 | kmh |
| Stalling speed | 45 | mph | 72 | kmh |
| Climb rate | 750 | ft/min | 231 | m/min |
| Range | 364 | mls | 583 | km |

As the Morane Sauinier MS 880 Rallye, this all metal French three seater first flew in 1959 with an unswept fin, powered by a 90 hp Continental.

Variants with more powerful engines, up to the 150 hp Lycoming and with four seats have produced a spate of type numbers for look-a-like aeroplanes with low parallel chord wings of pronounced dihedral with full span leading edge slots, tubby cabins and fixed trike undercarriages.

Nearly 600 were produced by Morane Saulnier before SOCATA took over in 1966.

The SOCATA built Rallyes type numbers indicate the engine power, ie Rallye 100T and Rallye 235GT have 100 hp and 235 hp respectively.

SOCATA have outstripped MS production with over 2000 Rallyes built to date (111 on UK Register).

The SOCATA Caribbean range, in some ways similar is a more recent design. Data below is for our MS893, 180hp.

Now built in Poland as PZL Koliber.

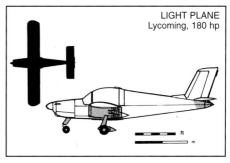

LIGHT PLANE
Lycoming, 180 hp

| DATA | IMPERIAL | | METRIC | |
|---|---|---|---|---|
| Span | 31.5 | ft | 9.7 | m |
| Wing area | 132 | sq ft | 12.4 | sq m |
| Aspect ratio | 7.5 | | 7.5 | |
| Empty Weight | 1265 | lb | 574 | kg |
| Loaded weight | 2315 | lb | 1051 | kg |
| Wing loading | 17.5 | lb/sq ft | 85.4 | kg/sq m |
| Max speed | 142 | mph | 227 | kmh |
| Cruise speed | 128 | mph | 205 | kmh |
| Stalling speed | 50 | mph | 80 | kmh |
| Climb rate | 800 | ft/min | 308 | m/min |
| Range | 620 | mls | 992 | km |

This chunky little two seater was the winner of the 1953 Royal Aero Club of Great Britain light aircraft design competition. It went into production in Australia in 1959 an all wood prototype first flying in1959. Production aircraft were all metal trainer/tourers. A modified and 'up motored' version was produced by AESL, ninety-six being delivered to the armed forces as the Airtrainer.

Production by Victa and AESL, in New Zealand, has placed 250 on the civil market.

Designer Henry Millicer went on to create a four seat version, the Aircruiser which never went into production. Both these aircraft have highly efficient, low drag, laminar flow wings which combined with the small span and dumpy, but clean fuselage, give the Airtourer a good performance on 100 hp.

Various models acquired more power, up to 210 hp production ceased in 1966, though plans are a-foot-to re-start production), there are sixteen on the UK Register.

The data below is for the 100 hp Airtourer AT100.

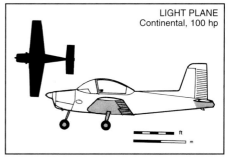

LIGHT PLANE
Continental, 100 hp

| DATA | IMPERIAL | | METRIC | |
|---|---|---|---|---|
| Span | 26 | ft | 8 | m |
| Wing area | 120 | sq ft | 11.3 | sq m |
| Aspect ratio | 5.6 | | 5.6 | |
| Empty Weight | 1058 | lb | 480 | kg |
| Loaded weight | 1650 | lb | 749 | kg |
| Wing loading | 13.8 | lb/sq ft | 67 | kg/sq m |
| Max speed | 137 | mph | 219 | kmh |
| Cruise speed | 116 | mph | 185 | kmh |
| Stalling speed | 50 | mph | 80 | kmh |
| Climb rate | 600 | ft/min | 185 | m/min |
| Range | 900 | mls | 1440 | km |

The Sundowner 180 has evolved from the Model 23 Musketeer which first flew in 1961 and had four seats, a fixed tricycle undercarriage and a 160 hp. Lycoming engine. The 5th variant, the C23, re-named Sundowner 180, proved the most popular with over 1000 being made.  Close relatives, the Model 24s, include the Sierra 200 and Musketeer Super R, all with retractable undercarriage and four-six seats.

The airframe is all metal incorporating bonded aluminium honeycomb in the wing structure, a roomy cabin and wide track tricycle undercarriage.  The elevator is of the all moving, or stabilator type, and cabin access is via car type doors front and rear.

There are twenty aircraft in this range on the UK Register, many more in the 'States where over 4500 have been made.

## BEECH
## SUNDOWNER 180

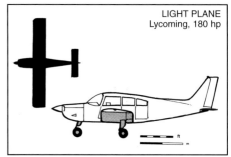

LIGHT PLANE
Lycoming, 180 hp

MUSKATEER

| DATA | IMPERIAL | | METRIC | |
|---|---|---|---|---|
| Span | 32.7 | ft | 10.1 | m |
| Wing area | 146 | sq ft | 13.7 | sq m |
| Aspect ratio | 7.3 | | 7.3 | |
| Empty Weight | 1375 | lb | 624 | kg |
| Loaded weight | 2400 | lb | 1089 | kg |
| Wing loading | 16.4 | lb/sq ft | 80 | kg/sq m |
| Max speed | 154 | mph | 246 | kmh |
| Cruise speed | 146 | mph | 233 | kmh |
| Stalling speed | 60 | mph | 96 | kmh |
| Climb rate | 805 | ft/min | 245 | m/min |
| Range | 678 | mls | 1085 | km |

Jim Bede the innovative designer of the BD4 BD5 etc designed the original AA1 Yankee as the BD1 which first flew in 1963. Production followed and 461 were built by the American Aviation corporation.

The Trainer model AA-1A with dual controls was produced in quantity, 500 being made up to 1973.

At this point Grumman Aerospace acquired American Aviation and continued production under the new badge of Grumman American, later to become the Gulfstream American Corporation.

This all metal two seater spans only 24.5ft whilst its look-a-like brother, the four seat AA5 Traveler has a 32.5ft wing (see elsewhere in the book). Construction embodies metal-to-bonding aluminum honeycomb elements and GRP undercarriage legs. The unusual nose wheel leg is distinguishing feature. There are sixteen AA1s on the UK Register.

## GULFSTREAM AMERICAN
## AA1 YANKEE

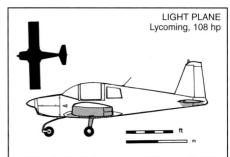

LIGHT PLANE
Lycoming, 108 hp

| DATA | IMPERIAL | | METRIC | |
|---|---|---|---|---|
| Span | 24.5 | ft | 7.54 | m |
| Wing area | 101 | sq ft | 9.5 | sq m |
| Aspect ratio | 6 | | 6 | |
| Empty Weight | 963 | lb | 437 | kg |
| Loaded weight | 1500 | lb | 681 | kg |
| Wing loading | 14.8 | lb/sq ft | 72.2 | kg/sq m |
| Max speed | 134 | mph | 214 | kmh |
| Cruise speed | 114 | mph | 182 | kmh |
| Stalling speed | 55 | mph | 88 | kmh |
| Climb rate | 720 | ft/min | 221 | m/min |
| Range | 515 | mls | 824 | km |

With over 30,000 fixed undercarriage P-28s built since 1961, the Cherokee tribe must be considered one of the most successful series of aeroplanes ever produced. The prototype, an all metal aircraft, designed by John Thorp and Fred Weick, first flew in 1960, had four seats and a fixed nose-wheel undercarriage; production followed a year later.

More than 40 variants have been produced, involving engine changes, seating, cockpit equipment, windows and wing plan and span changes. The main visible changes are, as follows - 180 Cherokee D,introduced three side windows; 180 Challenger, increased wing span and fuselage length plus stabilator (renamed Archer in '74);151 Warrior, tapered outer wing panels; 181 Archer II, tapered wing and new undercarriage fairings; the Archer III had re-styled engine air intakes;

NB- the suffix numbers are indicative of the model's engine horse power throughout the range, if the wing plan is tapered it is 'hp+1' - ie. odd numbers)

The PA28-235 Charger had a longer fuselage and bigger stabilator; PA28R-180 Cherokee Arrow had a retractable undercarriage and parallel chord wing; the PA28R-201 Arrow IV had a 'T' tail and tapered wing (6600 of the retractable PA28R models have been built - making it the most popular light 'retractable'.)

Two seat versions have been made, primarily for the training role, including the PA28-140 of 1964 , the '140 Fliteliner and the unusual Pillan with two seats in tandem under a big bubble canopy. (only two Piper built - 120 kitted for ENAER manufacture in Chile)

Turbo Arrows III and IV were the first in the range to be turbo-supercharged in 1976.

In 1978 the PA28-236 Dakota became turbo-supercharged as the '201T Turbo Dakota with a 200 hp Lycoming.

There are about a 1000 PA28s on the UK Register making it our most numerous light plane.

Although named Cherokee 6, the PA32 is an entirely new design, hence the change in prefix.

The order in which some of the variants appear is shown below -

| | | | |
|---|---|---|---|
| PA28-150/160/180 | 1961 | PA28 -151 Warrior | 1973 |
| PA28-235 | 1963 | PA28-180 Archer II | 1973 |
| PA28R-180 Arrow | 1967 | PA28R-201 Arrow III | 1976 |
| PA28-235 Charger | 1972 | PA28RT-201 Arrow IV | 1978 |
| PA28-180 Challenger | 1972 | PA28-236 Dakota | 1978 |

The photograph is of a PA28-181 Archer 2 and the sketches show a few of the variants, a bit like 'Spot the difference'!

The figures below are for the PA28-140B.

| DATA | IMPERIAL | | METRIC | |
|---|---|---|---|---|
| Span | 30 | ft | 9.24 | m |
| Wing area | 160 | sq ft | 15 | sq m |
| Aspect ratio | 5.6 | | 5.6 | |
| Empty Weight | 1180 | lb | 535 | kg |
| Loaded weight | 1950 | lb | 885 | kg |
| Wing loading | 12.2 | lb/sq ft | 59.5 | kg/sq m |
| Max speed | 144 | mph | 230 | kmh |
| Cruise speed | 134 | mph | 214 | kmh |
| Stalling speed | 54 | mph | 86 | kmh |
| Climb rate | 820 | ft/min | 259 | m/min |
| Range | 700 | mls | 1120 | km |

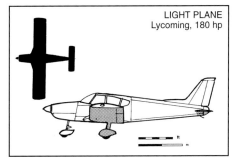

LIGHT PLANE
Lycoming, 180 hp

G-ODOG

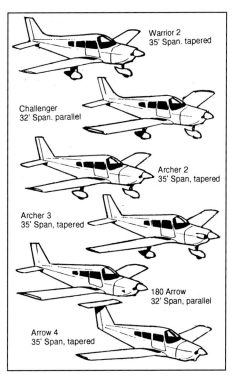

Warrior 2
35' Span. tapered

Challenger
32' Span. parallel

Archer 2
35' Span, tapered

Archer 3
35' Span, tapered

180 Arrow
32' Span, parallel

Arrow 4
35' Span, tapered

A six/seven seat partner to the hugely popular, two/four PA28 Cherokee became available in 1965, the PA32 Cherokee Six, in three fit standards, Custom, Executive and Sportsman. These early model PA32s all had the 32 ft span, parallel chord PA28 wing and 260 or 300 hp Lycoming engines.

In 1974 and extra side window was introduced, making four per side, and in 1975 the retractable gear PA32R-300 Cherokee Lance was added to the range, becoming just Lance in 1977. The PA32RT-300 was the retractable undercarriage Lance with a 'T' tail and parallel chord wings (turbo model PA32RT-300T).

The 36 ft span, semi tapered wing, based on the Warrior, lifted the 1980 Saratoga, PA32-301 into the range and was followed by the PA32-301T, turbo version and the retractable undercarriage version PA32R-301. There 103 of these fast six seaters on the UK Register, which is still in production and has included in its variants floatplane and COIN versions.

The figures below are for the PA32-300 Cherokee Six.

## PIPER
## PA 32 CHEROKEE SIX

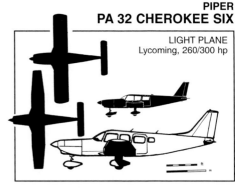

LIGHT PLANE
Lycoming, 260/300 hp

| DATA | IMPERIAL | | METRIC | |
|---|---|---|---|---|
| Span | 32.75 | ft | 10 | m |
| Wing area | 174.5 | sq ft | 16.4 | sq m |
| Aspect ratio | 6.1 | | 6.1 | |
| Empty Weight | 1818 | lb | 825 | kg |
| Loaded weight | 3394 | lb | 1541 | kg |
| Wing loading | 19.4 | lb/sq ft | 95 | kg/sq m |
| Max speed | 174 | mph | 278 | kmh |
| Cruise speed | 168 | mph | 269 | kmh |
| Stalling speed | 63 | mph | 101 | kmh |
| Climb rate | 1050 | ft/min | 323 | m/min |
| Range | 850 | mls | 1360 | km |

First flown in 1965 the Fuji FA-200 Subaru is one of the few Japanese light planes flying in this country.

When production ceased in 1986 a total of 274 had had been produced, about fifteen making it on to the UK Register.

the Subaru is of all metal construction and can carry four people, though in this mode its range is somewhat restricted and the FA200-160 hp Lycoming is a mite underpowered, hence the later FA200-180 with 180 hp Lycoming.

A reliable and well mannered aeroplane comparable to the small Cessnas. Stressed for +6-3g the Subaru is capable of limited aerobatics at a wight limitation of 1940 lb.

Rather like a Piper Tomahawk without the 'T' tail, the Fuji, a ten year older design has a marginally inferior performance to the Piper.

## FUJI
## FA200 SUBARU

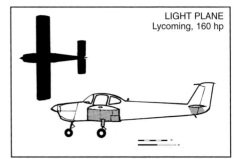

LIGHT PLANE
Lycoming, 160 hp

| DATA | IMPERIAL | | METRIC | |
|---|---|---|---|---|
| Span | 30.9 | ft | 9.5 | m |
| Wing area | 150 | sq ft | 14.1 | sq m |
| Aspect ratio | 6 | | 6 | |
| Empty Weight | 1497 | lb | 680 | kg |
| Loaded weight | 2137 | lb | 970 | kg |
| Wing loading | 14.2 | lb/sq ft | 69.3 | kg/sq m |
| Max speed | 120 | mph | 192 | kmh |
| Cruise speed | 95 | mph | 152 | kmh |
| Stalling speed | 58 | mph | 93 | kmh |
| Climb rate | 600 | ft/min | 185 | m/min |
| Range | 300 | mls | 480 | km |

An all metal four seater from Italy, looking a little like an early model Cherokee, the SIAI-Marchetti S205-18F, first flew in 1965 in fixed undercarriage form with a 180 hp. Lycoming; a 200 hp. retractable gear version, the S205-20R followed.

An agreement was reached with the Waco Aircraft Company to assemble 205s at their Pottstown, Pa. plant and 60 aircraft were completed and marketed as the 220 Sirius, powered by a 220 hp. Franklin engine.

A five seat version with retracting gear and a 260 hp Lycoming appeared in 1967 as the S208; 85 of these being built.

All 205/208 production ceased in 1972 but was restarted in '77 with an order for 40 from the Aero Club d'Italia which was completed by 1979.

SIAI-Marchetti are an old established firm who make parts for the Panavia Tornado and the Airbus A310 and have their own fighter trainer, the S211A.

There are five S205s on the UK Register. Data below for S205- 18F.

## SIA-MARCHETTI
# S-205

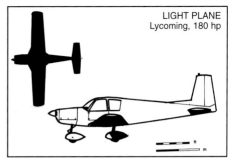

LIGHT PLANE
Lycoming, 180 hp

| DATA | IMPERIAL | | METRIC | |
|---|---|---|---|---|
| Span | 34.9 | ft | 10.7 | m |
| Wing area | 173 | sq ft | 16.2 | sq m |
| Aspect ratio | 7 | | 7 | |
| Empty Weight | 1490 | lb | 655 | kg |
| Loaded weight | 2645 | lb | 1163 | kg |
| Wing loading | 15.3 | lb/sq ft | 74.6 | kg/sq m |
| Max speed | 147 | mph | 235 | kmh |
| Cruise speed | 134 | mph | 214 | kmh |
| Stalling speed | 66 | mph | 105 | kmh |
| Climb rate | 787 | ft/min | 242 | m/min |
| Range | 745 | mls | 1192 | km |

An all metal American ultralight designed by Leon Davis the DA-2 is now produced, ready made or in kit form by D2 incorporated. It was first flown in 1966 and in the same year collected awards at the EAA Fly-in at Rockford for Outstanding Design and Popularity.

Of simple all metal construction, no double curvature panels, with an unusual all moving 'butterfly' tail, the two seat DA-2 has a fixed and spatted undercarriage with spring steel cantilever legs. Unusual again, for a small low wing cabin monoplane. Entry is made through a car type side door.

Though fitted, as standard, with a 65 hp Continental, the airframe is stressed for other motors up to 100 hp.

An official PFA approved design in the UK, there are over 100 flying in the USA, one on the UK Register.

## DAVIS
# DA-2

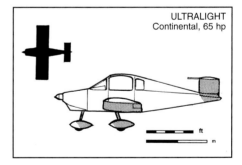

ULTRALIGHT
Continental, 65 hp

| DATA | IMPERIAL | | METRIC | |
|---|---|---|---|---|
| Span | 19.25 | ft | 5.86 | m |
| Wing area | 82.5 | sq ft | 7.66 | sq m |
| Aspect ratio | 4.5 | | 4.5 | |
| Empty Weight | 610 | lb | 277 | kg |
| Loaded weight | 1125 | lb | 510 | kg |
| Wing loading | 13.6 | lb/sq ft | 66.5 | kg/sq m |
| Max speed | 120 | mph | 193 | kmh |
| Cruise speed | 115 | mph | 185 | kmh |
| Stalling speed | 55 | mph | 88 | kmh |
| Climb rate | 900 | ft/min | 277 | m/min |
| Range | 450 | mls | 725 | km |

First flown in 1967 the DR400 is one of Pierre Robin's designs and is a four seater of all wood construction.

Robin not only designs the Robin ranged light planes, he has been a well known air race pilot and founder of the Centre Est Aeronautique in 1957 (Changed to Societe des Avions Pierre Robin in 1969) which produces the planes that bear his name, all based on the Jodel wing.

The DR400 is a highly successful aeroplane on the continent with over 1400 produced to date.

Variants include the DR400-100, a two seat trainer, the DR400-140, with forward sliding canopy, the DR400-180R, a glider tug and the DR400-180 Regent, featured here.

The second of the Robins to feature a tricycle undercarriage, the elegant and efficient DR400 has proved popular in the UK with over 128 on the Register.

# ROBIN
# DR 400 REGENT

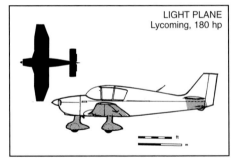

LIGHT PLANE
Lycoming, 180 hp

| DATA | IMPERIAL | | METRIC | |
|------|----------|--|--------|--|
| Span | 28.6 | ft | 8.72 | m |
| Wing area | 146 | sq ft | 13.6 | sq m |
| Aspect ratio | 5.6 | | 5.6 | |
| Empty Weight | 1301 | lb | 590 | kg |
| Loaded weight | 2425 | lb | 1100 | kg |
| Wing loading | 16.2 | lb/sq ft | 80.5 | kg/sq m |
| Max speed | 164 | mph | 264 | kmh |
| Cruise speed | 134 | mph | 215 | kmh |
| Stalling speed | 60 | mph | 96 | kmh |
| Climb rate | 825 | ft/min | 1320 | m/min |
| Range | 913 | mls | 1470 | km |

Zlinska Letecka, the pre war Czech company became Moravia after WW2 but the aircraft were still typed as Zlin. the most famous being the Trener, many hundreds of which were made right up to 1973.

In 1967 the Z42 first flew, a two seat aerobatic cabin monoplane, later with a new canopy and engine became the Z142, which in turn became the Z242 in 1990 with the installation of a 200 hp Lycoming driving a three blade Hoffman cls prop and straight parallel chord wings with upturned tip trailing edges. The construction is all metal with some GRP fairings and the fixed, spatted, tricycle undercarriage has cantilever steel spring legs and a steerable nose-wheel. The well-stocked panel includes a gauge reading gas pressure within the main wing spar, loss of pressure = crack in spar!(some helicopters have this safety feature on their rotor spars).

UK Flight tests have declared the cockpit, comfortable with parachute recesses in seats, good visibility and handling all combined in a very tough airframe. There are three Z242s on the UK Register.

# ZLIN
# Z 242

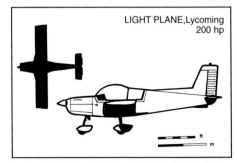

LIGHT PLANE,Lycoming
200 hp

| DATA | IMPERIAL | | METRIC | |
|------|----------|--|--------|--|
| Span | 30.6 | ft | 9.4 | m |
| Wing area | 147 | sq ft | 13.3 | sq m |
| Aspect ratio | 65.6 | | 6.6 | |
| Empty Weight | 1609 | lb | 730 | kg |
| Loaded weight | 2400 | lb | 1089 | kg |
| Wing loading | 17 | lb/sq ft | 82 | kg/sq m |
| Max speed | 198 | mph | 306 | kmh |
| Cruise speed | 173 | mph | 278 | kmh |
| Stalling speed | 58 | mph | 94 | kmh |
| Climb rate | 1200 | ft/min | 370 | m/min |
| Range | 425 | mls | 680 | km |

The original Pup was a two seater, developed from the Miles M117, with a 100 hp Continental engine and the series 2, which followed was powered by a 150 hp Lycoming and was a three/four seater. The Pup is an all metal aeroplane that was originally designed for composite construction.

Built like a battleship, the Pup has a keen following and an owners club, the sixty-eight aircraft being much prized.

The Pup features, well harmonized controls, sweet handling, and aerobatic capability, and a commodious and well laid out cockpit.

When Beagle folded in 1969, it dealt a body blow to the UK volume light aircraft industry from which it has never fully recovered. This aeroplane shows just what could be done, along with its sister, the twin engined 206, see elsewhere in book, which is a big hit in in the USA.

The RAF trainer version, bigger and more power, the Bulldog, built by Scottish Aviation, is being de-commissioned and over sixty are on the civil UK Register.

# BEAGLE
# PUP, SERIES 2

LIGHT PLANE
Lycoming 150 hp

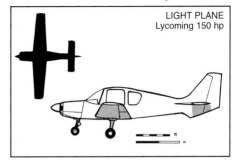

| DATA | IMPERIAL | | METRIC | |
|---|---|---|---|---|
| Span | 31 | ft | 9.5 | m |
| Wing area | 110 | sq ft | 10.3 | sq m |
| Aspect ratio | 8.7 | | 8.7 | |
| Empty Weight | 1265 | lb | 574 | kg |
| Loaded weight | 1925 | lb | 874 | kg |
| Wing loading | 17.5 | lb/sq ft | 85.4 | kg/sq m |
| Max speed | 140 | mph | 224 | kmh |
| Cruise speed | 120 | mph | 192 | kmh |
| Stalling speed | 57 | mph | 91 | kmh |
| Climb rate | 750 | ft/min | 231 | m/min |
| Range | 287 | mls | 460 | km |

An all metal single seater intended for sport flying and glider tugging, the Kittiwake was the brain child of Dr C Mitchell and Roy and Ann Proctor. It first flew in 1967 and the second one, built by Navy apprentices at Yeovilton and Lee -on -Solent, took to the air in 1971.

The Mitchell – Proctor team split up in 1968 and Proctor Aircraft Associates along with Yorkshire Sailplanes took on the marketing of plans and kit parts.

The construction is simple and self jigging with a single spar wing with extruded light alloy booms. The fuselage is a four longeron LA box and the cantilever undercarriage legs are spring steel with disc braked wheels. The nose wheel leg is rubber sprung on some versions and cantilevered on others. Fuel is carried in a tank integral with the wing leading edge structure.

A two seat version with a more powerful engine, the Petrel, was built by BAC apprentices and first flew in 1978

There are four Kittiwakes on the UK Register.

# MITCHELL PROCTOR
# KITTIWAKE

LIGHT PLANE
Continental, 100 hp

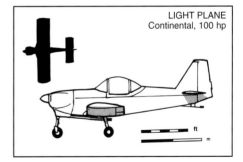

| DATA | IMPERIAL | | METRIC | |
|---|---|---|---|---|
| Span | 24 | ft | 7.32 | m |
| Wing area | 105 | sq ft | 9.75 | sq m |
| Aspect ratio | 5.3 | | 5.3 | |
| Empty Weight | 910 | lb | 413 | kg |
| Loaded weight | 1350 | lb | 612 | kg |
| Wing loading | 12.9 | lb/sq ft | 63 | kg/sq m |
| Max speed | 131 | mph | 211 | kmh |
| Cruise speed | 122 | mph | 196 | kmh |
| Stalling speed | 55 | mph | 88 | kmh |
| Climb rate | 1050 | ft/min | 320 | m/min |
| Range | 490 | mls | 790 | km |

Designed by J Smyth of Indiana, the Sidewinder, an all metal side-by-side two seater, first flew in 1969 and in that year it won the 'Outstanding Design' award at the EAA Fly In.

Intended for home building, the Sidewinder embodies a Thorp T18 canopy assembly and Wittman main gear. Engines of from 90 to 180 hp. may be fitted; the prototype having a 125 hp. Lycoming as has the only UK representative, G-BRVH, which was built in the UK by its owner. (G-JOPF also registered).

The wings are of two spar stressed skin construction and the fuselage has a welded steel tube framework with LA formers and skin. All skinning is flush rivetted. An unusual feature is the electrically operated under fuselage 'speed brake' or perforated flap – no wing flaps are fitted. Stabilator, ailerons and rudder have electrically operated trimmers and the Wittman spring undercarriage legs carry hydraulically braked wheels, the nose wheel being a steerable oleo.

The pretty Sidewinder, a PFA approved design, with its distinctive very swept fin, is a compact two seater with good performance and luggage space.

## SMYTH SIDEWINDER

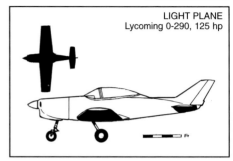

LIGHT PLANE
Lycoming 0-290, 125 hp

| DATA | IMPERIAL | | METRIC | |
|---|---|---|---|---|
| Span | 24.8 | ft | 7.57 | m |
| Wing area | 96 | sq ft | 8.92 | sq m |
| Aspect ratio | 6.83 | | | |
| Empty Weight | 988 | lb | 453 | kg |
| Loaded weight | 1450 | lb | 657 | kg |
| Wing loading | 15.8 | lb/sq ft | 77 | kg/sq m |
| Max speed | 185 | mph | 321 | kmh |
| Cruise speed | 134 | mph | 214 | kmh |
| Stalling speed | 59 | mph | 95 | kmh |
| Climb rate | 1000 | ft/min | 308 | m/min |
| Range | 360 | mls | 537 | km |

Mark Brown a designer with Fairchild formed Starlite Aircraft designed the all composites, single seat Starlite in the early eighties; the prototype first flew in 1983 with a 20 hp. Zenoak engine and won the Outstanding New Design award at OshKosh the same year. Also Best Composites Aircraft at PFA Rally 1990. The Starlite comes as a kit aeroplane, with a Rotax 447 of 40 hp. Nose wheel and tail dragger undercarriage versions are available with leaf spring main kegs and Azusa brakes.

Mark Brown went on to build a two seater, side by side Starlite look-a-like the Pulsar; which is marketed by Aero Designs. The Starlite is small, a 21-feet wing span of Aspect Ratio 9, giving a wing area of only 57 Square feet – but this allows it to cruise at 120 mph on only 40 hp. PFA approved, with four on the UK Register the economical and sleek Starlite was discontinued in 1990.

## STARLITE

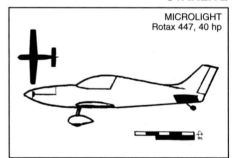

MICROLIGHT
Rotax 447, 40 hp

| DATA | IMPERIAL | | METRIC | |
|---|---|---|---|---|
| Span | 21.6 | ft | 6.55 | m |
| Wing area | 57 | sq ft | 5.3 | sq m |
| Aspect ratio | 9 | | | |
| Empty Weight | 230 | lb | 104 | kg |
| Loaded weight | 480 | lb | 218 | kg |
| Wing loading | 8.4 | lb/sq ft | 41 | kg/sq m |
| Max speed | 140 | mph | 225 | kmh |
| Cruise speed | 120 | mph | 193 | kmh |
| Stalling speed | 42 | mph | 68 | kmh |
| Climb rate | 1200 | ft/min | 366 | m/min |

Designed and built, initially, by SIAI in Italy and the Swiss firm FFA; the Italians made the wings and the Swiss made the rest. This arrangement did not last and FFA, later FWA, made the whole aeroplane.

The Bravo is a semi aerobatic two-three seat trainer of all metal construction with a fixed tricycle undercarriage. The wing has light alloy spars and ribs under a sheet and honeycomb sandwich skin, with slotted flaps over 60% of the span. The undercarriage is rubber sprung with hydraulic brakes and a steerable nose-wheel.

Motors range from 115 hp to 180 hp, the higher powered versions having the extra seat.

Around 250 Bravos have been made, going to several foreign air forces including Indonesia, Iraq and Oman. Ten were delivered in 1987 to BAe training at Prestwick, but they were all sold on to Finland recently.

Figures below are for the 150 hp AS202/15.

## FWA
## AS 202 BRAVO

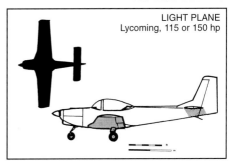

LIGHT PLANE
Lycoming, 115 or 150 hp

| DATA | IMPERIAL | | METRIC | |
|---|---|---|---|---|
| Span | 32 | ft | 9.8 | m |
| Wing area | 149 | sq ft | 14 | sq m |
| Aspect ratio | 6.5 | | 6.5 | |
| Empty Weight | 1388 | lb | 630 | kg |
| Loaded weight | 2000 | lb | 908 | kg |
| Wing loading | 14.8 | lb/sq ft | 72.2 | kg/sq m |
| Max speed | 131 | mph | 209 | kmh |
| Cruise speed | 126 | mph | 201 | kmh |
| Stalling speed | 56 | mph | 90 | kmh |
| Climb rate | 633 | ft/min | 195 | m/min |
| Range | 574 | mls | 918 | km |

Virtually, a four seat version of the two seat AA-1 Yankee of 1970, the AA-5 first flew in the same year and was type named, Traveler and had a smaller rear window and dorsal fin than later models.

Over 800 of the Traveler version were built to be superseded by the de Luxe AA-5A Cheetah (900 built) which introduced the longer fin and window.

The AA-5B Tiger, which first flew in 1974, stepped up the power from 150 hp to 180 hp (Lycoming 0-360-4AK) and is currently back in production with over 1300 produced.

The original design was by American Aviation which then became, successively, Grumman American, Gulfstream American and - to date, American General Aircraft Corporation!

The airframe is all metal, but differs from the norm in being 'rivetless' - the major part of the structure being glued together. The single main wing spar is a massive aluminium tube.

There are over 140 AA-5s on the UK Register.

## GULFSTREAM AMERICAN
## AA-5 TIGER

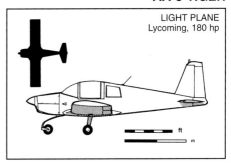

LIGHT PLANE
Lycoming, 180 hp

| DATA | IMPERIAL | | METRIC | |
|---|---|---|---|---|
| Span | 31.5 | ft | 9.7 | m |
| Wing area | 145 | sq ft | 13.6 | sq m |
| Aspect ratio | 6.8 | | 6.8 | |
| Empty Weight | 1311 | lb | 595 | kg |
| Loaded weight | 2400 | lb | 1089 | kg |
| Wing loading | 16.6 | lb/sq ft | 81 | kg/sq m |
| Max speed | 170 | mph | 272 | kmh |
| Cruise speed | 164 | mph | 262 | kmh |
| Stalling speed | 64 | mph | 102 | kmh |
| Climb rate | 850 | ft/min | 262 | m/min |
| Range | 600 | mls | 960 | km |

First flown in 1971 the two seat HR 200 is contemporary with the HR 100 a look - alike four seater. Both aeroplanes are all metal, unlike the 'DR' Robin range of wooden 'crank wings'.

The HR 200 has an extensive blown and tinted canopy which slides forward to open and distinguishes it from the HR 100 which has a 'roof and windows'.

With full dual controls and comprehensive instrumentation the '200 is an ideal club trainer in the same category as the Cessna 152, compared to which it is smaller and faster, with a greater range.

Variants are, HR 200/100 S, the basic version, and the HR 200/100 Club, with wheel fairings and Hoffman airscrew, HR 200/120 has 118 hp. Lycoming and HR 200/160 has a 160 hp. Lycoming.

Production ceased in 1981 when 200 had been built - however - it is back in production again (1993) with the 118 hp. Lycoming. (Details below)

There are twenty-seven on the UK Register.

## ROBIN
## HR 200

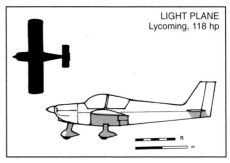

LIGHT PLANE
Lycoming, 118 hp

| DATA | IMPERIAL | | METRIC | |
|------|----------|--|--------|--|
| Span | 27.5 | ft | 8.4 | m |
| Wing area | 135 | sq ft | 12.7 | sq m |
| Aspect ratio | 5.5 | | 5.5 | |
| Empty Weight | 1158 | lb | 502 | kg |
| Loaded weight | 1720 | lb | 746 | kg |
| Wing loading | 12.78 | lb/sq ft | 62 | kg/sq m |
| Max speed | 145 | mph | 232 | kmh |
| Cruise speed | 138 | mph | 220 | kmh |
| Stalling speed | 57 | mph | 91 | kmh |
| Climb rate | 770 | ft/min | 237 | m/min |
| Range | 650 | mls | 1040 | km |

Marketed in the USA by Macfam and in Canada by K and S (Kay and Stan Mc Leod) the Cavalier 102.5 is a side by side two seater of all wood construction. Listed as 'plans only' for home build, parts and back up are available

The design is based on the Gardan Minicab, of 1949, with modifications, which include, a nose wheel tricycle undercarriage in place of the original tail-dragger gear, a swept back fin and rudder, and a canopy that slides bodily forward in place of the forward and upward pivoting original. There is also additional cabin glazing aft of the main hood.

An unusual feature, and a boon to spotters, are the upswept wing tip fuel tanks which hold all the aircraft's fuel.

Some of the early models were built as tail draggers and later modified to trikes.

There are five on the UK Register. It is PFA approved.

Various engines are fitted, from 85 to 135 hp. - the figures below are for the 100 hp. model.

## K AND S
## CAVALIER 102.5

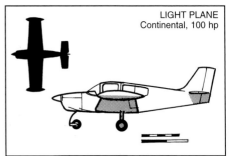

LIGHT PLANE
Continental, 100 hp

| DATA | IMPERIAL | | METRIC | |
|------|----------|--|--------|--|
| Span | 27.6 | ft | 8.39 | m |
| Wing area | 118 | sq ft | 10.9 | sq m |
| Aspect ratio | 6.4 | | 6.4 | |
| Empty Weight | 950 | lb | 431 | kg |
| Loaded weight | 1800 | lb | 817 | kg |
| Wing loading | 15.3 | lb/sq ft | 74.4 | kg/sq m |
| Max speed | 150 | mph | 240 | kmh |
| Cruise speed | 138 | mph | 222 | kmh |
| Stalling speed | 50 | mph | 80 | kmh |
| Climb rate | 1200 | ft/min | 366 | m/min |
| Range | 830 | mls | 1328 | km |

The all metal PA 38 Tomahawk has been produced in considerable numbers – over 2500 – and is a hardworking and durable trainer, with 166 flying in this country.

Introduced in 1978 (first flew 1977), the Tomahawk's high mounted tailplane and all round vision canopy are identification features, as is the fairly high aspect ratio wing.

The Tomahawk is a fully aerobatic trainer/tourer, well liked by its pilots.

It has a striking similarity to the Beechcraft Skipper (not in this book) but if you see a Skipper it is almost certainly a Tomahawk as there are none of the former on the UK Register.

The fashion for 'T' tails comes and goes, the claimed advantage being improved rudder control at high angles and better spin recovery.

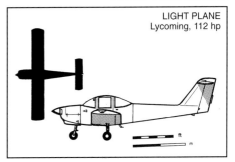

LIGHT PLANE
Lycoming, 112 hp

| DATA | IMPERIAL | | METRIC | |
|---|---|---|---|---|
| Span | 34 | ft | 10.36 | m |
| Wing area | 124.7 | sq ft | 11.6 | sq m |
| Aspect ratio | 9.3 | | 9.3 | |
| Empty Weight | 1128 | lb | 512 | kg |
| Loaded weight | 1670 | lb | 757 | kg |
| Wing loading | 13.4 | lb/sq ft | 65.4 | kg/sq m |
| Max speed | 126 | mph | 202 | kmh |
| Cruise speed | 97 | mph | 156 | kmh |
| Stalling speed | 60 | mph | 96 | kmh |
| Climb rate | 725 | ft/min | 221 | m/min |
| Range | 520 | mls | 838 | km |

A small, attractive and innovative design with a good performance, initiated by the PILOT magazine in 1968. It was an all metal two seater intended for kit construction.

The prototype was built by P. Burril over a period of years, 1969-76, to the designs of Lloyd Jenkinson and Peter Sharman and then taken on by Practavia Ltd at Wycombe Air Park, Booker. The first flight being made in 1976.

During the following years 150 kits were sold, eight of them eventually flying with four still on the UK Register.

Practavia were geared up to sell the 'Sprite ready made when they went out of business in 1982.

The wing, constructed in three units had leading edge fuel tanks on production models, the home-builts having tip tanks. The semi-monocoque fuselage had no double curvature panels, the u/c legs were rubber sprung and the brakes were hydraulic.

Another lost opportunity for the British light aircraft industry.

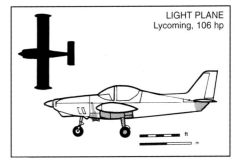

LIGHT PLANE
Lycoming, 106 hp

| DATA | IMPERIAL | | METRIC | |
|---|---|---|---|---|
| Span | 27 | ft | 8.23 | m |
| Wing area | 108 | sq ft | 10.03 | sq m |
| Aspect ratio | 6.75 | | 6.75 | |
| Empty Weight | 1050 | lb | 476 | kg |
| Loaded weight | 1650 | lb | 748 | kg |
| Wing loading | 15.3 | lb/sq ft | 74.7 | kg/sq m |
| Max speed | 139 | mph | 224 | kmh |
| Cruise speed | 124 | mph | 200 | kmh |
| Stalling speed | 56 | mph | 91 | kmh |
| Climb rate | 720 | ft/min | 219 | m/min |
| Range | 625 | mls | 1006 | km |

Related to the Christophe Heintz designed Robin HR 200 and the R 2100 Super Club, the R2160 is an all metal two seat aerobatic/ trainer, certificated in 1978.

107 were sold before production ceased in 1984, Avions Pierre Robin of Canada being involved in the assembly of some of these. In 1993 production was resumed.

The R 2160, distinctive for its long ventral fin, is an all metal aeroplane powered by a 160 hp. Lycoming. The flying control surfaces comprise an 'all moving' tailplane, horn balanced rudder and balanced slotted ailerons plus electrically operated flaps. The well faired tricycle undercarriage is oleo sprung with disc brakes and a steering nose wheel.

When not aerobatting the R 2160 is a useful fast tourer with a well equipped panel and a range of nearly 600 miles at 150 mph.

There are twenty-three on the UK Register including R2100, R2112, R2120, R2160. Distributed in the UK by Mistral Aviation of Gloucester Airport.

## ROBIN R 2160

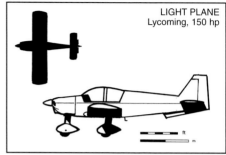

LIGHT PLANE
Lycoming, 150 hp

| DATA | IMPERIAL | | METRIC | |
|---|---|---|---|---|
| Span | 26.3 | ft | 8.33 | m |
| Wing area | 140 | sq ft | 13.01 | sq m |
| Aspect ratio | 5.33 | | 5.33 | |
| Empty Weight | 1235 | lb | 560 | kg |
| Loaded weight | 1764 | lb | 800 | kg |
| Wing loading | 12.6 | lb/sq ft | 61.5 | kg/sq m |
| Max speed | 160 | mph | 257 | kmh |
| Cruise speed | 150 | mph | 241 | kmh |
| Stalling speed | 60 | mph | 96 | kmh |
| Climb rate | 1025 | ft/min | 312 | m/min |
| Range | 590 | mls | 950 | km |

This smart four seat tourer from France has proved to be a best seller with over a 1000 of the Tobago and its variants, Tampico, Trinidad etc, produced to date.

From the same stable as the Rallye, the Tobago is a completely new and more streamlined airframe.

The Trinidad TB 20 is the retractable undercarriage version of the Tobago and the TB 200 version, illustrated. Has a 200 hp Lycoming as opposed to the standard TB 10 Tobago's 180 hp.

The prototype first flew in 1977 and steady refining of the design has ensured an ever full order book.

The airframe is of aluminium alloy with parallel chord wings with fairly pronounced dihedral, a much swept large fin and rudder and an all moving tailplane.

A pair of belly strakes just aft of the wing are an unusual feature.

There are about 140 of the Tobago family on the UK Register, and it is still in production.

## SOCATA TB 10 TOBAGO

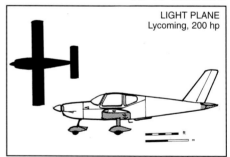

LIGHT PLANE
Lycoming, 200 hp

| DATA | IMPERIAL | | METRIC | |
|---|---|---|---|---|
| Span | 31.7 | ft | 9.76 | m |
| Wing area | 135 | sq ft | 12.7 | sq m |
| Aspect ratio | 7.5 | | 7.5 | |
| Empty Weight | 1576 | lb | 715 | kg |
| Loaded weight | 2535 | lb | 1146 | kg |
| Wing loading | 18.8 | lb/sq ft | 91.6 | kg/sq m |
| Max speed | 161 | mph | 257 | kmh |
| Cruise speed | 150 | mph | 240 | kmh |
| Stalling speed | 61 | mph | 98 | kmh |
| Climb rate | 940 | ft/min | 290 | m/min |
| Range | 745 | mls | 1192 | km |

An advanced design from Avions Pierre Robin that has not, as yet, made its mark on this side of the channel.

The design team set out to produce a cheap, light weight, two seat trainer, in the best Jodel tradition.

After two years work the prototype ATL first flew in 1983 powered by a 47 hp. JPX PAL engine - a three cylinder air cooled unit. The power was soon increased to 56 hp. using a JPX/VW unit and in its initial production form a 65 hp. unit was installed, necessitating a swept forward wing to accommodate the, now, more forward CG position due to the heavier motor.

Deliveries began in 1985, thirty were ordered, but all were recalled within a year for 'full certification mods'.

Full certification being obtained in 1986.

A German built version was powered by a 70 hp. Limbach engine and this became the standard production version in France, where it is defined as the ATL Club 89, being certificated in 1989.

The wings and 'V' tail are wooden with fabric covering and the pod and boom fuselage is of GRP/composites.

Over 150 have been delivered, some UK based, but none appear on the UK Register.

### ROBIN ATL

Limbach, 70 hp

| DATA | IMPERIAL | METRIC |
|---|---|---|
| Span | 33.6 ft | 10.25 m |
| Wing area | 130.8 sq ft | 12.15 sq m |
| Aspect ratio | 8.65 | 8.65 |
| Empty Weight | 794 lb | 360 kg |
| Loaded weight | 1278 lb | 580 kg |
| Wing loading | 9.8 lb/sq ft | 47.7 kg/sq m |
| Max speed | 121 mph | 195 kmh |
| Cruise speed | 104 mph | 167 kmh |
| Stalling speed | 47 mph | 75 kmh |
| Climb rate | 600 ft/min | 183 m/min |
| Range | 624 mls | 1004 km |

### FLS AEROSPACE SPRINT

Designed by S.A.Holloway, its initial designation was SAH-1, and built at Bodmin, the Sprint trainer first flew in 1983. Originally funded by Trago Mills Supermarkets, the aeroplane has had a chequered history since TMS pulled out.

The Sprint, at one time named Orca, has been much praised by all who have flown it, including RAF Central Flying School and pilots from various foreign firms.

Five were produced by FLS but further examples are not planned. The Sprint is of simple all metal construction, it has manually operated slotted flaps, steerable nose wheel, and cantilever spring legs.

Comparisons with its nearest rivals, the Cessna 152 and the Tomahawk, show it to be roomier, carry more, fly further and faster and out climb them. Why, then, are we not making thousands of them?

Two versions are flying, one with a 118 hp motor and the other has 160 hp. There are six Sprints on the UK Register.

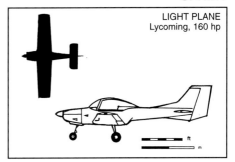

LIGHT PLANE
Lycoming, 160 hp

| DATA | IMPERIAL | METRIC |
|---|---|---|
| Span | 30.6 ft | 9.4 m |
| Wing area | 120 sq ft | 11.3 sq m |
| Aspect ratio | 7.8 | 7.8 |
| Empty Weight | 1100 lb | 500 kg |
| Loaded weight | 1750 lb | 794 kg |
| Wing loading | 14.5 lb/sq ft | 71.1 kg/sq m |
| Max speed | 140 mph | 224 kmh |
| Cruise speed | 138 mph | 221 kmh |
| Stalling speed | 53 mph | 85 kmh |
| Climb rate | 815 ft/min | 251 m/min |
| Range | 713 mls | 1141 km |

Aero Designs Inc. of Texas produced a prize winning single seater for Oshkosh 1983 from which designer Mark Brown developed the two seater Pulsar using the same construction methods, composites fuselage and plywood covered wooden spar wing with foam ribs at 8 inch (20cm) spacing.

First flown in 1989 the Pulsar's stylish lines and lively performance on only 64 hp make this a very desirable kit plane. Launched in kit form in 1991 over 100 were sold in the first two years.

A Rotax 912, 80 hp, version is now available giving an even more spectacular performance combined with the lower noise/vibration level of the four cylinder water cooled engine.

The Pulsar is a PFA approved design and is available as a trike or a tail-dragger, twenty-nine are on the UK Register and six are being built.

# AERO DESIGNS
# PULSAR

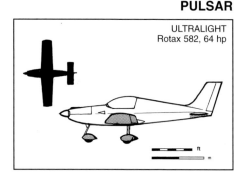

ULTRALIGHT
Rotax 582, 64 hp

| DATA | IMPERIAL | | METRIC | |
|---|---|---|---|---|
| Span | 25 | ft | 7.7 | m |
| Wing area | 104 | sq ft | 9.8 | sq m |
| Aspect ratio | 6 | | 6 | |
| Empty Weight | 430 | lb | 195 | kg |
| Loaded weight | 870 | lb | 395 | kg |
| Wing loading | 8.4 | lb/sq ft | 41 | kg/sq m |
| Max speed | 150 | mph | 240 | kmh |
| Cruise speed | 130 | mph | 208 | kmh |
| Stalling speed | 40 | mph | 64 | kmh |
| Climb rate | 1200 | ft/min | 370 | m/min |
| Range | 400 | mls | 640 | km |

French Canadian Chris Heintz designed the Zenair Zodiac CH601, a small but nippy metal two seater, for ease of construction by home builders.

The ease of construction was well demonstrated at the Sun'n Fun Rally 1993 when one was completed and flown within the week! There is no double curvature forming of the skins which are attached using mainly 'pop' blind rivets.

The thick single spar wing has a constant chord and the rudder/fin is all moving.

The prototype first flew in 1984 and the first 200 Zodiacs were powered by 65 hp VW engines and were either trike or trail-dragger. Later models had Rotax units. the CH 601 HDS has a tapered wing and a claimed cruise of 140 mph.

The CH 601 UL is an ultralight model grossing at under 1000lb.

There are thirty-two CH 601s on the UK Register and the type is on the PFA approved list.

# HEINTZ/ZENAIR
# CH 601 ZODIAC

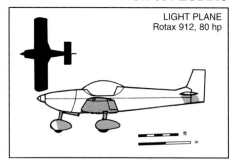

LIGHT PLANE
Rotax 912, 80 hp

| DATA | IMPERIAL | | METRIC | |
|---|---|---|---|---|
| Span | 27 | ft | 8.32 | m |
| Wing area | 130 | sq ft | 12.2 | sq m |
| Aspect ratio | 5.6 | | 5.6 | |
| Empty Weight | 550 | lb | 250 | kg |
| Loaded weight | 1058 | lb | 480 | kg |
| Wing loading | 8.1 | lb/sq ft | 39.7 | kg/sq m |
| Max speed | 140 | mph | 224 | kmh |
| Cruise speed | 120 | mph | 192 | kmh |
| Stalling speed | 50 | mph | 80 | kmh |
| Climb rate | 1200 | ft/min | 370 | m/min |
| Range | 500 | mls | 880 | km |

A product of the Tri-R Technologies of California – KIS stands for 'keep it simple', was at one time marketed in the UK by ABC Aviation. It is a neat, two seat, side-by-side kit plane with GRP and Carbon fibre pre moulded components on honeycomb cores, the metal parts are all pre-formed and welded.

The stateside KIS was powered either by a Limbach L2000 or a 125 hp Continental. The UK prototype has a modified Honda Civic car engine, the CAM 100, 100 hp, by Lycomings and Continentals are now more usual.

A cool performer the KIS cruises at 170 mph and climbs at 1600 feet a minute, solo.

The spatted tricycle gear is non retracting and the upturned vortex control wing tips are a distinguishing feature. It may also be seen as a tail-dragger.

There are ten flying in the UK and several are under construction with PFA blessing. The four-seat KIS Cruiser is a development but is currently limited in the UK to two seats under PFA Regulations.

**TRI-R**
**KIS**

LIGHT PLANE
CAM 100, 100hp

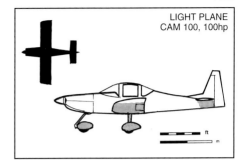

| DATA | IMPERIAL | | METRIC | |
|---|---|---|---|---|
| Span | 23 | ft | 7.1 | m |
| Wing area | 88 | sq ft | 8.3 | sq m |
| Aspect ratio | 6 | | 6 | |
| Empty Weight | 680 | lb | 308 | kg |
| Loaded weight | 1400 | lb | 635 | kg |
| Wing loading | 16 | lb/sq ft | 77.6 | kg/sq m |
| Max speed | 180 | mph | 288 | kmh |
| Cruise speed | 170 | mph | 272 | kmh |
| Stalling speed | 50 | mph | 80 | kmh |
| Climb rate | 1600 | ft/min | 492 | m/min |
| Range | 600 | mls | 960 | km |

A product of the German company Burkhart Grob Luft und Raumfahrt, well known for their high performance GRP gliders. The G115 is no power glider though, with its 170 mph. top speed and 180 hp motor.

The latest model of the G115, the G115D, differs from the earlier models in having simpler canopy framing, a more swept back fin and rudder, and a more powerful fuel injected engine.

The Royal Navy, through Airwork, are replacing some of their Chipmunks with the G115D (the Navy will call it the Heron), and other orders have been received from flying clubs in Australia and the USA.

The earlier models are flying with UK flying clubs giving well instrumented side by side tuition, eighteen on the UK Register. In RAF service the G115 is the Tutor. Ex RAF G115s have swelled the number on the UK Register to over 100.

The G115 is an all composites aeroplane that looks set for a successful future.

**GROB**
**G 115**

LIGHT PLANE
Lycoming, 180 hp

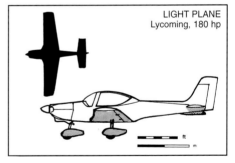

| DATA | IMPERIAL | | METRIC | |
|---|---|---|---|---|
| Span | 30.6 | ft | 9.42 | m |
| Wing area | 129 | sq ft | 12.1 | sq m |
| Aspect ratio | 7.25 | | 7.25 | |
| Empty Weight | 1630 | lb | 740 | kg |
| Loaded weight | 2182 | lb | 990 | kg |
| Wing loading | 17 | lb/sq ft | 83 | kg/sq m |
| Max speed | 168 | mph | 268 | kmh |
| Cruise speed | 135 | mph | 248 | kmh |
| Stalling speed | 53 | mph | 85 | kmh |
| Climb rate | 1350 | ft/min | 416 | m/min |
| Range | 600 | mls | 960 | km |

The origins of the Firefly lay in the Fournier RF-6B, an all wood French design of 1971, built under licence by Slingsby. Slingsby re-engineered the Fournier giving it a wider GRP fuselage and all composites wing and tail surfaces. Later developments include more powerful engines and constant speed prop.

Fully aerobatic at +6-3g, the Firefly has an inverted fuel system, fully comprehensive instrumentation and avionics making it a pretty expensive aeroplane for the average weekend flying though maintenance costs they say are low. There are eighty on the UK Register.

In 1994 the design won the British Design Council Award, specifically for the T3A version ordered by the USAF, it is the world's first training aircraft to be made largely from GRP and the first GRP aeroplane to get Transport Category certification from the CAA.

The American order for 113 aircrafts in conjunction with Northrop Aircraft is worth £37 million.

The T3 was grounded by the USAF in 1997 after a spate of crashes and though modified it has been dropped.

## SLINGSBY
## T67 FIREFLY

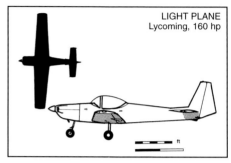

LIGHT PLANE
Lycoming, 160 hp

| DATA | IMPERIAL | | METRIC | |
|---|---|---|---|---|
| Span | 34.7 | ft | 10.62 | m |
| Wing area | 136 | sq ft | 12.6 | sq m |
| Aspect ratio | 8.9 | | 8.9 | |
| Empty Weight | 1543 | lb | 700 | kg |
| Loaded weight | 2250 | lb | 1020 | kg |
| Wing loading | 16.57 | lb/sq ft | 80.5 | kg/sq m |
| Max speed | 161 | mph | 259 | kmh |
| Cruise speed | 149 | mph | 240 | kmh |
| Stalling speed | 45 | mph | 72 | kmh |
| Climb rate | 1150 | ft/min | 350 | m/min |
| Range | 518 | mls | 833 | km |

Rene Fournier started in the aviation business in the '60s by producing a range of highly popular motor gliders. Turning to a higher powered trainer/tourer in 1974 with the RF-6, an all wood trike two seater. After only 43 had been made the Fournier factory was in financial trouble and split up (Slingsby at this stage obtained the rights to build the RF-6, which was later to become the successful Firefly).

When Fournier, restructured, got going again the RF-47 appeared in 1993, at first glance similar to the RF-6, it is a smaller, lighter and lower powered aeroplane.

Prototypes were all wood, but subsequent models have included composites (ie. for main spar) but retain part fabric covering.

Stressed for +4.4,-2.2, the RF-47 is semi aerobatic and has superb visibility through its backwards and upwards opening canopy.

## FOURNIER
## RF-47

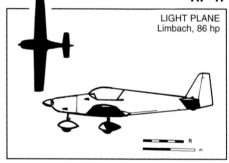

LIGHT PLANE
Limbach, 86 hp

| DATA | IMPERIAL | | METRIC | |
|---|---|---|---|---|
| Span | 32.8 | ft | 10 | m |
| Wing area | 117.6 | sq ft | 10.9 | sq m |
| Aspect ratio | 9.2 | | 9.2 | |
| Empty Weight | 870 | lb | 395 | kg |
| Loaded weight | 1376 | lb | 620 | kg |
| Wing loading | 11.6 | lb/sq ft | 57 | kg/sq m |
| Max speed | 124 | mph | 200 | kmh |
| Cruise speed | 112 | mph | 180 | kmh |
| Stalling speed | 49 | mph | 78 | kmh |
| Climb rate | 787 | ft/min | 240 | m/min |
| Range | 616 | mls | 985 | km |

This 'up and coming' two seater from France is based on the all metal Colomban Ban Bi, designed by Michel Colomban, which first flew in 1994.

The MCR 01 is of mixed construction, composites fuselage and a wing with alloy skin over foam ribs and composites spars. It is manufactured by Dyn Aero whose director is Christophe Robin son of the famous Pierre Robin, he of the delightful Robin range of light aircraft.

The three main versions of the MCR-01 are, the VLA, short span, 100 hp Rotax, capable of an incredible 190 mph., the Club, seen as a' trainer', bigger wing, flies and lands slower than the 'hot' VLA, but is just outside the SLA category, into which the MCR 01 SLA falls, which has more wing and less weight. The SLA has full span double slotted Fowler flaps and a stalling speed of 40 mph.

Twelve are on the UK Register at the time of writing – but I have a hunch we'll see many more.

Data below is for the MCR-01 SLA.

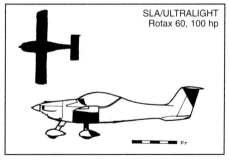

SLA/ULTRALIGHT
Rotax 60, 100 hp

| DATA | IMPERIAL | | METRIC | |
|---|---|---|---|---|
| Span | 25.5 | ft | 7.8 | m |
| Wing area | 80.7 | sq ft | 7.5 | sq m |
| Aspect ratio | 8 | | | |
| Empty Weight | 528 | lb | 240 | kg |
| Loaded weight | 991 | lb | 450 | kg |
| Wing loading | 12.3 | lb/sq ft | 60 | kg/sq m |
| Max speed | 111 | mph | 178 | kmh |
| Cruise speed | 95 | mph | 152 | kmh |
| Stalling speed | 40 | mph | 63 | kmh |
| Climb rate | 800 | ft/min | 126 | m/min |
| Range | 400 | mls | 640 | km |

This sleek modern two seater designed and built by the Austrian company HOAC (also made by Diamond aircraft in Canada) is marketed in this country by Diamond Aircraft UK who are based at Staverton.

Of all-composites construction, the Katana is powered by the economical Rotax 912 a four cylinder, four stroke which employs both air and water cooling.

The Katana, with its low operating costs, low maintenance and docile handling is seen by many as the way ahead in the mass training field, i.e. a long overdue replacement for the omnipresent, but ageing Cessna 150/152 and Tomahawk.

Based on the Super Dimona powered glider, with its aspect ratio of ten, up-turned wing tips, pod and boom fuselage and 'T' tail, the katana is easily identified.

Already in use at some flying schools, it is much praised by instructors who find that student dual time to solo can be as little as six hours.

A well stocked instrument panel, constant speed prop, and a very low noise level are all part of the package. A four seat version is being developed, Katana sales have burgeoned since our first edition and there are now thirty-two on the UK Register.

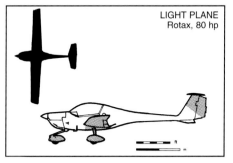

LIGHT PLANE
Rotax, 80 hp

| DATA | IMPERIAL | | METRIC | |
|---|---|---|---|---|
| Span | 31.1 | ft | 10.8 | m |
| Wing area | 114.8 | sq ft | 11.6 | sq m |
| Aspect ratio | 10 | | 10 | |
| Empty Weight | 1090 | lb | 494 | kg |
| Loaded weight | 1610 | lb | 730 | kg |
| Wing loading | 14.1 | lb/sq ft | 70 | kg/sq m |
| Max speed | 160 | mph | 256 | kmh |
| Cruise speed | 137 | mph | 219 | kmh |
| Stalling speed | 57 | mph | 91 | kmh |
| Climb rate | 730 | ft/min | 225 | m/min |
| Range | 600 | mls | 962 | km |

Ten years in development, the Cirrus SR20 is an advanced four seater of composites construction. The first production aircraft flew in 1999 and since then several hundred have been delivered from plants at Deluth, Hibbing and Grand Forks, USA. Brain-child of the Klapmeir brothers, whose firm was founded in 1954 producing kit planes. Development of the SR20 began in 1990 as a factory built aeroplane..

The roomy cockpit (50 inches wide) contains an ARNAV LCD panel with GPS moving map and a Meggitt Systems autopilot backing up the side stick control. An advanced feature is the ballistic recovery parachute gun situated behind the baggage compartment – eight test deployments were carried out during development flying.

The similar but improved SR22 is now in production Cirrus have a very full order book for this all composites speedster which seems set for worldwide acclaim, several examples of which are already in the UK. There are twenty on the UK Register.

## CIRRUS SR20/22

LIGHT PLANE
Continental 200/310 hp

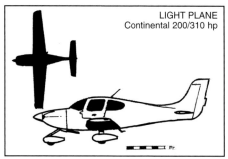

| DATA | IMPERIAL | | METRIC | |
|---|---|---|---|---|
| Span | 35.5 | ft | 10.82 | m |
| Wing area | 135 | sq ft | 12.5 | sq m |
| Aspect ratio | 9 | | 9 | |
| Empty Weight | 1950 | lb | 885 | kg |
| Loaded weight | 2900 | lb | 1315 | kg |
| Wing loading | 21.45 | lb/sq ft | 105 | kg/sq m |
| Max speed | 200 | mph | 320 | kmh |
| Cruise speed | 184 | mph | 296 | kmh |
| Stalling speed | 74 | mph | 118 | kmh |
| Climb rate | 1000 | ft/min | 305 | m/min |
| Range | 800 | mls | 1280 | km |

This sleek 450kg ultralight two seater is a kit plane produced in Spain. the Esqual has a welded steel centre section within a GRP monocoque fuselage and glass fibre or carbon fibre main spar within a glass fibre sandwich skin. The standard fixed tricycle gear version has a sister with a retracting tail-dragger configuration which first flew in 2002. Power units are, the Rotax 912 (98hp) or the Jabiru 3300 (120hp) – the figures are for the Rotax powered model. The Esquals flaps and elevator trim are electric and the nose wheel castors for the differential hydraulic bakes. A ballistic parachute recovery system may be included as an optional extra. No Esquals yet on the UK Register – PFA approval has yet to be gained as a microlight. A pretty kit-plane that looks as though it means business.

## VOL MEDITERRANI VM-1 ESQUAL

ULTRALIGHT
Rotax 912, 98hp

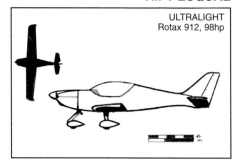

| DATA | IMPERIAL | | METRIC | |
|---|---|---|---|---|
| Span | 30.3 | ft | 9.25 | m |
| Wing area | 96.9 | sq ft | 9 | sq m |
| Aspect ratio | 9.4 | | | |
| Empty Weight | 569 | lb | 285 | kg |
| Loaded weight | 992 | lb | 450 | kg |
| Wing loading | 10.2 | lb/sq ft | 50 | kg/sq m |
| Max speed | 161 | mph | 260 | kmh |
| Cruise speed | 143 | mph | 230 | kmh |
| Stalling speed | 38 | mph | 60 | kmh |
| Climb rate | 1500 | ft/min | 457 | m/min |
| Range | 652 | mls | 1050 | km |

The Austrian company Diamond Aircraft, previously Hoffman and then HOAG, have produced a range of sleek GRP and composites aeroplanes including, the HK36 Katana two seater powered by a Rotax 914 which has obtained certification in many countries and has world-wide sales of over 2000 units. The Diamond Aircraft Corp. in Canada produces the HK36. The DA40 Star first flown 1997 is a four seat development of the HK36 (Katana/Super Dimona); similar in appearance, it has extended cabin framing with an arch. The diesel engined version, the DA40-TD1 is set to become the most popular model and trend-setter with its greater economy (50% of normal carburettor/four stroke consumption). With automatic mixture and airscreen pitch control the TDI's engine is managed with a single lever. Within the same price bracket as the Lycoming version the Thielert TAE 125 diesel engined model's figures are given below.

DIAMOND
# DA40
LIGHT PLANE
Thielert TAE 125, 135hp

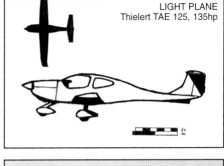

| DATA | IMPERIAL | | METRIC | |
|---|---|---|---|---|
| Span | 39.1 | ft | 11.9 | m |
| Wing area | 145.3 | sq ft | 13.5 | sq m |
| Aspect ratio | 10.6 | | | |
| Empty Weight | 1653 | lb | 750 | kg |
| Loaded weight | 2535 | lb | 1150 | kg |
| Wing loading | 17.45 | lb/sq ft | 85.2 | kg/sq m |
| Max speed | 177 | mph | 285 | kmh |
| Cruise speed | 152 | mph | 244 | kmh |
| Stalling speed | 57 | mph | 91 | kmh |
| Climb rate | 780 | ft/min | 238 | m/min |
| Range | 863 | mls | 1389 | km |

Michel Colomban, the French designer of the Innovative and minuscule Cri Cri has turned his hand to a rather more traditional configuration. The Banbi is a side by side two seater with a fixed tricycle undercarriage and a 'T' tail. The prototype aircraft are of all metal construction - and a metal kit is available - but a composites kit version is produced by Messrs Robin.

The Banbi first flew in 1994 and has been well liked by the pundits, especially its 190 mph (304 km p h) on 80 hp, supplied by a water cooled Rotax 912.

It is a small aeroplane 21ft (6.6 m) span and almost qualifies as a microlight weight-wise.

The smooth skin finish is achieved by much of the skin being bonded to the structure instead of riveting. The large flaps are electrically operated and reduce the stall from 64 mph (102 kmh) to 52 mph (83 kmh).

With its high wing loading the, as yet non-aerobatic, Banbi is not for the tyro, but a joy for the more experienced pilot.

PFA approval pending.

COLOMBAN
# MC 100 BANBI
ULTRALIGHT
Rotax 912, 80 hp

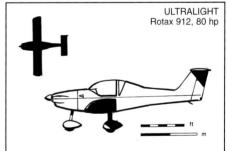

| DATA | IMPERIAL | | METRIC | |
|---|---|---|---|---|
| Span | 21.6 | ft | 6.6 | m |
| Wing area | 56 | sq ft | 5.2 | sq m |
| Aspect ratio | 8.3 | | 8.3 | |
| Empty Weight | 444 | lb | 201 | kg |
| Loaded weight | 946 | lb | 429 | kg |
| Wing loading | 16.8 | lb/sq ft | 82 | kg/sq m |
| Max speed | 190 | mph | 304 | kmh |
| Cruise speed | 181 | mph | 289 | kmh |
| Stalling speed | 64 | mph | 102 | kmh |
| Climb rate | 980 | ft/min | 301 | m/min |
| Range | 500 | mls | 800 | km |

This Czech designed ultralight kit plane is a two seat development of the French designed Pottier P220S three seater.

Hordes of modern, simple and economic light planes exist on the Continent but most are kept from the UK builder/owner by rigorous BCAR requirements. The Eurostar looks like breaking through the red tap, the PFA are reviewing the design and one has been built and is flying in the UK.

Of all metal construction, the Eurostar prototype first flew in 1997 and the type has since received certification in most Euro-countries.

The fixed tricycle gear has GRP cantilever legs with hydraulically braked wheels and a steerable or castoring nose-wheel. The wings, optional folding, carry three position flaps. Another option is a Ballistic parachute.

A two bladed wooden propeller is driven by a Rotax 912 of 80 hp.

The kit comes pre-formed and ready to rivet together with the front and rear fuselages already party assembled.

The chamfered lower edge of the rudder is a distinctive feature.

## AERO TECHNIK
# EV97 EUROSTAR

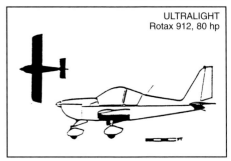

ULTRALIGHT
Rotax 912, 80 hp

| DATA | IMPERIAL | | METRIC | |
|------|----------|--|--------|--|
| Span | 26.5 | ft | 8.1 | m |
| Wing area | 106 | sq ft | 6 | sq m |
| Aspect ratio | 6.6 | | | |
| Empty Weight | 577 | lb | 262 | kg |
| Loaded weight | 992 | lb | 450 | kg |
| Wing loading | 9.37 | lb/sq ft | 45.7 | kg/sq m |
| Max speed | 141 | mph | 225 | kmh |
| Cruise speed | 113 | mph | 180 | kmh |
| Stalling speed | 41 | mph | 65 | kmh |
| Climb rate | 1079 | ft/min | 332 | m/min |
| Range | 435 | mls | 700 | km |

Europa's have gone from strength to strength with over 400 flying or in build since the '97 edition of this book.

The model covered here is the tri-gear version, in place of the original model's mono-wheel (the mono-wheel option is still available).

The more familiar 'trike' will appeal to many - the mono still being an undercarriage rarity, which, although good for rough strips, needs special take off and crosswind techniques.

The penalty for having three long legs is a reduction in maximum speed, in the order of 15 mph. Flight handling is just as good as the earlier model, and in the cockpit a wider seat is possible as the mono' housing is empty.

Europa kits are renowned for their quality as is the factory back-up. Ivan Shaw and his team have put British light planes 'on the map' with sales world-wide.

A big winged motor-glider model and the 200 mph XS (new wing and clean up) are the latest Europas .

Deliveries of a developed factory built model, the Liberty XL-2 are now US certificated.

## EUROPA AVIATION
# EUROPA TRI-GEAR

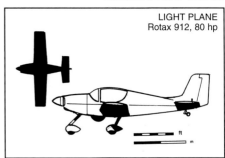

LIGHT PLANE
Rotax 912, 80 hp

| DATA | IMPERIAL | | METRIC | |
|------|----------|--|--------|--|
| Span | 19.2 | ft | 5.9 | m |
| Wing area | 95 | sq ft | 8.9 | sq m |
| Aspect ratio | 6.6 | | 6.6 | |
| Empty Weight | 730 | lb | 331 | kg |
| Loaded weight | 1370 | lb | 622 | kg |
| Wing loading | 14.4 | lb/sq ft | 70.3 | kg/sq m |
| Max speed | 150 | mph | 240 | kmh |
| Cruise speed | 103 | mph | 168 | kmh |
| Stalling speed | 56 | mph | 89 | kmh |
| Climb rate | 600 | ft/min | 185 | m/min |
| Range | 575 | mls | 920 | km |

Designed by Herman Mylius when Bolkow was part of the Messerschmit-Bolkow-Blohm organisation, the Monsun is essentially a low wing version of the BO208 Junior. first flown as the MHK 101 in 1987 the BO209 production version flew in 1969.

A clean, all metal, two seat aeroplane with a square section rear fuselage, all flying tailplane, a retractable nose wheel option and wings that fold alongside the fuselage for storage. This feature is not available on all models.

Semi-aerobatic, a pleasant, viceless aeroplane to fly the Monsun is much coveted by its ten UK Registered owners, 102 were built.

Production was resumed in 1979 by Monsun Flugzeubau at Weiden.

Data below are for the 150 hp Lycoming version.

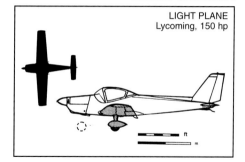

## BOLKOW
## BO209 MONSUN

LIGHT PLANE
Lycoming, 150 hp

| DATA | IMPERIAL | | METRIC | |
|---|---|---|---|---|
| Span | 27.5 | ft | 8.4 | m |
| Wing area | 110 | sq ft | 10.22 | sq m |
| Aspect ratio | 6.9 | | 6.9 | |
| Empty Weight | 1045 | lb | 474 | kg |
| Loaded weight | 1808 | lb | 820 | kg |
| Wing loading | 16.4 | lb/sq ft | 80.2 | kg/sq m |
| Max speed | 146 | mph | 233 | kmh |
| Cruise speed | 127 | mph | 203 | kmh |
| Stalling speed | 57 | mph | 91 | kmh |
| Climb rate | 896 | ft/min | 276 | m/min |
| Range | 618 | mls | 990 | km |

The most numerous flying machines in our skies, the flex wing (some say 'powered hang glider') comes in many models and variants, too many, I fear, for me to cover in this small book. I have, therefore, picked a Mainair Blade as typical of the breed.

Developed in the 1970s from the Rogallo foldable wing glider developed by NASA for the safe earth landing of space vehicles, the wing plan was rather like this - A. The modern wing plan is of a much higher aspect ratio with subsequent higher efficiency.

An essential difference between flexible and stiff wings is that the flex-wing dispenses with three axis controls and relies on pilot weight shift via a hanging control yoke.

Many remarkable distance flights have been made by these minimalist flying machines which represent the cheapest form of powered flying.

The BMAA (British Microlight Aircraft Association) is the controlling body for the close-knit flex wing fraternity.

## FLEX-WINGS

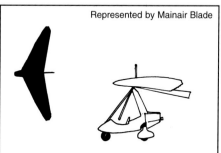

Represented by Mainair Blade

| DATA | IMPERIAL | | METRIC | |
|---|---|---|---|---|
| Span | 34 | ft | 10.6 | m |
| Wing area | 164 | sq ft | 15.4 | sq m |
| Aspect ratio | 7.2 | | 7.2 | |
| Empty Weight | 381 | lb | 173 | kg |
| Loaded weight | 858 | lb | 390 | kg |
| Wing loading | 5.12 | lb/sq ft | 25 | kg/sq m |
| Max speed | 101 | mph | 176 | kmh |
| Cruise speed | 70 | mph | 112 | kmh |
| Stalling speed | 30 | mph | 48 | kmh |
| Climb rate | 800 | ft/min | 246 | m/min |
| Range | 300 | mls | 480 | km |

A popular choice for a WW1 replica, the Dr1 has been built many times – there are two on the UK Register, plus others in many parts of the world. A small and fairly simple aeroplane, the Triplane is usually built actual size using the same construction as that drawn by Anthony Fokker and Reinhold Platz. Various engines are used (none rotaries!?) but the Warner Scarab of 145 hp. seems to fit it like a glove – performance figs below are for this combination.

The plans-built Redfern Fokker Dr1 is very popular and a Rotax engined microlight version is also built in the 'States.

A favourite mount of Baron Von Richtofen – in fact, his last mount – the Triplane is, by modern standards, a difficult aeroplane to fly and with its original 104 hp engine was not half as agile as our film makers would let us believe! Manoeuvrable, yes, but with limitations.

The fact that the performance and physical characteristics are similar to the 'real thing' engenders respect from today's pilots for the men who flew for their lives in such machines in that far-away war. There are five replicas in UK museums, plus two flying examples in the UK.

# FOKKER
# Dr1 TRIPLANE

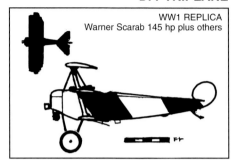

WW1 REPLICA
Warner Scarab 145 hp plus others

| DATA | IMPERIAL | | METRIC | |
|---|---|---|---|---|
| Span | 19 | ft | 5.86 | m |
| Wing area | 202 | sq ft | 18.8 | sq m |
| Aspect ratio | 5 | | | |
| Empty Weight | 1112 | lb | 505 | kg |
| Loaded weight | 1456 | lb | 661 | kg |
| Wing loading | 7.2 | lb/sq ft | 35.2 | kg/sq m |
| Max speed | 135 | mph | 216 | kmh |
| Cruise speed | 100 | mph | 161 | kmh |
| Stalling speed | 40 | mph | 64 | kmh |
| Climb rate | 2000 | ft/min | 610 | m/min |
| Range | 1700 | mls | 272 | km |

The original Nieuport single seat fighter of WW1 was extensively used by the RFC and many of our aces flew this French 'V strutter', including Ball, Bishop and Mannock.

The Germans, at one stage in the war, were so impressed with the Nieuport that they started to build them by copying captured aircraft; but none saw action.

Several full size replicas have been built – one flying in the UK and another nearing completion. Original aircraft exist in museums in France, Italy and the USA.

The first Nieuports had a novel trimming device – the high aspect ratio lower wing, pivoting on the 'V' strut, was adjustable in incidence in flight!

The UK replica has a welded steel tube fuselage, instead of wood, but the wings are as original wood and fabric. For safety's sake and to aid manoeuvring, the spoked wheels contain drum brakes, unlike the unbraked original.

The Scarab develops 110 hp with the bespoke prop, is about the right size and is more reliable!

Data for replica below is very similar to original.

# NIEUPORT
# 17/23 SCOUT

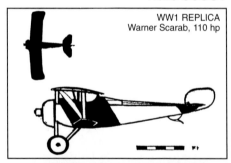

WW1 REPLICA
Warner Scarab, 110 hp

| DATA | IMPERIAL | | METRIC | |
|---|---|---|---|---|
| Span | 27 | ft | 8.3 | m |
| Wing area | 159 | sq ft | 15 | sq m |
| Aspect ratio | 9 | | | |
| Empty Weight | 1085 | lb | 492 | kg |
| Loaded weight | 1038 | lb | 626 | kg |
| Wing loading | 8.7 | lb/sq ft | 42 | kg/sq m |
| Max speed | 110 | mph | 176 | kmh |
| Cruise speed | 92 | mph | 147 | kmh |
| Stalling speed | 52 | mph | 83 | kmh |
| Climb rate | 800 | ft/min | 246 | m/min |
| Range | 180 | mls | 288 | km |

There are many replicas of this famous WW1 fighter worldwide – 13 are on the UK Register, half a dozen of which are airworthy; others are static display replicas in museums. Three originals exist in collection, including, the one at Old Warden – still flying after 82 years!

Many SE5s, redundant after the war, came on to the civil market and were used for banner towing, sky-writing and, two seat versions, for joy riding.

The UK replicas are built to the Slingsby design, based on the all wood Currie Wot (used in several films on WW1), or the Canadian Replica Plans version.

Replicas are usually 7/8 scale, about half the weight of the original and powered by Lycoming engines of around 100 hp. – half the power.

The modern engine, being much lighter than the WW1 unit, makes a longer than scale nose necessary to achieve the correct cg. – but the general appearance of these olive green replicas is very authentic – they even seem to sound right!

The Replica Plans version is a PFA approved design (PFA-20F) and two, at least, are under construction. Eight on the UK Register.

Data below is typical for this replica.

# SE5

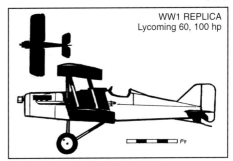

WW1 REPLICA
Lycoming 60, 100 hp

| DATA | IMPERIAL | METRIC |
|---|---|---|
| Span | 22 ft | 6.7 m |
| Wing area | 180 sq ft | 16.2 sq m |
| Aspect ratio | 5.4 | |
| Empty Weight | 850 lb | 385 kg |
| Loaded weight | 1200 lb | 545 kg |
| Wing loading | 6.6 lb/sq ft | 32 kg/sq m |
| Max speed | 100 mph | 160 kmh |
| Cruise speed | 85 mph | 136 kmh |
| Stalling speed | 40 mph | 64 kmh |
| Climb rate | 500 ft/min | 154 m/min |
| Range | 300 mls | 480 km |

One of the most successful and long lived of aeroplanes. the original A.V. Roe design the 504 became the classic 504K in 1913, serving in the RFC as night fighter, trainer and occasional bomber.

After the 1914-18 war 319 504Ks were sold on to the civil market where they served as trainers, joy riders, banner towers and wing walker mounts.

The structure was the wire braced wooden girder type with fabric covering. Some later models had welded tube fuselages. Power was supplied by a rotary engine. 100 hp, Gnome, 110 hp Le Rhone, 150 hp Bentley.

At a time when lateral control was achieved in many cases by wing warping the 504 had the luxury of ailerons on all wings!

The single skid, or toothpick between the main wheels to prevent nosing over, is unique feature.

8000 504s were built, the RAF kept theirs until 1932 and seven were impressed at the start of WW2.

One is still flying with the Shuttleworth Trust, two originals are in UK museums, six abroad, and four replicas.

# AVRO
# 504 K

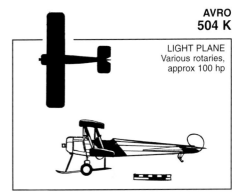

LIGHT PLANE
Various rotaries,
approx 100 hp

| DATA | IMPERIAL | METRIC |
|---|---|---|
| Span | 36 ft | 11.1 m |
| Wing area | 330 sq ft | 31 sq m |
| Aspect ratio | 7.8 | 7.8 |
| Empty Weight | 1231 lb | 559 kg |
| Loaded weight | 1829 lb | 830 kg |
| Wing loading | 5.5 lb/sq ft | 27 kg/sq m |
| Max speed | 95 mph | 152 kmh |
| Cruise speed | 75 mph | 120 kmh |
| Stalling speed | 30 mph | 48 kmh |
| Climb rate | 700 ft/min | 215 m/min |
| Range | 225 mls | 360 km |

Two Hawker Cygnets were built for the Lympne Light Aeroplane Trials of 1924, they were two seat ultralight biplanes, one powered by a 30 hp. ABC Scorpion and the other by a Bristol Cherub of 32 hp. Let down by erratic engine performance on their first appearance in the '24 Trials, they both won prizes at the Lympne Trials in 1926.

One, G-EBMB, survives to this day in the RAF Museum at Cosford, the other, G-EBJH was destroyed in a crash at Lympne in 1927.

Unlike many 'replica' aeroplanes that are compromises of scale and proportion, the Cygnet is a true replica, not only in scale but in its construction - in fact the replicas have been built, largely, from original Hawker drawings.

The design, which is a bit marginal in flight as a two seater, is PFA approved - Sydney Camm would have turned in his grave if it hadn't been!

One replica has been built powered by a 35 hp. Mosler engine and another is on long term construction (G-EBJI).

# HAWKER
# CYGNET Replica

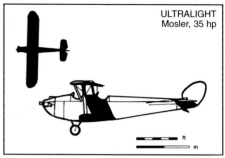

ULTRALIGHT
Mosler, 35 hp

| DATA | IMPERIAL | | METRIC | |
|---|---|---|---|---|
| Span | 28 | ft | 8.6 | m |
| Wing area | 172 | sq ft | 16 | sq m |
| Aspect ratio | 6.6 | | 6.6 | |
| Empty Weight | 373 | lb | 169 | kg |
| Loaded weight | 730 | lb | 331 | kg |
| Wing loading | 4.2 | lb/sq ft | 20.5 | kg/sq m |
| Max speed | 82 | mph | 131 | kmh |
| Cruise speed | 60 | mph | 96 | kmh |
| Stalling speed | 30 | mph | 48 | kmh |
| Climb rate | 275 | ft/min | 85 | m/min |
| Range | 400 | mls | 640 | km |

The first DH60 Moth, with an upright Cirrus engine, flew in 1925, subsequently the upright Gypsy Major engined DH60g Moth was launched three years later.

This father of the famous DH82 Tiger Moth was a sensation in it's day, winning many races and setting class records for speed, altitude, and engine reliability.

Jean Batten, Amy Johnson and Francis Chichester all became famous flying the DH60 Moth, Amy's Jason is in the Science Museum in London.

The 60G Moth was all wood with fabric covered wings and control surfaces and a plywood skinned fuselage, many hundreds being manufactured up to the advent of the Tiger Moth.

The 60M had a welded steel tube fuselage with fabric covering over wooden stringers, a (close up!) recognition give away.

The success of the '60 Moths boosted De Haviland's fortunes who in 1930 opened a new factory at Hatfield and issued licences for overseas manufacturers.

There are twenty-three DH60 Moths on the UK Register, thirteen of which are triumphantly airworthy.

# DE HAVILAND
# DH 60G MOTH

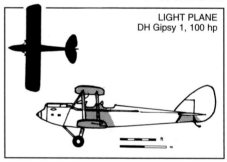

LIGHT PLANE
DH Gipsy 1, 100 hp

| DATA | IMPERIAL | | METRIC | |
|---|---|---|---|---|
| Span | 30 | ft | 9.24 | m |
| Wing area | 243 | sq ft | 22.81 | sq m |
| Aspect ratio | 7.4 | | 7.4 | |
| Empty Weight | 962 | lb | 437 | kg |
| Loaded weight | 1650 | lb | 749 | kg |
| Wing loading | 6.8 | lb/sq ft | 33.2 | kg/sq m |
| Max speed | 98 | mph | 157 | kmh |
| Cruise speed | 83 | mph | 133 | kmh |
| Stalling speed | 40 | mph | 64 | kmh |
| Climb rate | 700 | ft/min | 215 | m/min |
| Range | 290 | mls | 464 | km |

The two seat Avro 594 Avian was designed and built for the 1926 Lymne Light Aeroplane Trials and was powered by a 75hp. AS Genet engine.

Though only moderately successful at Lymne, eighteen months later Bert Hinkler flew one from Croydon to Darwin in a record fifteen days. Avians made other long distance flights in the late 1920s and in 1930 an Avian Mk3 won the Kings Cup air race.

Various marks and model numbers covered engine changes, wing tip shapes and undercarriage configuration. The main engines fitted were the Genet (75hp), Cirrus 2 (85hp), and Cirrus 3 (95hp).

About 80 Avians were built, many surviving up to WW2, when they were impressed – four survived the conflict. One is still flying – restored by Lang Kidby in Australia and air freighted to the UK. Whilst flying in the UK it crashed badly, but was rebuilt in two months and flown back to Oz by Kidby.

Three are on the UK Register Two in museums and one on long-term restoration.

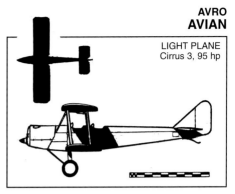

**AVRO AVIAN**

LIGHT PLANE
Cirrus 3, 95 hp

| DATA | IMPERIAL | | METRIC | |
|---|---|---|---|---|
| Span | 28 | ft | 8.6 | m |
| Wing area | 245 | sq ft | 23 | sq m |
| Aspect ratio | 6.4 | | 6.4 | |
| Empty Weight | 907 | lb | 411 | kg |
| Loaded weight | 1467 | lb | 666 | kg |
| Wing loading | 6.0 | lb/sq ft | 29.3 | kg/sq m |
| Max speed | 98 | mph | 157 | kmh |
| Cruise speed | 82 | mph | 131 | kmh |
| Stalling speed | 30 | mph | 48 | kmh |
| Climb rate | 650 | ft/min | 200 | m/min |
| Range | 325 | mls | 520 | km |

Simmonds Aircraft Ltd built the Spartan, two-seat biplane in 1928 with symmetrical section wings interchangeable for ease of manufacture and spares holding. though fairly successful there was a prejudice against the symmetrical wing section, so Simmonds, re-named Spartan Aircraft Ltd, built a Clark Y section winged model called the Spartan Arrow. Interchangeability continued with the rudder doubling as half an elevator. A napier Javelin test bed version, G-ABST, had a non-standard fin and rudder.

All wood with fabric covered wings that folded backwards the Arrow first flew in 1930 and was usually powered by a Hermes 105 hp engine.

Although raced in several Kings Cup races the Arrow was never well placed.

Fifteen Arrows were built all either being sold abroad or destroyed before WW2, except one, G-ABWP, bought in 1936 by Shuttleworth, stored for many years, it is now privately owned and airworthy.

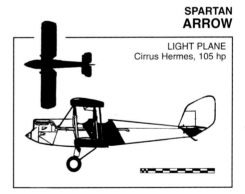

**SPARTAN ARROW**

LIGHT PLANE
Cirrus Hermes, 105 hp

| DATA | IMPERIAL | | METRIC | |
|---|---|---|---|---|
| Span | 30.6 | ft | 9.4 | m |
| Wing area | 251 | sq ft | 23.6 | sq m |
| Aspect ratio | 7.4 | | | |
| Empty Weight | 965 | lb | 438 | kg |
| Loaded weight | 1750 | lb | 794 | kg |
| Wing loading | 7 | lb/sq ft | 34.2 | kg/sq m |
| Max speed | 106 | mph | 170 | kmh |
| Cruise speed | 92 | mph | 147 | kmh |
| Stalling speed | 40 | mph | 64 | kmh |
| Climb rate | 830 | ft/min | 255 | m/min |
| Range | 432 | mls | 691 | km |

One of F G Miles first ventures when starting out at Shoreham in 1929 was the conversion of a 1918 Avro Baby into a Southern Martlet. The Baby's fuselage and wings were retained and a new tail, undercarriage and engine were fitted, plus detail improvements produced a lively aerobatic biplane – which was initially called the Hornet Baby.

Six Martlets were built with a variety of engines. The prototype, with an ABC Hornet (85hp) and others included. AS Genet 2 (80hp), Genet Major (100hp), Gipsy 1 (100hp) and Gipsy 2 (120hp).

The only surviving Martlet, G-AAYX, recently restored to airworthy condition at Old Warden, was stored throughout WW2, bought by Billy Butlin in 1947 and restored by Miles, at Woodley, and used to give aerobatic displays at his holiday camps. Alan Cobham's National Air Displays owned one as a workhorse and Mrs F G Miles as a hack, the latter was given to the ATC in 1940.

A final version, the Metal Martlet, had a steel tube fuselage frame and a split axle undercarriage; it was flown in 1931 and, inexplicably, scrapped the following year.

Details below for Genet 2 version.

## SOUTHERN MARTLET

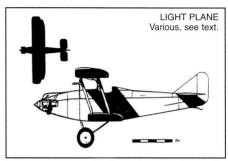

LIGHT PLANE
Various, see text.

| DATA | IMPERIAL | | METRIC | |
|---|---|---|---|---|
| Span | 25 | ft | 7.6 | m |
| Wing area | 180 | sq ft | 17 | sq m |
| Aspect ratio | 7 | | | |
| Empty Weight | 705 | lb | 320 | kg |
| Loaded weight | 1030 | lb | 467 | kg |
| Wing loading | 5.7 | lb/sq ft | 28 | kg/sq m |
| Max speed | 112 | mph | 170 | kmh |
| Cruise speed | 95 | mph | 180 | kmh |
| Stalling speed | 35 | mph | 56 | kmh |
| Climb rate | 1100 | ft/min | 339 | m/min |
| Range | 280 | mls | 448 | km |

## AVRO 621 TUTOR

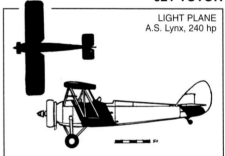

LIGHT PLANE
A.S. Lynx, 240 hp

Designed as a replacement for the venerable Avro 504, the Tutor first flew in 1929. Fabric covered, it had a steel tube fuselage, single piece LA wing ribs over steel spars. The usual power plant was a seven cylinder, 240 hp Lynx, which was originally uncowled.

It became the standard RAF trainer, about 200 being delivered and nineteen were civil registered. Several were sold abroad including Irish and Greek air forces. The famous pre-war Alan Cobham Circus had two Tutors in its fleet.

Three of the civil Tutors were impressed in 1939 and were not seen again, but three ex RAF models were civilianised after the conflict, one of which, G-AHSA, is still flying with the Shuttleworth Trust.

Replaced, finally by the more economic Tiger Moth the Tutor is a fine example of a typical 1930s biplane and long may it enthral us at Old Warden.

| DATA | IMPERIAL | | METRIC | |
|---|---|---|---|---|
| Span | 28.5 | ft | 8.8 | m |
| Wing area | 238 | sq ft | 22.4 | sq m |
| Aspect ratio | 6.8 | | 6.8 | |
| Empty Weight | 1100 | lb | 500 | kg |
| Loaded weight | 2100 | lb | 953 | kg |
| Wing loading | 8.8 | lb/sq ft | 43 | kg/sq m |
| Max speed | 124 | mph | 198 | kmh |
| Cruise speed | 105 | mph | 168 | kmh |
| Stalling speed | 45 | mph | 72 | kmh |
| Climb rate | 1000 | ft/min | 308 | m/min |
| Range | 350 | mls | 560 | km |

Designed as a trainer for the RAF the Tomtit first flew in 1929 some being sold onto the civil market, plus four to the RNZAF.

An all-metal airframe with fabric covering, heavily staggered wings and a 150 hp. Mongoose engine the Tomtit competed in several Kings Cup air races.

In 1935 the Tomtit was phased out of RAF service and nine were 'civilianised' – one being operated by Campbell Black's British Empire Air Displays.

During WW2 six Tomtits operated on vital communications work, camouflaged and with civil markings, but were never officially 'impressed'. Alex Henshaw, the famous test pilot, had a Tomtit as his personal hack during that war.

Three seem to have survived the conflict, one crashed one was scrapped and one (G-AFTA) survives at that Valhalla for historic aeroplanes, Old Warden, where it is maintained in an airworthy condition.

Other engines fitted were, Cirrus Hermes, Wolseley AIR9, Aquarius and Aries (225 hp).

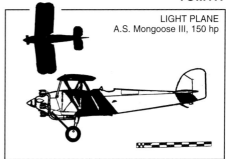

# HAWKER
# TOMTIT

LIGHT PLANE
A.S. Mongoose III, 150 hp

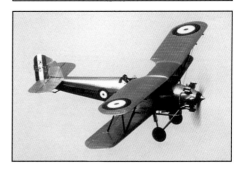

| DATA | IMPERIAL | | METRIC | |
|---|---|---|---|---|
| Span | 28.5 | ft | 8.8 | m |
| Wing area | 238 | sq ft | 22.4 | sq m |
| Aspect ratio | 6.8 | | | |
| Empty Weight | 1100 | lb | 500 | kg |
| Loaded weight | 2100 | lb | 953 | kg |
| Wing loading | 8.8 | lb/sq ft | 43 | kg/sq m |
| Max speed | 124 | mph | 198 | kmh |
| Cruise speed | 105 | mph | 168 | kmh |
| Stalling speed | 45 | mph | 72 | kmh |
| Climb rate | 1000 | ft/min | 308 | m/min |
| Range | 350 | mls | 560 | km |

First flown in 1930, the all wood Redwing was a side- by-side two seater powered by an air cooled flat four ABC Hornet of 75 hp. The fuselage was plywood covered, the rest of the airframe fabric. The sturdy divided axle undercarriage had long shock struts, which were attached to the top longerons.

The Mk2 Redwing was fitted with a Genet 2A of 80 hp, all subsequent models used this unit. The Mk 3 with reduced span and spatted wheels was built but never certificated and later converted to a Mk 2.

Twelve Redwings in all were built between 1930/33.

In 1934 a Mrs K Miller attempted to fly from Croydon to Cape Town but came to grief after a creditable flight across the Sahara when it was wrecked in a forced landing in Dahomey after a flight of 10,000 miles.

G-ABNX, a privately owned Redwing, was stored throughout the war. Maintained post-war by John Pothecary, he has now passed it to a Charitable Trust in an airworthy condition.

With its 250 sq ft. of wing the Redwing has stately flying characteristics and a slow landing speed and with its sociable seating it is a true 'gentleman's aerial carriage'.

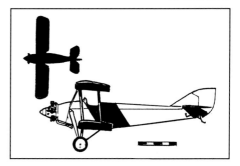

# ROBINSON
# REDWING

| DATA | IMPERIAL | | METRIC | |
|---|---|---|---|---|
| Span | 30.5 | ft | 9.3 | m |
| Wing area | 250 | sq ft | 23.2 | sq m |
| Aspect ratio | 7 | | | |
| Empty Weight | 870 | lb | 395 | kg |
| Loaded weight | 1450 | lb | 658 | kg |
| Wing loading | 5.8 | lb/sq ft | 28.3 | kg/sq m |
| Max speed | 95 | mph | 153 | kmh |
| Cruise speed | 85 | mph | 137 | kmh |
| Stalling speed | 35 | mph | 56 | kmh |
| Climb rate | 800 | ft/min | 244 | m/min |
| Range | 275 | mls | 442 | km |

The Tiger Moth, De Haviland's 82nd design, first flew in 1931. It was the mainstay of the pre war flying clubs and with the advent of WW2 it got into camouflage and became the RAFs main *ab initio* trainer, practically every pilot who flew in the war learned his basic skills on this aeroplane.

8,500 Tigers were built, mainly in Britain, 4,000 during the war. There were also production units in Canada, New Zealand and Australia.

A four seat version with enclosed cockpit, called the Jackaroo, was produced at Thruxton in limited number, using ex RAF models.

Some Canadian models were powered by a Menasco Pirate engine of 160 hp.

The wings are a fabric covered wooden structure and the fuselage is plywood covered welded steel tube. Sixty-four years old and still going strong. 200 still on the UK Register.

## DE HAVILAND
## TIGER MOTH

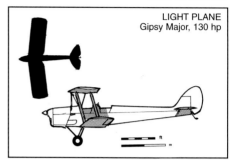

LIGHT PLANE
Gipsy Major, 130 hp

| DATA | IMPERIAL | | METRIC | |
|---|---|---|---|---|
| Span | 29.3 | ft | 9.2 | m |
| Wing area | 239 | sq ft | 22.5 | sq m |
| Aspect ratio | 7.2 | | 7.2 | |
| Empty Weight | 1115 | lb | 506 | kg |
| Loaded weight | 1825 | lb | 828 | kg |
| Wing loading | 7.6 | lb/sq ft | 37.1 | kg/sq m |
| Max speed | 109 | mph | 174 | kmh |
| Cruise speed | 90 | mph | 144 | kmh |
| Stalling speed | 40 | mph | 64 | kmh |
| Climb rate | 673 | ft/min | 305 | m/min |
| Range | 285 | mls | 456 | km |

First flown in 1932 the De Haviland Fox Moth embodied many Tiger Moth components - wings, tail unit and undercarriage. It could carry four passengers + pilot on short flights and three passengers on longer journeys. An early production version with a Gipsy 3A engine (later named Gipsy Major) won the 1933 Kings Cup Air Race at an average speed of 124 mph. The Prince of Wales owned one, briefly, before it was sold to Belgium as OO-ENC.

98 Fox Moths were built at Stag Lane, forty-nine were UK Registered and production was also undertaken post-war at DH's Toronto works. Several small airlines used them as well as air display companies, who used them for joy-riding and one was attached to the 1933 British Everest Flight Expedition.

Eleven of the UK Registered. Foxes that were around in 1939 were impressed, mainly for ATA taxi work; none of these survived. Today there are three on the UK Registered two airworthy and one being restored, other examples exist in Switzerland, Australia, New Zealand and Canada.

The Fox Moth with its 120/130 hp. engine was a fine performer, cruising with five people at nearly 100 mph.

## DE HAVILAND
## DH 83 FOX MOTH

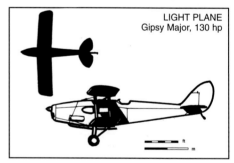

LIGHT PLANE
Gipsy Major, 130 hp

| DATA | IMPERIAL | | METRIC | |
|---|---|---|---|---|
| Span | 30.9 | ft | 9.5 | m |
| Wing area | 261 | sq ft | 24.5 | sq m |
| Aspect ratio | 7.3 | | 7.3 | |
| Empty Weight | 1100 | lb | 499 | kg |
| Loaded weight | 2070 | lb | 939 | kg |
| Wing loading | 7.9 | lb/sq ft | 38 | kg/sq m |
| Max speed | 113 | mph | 181 | kmh |
| Cruise speed | 90 | mph | 144 | kmh |
| Stalling speed | 45 | mph | 72 | kmh |
| Climb rate | 492 | ft/min | 151 | m/min |
| Range | 360 | mls | 576 | km |

The two seat, side by side, B2 was developed from the
Bluebird IV of 1929, both metal framed biplanes with fabric
covering. First flown in 1932 the B2 had a redesigned fin
and rudder and Alclad covered fuselage. Cirrus Hermes IV
engines were usually fitted though other installations
included Gipsy III and Gipsy Major.

Entered for the 1932 and 1934 Kings Cup Air Races, G-
ACAH finished fourth in '34.

The B2 was taken up by several flying schools and the
RAF, doing sterling service as a trainer in the early war
years.

Thirty six were built, but by 1942 they had been
relegated to 'instructional airframes' and 24 were
distributed to ATC squadrons. Seven were written off in
crashes before 1942.

There are still two on the UK Register, G-AEBJ airworthy
and still flying, one other stored and (hopefully) under
restoration. I wonder if any of the twenty-four that went to
ATC huts up and down the country in1942 still exist, whole
or in pieces?)

# BLACKBURN
# B2

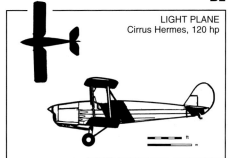

LIGHT PLANE
Cirrus Hermes, 120 hp

| DATA | IMPERIAL | | METRIC | |
|---|---|---|---|---|
| Span | 30.1 | ft | 9.3 | m |
| Wing area | 246 | sq ft | 23.1 | sq m |
| Aspect ratio | 7.3 | | 7.3 | |
| Empty Weight | 1175 | lb | 528 | kg |
| Loaded weight | 1850 | lb | 840 | kg |
| Wing loading | 7.5 | lb/sq ft | 36.7 | kg/sq m |
| Max speed | 112 | mph | 179 | kmh |
| Cruise speed | 95 | mph | 152 | kmh |
| Stalling speed | 45 | mph | 72 | kmh |
| Climb rate | 700 | ft/min | 215 | m/min |
| Range | 320 | mls | 512 | km |

A heavyweight for this book, but a truly classic 'light plane'.
The Beech 17 was the first design to come out of Walter
Beech's own factory at Wichita, Kansas in 1932, his previous
designs were under the Travel Air label.

The prototypes had a fixed undercarriage (the retractable
gear coming a year later) and five seats, and by 1934
production had reached a modest 18.

But the back staggered biplane with the big engine had
proved an extremely nifty performer and clocked up a lot of air
race wins and further enhanced production.

During WW2 the '17 was ordered in quantity by the USAAF
and USN as a personnel and utility transport, and with the
peace a short run of improved civilian models were produced.

So here we have a 60 year old biplane that cruises at 200
mph., climbs at 1500 fpm., has a range of nearly 1000 miles
and a cabin like a limo'! (It makes you think!)

At one time there were twelve on the UK Register (including
one Amy Johnson) there are now two with UK Register and
two with USA registration based here.

Look out for this lovely 'gas guzzler'.

# BEECH
# 17 STAGGERWING

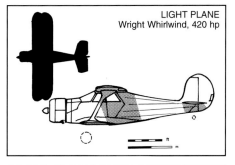

LIGHT PLANE
Wright Whirlwind, 420 hp

| DATA | IMPERIAL | | METRIC | |
|---|---|---|---|---|
| Span | 32 | ft | 9.24 | m |
| Wing area | 267 | sq ft | 25.1 | sq m |
| Aspect ratio | 7.73 | | 7.7 | |
| Empty Weight | 2226 | lb | 1011 | kg |
| Loaded weight | 3900 | lb | 1771 | kg |
| Wing loading | 14.6 | lb/sq ft | 71.25 | kg/sq m |
| Max speed | 230 | mph | 368 | kmh |
| Cruise speed | 202 | mph | 323 | kmh |
| Stalling speed | 55 | mph | 88 | kmh |
| Climb rate | 1500 | ft/min | 462 | m/min |
| Range | 700 | mls | 1120 | km |

Co-designed by Jean Stampe, the DH agent in Belgium, this Tiger Moth look-a-like first flew in 1933 and was adopted by the Belgian French Air Forces as their ab initio trainer.

Production ceased until after the war when production was undertaken by Nord and 700 were built. Stampe, himself, formed Stampe et Renard and continued a small production run in Belgium.

Very popular in post war aerobatic circles right up to the advert of the more specialised Pitts and Zlins.

Made famous in the 1960s by the daring Rothman Aerobatic Team the Stampe is still a useful aerobat and there are fifty or more on the British Register.

The Stampe SV-48s rounded wing tips help in sorting it out from The Tiger Moth.

Both Renault and De Haviland Gipsy major engines are fitted. (Ed. Plus some Lycoming 150/180 hp.).

## STAMPE SV 4

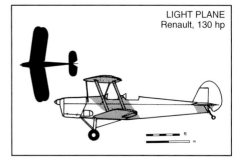

LIGHT PLANE
Renault, 130 hp

| DATA | IMPERIAL | | METRIC | |
|---|---|---|---|---|
| Span | 27.5 | ft | 8.4 | m |
| Wing area | 194 | sq ft | 18 | sq m |
| Aspect ratio | 7.8 | | 7.8 | |
| Empty Weight | 1056 | lb | 480 | kg |
| Loaded weight | 1716 | lb | 780 | kg |
| Wing loading | 8.8 | lb/sq ft | 43.2 | kg/sq m |
| Max speed | 127 | mph | 204 | kmh |
| Cruise speed | 109 | mph | 175 | kmh |
| Stalling speed | 45 | mph | 72 | kmh |
| Climb rate | 900 | ft/min | 277 | m/min |
| Range | 250 | mls | 400 | km |

In 1934 Alex Henshaw, air racer and famous Spitfire test pilot, bought a Mk 1 Arrow Active and proceeded to teach himself aerobatics. He liked the little biplane and claimed that he learned more about flying in it than any other aeroplane. Only two Actives were built by Arrow aircraft Ltd at Yeadon during 1931/32, the airframe was all metal and the covering mainly fabric.

The Mk 1 (G-ABIX) had a 115hp Cirrus Hermes engine and the Mk 2 a 120hp Gipsy Major 3; the other difference was the Mk 1s top plane was attached to the fuselage by a pylon and the Mk 2s by struts.

Both Arrows raced in the 1932 Kings Cup and the Mk 2 in the 1933 race. Two years later the Mk 1 caught fire in the air and crashed, Henshaw paracuted to safety.

The Mk 2 (G-ABVE) survives, having been discovered in a loft at the Slingsby works in 1957, now based at Breighton.

A tough little aerobatic biplane, which had it been developed could have become the British Pitts!

## ARROW ACTIVE

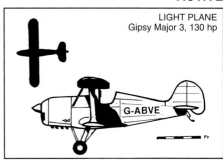

LIGHT PLANE
Gipsy Major 3, 130 hp

| DATA | IMPERIAL | | METRIC | |
|---|---|---|---|---|
| Span | 24 | ft | 7.4 | m |
| Wing area | 120 | sq ft | 11.3 | sq m |
| Aspect ratio | 8.2 | | 8.2 | |
| Empty Weight | 825 | lb | 420 | kg |
| Loaded weight | 1325 | lb | 602 | kg |
| Wing loading | 11.1 | lb/sq ft | 54 | kg/sq m |
| Max speed | 144 | mph | 230 | kmh |
| Cruise speed | 129 | mph | 206 | kmh |
| Stalling speed | 55 | mph | 88 | kmh |
| Climb rate | 1000 | ft/min | 454 | m/min |
| Range | 420 | mls | 772 | km |

This pre WW2 German trainer which first flew in 1934, a close contemporary of our Tiger Moth, has been built under licence in various countries and is, in a single seat form, the Jungmeister, a popular aerobat. (The Jungmeister differs in as much that its fuselage is of a completely different design).Having retained its appeal over the years, limited production was resumed in 1956 by CASA in Spain. It has also been built in Czechoslovakia and Switzerland. in 1968 a production line was set up in West Germany and it looks as if its going to go on forever. Total production is approximately 2,000.

fitted either with a Hirth inverted or Tigre in-line engine (CASA). the Jungman's structure is of mixed wood and metal, welded tube fuselage and is largely fabric covered.

The swept back biplane wings and raked forward, leggy, undercarriage are distinctive features.

There are thirty-eight on the British Register.

LIGHT PLANE
Hirth, 105 hp

| DATA | IMPERIAL | | METRIC | |
|---|---|---|---|---|
| Span | 24.25 | ft | 7.5 | m |
| Wing area | 145 | sq ft | 13.63 | sq m |
| Aspect ratio | 8.3 | | 8.3 | |
| Empty Weight | 836 | lb | 380 | kg |
| Loaded weight | 1474 | lb | 670 | kg |
| Wing loading | 10.2 | lb/sq ft | 49.6 | kg/sq m |
| Max speed | 115 | mph | 184 | kmh |
| Cruise speed | 106 | mph | 170 | kmh |
| Stalling speed | 45 | mph | 72 | kmh |
| Climb rate | 600 | ft/min | 184 | m/min |
| Range | 400 | mls | 640 | km |

Starting out as the Stearman 75 Kaydet in 1934 this venerable biplane became the classic wartime trainer of the USAF, and was produced in considerable numbers as the Boeing Stearman 75-10,000 being the final total.

Still to be seen working for it's living as a stunt plane, carrying wing walkers and joy riding; there are over twenty on the UK Register.

Of rugged construction, with sharply staggered wings, wire braced and 'N' strutted, the '75 has a clean single leg oleo undercarriage, open cockpits (of course!) and an often uncowled radial engine. The engine type varies; Lycoming, Continental, Jacobs and Pratt and Whitney have all been fitted.

In the post war years many of the trainers found work as crop dusters - for which metal fuselage panels replace the fabric covering.

Single seat versions have appeared and a closed cockpit version for the RCAF.

This chunky classic with the big radial growl is a star!

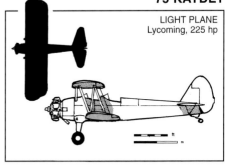

LIGHT PLANE
Lycoming, 225 hp

| DATA | IMPERIAL | | METRIC | |
|---|---|---|---|---|
| Span | 32.15 | ft | 9.8 | m |
| Wing area | 297.4 | sq ft | 27.6 | sq m |
| Aspect ratio | 7 | | 7 | |
| Empty Weight | 1931 | lb | 876 | kg |
| Loaded weight | 2635 | lb | 1196 | kg |
| Wing loading | 8.9 | lb/sq ft | 43.3 | kg/sq m |
| Max speed | 124 | mph | 200 | kmh |
| Cruise speed | 106 | mph | 170 | kmh |
| Stalling speed | 48 | mph | 77 | kmh |
| Climb rate | 1000 | ft/min | 308 | m/min |
| Range | 375 | mls | 600 | km |

Next to the Tiger Moth the Hornet is the greatest survivor of the pre WW2 de Haviland's. First flown in 1934 as an experimental aircraft for biplane wing research, it had elliptical wings and side by side seating in a well upholstered cabin.

The construction is all wood with mainly fabric covering; the rear fuselage is fabric covered over a conventional ply covered box structure to give a more pleasing/streamlined section.

In production by 1935 it was shortly modified to have square tipped, slightly tapered wings and sub typed as the DH 87B - as drawing.

The elliptical/tapered wings had some nasty habits and owners were invited to trade them in for square ones.

165 were eventually made and most were pressed into military service - three were, in fact, delivered new to the RAF - 24 survived to become 'civilians' again and today I count fifteen on the Register.

A quiet and gentle aeroplane and accepted as a valuable touring aircraft.

# DE HAVILAND
# DH 87B HORNET MOTH

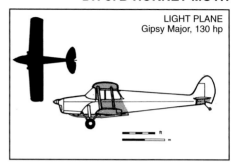

LIGHT PLANE
Gipsy Major, 130 hp

| DATA | IMPERIAL | | METRIC | |
|---|---|---|---|---|
| Span | 32 | ft | 9.8 | m |
| Wing area | 244.5 | sq ft | 23 | sq m |
| Aspect ratio | 8.4 | | 8.4 | |
| Empty Weight | 1304 | lb | 592 | kg |
| Loaded weight | 2000 | lb | 908 | kg |
| Wing loading | 8.2 | lb/sq ft | 40 | kg/sq m |
| Max speed | 124 | mph | 198 | kmh |
| Cruise speed | 105 | mph | 168 | kmh |
| Stalling speed | 45 | mph | 72 | kmh |
| Climb rate | 690 | ft/min | 212 | m/min |
| Range | 620 | mls | 992 | km |

Two Wots powered by Aeronca JAP engines were built to the design of J. R. Currie at Lympne in 1937 and were operated by Cinque Ports Aviation until both were destroyed by enemy bombing in WW2.

The Hampshire Aero Club in 1958, resurrected Currie's design and built the third Wot, and then a fourth powered by a Walter Mikron engine of 60 hp. Having given the Wot new life, plans were put on the market for home builders and there are now sixteen on the British Register, plus others being built.

The Wot is a sturdy good looking biplane with aerobatic strength and has been variously powered by VW, Continental and even, experimentally, with a Rover gas turbine.

Various scale SE5A replicas are based on the Wot airframe.

Of conventional wood and fabric construction the Wot carries te PFA seal of approval.

# CURRIE
# WOT

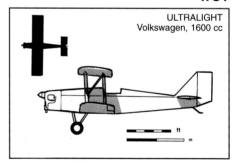

ULTRALIGHT
Volkswagen, 1600 cc

| DATA | IMPERIAL | | METRIC | |
|---|---|---|---|---|
| Span | 22.1 | ft | 6.73 | m |
| Wing area | 140 | sq ft | 13 | sq m |
| Aspect ratio | 7 | | 7 | |
| Empty Weight | 550 | lb | 250 | kg |
| Loaded weight | 900 | lb | 408 | kg |
| Wing loading | 6.4 | lb/sq ft | 31.3 | kg/sq m |
| Max speed | 95 | mph | 153 | kmh |
| Cruise speed | 90 | mph | 145 | kmh |
| Stalling speed | 40 | mph | 65 | kmh |
| Climb rate | 600 | ft/min | 183 | m/min |
| Range | 240 | mls | 385 | km |

Designed and first flown in 1945 by Curtis Pitts the Special is an out and out aerobat, that's what Pitts built it for and that's what it does best.

Originally only available in plans or kit form, the little biplane went into formal production in 1970 and to date in the region of 2000 are flying world-wide.

The main changes, over the years, have been to engine size, in 1945 the prototype had a 55 hp motor and in 1994 some are flying with 260 hp Lycomings, the most common power plant, however, is the 180 hp Lycoming.

Of standard American construction, all wood wings with metal or plywood nosing and fabric covering aft of the main spar, welded steel tube fuselage also fabric covered. The landing gear is bungee sprung with disc braked wheels.

A PFA approved type with amost 100 on the UK Register including the S2, two seater.

## PITTS
## S1 SPECIAL

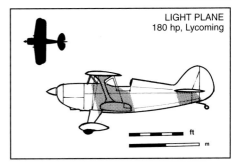

LIGHT PLANE
180 hp, Lycoming

| DATA | IMPERIAL | | METRIC | |
|---|---|---|---|---|
| Span | 17.4 | ft | 5.4 | m |
| Wing area | 96 | sq ft | 9 | sq m |
| Aspect ratio | 6.2 | | 6.2 | |
| Empty Weight | 720 | lb | 327 | kg |
| Loaded weight | 1050 | lb | 477 | kg |
| Wing loading | 11 | lb/sq ft | 54 | kg/sq m |
| Max speed | 165 | mph | 264 | kmh |
| Cruise speed | 145 | mph | 232 | kmh |
| Stalling speed | 57 | mph | 91 | kmh |
| Climb rate | 3000 | ft/min | 1362 | m/min |
| Range | 120 | mls | 192 | km |

The first Starduster was designed by Lou Stolp and George Adams for the homebuilt market in the 1950s. A two seat aerobatic sport biplane of the type that the Americans are rather good at. The fully aerobatic scaled down version is called the Acroduster.

Traditional USA construction, welded steel tube fuselage, wooden two spar wings of elliptical plan, bit of a builders headache all those ribs of different length, all fabric covered.

Ailerons may be fitted to both planes or lower plane only, in the former layout the interconnecting operating strut is apparent.

The tailplane is fully wire braced and the large vertical surfaces are a distinct feature.

The Starduster is PFA approved, fourteen are on the UK Register, mainly the Starduster Too.

## STOLP
## STARDUSTER

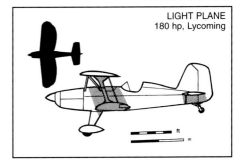

LIGHT PLANE
180 hp, Lycoming

| DATA | IMPERIAL | | METRIC | |
|---|---|---|---|---|
| Span | 24 | ft | 7.4 | m |
| Wing area | 165 | sq ft | 15.5 | sq m |
| Aspect ratio | 7 | | 7 | |
| Empty Weight | 1000 | lb | 454 | kg |
| Loaded weight | 1704 | lb | 773 | kg |
| Wing loading | 10.3 | lb/sq ft | 50 | kg/sq m |
| Max speed | 148 | mph | 237 | kmh |
| Cruise speed | 104 | mph | 166 | kmh |
| Stalling speed | 50 | mph | 90 | kmh |
| Climb rate | 1500 | ft/min | 462 | m/min |
| Range | 250 | mls | 400 | km |

John Isaac's, one time of Supermarine, designed and built this 7/10 scale replica of the RAFs famous Fury single seat fighter of the 1930s. It first flew at Thruxton in 1963 with a 65 hp Walter Mikron engine which rather spoiled the pointed cowling lines. later a flat four Lycoming engine allowed he classic fine fuselage lines to be more closely represented.

Of all wood construction with fabric covered wings the Fury has ailerons on the top plane only and like its forebear no flaps. the landing gear is bungee sprung at the axle 'V' strut intersection.

Fully aerobatic the plans have been sold world-wide and completed aircraft are flying in Australia and the USA.

It is a PFA approved design and fifeen are on the UK Register.

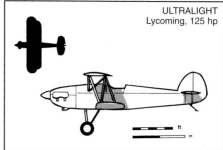

ULTRALIGHT
Lycoming, 125 hp

| DATA | IMPERIAL | | METRIC | |
|------|------|------|------|------|
| Span | 21 | ft | 6.4 | m |
| Wing area | 124 | sq ft | 11.5 | sq m |
| Aspect ratio | 6 | | 6 | |
| Empty Weight | 710 | lb | 382 | kg |
| Loaded weight | 1000 | lb | 450 | kg |
| Wing loading | 8.1 | lb/sq ft | 39.3 | kg/sq m |
| Max speed | 115 | mph | 185 | kmh |
| Cruise speed | 98 | mph | 157 | kmh |
| Stalling speed | 38 | mph | 61 | kmh |
| Climb rate | 1600 | ft/min | 488 | m/min |
| Range | 170 | mls | 272 | km |

The prototype Baby Great Lakes single seat biplane first flew in 1964 and is a scaled down version of the Great Lakes Sport Trainer of 1929 vintage, which went back into limited production in 1980.

It was designed by Andrew Oldfield of Great Lakes Airplanes in the traditional manner, welded steel tube fuselage, wooden wings and fabric covering, and when he died in 1970 the operation was taken over by Barney Oldfield and the company renamed Barney Oldfield Aircraft Co.

This tiny biplane is a nimble performer on its 80 hp., cruising at nearly 120 mph. and an initial climb rate of 2000 ft/min.

Limited aerobatics are permitted on the standard Baby' but a Super Baby Great Lakes, first flown in 1976, is fully aerobatic and has a 115 hp. Continental engine.

The design is PFA approved, ten are on the 'Register and others are under construction.

**OLDFIELD**
# BABY GREAT LAKES

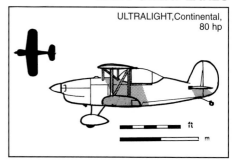

ULTRALIGHT,Continental, 80 hp

| DATA | IMPERIAL | | METRIC | |
|------|------|------|------|------|
| Span | 16.6 | ft | 5.1 | m |
| Wing area | 86 | sq ft | 8.1 | sq m |
| Aspect ratio | 6.4 | | 6.4 | |
| Empty Weight | 475 | lb | 216 | kg |
| Loaded weight | 850 | lb | 386 | kg |
| Wing loading | 9.9 | lb/sq ft | 48.2 | kg/sq m |
| Max speed | 135 | mph | 216 | kmh |
| Cruise speed | 118 | mph | 189 | kmh |
| Stalling speed | 50 | mph | 80 | kmh |
| Climb rate | 2000 | ft/min | 616 | m/min |
| Range | 250 | mls | 400 | km |

Designed by Bjorn Andreasson, the prototype was built by students at Malmo Flygindustri, Sweden and first flew in 1965.

A very small aerobatic biplane powered by a Lycoming or continental engine of 100/150 hp, the BA-4 has a sparkling performance, with a spectacular rate of climb of 2000 feet a minute and a cruising speed of 120 mph.

The metal fuselage can be married to wooden or metal wings which are spaced by a single 'I' strut. both the upper and lower wings carry ailerons for maximum roll rate. Spatted wheels are standard and later variants have a bubble canopy over the previously open cockpit.

Sound design and good record have earned the BA-4 Crosby PFA approval. Six examples of the UK licensed built Crosby BA-4 flew in 1970 and several plans-built machines are current.

ULTRALIGHT
Volkswagen, 30 hp

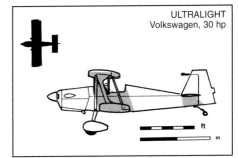

| DATA | IMPERIAL | METRIC |
|---|---|---|
| Span | 17.6 ft | 5.42 m |
| Wing area | 89.3 sq ft | 8.4 sq m |
| Aspect ratio | 7 | 7 |
| Empty Weight | 500 lb | 227 kg |
| Loaded weight | 827 lb | 45 kg |
| Wing loading | 9.26 lb/sq ft | 375 kg/sq m |
| Max speed | 140 mph | 224 kmh |
| Cruise speed | 120 mph | 142 kmh |
| Stalling speed | 45 mph | 72 kmh |
| Climb rate | 2000 ft/min | 616 m/min |
| Range | 250 mls | 320 km |

First flown in 1968, the two seat CB-1 is a PFA approved plans-built biplane, three of which are on the UK Register and others are under construction.

The fabric covered, 'N' strut braced, wings are of all wood construction. There are ailerons on all wings, no flaps and the top plane has zero dihedral. The fuselage is of welded steel tube with fabric covering, as is the tail unit, which is wire braced.

A Piper J3, bungee sprung, undercarriage is employed in the tail-dragger configuration with a steerable tail-wheel. The main wheels contain Piper J3 brakes, are usually spatted and many have the u/c 'V' struts faired together.

The style of the CB-1 is distinctly 'retro' and it is extremely popular in the USA where many are flying and a thriving Hatz CB-1 association – and web site – supplies plans, advice and news.

The prototype was powered by a Continental C85 of 85 hp. but the design is cleared for engines up to 150 hp. (Figures below for 150 hp. model). Five are on the UK Register.

LIGHT PLANE
Lycoming, 150 hp

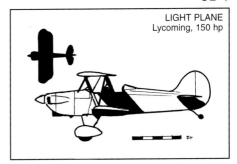

| DATA | IMPERIAL | METRIC |
|---|---|---|
| Span | 26 ft | 7.9 m |
| Wing area | 190 sq ft | 17.6 sq m |
| Aspect ratio | 6.7 | |
| Empty Weight | 996 lb | 438 kg |
| Loaded weight | 1600 lb | 726 kg |
| Wing loading | 8.4 lb/sq ft | 41 kg/sq m |
| Max speed | 130 mph | 208 kmh |
| Cruise speed | 87 mph | 100 kmh |
| Stalling speed | 45 mph | 72 kmh |
| Climb rate | 1200 ft/min | 366 m/min |
| Range | 270 mls | 434 km |

Designed by Ed Marquart in the USA and first flown in 1970, the MA-5 Charger is a 'classic' American bi-plane with a welded steel tube fuselage, twin solid wood wing spars and fabric covering. The neat undercarriage comprises a steel box leg with rubber in compression blocks within the fuselage.

It is a plans-only aeroplane and not for the first time builder, but when completed it is a beautiful two seater with aerobatic capability.

All the wings are swept back, in the manner of a Bucker, and mount four ailerons which are push rod operated, as are the elevators - the rudder relies on cable operation.

Toe brakes and a steerable tail-wheel make for ease of taxying.

A range of engines have been fitted to the hundred, or so, that have been built with powers of 125 to 180 hp.

There are two on the UK Register.

## MARQUART
## MA-5 CHARGER

LIGHT PLANE
Lycoming, 125 hp

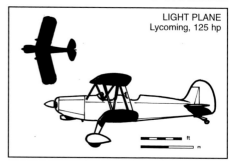

| DATA | IMPERIAL | METRIC |
|---|---|---|
| Span | 24 ft | 7.4 m |
| Wing area | 172 sq ft | 16.1 sq m |
| Aspect ratio | 5 | 5 |
| Empty Weight | 1000 lb | 454 kg |
| Loaded weight | 1550 lb | 704 kg |
| Wing loading | 10.6 lb/sq ft | 52 kg/sq m |
| Max speed | 1250 mph | 200 kmh |
| Cruise speed | 1160 mph | 185 kmh |
| Stalling speed | 43 mph | 69 kmh |
| Climb rate | 12000 ft/min | 308 m/min |
| Range | 345 mls | 552 km |

Lamar Steen, an aerospace teacher in Denver, Colorado, designed the Skybolt in 1968, as a project for his students! the resulting two seater aerobatic biplane first took to the air in 1970 with a 180 hp Lycoming and an airframe stressed for +12-10g. It was, in fact, the first two seat aerobatic plane to get type approval.

The construction is typical American Classic welded steel tube fuselage with fabric covering, two spar wooden wing with aluminium leading edge and fabric covering aft of the front spar and ailerons on upper and lower planes. The wheels are bungee sprung and hydraulically braked with spats as standard fit.

Steen claims that 600 Skybolts are flying in twenty-two countries and that includes fourteen in the UK where it is PFA approved.

## STEEN
## SKYBOLT

LIGHT PLANE
Lycoming, 85-200 hp

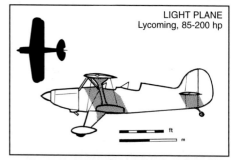

| DATA | IMPERIAL | METRIC |
|---|---|---|
| Span | 24 ft | 7.4 m |
| Wing area | 152 sq ft | 14.3 sq m |
| Aspect ratio | 7.5 | 7.5 |
| Empty Weight | 1250 lb | 567 kg |
| Loaded weight | 1800 lb | 817 kg |
| Wing loading | 11.8 lb/sq ft | 58 kg/sq m |
| Max speed | 145 mph | 232 kmh |
| Cruise speed | 115 mph | 184 kmh |
| Stalling speed | 55 mph | 88 kmh |
| Climb rate | 1600 ft/min | 493 m/min |
| Range | 250 mls | 400 km |

Paul Poberezny, founder of the Experimental Aircraft Association (EAA), designed the Acrosport as an easy build aerobatic single seater the prototype flying in 1972 - this aeroplane is now in the Air Adventure Museum at Oshkosh.

Many Acrosports were subsequently built, mainly in the USA, including the two seat Acrosport 2 - slightly bigger but virtually identical in appearance. Eleven are on the UK Register with another four under construction.

The construction is 'standard American' i.e.. welded steel tube fuselage with light wooden fabric covered fairings, wooden spar wings with wood and metal ribs all fabric covered. There are inset ailerons on both upper and lower planes, linked by a strut, and the two fuel tanks have a capacity of 27 gall.(85 Lt).

The upper plane has an extensive cut out to improve upward vision.

Data below is for the 180 hp. single seat version, note the spectacular rate of climb!

# EAA ACROSPORT

LIGHT PLANE
Lycoming, 85-200 hp

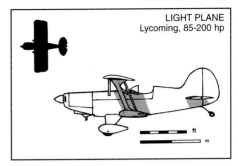

| DATA | IMPERIAL | | METRIC | |
|---|---|---|---|---|
| Span | 19.6 | ft | 6 | m |
| Wing area | 115 | sq ft | 10.8 | sq m |
| Aspect ratio | 6.6 | | 6.6 | |
| Empty Weight | 739 | lb | 335 | kg |
| Loaded weight | 1178 | lb | 534 | kg |
| Wing loading | 10.2 | lb/sq ft | 49.7 | kg/sq m |
| Max speed | 150 | mph | 240 | kmh |
| Cruise speed | 130 | mph | 208 | kmh |
| Stalling speed | 55 | mph | 88 | kmh |
| Climb rate | 3500 | ft/min | 1078 | m/min |
| Range | 400 | mls | 640 | km |

The all metal Scamp is manufactured and kitted in the USA by Aerosport Ltd and is a NASAD (National Association Sport aircraft Designers) approved design.

First flown in 1973, its simple construction soon gained many fans and by 1985 over 800 plans had been sold, thirty-six were flying in the USA, three on the UK Register and one being built to PFA approval.

Designed to operate from grass strips it has light alloy cantilever sprung main wheels and the whole ship is stressed to +6-3g, giving it a limited aerobatic category. A crop sprayer version, the Scamp B, was put into production in Columbia in 1983.

The all metal biplane wings are wire braced, the centre section being supported by a single sturdy strut it has no flaps or trim tabs.

# AEROSPORT SCAMP

ULTRALIGHT
Volkswagen, 60 hp

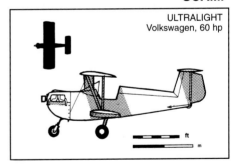

| DATA | IMPERIAL | | METRIC | |
|---|---|---|---|---|
| Span | 17.5 | ft | 5.4 | m |
| Wing area | 105 | sq ft | 9.8 | sq m |
| Aspect ratio | 5.8 | | 5.8 | |
| Empty Weight | 630 | lb | 240 | kg |
| Loaded weight | 780 | lb | 354 | kg |
| Wing loading | 7.4 | lb/sq ft | 36 | kg/sq m |
| Max speed | 105 | mph | 168 | kmh |
| Cruise speed | 90 | mph | 144 | kmh |
| Stalling speed | 45 | mph | 72 | kmh |
| Climb rate | 800 | ft/min | 246 | m/min |
| Range | 125 | mls | 200 | km |

Developed from a range of light biplanes the SN7 is the kit plane version of the SN6 which was a design prize winner at Oshkosh in 1973, the year the prototype SN7 first flew.

The fuselage is of welded steel tube with fabric and GRP panel covering, as is the empennage. The back-staggered wings are all wood with plywood skin, the inter-plane struts are steel.

The landing gear has spring steel Wittman legs and disc brakes, the steerable tail wheel is by Maule. Metal flaperons are fitted to both planes and are operated by torque tubes from the standard dual controls. The fuselage tapers in side view but is untapered in plan. the tailplane shape is reminiscent of Concorde!

A fast cruising biplane of distinctive lines, only one of which is on the British Register, many more in the US.

### SORRELL
### SN-7 HIPERBIPE

LIGHT PLANE
Lycoming, 180 hp

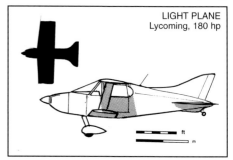

| DATA | IMPERIAL | | METRIC | |
|---|---|---|---|---|
| Span | 22.8 | ft | 9.76 | m |
| Wing area | 135 | sq ft | 12.7 | sq m |
| Aspect ratio | 7.5 | | 7.5 | |
| Empty Weight | 1576 | lb | 715 | kg |
| Loaded weight | 2535 | lb | 1146 | kg |
| Wing loading | 18.8 | lb/sq ft | 91.6 | kg/sq m |
| Max speed | 161 | mph | 257 | kmh |
| Cruise speed | 150 | mph | 240 | kmh |
| Stalling speed | 61 | mph | 98 | kmh |
| Climb rate | 940 | ft/min | 290 | m/min |
| Range | 745 | mls | 1192 | km |

First flown in 1977 and supplied in kit form from that year, the Eagle, a two seat aerobatic biplane, was developed from the single seat Eagle 1.

The designer Frank Christensen of Wyoming, who later acquired the Pitts Company, had a Pitts replacement in mind when he draughted the Eagle specifically for the home build market.

The structure of the Eagle is conventional american i.e. welded steel tube fuselage, part metal and part fabric covered, the wings have wooden spars and ribs, metal leading and trailing edges and is all fabric covered.

The interplane 'I' struts are steel as are the undercarriage legs.

Christensen manufactured both Pitts and Eagle kits in to the mid 1980s.

Over 700 kits have been sold, half of which are flying. the type is a PFA approved design with seven on the UK Register.

### CHRISTEN
### EAGLE 2

LIGHT PLANE
Lycoming, 200 hp

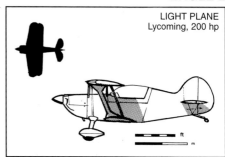

| DATA | IMPERIAL | | METRIC | |
|---|---|---|---|---|
| Span | 19.9 | ft | 6.13 | m |
| Wing area | 125 | sq ft | 11.7 | sq m |
| Aspect ratio | 6.3 | | 6.3 | |
| Empty Weight | 1081 | lb | 491 | kg |
| Loaded weight | 1600 | lb | 726 | kg |
| Wing loading | 12.8 | lb/sq ft | 62.6 | kg/sq m |
| Max speed | 184 | mph | 294 | kmh |
| Cruise speed | 165 | mph | 264 | kmh |
| Stalling speed | 58 | mph | 93 | kmh |
| Climb rate | 2100 | ft/min | 647 | m/min |
| Range | 380 | mls | 608 | km |

One of the earlier UK microlights, the Tiger Cub was designed by Tom Wright and originally known as the Micro Bipe.

Initially powered by a 35 hp Fuji Robin engine the Tiger Cub was a single seat tail-dragger as shown in the drawing. Two seat and tricycle undercarriage versions were projected, some of the latter, in fact, flying, but the company, Micro Biplane Aviation of Nottingham went into liquidation in 1984 after 150 kits had been sold.

An export version failed, initially, to meet foreign airworthiness requirements resulting in much delay and aeronautical angst.

The wings have light alloy spars with a foam aerofoil section infill, the whole being covered in heat shrink fabric giving smooth and stiff wings.

On early models an all moving tailplane and rudder were fitted with ailerons on the lower plane only. Later models had flaperons on the lower plane and ailerons on the top and a large fin in front of the rudder but retained the all moving tailplane.

There are thirty-four on the UK Register, only one of which appears to be airworthy.

# MBA
# TIGER CUB

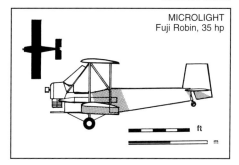

MICROLIGHT
Fuji Robin, 35 hp

| DATA | IMPERIAL | | METRIC | |
|------|----------|---|--------|---|
| Span | 21 | ft | 6.4 | m |
| Wing area | 140 | sq ft | 13 | sq m |
| Aspect ratio | 6.6 | | 6.6 | |
| Empty Weight | 284 | lb | 129 | kg |
| Loaded weight | 551 | lb | 250 | kg |
| Wing loading | 3.9 | lb/sq ft | 19.2 | kg/sq m |
| Max speed | 69 | mph | 111 | kmh |
| Cruise speed | 52 | mph | 83 | kmh |
| Stalling speed | 29 | mph | 47 | kmh |
| Climb rate | 490 | ft/min | 150 | m/min |
| Range | 75 | mls | 120 | km |

Developed from the Renegade 2, the Spirit is a Canadian design that has found a firm following in the UK.

Surprisingly, for such a sturdy two seat biplane, +1-16g, the Spirit is a microlight, but only when fitted with the Rotax 503. The Rotax 912 engined Renegade fails outside the microlight limit.

The airframe is all metal with rivetted light alloy tubes incorporating patented extruded alloy joints. Alloy tube main spars with pressed alloy ribs form the wings, the whole being covered in Stits fabric.

There are ailerons on both sets of wings linked by a connecting strut and the landing gear has a steerable tail wheel and braked wheels.

A Subaru car engined version has recently flown in the USA. There are thirty-four on the UK Register and four being built.

# MURPHY
# RENEGADE SPIRIT

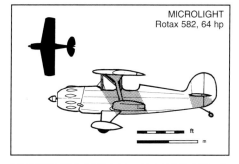

MICROLIGHT
Rotax 582, 64 hp

| DATA | IMPERIAL | | METRIC | |
|------|----------|---|--------|---|
| Span | 24.5 | ft | 7.54 | m |
| Wing area | 172 | sq ft | 16.2 | sq m |
| Aspect ratio | 7 | | 7 | |
| Empty Weight | 390 | lb | 177 | kg |
| Loaded weight | 850 | lb | 386 | kg |
| Wing loading | 5 | lb/sq ft | 24.4 | kg/sq m |
| Max speed | 90 | mph | 144 | kmh |
| Cruise speed | 80 | mph | 128 | kmh |
| Stalling speed | 33 | mph | 53 | kmh |
| Climb rate | 1300 | ft/min | 400 | m/min |
| Range | 240 | mls | 384 | km |

The BGP-1 is an all wood single seat sport biplane, designed and built by Barry Plumb of Leighton Buzzard, Bedfordshire. The prototype aircraft was first flown in 1986 and received a full Permit to Fly in 1987.

The aircraft was powered by a 55 hp. 1834cc. Volkswagen until a 80 hp. Jabiru engine was installed.

The aircraft has an open cockpit and a small luggage bay behind the pilot's seat. Ailerons are fitted to the top wing only and all controls are sensitive and well harmonised. An unusual feature is the single lift strut in place of conventional wire bracing for the wings. Construction is all wood with birch ply and fabric covering to the fuselage and fabric covering of the open structure flying surfaces.

A second example is currently under construction in Cornwall, being built from updated drawings. The updated aircraft has increased span but retains the same wing area and general appearance as the prototype. The updated design is currently undergoing approval scrutiny by the PFA, following which plans will be made available

**PLUMB**
# BGP-1 BIPLANE

ULTRALIGHT
Volkswagen, 55 hp

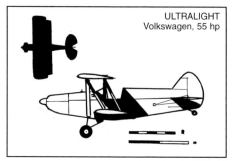

| DATA | IMPERIAL | | METRIC | |
|---|---|---|---|---|
| Span | 16 | ft | 4.9 | m |
| Wing area | 100 | sq ft | 9.8 | sq m |
| Aspect ratio | 4.6 | | 4.6 | |
| Empty Weight | 525 | lb | 231 | kg |
| Loaded weight | 800 | lb | 363 | kg |
| Wing loading | 8 | lb/sq ft | 39 | kg/sq m |
| Max speed | 103 | mph | 165 | kmh |
| Cruise speed | 78 | mph | 125 | kmh |
| Stalling speed | 45 | mph | 72 | kmh |
| Climb rate | 650 | ft/min | 200 | m/min |
| Range | 150 | mls | 240 | km |

A popular ultralight in France with eleven now on the UK Register.

The extremely short build time, due to many pre-assembled units, caused it to be de-classified as a kit plane in 1993. In his home country or more are flying, not only as ARV, but being capable of cropdusting, aerial TV and police work.

Of unusual appearance, the Mistral has swept forward wings, spatted tricycle undercarriage and an un-biplane-like pod and boom fuselage and an enclosed cockpit.

The wings have Dural spars, wooden ribs and Dacron covering, the lower planes are all-moving and act as ailerons. The tailplane/elevator is all-moving and of similar construction.GRP and composites are used for the pod and boom, which houses the three axis controls. The landing gear is sprung and braked.

**AVIASUD**
# MISTRAL

ULTRALIGHT
Rotax 532, 63 hp

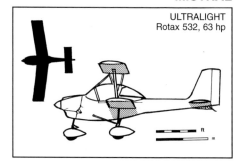

| DATA | IMPERIAL | | METRIC | |
|---|---|---|---|---|
| Span | 30.8 | ft | 9.4 | m |
| Wing area | 192.7 | sq ft | 17.9 | sq m |
| Aspect ratio | 9.3 | | 9.3 | |
| Empty Weight | 383 | lb | 174 | kg |
| Loaded weight | 882 | lb | 400 | kg |
| Wing loading | 4.58 | lb/sq ft | 22.3 | kg/sq m |
| Max speed | 93 | mph | 150 | kmh |
| Cruise speed | 84 | mph | 135 | kmh |
| Stalling speed | 38 | mph | 60 | kmh |
| Climb rate | 785 | ft/min | 240 | m/min |
| Range | 310 | mls | 500 | km |

The all British Sherwood Ranger, developed by Russell Light of TCD Ltd. at Larkfield, South Yorkshire, first flew in 1993, and is a very tidy biplane of vintage, yet modern lines.

Available in the microlight category as the LW and the more powerful and heavier ST ultralight. Both are two seaters, though single seat versions are available in both types. A further model, the XP, which is fully aerobatic, is currently under development.

The Ranger's fuselage is built up with light alloy tubing, the joining fish plates and brackets being secured with 'pop' rivets. A fabric skin is smoothly streamlined over light wooden formers. The wings, have light alloy spars and plywood ribs, and are fabric covered, with ailerons on both upper and lower planes.

The wings fold, a la 'Moth, alongside the fuselage and re-rigging takes only three minutes!

The undercarriage is bungee sprung and has differentially braked wheels plus a castoring tail wheel.

The prototype, G-WND, is shortly to be joined by several homebuilt, one of which is flying in the USA.

There are eight on the UK Register.

## SHERWOOD RANGER

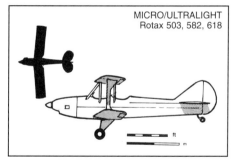

MICRO/ULTRALIGHT
Rotax 503, 582, 618

| DATA | IMPERIAL | | METRIC | |
|---|---|---|---|---|
| Span | 26 | ft | 8 | m |
| Wing area | 168 | sq ft | 15.8 | sq m |
| Aspect ratio | 8 | | 7 | |
| Empty Weight | 400 | lb | 181 | kg |
| Loaded weight | 860 | lb | 390 | kg |
| Wing loading | 5.1 | lb/sq ft | 24.8 | kg/sq m |
| Max speed | 80 | mph | 130 | kmh |
| Cruise speed | 67 | mph | 107 | kmh |
| Stalling speed | 40 | mph | 64 | kmh |
| Climb rate | 650 | ft/min | 200 | m/min |
| Range | 350 | mls | 560 | km |

Designed by Lynn Williams and built by Sky Craft Ltd, the Flitzer first flew in 1995 powered by a 1600 cc. VW engine. William's aim was to design a 'vintage' looking aeroplane of simple construction unrestrained by the slavish following of true scale/replica work. This has been achieved in the truly distinctive shape of the Flitzer, which is badged as Staaken, the WW1 German aircraft manufacturer.

The Flitzer is powered by a 1834 cc. VW engine (prototype had the 1600) and has the 'registration' D692 displayed on its wings and fuselage - its official UK registration is G-BVAW. A second aircraft is being built with Bell Aeromarine backing at time of writing, and another privately. (Five now on UK Register).

The wooden structure with fabric covering has the minimum of metal fittings and has, with its single 'I' struts , 'A' frame cabin and unswept wings, simple rigging requirements. The stalky 'gear is 'classic', three axles, two fixed and one moving with bungee wrap around.

## STAAKEN FLITZER

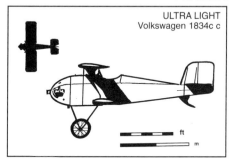

ULTRA LIGHT
Volkswagen 1834c c

| DATA | IMPERIAL | | METRIC | |
|---|---|---|---|---|
| Span | 18 | ft | 5.5 | m |
| Wing area | 97 | sq ft | 9.1 | sq m |
| Aspect ratio | 6.5 | | 6.5 | |
| Empty Weight | 480 | lb | 218 | kg |
| Loaded weight | 750 | lb | 337 | kg |
| Wing loading | 7.51 | lb/sq ft | 24.8 | kg/sq m |
| Max speed | 86 | mph | 138 | kmh |
| Cruise speed | 75 | mph | 120 | kmh |
| Stalling speed | 42 | mph | 67 | kmh |
| Climb rate | 700 | ft/min | 216 | m/min |
| Range | 300 | mls | 480 | km |

An early British light twin, the Monospar evolved around the novel monospar wing designed by the Swiss H J Stieger. The first version, the ST3 was built by Gloster's for the Monospar Wing Co in 1929. The ST3 was encouraging and General Aircraft was formed to build Monospars, based briefly at Croydon and finally at Hanworth.

The subsequent models were all rather similar except for the ST6 and ST11 which had retractable undercarriages and an experimental model with a, fixed nose wheel, tricycle undercarriage. The last in the range the ST25 had twin fins.

The Monospars were four seaters of mixed wood and metal construction with fabric covering and the engines were usually Pobjoy radials though the ST12 had Gipsy Majors.

Used by small airlines and taxi firms, 57 of the distinctive and sturdy Monospars were built – about half of them going abroad. With WW2 twelve assorted Monospars were impressed but did not survive the war.

In 1961 an Australian ST12 made an epic flight back to the UK and now, after many years storage, is being restored at Newark. In museums, Denmark one, New Zealand one.

# GENERAL AIRCRAFT
# MONOSPAR

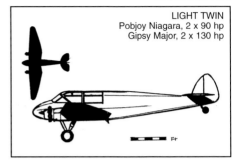

LIGHT TWIN
Pobjoy Niagara, 2 x 90 hp
Gipsy Major, 2 x 130 hp

| DATA | IMPERIAL | | METRIC | |
|---|---|---|---|---|
| Span | 40.16 | ft | 12.3 | m |
| Wing area | 217 | sq ft | 20.4 | sq m |
| Aspect ratio | 7.4 | | | |
| Empty Weight | 1840 | lb | 835 | kg |
| Loaded weight | 2875 | lb | 1305 | kg |
| Wing loading | 13.2 | lb/sq ft | 64 | kg/sq m |
| Max speed | 158 | mph | 253 | kmh |
| Cruise speed | 142 | mph | 227 | kmh |
| Stalling speed | 55 | mph | 88 | kmh |
| Climb rate | 1233 | ft/min | 380 | m/min |
| Range | 410 | mls | 656 | km |

The Percival P16 Q6 a pre war light twin carried four or five passengers and a crew of two; it was of all wood construction and beautiful lines.

First flown in 1937, the Q6 had a trousered undercarriage, split trailing edge flaps, VP airscrews and radio as standard. Four of the 22 aircraft built had retractable undercarriages resulting in a very sleek and crisp performer (183 mph cruise).

Five Q6s were sold abroad, two going to Lithuania and others to India, Iraq and Belgium. (French and Australian registrations were taken out for two but these were never delivered).

The Q6s had just about got into service with various companies and small charter airlines when war broke out and most were impressed for RAF and Navy communications work. They later acquired military marks and were referred to as the Petrel – this appellation was, it is said, never 'official').

Three 'Petrels' survived the war plus four others, but their numbers quickly diminished, the last 'flyer' retiring in 1954. One, G-AFFD, has been resurrected and is on long-term restoration on the Isle of Man. (Two others, or parts thereof, may exist in storage).

The data below is for the fixed gear version.

# PERCIVAL
# Q6

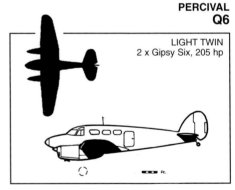

LIGHT TWIN
2 x Gipsy Six, 205 hp

| DATA | IMPERIAL | | METRIC | |
|---|---|---|---|---|
| Span | 46.8 | ft | 14.3 | m |
| Wing area | 278 | sq ft | 26 | sq m |
| Aspect ratio | 7.8 | | | |
| Empty Weight | 3500 | lb | 1569 | kg |
| Loaded weight | 5500 | lb | 2497 | kg |
| Wing loading | 19.8 | lb/sq ft | 96 | kg/sq m |
| Max speed | 195 | mph | 312 | kmh |
| Cruise speed | 175 | mph | 260 | kmh |
| Stalling speed | 50 | mph | 80 | kmh |
| Climb rate | 1150 | ft/min | 354 | m/min |
| Range | 750 | mls | 1200 | km |

A light twin from the 1930s, the 6/8 seat Dragon is the same weight as a Piper Seneca.

First flown in 1932 the big wood and fabric biplane with high aspect ratio wings has two Gipsy Major engines and was the mainstay of many of the UK's smaller airlines. Over 100 were built at Hatfield and somewhat fewer at DH in Australia. The Mk 2 had faired main-wheels and separate cabin windows, and was slightly faster than the MK 1.

In 1933 Jim and Amy Mollison used a Dragon for an attempt on the World Long Distance Record, but after flying across the Atlantic, crashed in Connecticut. The rebuilt Dragon was flown back to the UK by J. Ayling and L. Reid and became the first aircraft to fly non-stop from Canada to Great Britain.

Twenty Dragons were impressed at the outbreak of WW2, very few survived, one actually being shot down by a German aircraft. One Dublin based Dragon is still flying, G-ECAN, an Australian-built Dragon is now flying in the UK. One is on re-build and another is at Wroughton. Three in museums abroad Australia, New Zealand and United States.

Figures below are for the Mk 2.

## DE HAVILAND
## DH84 DRAGON

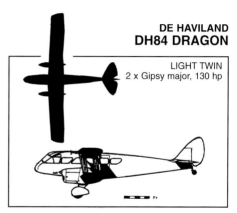

LIGHT TWIN
2 x Gipsy major, 130 hp

| DATA | IMPERIAL | | METRIC | |
|---|---|---|---|---|
| Span | 47.3 | ft | 14.6 | m |
| Wing area | 376 | sq ft | 35.3 | sq m |
| Aspect ratio | 12 | | | |
| Empty Weight | 2336 | lb | 1060 | kg |
| Loaded weight | 4500 | lb | 2043 | kg |
| Wing loading | 12 | lb/sq ft | 58.5 | kg/sq m |
| Max speed | 134 | mph | 214 | kmh |
| Cruise speed | 114 | mph | 182 | kmh |
| Stalling speed | 50 | mph | 80 | kmh |
| Climb rate | 565 | ft/min | 174 | m/min |
| Range | 545 | mls | 872 | km |

When the Miles M65 Gemini prototype first flew in 1945, powered by a 100 hp Cirrus Minor, fast four seat civil twins were thin on the ground, the American twin invasion being some years in the future.

In the region of 160 Geminis, virtually a twin engined M28 messenger, were built at Reading, many of them being exported world wide.

Of all wooden construction the Gemini had an electrically operated retractable undercarriage, auxiliary aerofoil flaps and twin fins combined with a luxurious cabin interior.

Many large companies bought them including Shell, and it was the executive fast twin on its day. Fast indeed, G-AKDC won the 1949 Kings Cup at 165 mph.

Various engines were fitted including the 125 hp Continental C-125-2 and the Cirrus Major of 155 hp.

Ten are still shown on the UK Register,four still flying as a reminder of a ground breaking design by a company of brilliant designers and not so brilliant bookkeepers. Miles folded in 1948.

## MILES
## M65 GEMINI

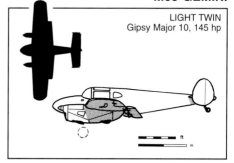

LIGHT TWIN
Gipsy Major 10, 145 hp

| DATA | IMPERIAL | | METRIC | |
|---|---|---|---|---|
| Span | 36.2 | ft | 11.1 | m |
| Wing area | 191 | sq ft | 17.9 | sq m |
| Aspect ratio | 6.8 | | 6.8 | |
| Empty Weight | 1896 | lb | 860 | kg |
| Loaded weight | 3000 | lb | 1362 | kg |
| Wing loading | 15.7 | lb/sq ft | 76.6 | kg/sq m |
| Max speed | 140 | mph | 224 | kmh |
| Cruise speed | 125 | mph | 200 | kmh |
| Stalling speed | 50 | mph | 80 | kmh |
| Climb rate | 550 | ft/min | 170 | m/min |
| Range | 820 | mls | 1312 | km |

A Czechoslovakian twin designed to replace the ageing tail-dragger the Aero 145 (first flew 1947).

The LET 200A first flew in 1969 powered by 160 hp. Walter Minors; after 160 had been built the engine was changed to the more powerful Walter M337 of 210 hp. this remained the standard power unit for the rest of the production run of 1000. These later aircraft were designated LET 200D.

The Morava is a distinctive twin, having inverted in-line engines, Dornier-like twin fins and a retractable tricycle undercarriage. The substantially framed dome-like cabin houses a pilot and 'co-pilot' in the front seats and three passengers on a rear bench seat. There is also an arrangement for loading two stretcher cases.

The construction is all metal, the wing has a high-ish aspect ratio and the 200Ds have three blade constant speed props.

Supplied in some quantity to Aeroflot and built under licence in Yugoslavia, there are two on the UK Register.

# LET
# MORAVA

LIGHT TWIN
2 x Walte, 210 hp

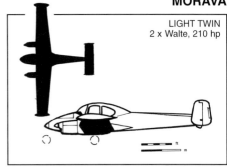

| DATA | IMPERIAL | | METRIC | |
|---|---|---|---|---|
| Span | 40.5 | ft | 12.3 | m |
| Wing area | 186 | sq ft | 17.3 | sq m |
| Aspect ratio | 8.8 | | 8.8 | |
| Empty Weight | 2932 | lb | 1330 | kg |
| Loaded weight | 4300 | lb | 1950 | kg |
| Wing loading | 23.1 | lb/sq ft | 113 | kg/sq m |
| Max speed | 157 | mph | 290 | kmh |
| Cruise speed | 138 | mph | 256 | kmh |
| Stalling speed | 60 | mph | 96 | kmh |
| Climb rate | 1260 | ft/min | 388 | m/min |
| Range | 1068 | mls | 1710 | km |

Developed from the Twin Stinson, the Apache is a senior member of the light American twin fraternity having first flown in 1952. It was Pipers first twin and had a 'rag and pipe' fuselage and a fixed tricycle undercarriage. Production models were all metal stressed skin construction and powered by 160 hp Lycoming O-320s.

Apache models followed with the suffix denoting engine horse power, though not always, i.e. the PA-23-160 appearing in 1959 and the most powerful PA-23-235 coming in 1962.

The Apache is a four seater with provision for an occasional fifth, a cruising speed of 200 mph and a production tally of over 2000, eighty-eight of which are on the UK Register, including Aztecs.

The Apache blurred into the PA 23 Aztec, the intermediate models being externally identical until the Aztec developed a longer nose and could carry up to six people, all Aztecs have higher powered engines including turbo charged versions and have overtaken the Apache with 5000 produced, over 100 being on the UK Register. Apache had rounded fin but the Apache 235 had the swept fin used on the Aztec. Data below for PA-23-235.

# PIPER
# PA 23 APACHE

LIGHT TWIN
Lycoming, 235 hp

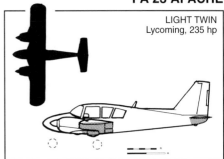

AZTEC

| DATA | IMPERIAL | | METRIC | |
|---|---|---|---|---|
| Span | 37.1 | ft | 11.4 | m |
| Wing area | 207 | sq ft | 19.5 | sq m |
| Aspect ratio | 6.6 | | 6.6 | |
| Empty Weight | 2735 | lb | 1241 | kg |
| Loaded weight | 4800 | lb | 2179 | kg |
| Wing loading | 23.2 | lb/sq ft | 113 | kg/sq m |
| Max speed | 202 | mph | 323 | kmh |
| Cruise speed | 191 | mph | 305 | kmh |
| Stalling speed | 70 | mph | 112 | kmh |
| Climb rate | 1485 | ft/min | 446 | m/min |
| Range | 1185 | mls | 1896 | km |

The first new De Haviland aircraft to fly after WW2. the aptly named Dove, an all metal twin, first flew in September 1945.

Though this was sixty years ago the Dove still looks good and as testimony to the sound desing, there are still thirty on the UK Civil Register.

As the Devon, the military version, it was supplied to many overseas air forces as well as thirty-nine for the RAF. Many of these military models are still in active service in far flung parts of the globe. UK production ceased in 1957 but in the 1960s two U.S. companies thought there was more mileage in the hard working Dove and built re-engined and lengthened version, some of which are still operating. The Dove carried two pilots, side by side, and eight passengers, cruised at 179mph and had a range of 500 miles. 528 in all were built.

# DE HAVILAND
# DH 104 DOVE

LIGHT TWIN
2 x Gipsy Queens 2 x 340hp

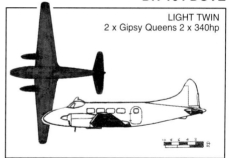

| DATA | IMPERIAL | | METRIC | |
|---|---|---|---|---|
| Span | 57 | ft | 17.4 | m |
| Wing area | 335 | sq ft | 31.5 | sq m |
| Aspect ratio | 9.6 | | 9.6 | |
| Empty Weight | 5650 | lb | 2565 | kg |
| Loaded weight | 8500 | lb | 3859 | kg |
| Wing loading | 25.4 | lb/sq ft | 123.8 | kg/sq m |
| Max speed | 210 | mph | 336 | kmh |
| Cruise speed | 179 | mph | 286 | kmh |
| Stalling speed | 65 | mph | 104 | kmh |
| Climb rate | 750 | ft/min | 228 | m/min |
| Range | 500 | mls | 800 | km |

Another classic American twin, the Beech 55 Baron which first flew in 1960 was developed from the Model 95 Travel Air of 1956, which, though similar, had a vertical fin and rudder and the lower powered 180 hp. Lycomings. In 1962 the improved A55 appeared, followed in '64 by the B55 with lengthened fuselage.

In 1965 came the C55 with 260 hp. Continentals, which is illustrated here.

A military version, designated T42 A, serves in the USAAF as an instrument trainer.

The Baron is all metal and can carry 5 to 6 passengers (plus pilot), can cruise at 230 mph. and has had a production run of over 6000 - including all variants.

Variants are, the A56 Turbo Baron, the model 58 with longer cabin and the 58P, which is pressurised.

There are more than thirty-seven Barons, including three Model 95 Travel Airs, on the UK Register flying as company or taxi aircraft.

Very similar to the Piper PA 30 Navajo and PA 31 Twin Comanche, the Baron has a slightly lower aspect ratio fin and rudder.

# BEECH
# C55 BARON

LIGHT TWIN
2 x Continental, 260 hp

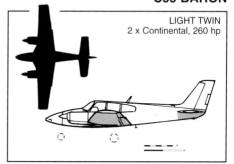

| DATA | IMPERIAL | | METRIC | |
|---|---|---|---|---|
| Span | 37.8 | ft | 11.6 | m |
| Wing area | 199.2 | sq ft | 18.7 | sq m |
| Aspect ratio | 7.2 | | 7.2 | |
| Empty Weight | 3025 | lb | 1373 | kg |
| Loaded weight | 5300 | lb | 2405 | kg |
| Wing loading | 26.6 | lb/sq ft | 130 | kg/sq m |
| Max speed | 242 | mph | 387 | kmh |
| Cruise speed | 230 | mph | 368 | kmh |
| Stalling speed | 70 | mph | 112 | kmh |
| Climb rate | 1670 | ft/min | 514 | m/min |
| Range | 1143 | mls | 1828 | km |

Since the prototype first flew in 1953 (forty six years ago!) 10,000 had been made when production ceased in 1981, many thousands of which are still flying world wide; one of the all time successful private light twins.

Of all metal construction, the first '310s had a vertical fin and rudder, 240 hp. Continental 0-470-B engines, five seats and wing tip tanks. The 310 D followed, introducing the swept fin and rudder; the 310 G was a six seater and introduced the 310's 'trade mark' - the upswept tip tanks. The 310 G has a longer nose baggage compartment.

The six seat versions have an extra window at the rear.

Looking similar, the '320 Skyknight is a stretched six seater with turbocharged engines and the '340 is pressurised - easily identified by its circular cabin windows.

Military versions in service with the USAAF are typed as U3-A and U3-B.

Access is by a car type door on the starboard side, full dual control and lavish instrumentation, split flaps plus the smooth American automobile interior finish make this a real little airliner.

There are around forty-nine on the UK Register.

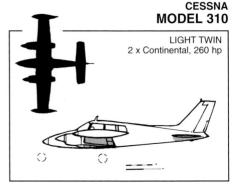

## CESSNA
# MODEL 310

LIGHT TWIN
2 x Continental, 260 hp

| DATA | IMPERIAL | | METRIC | |
|---|---|---|---|---|
| Span | 36.7 | ft | 11.3 | m |
| Wing area | 179 | sq ft | 16.8 | sq m |
| Aspect ratio | 7.5 | | 7.5 | |
| Empty Weight | 3125 | lb | 1418 | kg |
| Loaded weight | 5200 | lb | 2360 | kg |
| Wing loading | 29 | lb/sq ft | 141.7 | kg/sq m |
| Max speed | 222 | mph | 355 | kmh |
| Cruise speed | 179 | mph | 286 | kmh |
| Stalling speed | 74 | mph | 118 | kmh |
| Climb rate | 1540 | ft/min | 474 | m/min |
| Range | 966 | mls | 1545 | km |

A post war British aviation success story. The boxy ten-seat Islander the brain-child of John Britten and Des Norman, first saw the light of day on the Isle of Wight in 1964, since then over 1,250 have been built and are operating all over the world.

The Islander is, in effect, a modern replacement for the pre-war work-horse the DH Rapide – but is an all-metal monoplane mainly produced with Lycoming 260 hp but the BN-2T has an Allison 250 turbine. In 1966 a deal was made with IRMA the Rumanian firm to build bare Islander airframes, which were then flown to the IOW for completion. In 1978 Pilatus joined Birtten-Norman and moved production back to the IOW. The Pilatus deal was superseded by the Rumanian contract which is still current.

In the same weight class as the US twins (Navajo, Aerostar, Soneca) the Islander is far more versatile. There are more than sixty on the UK Register.

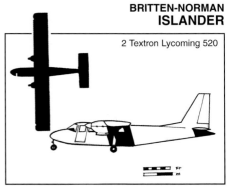

## BRITTEN-NORMAN
# ISLANDER

2 Textron Lycoming 520

| DATA | IMPERIAL | | METRIC | |
|---|---|---|---|---|
| Span | 49 | ft | 14.9 | m |
| Wing area | 325 | sq ft | 30.2 | sq m |
| Aspect ratio | 7.4 | | | |
| Empty Weight | 3024 | lb | 2280 | kg |
| Loaded weight | 6600 | lb | 2994 | kg |
| Wing loading | 20.3 | lb/sq ft | 99 | kg/sq m |
| Max speed | 175 | mph | 280 | kmh |
| Cruise speed | 143 | mph | 265 | kmh |
| Stalling speed | 50 | mph | 93 | kmh |
| Climb rate | 1130 | ft/min | 344 | m/min |
| Range | 503 | mls | 932 | km |

Beagle were formed in 1960, combining Pressed Steel Co, Auster and F G Miles Ltd. The Miles design team came up with the slick B206, a 5/7 seater which first flew at Shoreham in 1961. A military version, the B206R Bassett was built alongside the civil versions some of which were the turbo charged B206S. Fifty-seven civil aircraft were built and a further twenty-two for the RAF.

The B206 cruised at over 200 mph. and had a range of 1500 miles, comparing favourably with the 'American twins that were being developed at about the same time. The '206 may have been somewhat 'over-engineered', (in other words, it was a quality product) and in the climate of the time it was under-funded and eventually dropped. The assets of Beagle (after a brief period of State ownership) were transferred to Scottish Aviation in 1969.

An 'American fan of the '206 reputedly bought the entire stock of airframes and spares from Scottish Aviation and set up a stateside '206 'agency'!

There are five on the UK Register two airworthy, the others in collections.

# BEAGLE
# B 206

LIGHT TWIN
2 x Continental, 310 hp

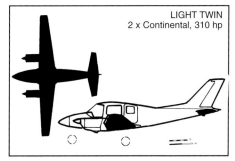

| DATA | IMPERIAL | | METRIC | |
|---|---|---|---|---|
| Span | 45.7 | ft | 14 | m |
| Wing area | 213 | sq ft | 20 | sq m |
| Aspect ratio | 9.8 | | 9.8 | |
| Empty Weight | 4444 | lb | 2017 | kg |
| Loaded weight | 7500 | lb | 3405 | kg |
| Wing loading | 35.2 | lb/sq ft | 172 | kg/sq m |
| Max speed | 220 | mph | 352 | kmh |
| Cruise speed | 214 | mph | 342 | kmh |
| Stalling speed | 77 | mph | 123 | kmh |
| Climb rate | 1170 | ft/min | 360 | m/min |
| Range | 1645 | mls | 3632 | km |

First flown in 1961 the PA 30 was a twin engined version of the PA 24 single engined Comanche and used many of the PA 24 jigs and fixtures, it was a 4 to 6 seater and ran to many variants.

The PA30 was the initial production version and was a four seater, the PA 30 B, of 1965, the 'Twin Comanche B', had extended cabin glazing and provision for six seats and was available as the Standard, Custom or Sportsman depending on equipment fit as were the Executive 222 and the Professional 422.

The PA 30 C had the improved Lycoming O-320 engines and the Comanche C/R had contra rotating props. and tip tanks as standard (optional on earlier models) - this was re-classified as the PA 39 in 1971.

Over 2000 of these all metal twins have been produced and there are currently thirty-eight on the UK Register.

Somewhat lighter and lower powered than other American Twins the PA 30 still cruises at nearly 200 mph. and has fuel for 1000 miles.

# PIPER
# PA 30 TWIN COMANCHE

LIGHT TWIN
Lycoming, 160 hp

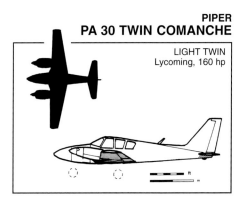

| DATA | IMPERIAL | | METRIC | |
|---|---|---|---|---|
| Span | 36 | ft | 11.1 | m |
| Wing area | 178 | sq ft | 16.1 | sq m |
| Aspect ratio | 7.3 | | 7.3 | |
| Empty Weight | 2160 | lb | 980 | kg |
| Loaded weight | 3600 | lb | 1634 | kg |
| Wing loading | 26.2 | lb/sq ft | 98.6 | kg/sq m |
| Max speed | 205 | mph | 328 | kmh |
| Cruise speed | 181 | mph | 290 | kmh |
| Stalling speed | 68 | mph | 109 | kmh |
| Climb rate | 1460 | ft/min | 450 | m/min |
| Range | 1025 | mls | 1640 | km |

A fast 6/8 seat twin from the Piper stable, first flown in 1964, as the Inca, it was the largest type produced by the firm at the time. The type was certificated in 1966 and remained in production until 1985 by which time 5000 PA31 variants had been built, including the Chieftain, Mojave and Cheyenne.

Variants too numerous to detail in this box include pressurised cabin, turbo props, stretched fuselages and wings – the final, top of the range model the Cheyenne 3 has a 'T' tail, 1000 shp Garrett turbo props and a maximum speed of 335 mph. (Much advanced from the original PA31, the Cheyenne 3 is re-typed as the PA42).

The pilot compartment is separated by a bulkhead from the passengers, who, in the executive version, enjoy the facilities of a bar and WC.

Ten and fifteen passengers are carried in certain short haul, high density versions.

Schafer Aircraft of Waco convert pressurised PA31s to turbo prop power with increased tankage and re-name them Comancheros.

Data below for PA31T Cheyenne, PT6A turboprops.

# PIPER
# PA31 NAVAJO

LIGHT TWIN
Various

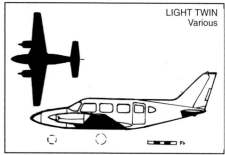

| DATA | IMPERIAL | | METRIC | |
|---|---|---|---|---|
| Span | 42.6 | ft | 13 | m |
| Wing area | 229 | sq ft | 21.3 | sq m |
| Aspect ratio | 7.9 | | 7.9 | |
| Empty Weight | 4983 | lb | 2260 | kg |
| Loaded weight | 9000 | lb | 4082 | kg |
| Wing loading | 39 | lb/sq ft | 191 | kg/sq m |
| Max speed | 322 | mph | 516 | kmh |
| Cruise speed | 282 | mph | 452 | kmh |
| Stalling speed | 70 | mph | 112 | kmh |
| Climb rate | 1750 | ft/min | 540 | m/min |
| Range | 1620 | mls | 2608 | km |

Cessna twins are legion – and all, pretty much, alike! The model 421 Golden Eagle has, however, a good foothold in the UK with 33 on the Register.

First flown in 1965, the '421 was developed from the 401 and the 411, with the difference that its new fuselage was pressurised.

Deliveries of production aircraft did not begin until 1967 and nearly 2000 were made before production ceased in 1984.

Four variants were made, the 421 and the 421A, 358 built; the 421B had an increased span, a longer fuselage, a fifth window and 600lb AUW increase. (699 built). The421C has a higher aspect ratio fin/rudder, 'wet' wings and no tip tanks – 859 of these were made, powered by Continental GTS10-520N flat six engines developing 375 hp each.

A purposeful 6/10 seater, all except the 421C, having distinctive upturned wing tip fuel tanks, the latter having plain square wing tips.

These aircraft cruise at nearly 300 mph and have an enormous range.

Details below for 421C.

# CESSNA
# 421 GOLDEN EAGLE

LIGHT TWIN
2 x Continental, 375 hp

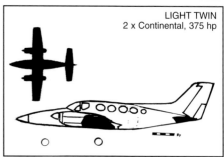

| DATA | IMPERIAL | | METRIC | |
|---|---|---|---|---|
| Span | 41.1 | ft | 12.5 | m |
| Wing area | 215 | sq ft | 19.9 | sq m |
| Aspect ratio | 7.9 | | | |
| Empty Weight | 4640 | lb | 2105 | kg |
| Loaded weight | 7450 | lb | 3379 | kg |
| Wing loading | 34.6 | lb/sq ft | 169 | kg/sq m |
| Max speed | 297 | mph | 478 | kmh |
| Cruise speed | 279 | mph | 450 | kmh |
| Stalling speed | 70 | mph | 112 | kmh |
| Climb rate | 1940 | ft/min | 591 | m/min |
| Range | 1710 | mls | 2752 | km |

One of the most popular of the American light twins, the prototype Seneca first flew in 1968. Introduced in 1971, over 4,500 have been produced and they are manufactured under licence in Poland for the Eastern European market - the power units for these versions being PZL, Franklins instead of the USA's turbo, charged Continentals.

Of all metal construction, the Seneca has Three bladed fully feathering airscrews, electrically operated slotted flaps and retractable tricycle undercarriage, Frise type ailerons, comprehensive instrumentation and radio aids.

The wings and empennage have de-icing boots, essential for its ability to cruise up to 25,000 ft.

Pitch control is by a stabilator positioned slightly aft of the rudder.

Much admired for it's wide cabin and comfortable seating, there are 136 on the UK Register.

### PIPER
### PA34 SENECA

LIGHTPLANE
Continental, 200 hp

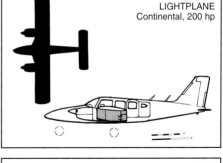

| DATA | IMPERIAL | | METRIC | |
|------|----------|--|--------|--|
| Span | 38.9 | ft | 12 | m |
| Wing area | 208.7 | sq ft | 19.6 | sq m |
| Aspect ratio | 7.2 | | 7.2 | |
| Empty Weight | 3333 | lb | 1513 | kg |
| Loaded weight | 4513 | lb | 2049 | kg |
| Wing loading | 21.7 | lb/sq ft | 106 | kg/sq m |
| Max speed | 225 | mph | 360 | kmh |
| Cruise speed | 205 | mph | 329 | kmh |
| Stalling speed | 73 | mph | 118 | kmh |
| Climb rate | 1400 | ft/min | 431 | m/min |
| Range | 1040 | mls | 1661 | km |

Italian company Partenavia's first twin the P68 Victor first flew in 1969 and was aimed to compete with the flood of US twins. Competing with but not imitating the USA product, Partenavia went for a high wing and fixed undercarriage.

Employed in many tasks including aerial survey, met and police work plus charter and taxi, the P68 has been exported in quantity.

Over 400 aircraft had been produced by the mid 1970s and a part-kitted version is built in India.

Of metal and composites construction the Victor is a clean good looking aeroplane with a useful performance, carrying six passengers 1000 miles at nearly 200 mph.

200 hp Lycomings are the standard fit but variants have 210 hp turbo charged Lycomings and the Spartacus version has 330 hp Allison turbo-props and a retractable undercarriage.

There are seventeen on the UK Register.

Performance figures are for the 200 hp version.

### PARTENAVIA
### P68 VICTOR

LIGHT TWIN
Lycoming, 200 hp

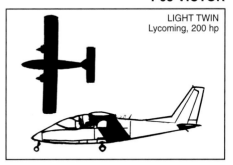

| DATA | IMPERIAL | | METRIC | |
|------|----------|--|--------|--|
| Span | 39.3 | ft | 12 | m |
| Wing area | 200 | sq ft | 18.6 | sq m |
| Aspect ratio | 7.7 | | 7.7 | |
| Empty Weight | 2425 | lb | 1100 | kg |
| Loaded weight | 4100 | lb | 1860 | kg |
| Wing loading | 20.5 | lb/sq ft | 100 | kg/sq m |
| Max speed | 208 | mph | 334 | kmh |
| Cruise speed | 186 | mph | 299 | kmh |
| Stalling speed | 60 | mph | 96 | kmh |
| Climb rate | 1700 | ft/min | 523 | m/min |
| Range | 1045 | mls | 1681 | km |

Having designed the Aero Commander, a ground breaking, fast, executive six- to eight-seat twin, the first model flying in 1948,Ted Smith moved on and set up Ted Smith Aircraft Co. Ltd in 1966. The result was the Aerostar with twin turbocharged Lycoming engines giving a total of 600 hp and 250 mph cruising. Between 1968 and 1976 several changes of company ownership took place finishing up where it started as the Ted Smith Aerostar Corporation in 1976. Two years later Piper's acquired the Aerostar and produced three models, until 1984 when all work ceased. In 1991 Aerostar Aircraft bought back the Aerostar rights from Piper and began work on a jet powered version with Williams FJ33 jets. the Aerostar is of all-metal construction with a mid wing and hydraulically operated retractable tricycle undercarriage. The various models have five or six seats and Lycoming flat six engines of 290 hp and 350 hp. The late model Aerostars are pressurised.

Three are flying in the UK with US registrations.

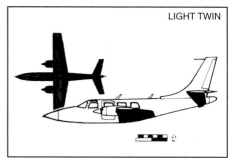

| DATA | IMPERIAL | | METRIC | |
|---|---|---|---|---|
| Span | 36.6 | ft | 11.18 | m |
| Wing area | 178 | sq ft | 16.54 | sq m |
| Aspect ratio | 7.55 | | 7.55 | |
| Empty Weight | 4000 | lb | 1814 | kg |
| Loaded weight | 6000 | lb | 2721 | kg |
| Wing loading | 33.7 | lb/sq ft | 164.5 | kg/sq m |
| Max speed | 290 | mph | 467 | kmh |
| Cruise speed | 270 | mph | 434 | kmh |
| Stalling speed | 82 | mph | 132 | kmh |
| Climb rate | 1530 | ft/min | 466 | m/min |

This remarkable aeroplane designed by Aerospatiale aerodynamicist M. Colomban in 1972 is minute, smaller than the Flying Flea and certainly the smallest twin engined aeroplane. With a wing span of 16ft and 2ft chord the Cri Cri's wing is about the size of a large model glider!

Early aircraft were powered by various chainsaw engines but the latest models are powered by the JPX PUL 212 engines specially developed for it.

The Cri Cri won the Design Award at Oshkosh in 1981 and by 1984, 360 plans had been sold, thirty of which were soon flying. The design has proved popular all over the world and there are six currently on the British Register.

Of all metal, ultra simple construction, the Cri Cri is PFA approved and two are being built. A twin jet version has flown recently, the coffee pot sized jets being started with a cigarette lighter.

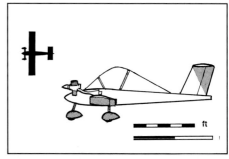

| DATA | IMPERIAL | | METRIC | |
|---|---|---|---|---|
| Span | 16 | ft | 14.9 | m |
| Wing area | 33.4 | sq ft | 3.1 | sq m |
| Aspect ratio | 7.75 | | 7.75 | |
| Empty Weight | 165 | lb | 74.9 | kg |
| Loaded weight | 375 | lb | 170 | kg |
| Wing loading | 11.2 | lb/sq ft | 54.8 | kg/sq m |
| Max speed | 137 | mph | 219 | kmh |
| Cruise speed | 124 | mph | 198 | kmh |
| Stalling speed | 45 | mph | 72 | kmh |
| Climb rate | 1280 | ft/min | 394 | m/min |
| Range | 248 | mls | 396 | km |

Grumman Aircraft's first civil twin, the GA7 first flew in 1974; it can seat four/six people and is in operation as an executive transport and trainer.

Although the prototype first flew in 1974 it was not until 1977 that the production model was finalised, considerable re-design having gone into the Cougar in the intervening three years.

An all metal design that was taken over by Gulfstream American, it has an outward retracting undercarriage and a parallel chord wing, which is a recognition feature, as most of its near look alikes have tapered wing plan forms.

The all metal construction is rivetless, most joints being glue/bonded. The wing has two spars and electrically operated Fowler type flaps, the 'gear retracts hydraulically and the nose wheel is steerable.

Production appears to be in the region of 120, of which a high proportion, ie. twenty-five are on the UK Register.

## GULFSTREAM AMERICAN
## GA7 COUGAR

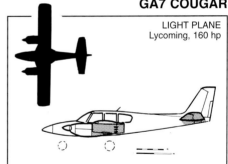

LIGHT PLANE
Lycoming, 160 hp

| DATA | IMPERIAL | | METRIC | |
|---|---|---|---|---|
| Span | 36.9 | ft | 11.4 | m |
| Wing area | 184 | sq ft | 17.3 | sq m |
| Aspect ratio | 7.4 | | 7.4 | |
| Empty Weight | 2515 | lb | 1142 | kg |
| Loaded weight | 3800 | lb | 1725 | kg |
| Wing loading | 20.65 | lb/sq ft | 100.8 | kg/sq m |
| Max speed | 193 | mph | 309 | kmh |
| Cruise speed | 184 | mph | 294 | kmh |
| Stalling speed | 82 | mph | 131 | kmh |
| Climb rate | 1200 | ft/min | 370 | m/min |
| Range | 1336 | mls | 2137 | km |

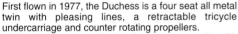

First flown in 1977, the Duchess is a four seat all metal twin with pleasing lines, a retractable tricycle undercarriage and counter rotating propellers.

The high aspect ratio wing has a commonalty with the single engined Sierra and the tailplane is mounted on top of the large chord fin and rudder.

The parallel chord wing helps distinguish the Duchess from other 'T' tailed twins, ie. Seminole, Cheyenne, King Air, which all have tapered wing plans.

At the lower powered end of the small twin range, the Duchess still manages a respectable cruise of nearly 190 mph. and a climb of over 1000 fpm.

As well as 'pilot doors either side, the Duchess has a baggage door aft of the trailing edge on the port side.

Slotted flaps run for 75% of the span and the Frise type ailerons are of metal/honeycomb construction. The undercarriage, flaps and brakes are operated by an electro-hydraulic system.

400 have been made and there are thirty on our UK Register.

## BEECHCRAFT
## 76 DUCHESS

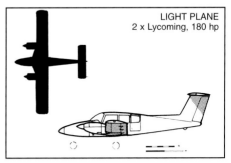

LIGHT PLANE
2 x Lycoming, 180 hp

| DATA | IMPERIAL | | METRIC | |
|---|---|---|---|---|
| Span | 38 | ft | 11.6 | m |
| Wing area | 181 | sq ft | 16.8 | sq m |
| Aspect ratio | 8 | | 8 | |
| Empty Weight | 2466 | lb | 1119 | kg |
| Loaded weight | 3900 | lb | 1769 | kg |
| Wing loading | 21.5 | lb/sq ft | 105.2 | kg/sq m |
| Max speed | 197 | mph | 317 | kmh |
| Cruise speed | 182 | mph | 293 | kmh |
| Stalling speed | 81 | mph | 130 | kmh |
| Climb rate | 1248 | ft/min | 384 | m/min |
| Range | 717 | mls | 1155 | km |

Designed by the late Peter Phillips, ex RAF and Britten Norman test pilot, the Speedtwin first flew in 1992 after many years of development - carried out with some degree of secrecy. Its debut was at the Biggin Hill Air Fair in '92 where its rakish, new appearance caused quite a stir.

Handled by Speedtwin Developments Ltd. of Monmouth, the Aircraft is of all metal construction, the mainplane being based on a Victa Airtourer wing and the fixed tail-dragger undercarriage being that of a Chipmunk. The twin engines are Continental 0-200s of 100 hp. with fixed pitch propellers; a Mk 2 is listed with Textron Lycomings of 160 hp.

Designed for kit building the airframe is stressed for +6,-3g and is cleared for aerobatics - the only light twin to be so. Small for a twin- 26 ft span - the Speedtwin has a short take off run, a high rate of climb and a range of over 1000 ml. at 160 mph.

Only one on the UK Register, it will be a pity if no more are built.

## PHILLIPS SPEEDTWIN

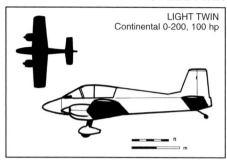

LIGHT TWIN
Continental 0-200, 100 hp

| DATA | IMPERIAL | | METRIC | |
|---|---|---|---|---|
| Span | 26 | ft | 8 | m |
| Wing area | 120 | sq ft | 11.3 | sq m |
| Aspect ratio | 5.6 | | 5.6 | |
| Empty Weight | 1410 | lb | 640 | kg |
| Loaded weight | 2250 | lb | 1202 | kg |
| Wing loading | 18.8 | lb/sq ft | 91.5 | kg/sq m |
| Max speed | 178 | mph | 286 | kmh |
| Cruise speed | 160 | mph | 257 | kmh |
| Stalling speed | 68 | mph | 110 | kmh |
| Climb rate | 1200 | ft/min | 366 | m/min |
| Range | 1129 | mls | 2092 | km |

The British Aircraft Co. of Maidstone manufactured gliders before WW2, and in 1932 C.H. Lowe-Wylde, their designer director fitted one with wheels and a pylon mounted pusher engine and called it the Planette. This early powered glider proved to be a docile performer over its 15 to 40 mph. speed range and more were built, 28 in all before the firm closed down in 1937. A year before this one was flown from Croydon to Berlin in eleven hours at the cost of £1.25!

Several were de-motored and reverted to gliders, others became popular performers at the pre war air shows - and thence in to storage 'for the duration'.

Eight Drones came out of storage, and three flew again, though none currently - this old lady is happier with her feet up!

The Douglas motor cycle engine that powered the prototype was developed into a small aero engine, the Sprite, which developed 23 hp, very noisily!

## BAC DRONE

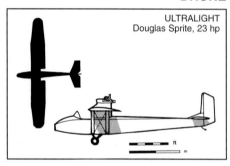

ULTRALIGHT
Douglas Sprite, 23 hp

| DATA | IMPERIAL | | METRIC | |
|---|---|---|---|---|
| Span | 39.6 | ft | 12.2 | m |
| Wing area | 172 | sq ft | 16.2 | sq m |
| Aspect ratio | 9.1 | | 9.1 | |
| Empty Weight | 390 | lb | 177 | kg |
| Loaded weight | 460 | lb | 209 | kg |
| Wing loading | 2.7 | lb/sq ft | 13.0 | kg/sq m |
| Max speed | 70 | mph | 112 | kmh |
| Cruise speed | 60 | mph | 96 | kmh |
| Stalling speed | 20 | mph | 32 | kmh |
| Climb rate | 380 | ft/min | 117 | m/min |
| Range | 300 | mls | 480 | km |

After Miles Aircraft folded at Woodley in 1947 the Miles brothers, Fred and George, set up in business at Shoreham – where they had started twenty years earlier! It was here that they designed and built the Student, which first flew in 1957, a 300 mph, all metal, two seat jet trainer. Well ahead of its time – we have yet to see another British, small two seat private jet! Built as a private venture the Student lost out to the Hunting Percival Provost – which cost twice as much.

The Student put on some brilliant aerobatic displays at the SBAC shows where its excellent forward vision and low ground clearance were also admired.

In 1964 the prototype became the Mk 2 with a more powerful Marbore (1,540 lb thrust), which put its top speed up to 400 mph. A four seat version was planned as an 'executive jet' and with funds running low a deal to build it in South Africa looked attractive but this was scuttled by the, then, arms embargo.

Still an attractive and practical aeroplane, the Student had all the bad breaks.

Currently being restored by the Berkshire Museum of Aviation, after a forced landing in 1985.

## MILES
## M100 STUDENT

LIGHT PLANE
Turbomeca marbore, 880 lb Thrust

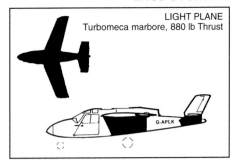

| DATA | IMPERIAL | METRIC |
|---|---|---|
| Span | 29 ft | 9 m |
| Wing area | 144 sq ft | 13.5 sq m |
| Aspect ratio | 5.9 | 5.9 |
| Empty Weight | 2400 lb | 1090 kg |
| Loaded weight | 3600 lb | 1634 kg |
| Wing loading | 25 lb/sq ft | 122 kg/sq m |
| Max speed | 300 mph | 478 kmh |
| Cruise speed | 260 mph | 416 kmh |
| Stalling speed | 70 mph | 112 kmh |
| Climb rate | 1780 ft/min | 548 m/min |
| Range | 444 mls | 710 km |

When is a twin not a twin? The push/pull one behind the other engines of the Skymaster eliminate the asymmetric trust hazard peculiar to wing engined twins. Although over 2000 Skymasters were made between 1964 and 1980 this was considered disappointing by Cessna standards.

Preceded by the Model 356 Skymaster, which had fixed gear, the 337 Super Skymaster is all metal, has six seats and retractable undercarriage and was first flown in 1964. A dozen variants followed, the main ones being, the 337P pressurised (identified by row of smaller windows), the 337B with belly pannier and the M337 military version, designated USAF 0-2A (513 of these were made). About 200 Skymasters were built in France by Reims, mainly the military FTB337G. Most models are powered by Continental 10-360 engines of 210 hp with 225 hp turbo option. Fifteen Super Skymasters and one Skymaster on the UK Register.

Data for standard 337, the turbo 337P is faster.

## CESSNA
## 337 SKYMASTER

LIGHT PLANE
Continental, 210 hp

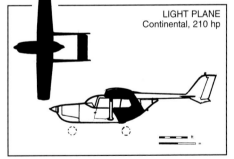

| DATA | IMPERIAL | METRIC |
|---|---|---|
| Span | 38.1 ft | 11.7 m |
| Wing area | 201 sq ft | 18.9 sq m |
| Aspect ratio | 7.2 | 7.2 |
| Empty Weight | 2695 lb | 1223 kg |
| Loaded weight | 4630 lb | 2102 kg |
| Wing loading | 23 lb/sq ft | 112 kg/sq m |
| Max speed | 199 mph | 318 kmh |
| Cruise speed | 180 mph | 288 kmh |
| Stalling speed | 70 mph | 112 kmh |
| Climb rate | 1100 ft/min | 339 m/min |
| Range | 1330 mls | 2128 km |

The Woody Pusher is named after its designer H. L. Woods formerly of Bensen Aircraft Corp. Woods also founded Aerosport, the company that builds the Pusher.

The Pusher first flew in 1970 with an all wood fuselage, later changed to welded steel tube with fabric covering over wooden formers. The wing has two wooden spars and ribs, fabric covered aft of the main spar, the nose is skinned with aluminium sheet. Flaps are standard and the undercarriage legs are spring steel, the spats are optional.

Engines of from 65 hp, to 85 hp give it a cruising speed of about 87 mph.

Many hundreds are flying in the USA but as yet few have appeared in the UK, four on the UK Register.

This sturdy two seater, in the ultralight category, is well liked by those who have flown it and maintained it.

# AEROSPORT
# WOODY PUSHER

ULTRALIGHT
Continental, 75 hp

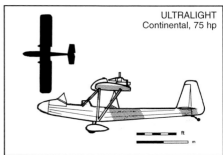

| DATA | IMPERIAL | | METRIC | |
|---|---|---|---|---|
| Span | 29 | ft | 8.84 | m |
| Wing area | 130 | sq ft | 12.1 | sq m |
| Aspect ratio | 6.5 | | 6.5 | |
| Empty Weight | 630 | lb | 285 | kg |
| Loaded weight | 1150 | lb | 522 | kg |
| Wing loading | 8.8 | lb/sq ft | 43 | kg/sq m |
| Max speed | 98 | mph | 158 | kmh |
| Cruise speed | 87 | mph | 140 | kmh |
| Stalling speed | 45 | mph | 72 | kmh |
| Climb rate | 600 | ft/min | 183 | m/min |
| Range | 225 | mls | 360 | km |

Designed by Bob Hovey in the USA (he also designed the Whing Ding) the Beta Bird is an aeroplane you sit on, rather than in.

Of wooden construction with strut braced fabric covered wings – an aluminium tube within the box tail boom carries the empenage. Bungee sprung main wheels with brakes and a steerable tail-wheel comprise the tail-dragger undercarriage.

A rare luxury for a microlight is the large landing light in the nose and wing tip navigation lights.

The controls comprise a normal joystick for elevator and flaperons and external pedals for the rudder and brakes.

The exposed pilot position was considered 'spooky' and almost impractical when it first appeared in the late 1970s but since then exposed flex wing and gyrocopter pilots have become legion.

The Beta Bird is PFA approved and is plans only, there is one on the UK Register.

# HOVEY
# BETA BIRD

MICROLIGHT
Rotax 503, 40 hp

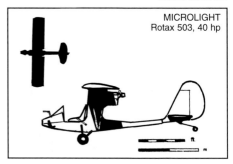

| DATA | IMPERIAL | | METRIC | |
|---|---|---|---|---|
| Span | 25.5 | ft | 7.8 | m |
| Wing area | 88 | sq ft | 8.3 | sq m |
| Aspect ratio | 7.4 | | 7.4 | |
| Empty Weight | 405 | lb | 184 | kg |
| Loaded weight | 650 | lb | 295 | kg |
| Wing loading | 7.4 | lb/sq ft | 36 | kg/sq m |
| Max speed | 90 | mph | 144 | kmh |
| Cruise speed | 80 | mph | 128 | kmh |
| Stalling speed | 40 | mph | 64 | kmh |
| Climb rate | 700 | ft/min | 215 | m/min |
| Range | 160 | mls | 256 | km |

First flown in 1971 the diminutive, single seat, BD-5 the brain child of *avant garde* designer Jim Bede had a stormy launch into the world of home building. The type having been certificated was offered on the North American market, over 6000 factory built models were ordered and 3000 kits, vast sums of money flowed in the form of deposits, but though parts of kits were delivered, no one got a complete set! Engine and sub contract problems plus mismanagement caused the BD-5 bubble to burst in 1979 when the company went bankrupt.

Fifty or so BD-5s were eventually built by persevering adherents of the type, there are six on the UK Register. (Ed. All now grounded).

The mainly metal aeroplane with a retractable tricycle undercarriage was only 13ft (4m) long and flew like a dream, cruising at 200 mph (320kph), but hitting the numbers at over 80mph (128kph).

An early model, had a butterfly tail and a jet powered version, the BD-5J, has been on the air show circuit.

**BEDE**
# BD-5

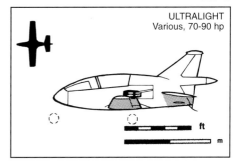

ULTRALIGHT
Various, 70-90 hp

| DATA | IMPERIAL | METRIC |
|---|---|---|
| Span | 17 ft | 5.23 m |
| Wing area | 38 sq ft | 3.6 sq m |
| Aspect ratio | 76 | 7.6 |
| Empty Weight | 410 lb | 186 kg |
| Loaded weight | 850 lb | 386 kg |
| Wing loading | 22.4 lb/sq ft | 109 kg/sq m |
| Max speed | 230 mph | 368 kmh |
| Cruise speed | 200 mph | 320 kmh |
| Stalling speed | 70 mph | 112 kmh |
| Climb rate | 1400 ft/min | 431 m/min |
| Range | 1130 mls | 1808 km |

One of the very first three axis, control Microlights, having taken to the air in 1972. Quicksilver, designed by American Bob Lovejoy set a standard which was immediately copied by other manufacturers, some under licence and some by derivation, and there are now literally thousands of the type flying world-wide.

The 'stick' controls pitch and yaw and a side lever looks after roll, though conventional three axis control is available as an option.

The wings are wire braced via a kingpost and have only a single surface section. Wheels are all torsion bar sprung and the nose wheel is braked. An extension shaft drives the airscrew from the under wing mounted motor.

There are twenty-seven on the UK Register. (Ed. in the USA a 'Police Interceptor' version has a searchlight, radio and siren!)

**EIPPER**
# QUICKSILVER

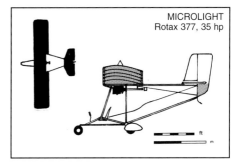

MICROLIGHT
Rotax 377, 35 hp

| DATA | IMPERIAL | METRIC |
|---|---|---|
| Span | 32 ft | 15.5 m |
| Wing area | 160 sq ft | 115 sq m |
| Aspect ratio | 6.4 | 6.4 |
| Empty Weight | 230 lb | 108 kg |
| Loaded weight | 525 lb | 238 kg |
| Wing loading | 3.28 lb/sq ft | 16 kg/sq m |
| Max speed | 52 mph | 84 kmh |
| Cruise speed | 46 mph | 74 kmh |
| Stalling speed | 24 mph | 38 kmh |
| Climb rate | 800 ft/min | 246 m/min |
| Range | 95 mls | 153 km |

The three seat Optica made its debut at the 1980 SBAC Show and stunned everyone with its originality and unusual configuration. Designed by John Edgley, who with a few friends began construction in Islington in 1976m moving later to Cranfield. Of all metal construction the Optica, which first flew in 1979, has a mid engine driving a five bladed prop/fan within an annular duct behind the helicopter-like cabin pod and twin booms to carry the twin fins and high mounted tailplane.

The Optica is designed for slow speed, helicopter type observation work (Police/Army) without the high operating costs of the rotorcraft.

The crash of the first delivered 'plane, followed by insolvency then re-birth, followed by a factory fire has hampered the Opticas progress; but over twenty were made, with six on the UK Register. Last batch were built by FLS Aerospace at Bournemouth.

**LOVAUX/FLX/AEROSPACE**
# OPTICA

LIGHT PLANE
Lycoming, 160 hp

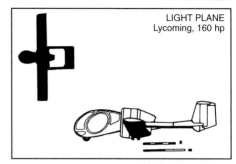

| DATA | IMPERIAL | | METRIC | |
|---|---|---|---|---|
| Span | 39.3 | ft | 12 | m |
| Wing area | 170 | sq ft | 15.8 | sq m |
| Aspect ratio | 9 | | 9 | |
| Empty Weight | 2090 | lb | 948 | kg |
| Loaded weight | 2899 | lb | 1316 | kg |
| Wing loading | 17 | lb/sq ft | 83 | kg/sq m |
| Max speed | 132 | mph | 211 | kmh |
| Cruise speed | 118 | mph | 189 | kmh |
| Stalling speed | 67 | mph | 107 | kmh |
| Climb rate | 810 | ft/min | 250 | m/min |
| Range | 655 | mls | 1048 | km |

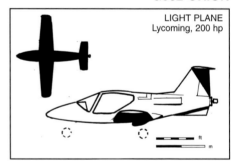

Jean Grinvalds began the design of this all composites 2+2 seater in 1975, a very early example of this type of construction. It first flew in 1981 as the G801 to be followed in 1983 by the kit version G802.

The three blade pusher constant speed prop is shaft driven by a turbocharged, fan cooled Lycoming T10-350 mounted midships. With its trike gear tucked away this super slippery homebuilt clocks up over 200 mph on its 200 hp. the deep glazed cabin provides, helicopter-like- superb 200 visibility and an enthusiast/builders club, Club Orion, exists in France. A company set up in the USA to kit G802s in a big way folded after Grinvalds died in the crash of the prototype in 1985.

The groovy looking speedster is reputed to be complicated and difficult to build, but its got to be worth it!

Two are flying in Belgium, two in the USA and six in France. A PFA Rally visitor. The data below is for the G802.

**GRINVALDS**
# G802 ORION

LIGHT PLANE
Lycoming, 200 hp

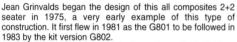

| DATA | IMPERIAL | | METRIC | |
|---|---|---|---|---|
| Span | 29.5 | ft | 9.1 | m |
| Wing area | 122 | sq ft | 11.5 | sq m |
| Aspect ratio | 7.1 | | 7.1 | |
| Empty Weight | 1340 | lb | 608 | kg |
| Loaded weight | 2310 | lb | 1049 | kg |
| Wing loading | 19.0 | lb/sq ft | 92.4 | kg/sq m |
| Max speed | 205 | mph | 328 | kmh |
| Cruise speed | 186 | mph | 298 | kmh |
| Stalling speed | 70 | mph | 112 | kmh |
| Climb rate | 885 | ft/min | 272 | m/min |
| Range | 1864 | mls | 2984 | km |

This sleek four seater designed by CMC, under Ian Chichester-Miles back in 1982, progressed through the mock-up stage to prototype first flight in 1988. The first prototype, powered by Noel Penny jets, was superseded by a second development aircraft with Williams FXJ-1, 700 lb thrust units plus cabin pressurisation and airframe liquid de-icing. The Leopard has no ailerons, roll control being effected by the differential incidence tailplane.

Of all composite construction, the CMC Leopard made a big impression at the 1996 Farnborough air show and is currently undergoing staged flight trials at Cranfield speeds up to 300 mph being completed, the next stage, up to its full potential of 500 mph are pending, in production form, with the new Williams FJX-2 engines its incredible performance figures will include a range of 2000 mls at 45,000 ft cruising at 500 mph and a fighter like climb of over 60000 fpm!

The electrifying Leopard is probably the most exciting British light plane since the DH88 Comet, let's hope its world-beating potential is recognised.

## CHICHESTER-MILES
# LEOPARD

LIGHT PLANE
2 x Williams FJX-2, 950 lb thrust

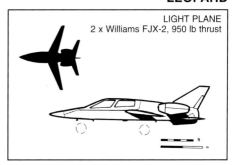

| DATA | IMPERIAL | | METRIC | |
|---|---|---|---|---|
| Span | 23.5 | ft | 7.16 | m |
| Wing area | 62.9 | sq ft | 5.9 | sq m |
| Aspect ratio | 8.7 | | 8.7 | |
| Empty Weight | 2200 | lb | 1000 | kg |
| Loaded weight | 4000 | lb | 1815 | kg |
| Wing loading | 63.5 | lb/sq ft | 310 | kg/sq m |
| Max speed | 525 | mph | 840 | kmh |
| Cruise speed | 500 | mph | 804 | kmh |
| Stalling speed | 100 | mph | 160 | kmh |
| Climb rate | 6430 | ft/min | 1980 | m/min |
| Range | 1725 | mls | 2760 | km |

The Kolb Company of Phoenixville, Penn, started in the microlight business in 1970, one of the earliest to do so.

First flown at Oshkosh in 1982 the TwinStar side-by-side two seater may be adapted to fly in the ultralight or microlight category. The 1982 model was a front engined tractor but later changed to the present pusher set up, and an enclosed cabin was added.

A useful 'garaging' feature are the quick folding wings, completed in minutes without the aid of tools. The all round visibility from the cockpit is impressive, as is the generous width of 45 inches, it is fitted with dual controls.

The construction is conventional tube, both steel and light alloy, at six-inch diameter tube being used for the wing main spar which has Stits fabric covering.

The large flaps and wide track undercarriage are noteworthy features. PFA approved, twenty-one are on the UK Register and four are being built.

## KOLB-MAINAIR
# TWINSTAR

MICROLIGHT
Rotax 503, 50 hp

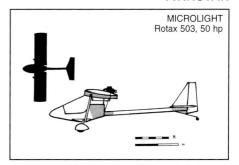

| DATA | IMPERIAL | | METRIC | |
|---|---|---|---|---|
| Span | 30.16 | ft | 9.3 | m |
| Wing area | 163 | sq ft | 15.3 | sq m |
| Aspect ratio | 5.6 | | 5.6 | |
| Empty Weight | 378 | lb | 172 | kg |
| Loaded weight | 1000 | lb | 454 | kg |
| Wing loading | 6.1 | lb/sq ft | 30 | kg/sq m |
| Max speed | 85 | mph | 136 | kmh |
| Cruise speed | 65 | mph | 104 | kmh |
| Stalling speed | 30 | mph | 48 | kmh |
| Climb rate | 850 | ft/min | 262 | m/min |
| Range | 150 | mls | 240 | km |

The two seat Arrow Hawk microlight first flew in 1982 and is very popular in its country of origin, the USA where most of the 1200 built are flying, three on the UK Register. The UK version of the Arrow Hawk is pretty spartan due to the 390 kg microlight weight limit. It has all fabric covering, including zip-up cabin sides, minimum instrumentation and a single carb Rotax 503.

The basic structure is aluminium tube and the wings and all flying surfaces are supplied assembled and ready for covering in the kit. The rest of the airframe is rivetted or bolted together, no gluing or welding.

Apart from being a pussy cat to fly, the Arrow Hawk's other pluses included, composites leaf spring main legs, +6-4g limits, steerable nose-wheel, braked man wheels, three notch flaps, three axis controls and quick set up from knock-down.

A tail-dragger version is available as is a float plane amphibian.

A tried and trusted design which will benefit from the 450 kg rule.

# CGS
# HAWK ARROW

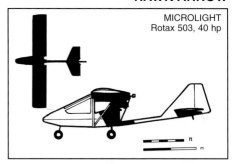

MICROLIGHT
Rotax 503, 40 hp

| DATA | IMPERIAL | | METRIC | |
|---|---|---|---|---|
| Span | 34 | ft | 10.5 | m |
| Wing area | 160 | sq ft | 15 | sq m |
| Aspect ratio | 7.2 | | 7.2 | |
| Empty Weight | 420 | lb | 191 | kg |
| Loaded weight | 820 | lb | 372 | kg |
| Wing loading | 5.1 | lb/sq ft | 25 | kg/sq m |
| Max speed | 90 | mph | 144 | kmh |
| Cruise speed | 60 | mph | 96 | kmh |
| Stalling speed | 30 | mph | 48 | kmh |
| Climb rate | 1000 | ft/min | 308 | m/min |
| Range | 100 | mls | 160 | km |

First flown in 1983 this rugged and good-looking British designed tandem seat microlight is constructed with composites and aluminium tube and is sold as a kit or factory-made. It is designed by pioneer 'microlighter' David Cook.

Shadows have made many notable long-distance flights including England-Australia. Thanks to the very clean aerodynamics, performance is outstanding with a climb of 1200 ft/min and an economic 30 mpg.

Sourced by Bella Aviation, Bentwaters, the Shadow, it is claimed, may be built in 500 hours using simple DIY tools.

The Streak Shadow, with a Rotax 532 engine has been added to the range, but is outside the microlight category.

This aeroplane has been highly successful and over 220 have been registered to date (1994).

# CFM
# SHADOW STREAK

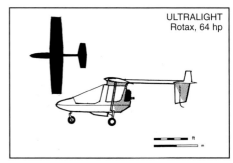

ULTRALIGHT
Rotax, 64 hp

| DATA | IMPERIAL | | METRIC | |
|---|---|---|---|---|
| Span | 28 | ft | 8.62 | m |
| Wing area | 140 | sq ft | 13.2 | sq m |
| Aspect ratio | 5.6 | | 5.6 | |
| Empty Weight | 388 | lb | 176 | kg |
| Loaded weight | 900 | lb | 408 | kg |
| Wing loading | 6.4 | lb/sq ft | 31.3 | kg/sq m |
| Max speed | 140 | mph | 224 | kmh |
| Cruise speed | 87 | mph | 140 | kmh |
| Stalling speed | 31 | mph | 50 | kmh |
| Climb rate | 1200 | ft/min | 370 | m/min |
| Range | 400 | mls | 640 | km |

Originating in the USA the Quad City Challenger is a microlight two seater, 500 of which have been built Stateside. The tandem seating enclosed cockpit gives a slim, smooth fuselage, the low drag of which enables its 55 hp motor to haul the Challenger through the air at a cruise of 75 mph, and using only 2.5 gallons of fuel an hour.

The construction is of light alloy tube with Stits fabric covering and the makers claim it can be put together in 500 hours.

The Challenger is a tough, good looking aeroplane which is easy to maintain and repair.

Full span ailerons or 'flaperons give good roll control, in flight trim and impressive short field landings, 200.

With forty-one on the UK Register and a dozen being built, the Challenger seems to be a hit and is PFA approved.

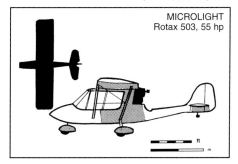

MICROLIGHT
Rotax 503, 55 hp

| DATA | IMPERIAL | | METRIC | |
|---|---|---|---|---|
| Span | 31 | ft | 9.5 | m |
| Wing area | 200 | sq ft | 19 | sq m |
| Aspect ratio | 4.8 | | 4.8 | |
| Empty Weight | 350 | lb | 159 | kg |
| Loaded weight | 840 | lb | 381 | kg |
| Wing loading | 4.2 | lb/sq ft | 20.5 | kg/sq m |
| Max speed | 85 | mph | 136 | kmh |
| Cruise speed | 75 | mph | 120 | kmh |
| Stalling speed | 25 | mph | 40 | kmh |
| Climb rate | 500 | ft/min | 154 | m/min |
| Range | 250 | mls | 400 | km |

Designed by Boeing engineer Chuck Herbst, the two seat Sparrowhawk first flew in 1986 as a product of Aero Dynamics of Arlington, Washington.

Sold in kit form, the Sparrowhawk has an all composites vacuum formed cockpit pod consisting mainly of Kevlar and foam. The tail booms are of similar construction whilst the wings are metal with fabric covering. The wing roots out to the boom intersection are integral with the fuselage pod, the outer sections are detachable for ease of storage.

The fixed, spatted undercarriage is rugged and practical, but is a retractable gear version on the cards? Its already cool lines and good performance would be enhanced enormously.

The airframe is stressed for +6-4g and will take engines from 60 to 100 hp. Data below for the 63 hp Rotax. There is one on UK Register and two here with US markings.

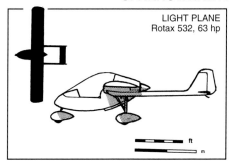

LIGHT PLANE
Rotax 532, 63 hp

| DATA | IMPERIAL | | METRIC | |
|---|---|---|---|---|
| Span | 34.5 | ft | 10.5 | m |
| Wing area | 143 | sq ft | 13.3 | sq m |
| Aspect ratio | 8.3 | | 8.3 | |
| Empty Weight | 700 | lb | 318 | kg |
| Loaded weight | 1400 | lb | 635 | kg |
| Wing loading | 10 | lb/sq ft | 48.8 | kg/sq m |
| Max speed | 120 | mph | 193 | kmh |
| Cruise speed | 100 | mph | 160 | kmh |
| Stalling speed | 36 | mph | 58 | kmh |
| Climb rate | 750 | ft/min | 229 | m/min |
| Range | 700 | mls | 1120 | km |

The side by side two seat RANS S12 Airaile is the first pod and boom pusher from RANS Aircraft of Kansas USA .and has been available since 1994 (the look alike S14, also named Airaile, is a single seater).

Three engine options are available, Rotax 503 (47 hp), Rotax 582 (63 hp) and the four cylinder water cooled Rotax 912 (80 hp)

The aircraft, which is an FAA approved 51% kit plane is not, at the time of writing, PFA approved.

The wings, which fold, are built around two tubular spars and are fabric covered, 'V' strut braced and have flaps and ailerons, the latter being push rod operated, as are the elevators. The main gear wheels are braked and sprung on steel cantilever legs, the nose wheel steers.

Cabin glazing may be fully enclosed or windscreen only - both versions have a 'perspex ' nose cone.

The empennage is carried on a 5 ins diameter tube with a nominal tail skid on to which it descends when 'empty'.

Data below for Rotax 912 version. One is shown on the UK Register.

# RANS
# S12 AIRAILE

ULTRALIGHT
Rotax 912, 80 hp

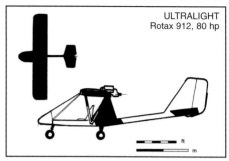

| DATA | IMPERIAL | | METRIC | |
|---|---|---|---|---|
| Span | 31 | ft | 9.5 | m |
| Wing area | 152 | sq ft | 14.3 | sq m |
| Aspect ratio | 6.3 | | 6.3 | |
| Empty Weight | 525 | lb | 238 | kg |
| Loaded weight | 1094 | lb | 497 | kg |
| Wing loading | 7.2 | lb/sq ft | 35 | kg/sq m |
| Max speed | 100 | mph | 160 | kmh |
| Cruise speed | 80 | mph | 128 | kmh |
| Stalling speed | 32 | mph | 51 | kmh |
| Climb rate | 1000 | ft/min | 308 | m/min |
| Range | 205 | mls | 328 | km |

In 1971 Grob began making a series of GRP sailplanes, graduating to motor-gliders in 1980 and in '82 to their first fully powered tourer/trainer the G109 - variants of which ran up to the G115. In 1991 Grob made a quantum leap and came up with the GF 200, a 4/5 seat all composites pusher with a retractable undercarriage a 'T' tail and 270 hp.

The Fowler flapped wing is of unusual plan form with a double swept back leading edge and tip fin/winglets.

The tall, small wheeled, undercarriage is necessary to give the prop clearance at high ground angles and retracts inwards, the nose-wheel forwards.

The engine on production models will be the 310 hp, water cooled, Continental as used in the globe circling Voyager. Only one GF 200 is flying, as I write. Other projected versions include the GF 300, pressurised, and the GF 350 with twin turbo shaft engines.

This fast, long legged, advanced aeroplane could be the shape of the future. Latest news is that the type has been abandoned.

# GROB
# GF-200

LIGHT PLANE
Continental, 310 hp

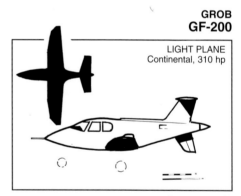

| DATA | IMPERIAL | | METRIC | |
|---|---|---|---|---|
| Span | 36 | ft | 11 | m |
| Wing area | 134 | sq ft | 12.5 | sq m |
| Aspect ratio | 9.7 | | 9.7 | |
| Empty Weight | 2422 | lb | 1100 | kg |
| Loaded weight | 3670 | lb | 1700 | kg |
| Wing loading | 28 | lb/sq ft | 136 | kg/sq m |
| Max speed | 270 | mph | 432 | kmh |
| Cruise speed | 230 | mph | 368 | kmh |
| Stalling speed | 80 | mph | 129 | kmh |
| Climb rate | 1221 | ft/min | 366 | m/min |
| Range | 1464 | mls | 2356 | km |

This good looking light plane from 3i Iniziative Industriali, Italy, first flew in 1992 and looks set to make inroads into the small 'plastic' two seater market.

ULTRALIGHT/LIGHT PLANE
Rotax 912/914, 79/100 hp

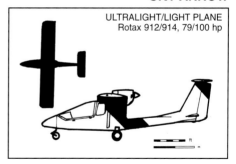

The two seats, with side stick dual controls, are within the well glazed nose pod and the rear boom carries a 'T' tail. The Rotax engine is mounted above the single strut braced wing and drives a two or three bladed (Airplast) prop. The fuselage and integral fin are all composites, the wing may be either all metal or composites. The main wheels are on a composites 'bow spring' and the nose wheel is castoring and rubber sprung.

The Sky Arrow comes in several variants, all outwardly the same (except the Exocet, which is a float plane amphibian) - they are all powered by Rotax 912 or 914 engines. In the UK, the plastic winged 650T has been PFA approved. Three 'ultralight' models with a much lighter structure weight are pending. Thirteen on the UK Register and others being built. Details below are for the 650T with a Rotax 912.

| DATA | IMPERIAL | | METRIC | |
|------|----------|--|--------|--|
| Span | 31.5 | ft | 9.7 | m |
| Wing area | 144 | sq ft | 13.5 | sq m |
| Aspect ratio | 6.9 | | 6.9 | |
| Empty Weight | 770 | lb | 350 | kg |
| Loaded weight | 1450 | lb | 658 | kg |
| Wing loading | 10 | lb/sq ft | 48.8 | kg/sq m |
| Max speed | 120 | mph | 192 | kmh |
| Cruise speed | 104 | mph | 166 | kmh |
| Stalling speed | 37 | mph | 60 | kmh |
| Climb rate | 890 | ft/min | 274 | m/min |
| Range | 145 | mls | 664 | km |

This delightful British one-off from the Mike Whittaker stable is currently in limbo, and I for one, hope that it is revived.

MICROLIGHT
Rotax 508, 43 hp

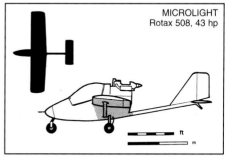

Built primarily for competition purposes, the MW8 which first flew in 1992 is powered by a Rotax 508 four-stroke engine with an extension shaft, in pusher configuration. It is a single seater with aerobatic capability and has a mid mounted strut braced wing based on the MW7. The cockpit is fully enclosed and contained in a neat wood and GRP nacelle.

The tricycle undercarriage has a steerable nose wheel and cantilever main legs carrying braked wheels. An all moving 'stabilator' is hinged on the end of a slender tubular boom, in a similar fashion to its predecessor.

The performance of this pretty microlight was considered disappointing, in spite of its more slippery shape, when compared with its older, more rugged brothers. There are no plans to produce plans or build other examples.

| DATA | IMPERIAL | | METRIC | |
|------|----------|--|--------|--|
| Span | 29.6 | ft | 9.1 | m |
| Wing area | 133 | sq ft | 12.5 | sq m |
| Aspect ratio | 6.6 | | 6.6 | |
| Empty Weight | 405 | lb | 184 | kg |
| Loaded weight | 680 | lb | 309 | kg |
| Wing loading | 5.1 | lb/sq ft | 25 | kg/sq m |
| Max speed | 85 | mph | 136 | kmh |
| Cruise speed | 70 | mph | 112 | kmh |
| Stalling speed | 30 | mph | 48 | kmh |
| Climb rate | 700 | ft/min | 215 | m/min |
| Range | 300 | mls | 480 | km |

Henri Mignet is the true father of home building, his 1934 HM14 was the first genuine small plane designed specifically for easy, cheap, amateur construction and fool-proof flying.

It had single stick control, fore and aft for mainplane incidence, and sideways for rudder control. It had no tailplane, elevator, or ailerons and the disposition of the tandem wings was supposedly proof against all aerodynamic screw ups. This,however, proved to be a fallacy when the home built Fleas took to the air, several fatal accidents caused the type to be grounded after they entered unrecoverable dives.

The fault was rectified and many flew on, in a redesigned form, retaining a following to the present day.

All wood with fabric covered wings and plywood fuselage the motor was anything you could get hold of between 0.5 and 1 litre, and in Mignet's book he even tells you how to carve the prop.

Twenty are on the UK Register, none flying here, but in France a few still spread their wings.

## MIGNET
## POU DU CEIL

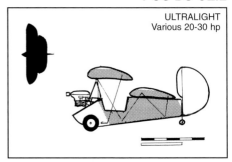

ULTRALIGHT
Various 20-30 hp

| DATA | IMPERIAL | | METRIC | |
|---|---|---|---|---|
| Span | 22 | ft | 6.7 | m |
| Wing area | 140 | sq ft | 13 | sq m |
| Aspect ratio | 5 | | 5 | |
| Empty Weight | 220 | lb | 100 | kg |
| Loaded weight | 450 | lb | 204 | kg |
| Wing loading | 3.2 | lb/sq ft | 15.7 | kg/sq m |
| Max speed | 70 | mph | 113 | kmh |
| Cruise speed | 50 | mph | 80 | kmh |
| Stalling speed | 30 | mph | 48 | kmh |
| Climb rate | 300 | ft/min | 92 | m/min |
| Range | 200 | mls | 320 | km |

Designed by Dan Maher the prototype Velocity first flew from its factory base, Sebastian 1985, Florida, USA becoming the first four seat composites kit plane to fly.

Its futuristic swept wing canard with four seats, the 173 Velocity's are of all composites construction and are supplied as a kit. The three versions available are the S.U.V. with fixed gear and a 160hp 10.360 Lycoming, the Elite, which has a 260 hp I0.540 Lycoming with options of retractable gear and large span wings. Finally there is the XL – with a wider and longer fuselage and taking a 300 hp Continental engine.

Hybrids between these option occur – our photograph is of an Elite 173 RG – an XL with a small fuselage and retracting gear.

The Velocity's are fast and flapless and need a fair bit of runway for both take off and landing. The range is excellent and the canard arrangement gives a self correcting stall capability. Over 200 are flying – mainly in the USA and others are being built. One is UK owned.

## VELOCITY AIRCRAFT
## VELOCITY 173

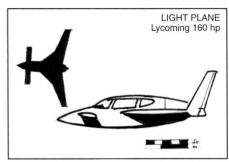

LIGHT PLANE
Lycoming 160 hp

| DATA | IMPERIAL | | METRIC | |
|---|---|---|---|---|
| Span | 31 | ft | 9.4 | m |
| Wing area | 192 | sq ft | 18 | sq m |
| Aspect ratio | 5 | | 5 | |
| Empty Weight | 1625 | lb | 737 | kg |
| Loaded weight | 2700 | lb | 1225 | kg |
| Wing loading | 14 | lb/sq ft | 68 | kg/sq m |
| Max speed | 215 | mph | 344 | kmh |
| Cruise speed | 195 | mph | 312 | kmh |
| Stalling speed | 70 | mph | 112 | kmh |
| Climb rate | 1500 | ft/min | 457 | m/min |
| Range | 1322 | mls | 2115 | km |

Designed in America by British born Craig Catto and first flown in 1974 the Goldwing is one of the pioneering microlights. With over 1000 flying, its streamlined shape and cantilever wing, in canard configuration, are still outstanding features among the microlights.

Nice to fly, a good safety record and an excellent engine off performance allied with the canard soft stall characteristic have made the Goldwing a popular aeroplane.

The wing is constructed of composites with aluminum honeycomb, foam and GRP whilst the fuselage is light alloy tube and GRP mouldings.

The main wheels are sprung and the nose wheel is steerable.

Several were produced in the UK by the now defunct Eurowing in Scotland in the early 1980s. Twenty-four are on the UK Register, only eight airworthy.

**CATTO**
# GOLDWING

MICROLIGHT
Rotax 277, 28 hp

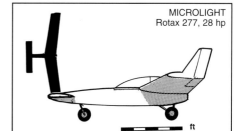

| DATA | IMPERIAL | METRIC |
|---|---|---|
| Span | 30 ft | 9.2 m |
| Wing area | 128 sq ft | 11.9 sq m |
| Aspect ratio | 7.8 | 7.8 |
| Empty Weight | 220 lb | 100 kg |
| Loaded weight | 480 lb | 218 kg |
| Wing loading | 3.75 lb/sq ft | 18.3 kg/sq m |
| Max speed | 70 mph | 113 kmh |
| Cruise speed | 60 mph | 97 kmh |
| Stalling speed | 24 mph | 38 kmh |
| Climb rate | 600 ft/min | 184 m/min |
| Range | 360 mls | 579 km |

Brain child of the brothers Rutan, Dick and Burt, the Long Eze is a fast two seater straight out of Star Wars and the first popular all composites homebuilt.

Preceded by the look-a-like VariEze that first flew in 1975, the improved LongEze is a plans only plane, all you need is a big block of expanded polystyrene, a roll of 'glass and a tin or two of epoxy resin and away you go! Construction of the sparless wing and the box like fuselage can be relatively quick but calls for a lot of expertise.

The Rutan Aircraft Factory (RAF) at Mojave, California, has become the mecca for avant garde homebuilders and from which emerged the Voyager to encircle the Globe.

Only the nose wheel is retractable on the Vari and Long Eze. An all retracting version with a 200 hp. engine, the Berkut, retains the Rutan main and fore plane. Three and four seat variants are the Puffer Cozy and Dan Mahers Velocity.

PFA approved and twenty-seven on the UK Register.

**RUTAN**
# LONG EZE

LIGHT PLANE
Lycoming, 100 hp

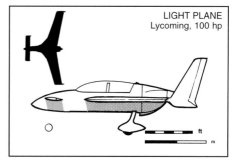

| DATA | IMPERIAL | METRIC |
|---|---|---|
| Span | 26.3 ft | 8.1 m |
| Wing area | 94.1 sq ft | 8.8 sq m |
| Aspect ratio | 7.4 | 7.4 |
| Empty Weight | 750 lb | 340 kg |
| Loaded weight | 1325 lb | 601 kg |
| Wing loading | 14.1 lb/sq ft | 68.8 kg/sq m |
| Max speed | 195 mph | 312 kmh |
| Cruise speed | 160 mph | 256 kmh |
| Stalling speed | 60 mph | 96 kmh |
| Climb rate | 1500 ft/min | 462 m/min |
| Range | 1100 mls | 1760 km |

This tiny two seater is developed from the even smaller Quickie 1 single seater designed by Burt Rutan which first flew in 1977 powered by an 18 hp. Onan engine.

The Quickie Q2 is an all composites tandem wing tractor powered by a 75 hp. Revmaster engine ( a VW relative) which, unlike the all composite Rutan range, is available in kit form. The Q1 to Q2 design hike was masterminded by Gene Sheenan and Tom Jewett in close collaboration with Rutan at RAF Mojave and appeared as the Quickie Aircraft Corporation Quickie Q2 in 1978.

Apart from the unusual arrangement of its lifting surfaces the Q2s main wheels are mounted on the fore plane wing tips and the flexibility of the wing provides the springing.

The performance is outstanding for its power - with a cruise of 170 mph. at 50 miles/gallon!

The type is PFA approved and there are eighteen, including Q1s, on the UK Register.

### QAC
# QUICKIE 2

ULTRALIGHT
Revmaster, 75 hp

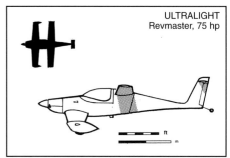

| DATA | IMPERIAL | | METRIC | |
|---|---|---|---|---|
| Span | 16.6 | ft | 5.1 | m |
| Wing area | 67 | sq ft | 6.3 | sq m |
| Aspect ratio | 8 | | 8 | |
| Empty Weight | 600 | lb | 272 | kg |
| Loaded weight | 1100 | lb | 499 | kg |
| Wing loading | 16.4 | lb/sq ft | 80 | kg/sq m |
| Max speed | 180 | mph | 288 | kmh |
| Cruise speed | 170 | mph | 272 | kmh |
| Stalling speed | 65 | mph | 104 | kmh |
| Climb rate | 700 | ft/min | 215 | m/min |
| Range | 1020 | mls | 1632 | km |

Great, great grandson of the famous Flying Flea of the 1930s, this high tech two seater follows the aerodynamic principles of its illustrious forebear. Mignet's close coupled tandem wings without ailerons and single stick control, rudder operated by sideways stock movement are all here in the 1984 Balerit.

Pierre Mignet, Henri's second son, set up Avions Mignet in 1983 to design and build updated Fleas, later Mignet Aviation.

There are eight on the UK Register and over 100 have been built in France, including twenty-four for the French Army and several for electricity grid surveillance.

To meet the UK microlight weight limit the British Balerit has had to be sparsely equipped, with an open cockpit, small fuel tank (90 miles range), and no electric engine start. The Balerit will now benefit from the new UK 450 kg limit.

The wings are fabric covered light alloy and the fuselage is clearly also light alloy tubing. The wheels are well sprung trailing link type fitted with brakes and mudguards.

### MIGNET AVIATION
# HM 1000 BALERIT

MICROLIGHT
Rotax, 582 64 hp

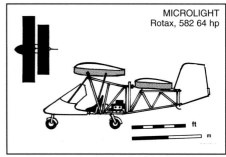

| DATA | IMPERIAL | | METRIC | |
|---|---|---|---|---|
| Span | 23.7 | ft | 7.3 | m |
| Wing area | 186 | sq ft | 17.5 | sq m |
| Aspect ratio | 6 | | 6 | |
| Empty Weight | 451 | lb | 205 | kg |
| Loaded weight | 859 | lb | 390 | kg |
| Wing loading | 4.6 | lb/sq ft | 22.5 | kg/sq m |
| Max speed | 90 | mph | 144 | kmh |
| Cruise speed | 72 | mph | 115 | kmh |
| Stalling speed | 37 | mph | 59 | kmh |
| Climb rate | 500 | ft/min | 154 | m/min |
| Range | 90 | mls | 144 | km |

The Cozy, a Nat Puffer design, is a 'wide bodied' version of the Rutan Long Ez, with side-by-side seating and an optional third seat in the rear. The Cozy 4 is a four seat model.

Uli and Linda Wolters acquired the Cozy design rights in 1987 and market it through Cozy Europe, a German company.

The standard Rutan wing is spar-less and rib-less, all the loads being taken by the GRP skin laid over a rigid foam core. The fuselage is mainly GRP with some plywood content.

The French company Stratifies Composites Aeronautiques supplies Cozy kits and the Cozy 4 is available, plans-only in the USA.

Six Cozys are on the UK Register and others are under construction as PFA approved.

The Cozy despite its wider body retains its sleek 'Star ship' appearance, and has the performance to prove it, with a cruise of nearly 200 mph and an initial climb rate of 1500 fpm.

# COZ/COZY

LIGHT PLANE
Textron lycoming 0-320, 160 hp

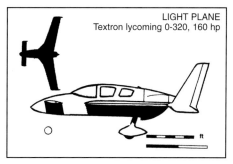

| DATA | IMPERIAL | | METRIC | |
|---|---|---|---|---|
| Span | 26.3 | ft | 8.03 | m |
| Wing area | 94.1 | sq ft | 8.8 | sq m |
| Aspect ratio | 7.4 | | 7.4 | |
| Empty Weight | 960 | lb | 435 | kg |
| Loaded weight | 1750 | lb | 794 | kg |
| Wing loading | 18.6 | lb/sq ft | 90.7 | kg/sq m |
| Max speed | 225 | mph | 362 | kmh |
| Cruise speed | 187 | mph | 301 | kmh |
| Stalling speed | 67 | mph | 108 | kmh |
| Climb rate | 1500 | ft/min | 457 | m/min |
| Range | 1000 | mls | 1609 | km |

Based on the Rutan LongEze, the Berkut has more roomy cockpits, a retractable undercarriage and an engine of twice the power.

Dave Ronnenburg, who has built seven LongEzes, masterminded the design of the super slick Berkut (name of an eagle) and it first flew in 1991.

Construction is a la Rutan – GRP over polystyrene foam and balsa wood, the skin taking all the loads in the spar-less wing.

The main gear legs are hydraulically operated and carry small disc braked wheels, whilst the nose leg is electrically operated independently to allow nose down parking – LongEze 'trademark'!

Renaissance Composites, having taken over from Experimental Aviation, produce the kits at their Santa Monica plant. A British built Berkut (G-REDX) won the Best Kit Built Aircraft at the 1999 PFA Rally – and is the only one on the UK Register.

A real eye-catcher, the super clean Berkut will cruise at over 200 mph on its 200 hp and keep it up for 1500 miles.

The longer nose, separate cockpit canopies and retracting undercarriage distinguish it from the Rutan Longeze.

# RENAISSANCE COMPOSITES
# BERKUT

LIGHT PLANE
Textron Lycoming, 200 hp

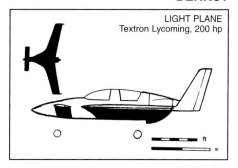

| DATA | IMPERIAL | | METRIC | |
|---|---|---|---|---|
| Span | 26.6 | ft | 8.13 | m |
| Wing area | 110 | sq ft | 10.2 | sq m |
| 748 | 7.4 | | 7.4 | |
| Empty Weight | 1035 | lb | 469 | kg |
| Loaded weight | 2000 | lb | 907 | kg |
| Wing loading | 18.2 | lb/sq ft | 88.8 | kg/sq m |
| Max speed | 248 | mph | 399 | kmh |
| Cruise speed | 239 | mph | 385 | kmh |
| Stalling speed | 62 | mph | 100 | kmh |
| Climb rate | 2000 | ft/min | 610 | m/min |
| Range | 1485 | mls | 2389 | km |

Originally designed and built in Australia the rakish Eagle X-ITS canard (or is it a much staggered biplane? - it's got a tailplane!) is now produced in Malaysia where a big joint venture project has borne fruit in the form of a large factory and production line.

An all-composites two seater of advanced design the Eagle spans only 23 ft (7.1 m). Seating is side by side under a single piece blown canopy in a well equipped cockpit which has a central console, between the seats. A central stubby 'joy stick' protrudes from the console - rather like a gear lever - and ground steering is affected by differential brakes and a castoring nose wheel.

All Canards claim to be 'stall proof' - they have, in effect, a different sort of stall. In a power-off, 'loss of lift situation', the Eagle's fore plane drops and in the subsequent dive, starts to lift again. If the stick is held back this continues in a series of nods until power is applied when recovery is immediate.

Much research flying and subsequent 'tweaking' has been carried out to bring this striking aeroplane up to JAR/VLA requirements and limited production is now under way. None yet in the UK

## EAM
## EAGLE X-TX

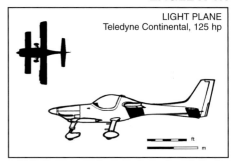

LIGHT PLANE
Teledyne Continental, 125 hp

| DATA | IMPERIAL | | METRIC | |
|---|---|---|---|---|
| Span | 23.5 | ft | 7.23 | m |
| Wing area | 91.5 | sq ft | 8.9 | sq m |
| 748 | 10 | | 10 | |
| Empty Weight | 948 | lb | 430 | kg |
| Loaded weight | 1433 | lb | 650 | kg |
| Wing loading | 15.7 | lb/sq ft | 76.6 | kg/sq m |
| Max speed | 150 | mph | 240 | kmh |
| Cruise speed | 127 | mph | 203 | kmh |
| Stalling speed | 63 | mph | 101 | kmh |
| Climb rate | 633 | ft/min | 194 | m/min |
| Range | 615 | mls | 985 | km |

In production for just one year, from1946 to '7; over 1000 Seabees were built by the company famous for its legendary P47 Thunderbolt fighter.

The prototype, RC1, first flew in 1944 as a three seater with a 175 hp Franklin engine, the developed RC3 followed as a four seater with a 215 hp Franklin.

All metal and of pleasing appearance, one is shown on the UK Register as waiting certification at Nottingham.

Republic had plans for a twin engined Seabee, a landplane version and a low powered two seat trainer – all came to nought as the company concentrated on the Thunderjet.

The Seabee has always been in need of a few more 'horses' and in 1966 United Consultants of Massachusetts produced the Twin Bee with two 180 hp Lycomings – and a fifth occupant where the central engine used to be. 24 of these conversions have been made.

Apart from those still operating, four reside in museums in Italy and New Zealand.

## REPUBLIC
## SEABEE

LIGHT AMPHIBIAN
Franklin 6A8, 215 hp

| DATA | IMPERIAL | | METRIC | |
|---|---|---|---|---|
| Span | 37.6 | ft | 11.5 | m |
| Wing area | 196 | sq ft | 18.2 | sq m |
| Aspect ratio | 7.2 | | 7.2 | |
| Empty Weight | 1950 | lb | 885 | kg |
| Loaded weight | 3000 | lb | 1360 | kg |
| Wing loading | 15.3 | lb/sq ft | 74.6 | kg/sq m |
| Max speed | 120 | mph | 193 | kmh |
| Cruise speed | 103 | mph | 166 | kmh |
| Stalling speed | 60 | mph | 96 | kmh |
| Climb rate | 700 | ft/min | 216 | m/min |
| Range | 543 | mls | 870 | km |

The Buccaneer is a development of the Colonial Aircraft Corporation XC1 Skimmer of 1948, forty-three of which were produced before CAC folded and Lake Aircraft Corporation retaining the original design team, acquired the right in 1959. The LA-4 went into production the following year.

A shoulder wing amphibian with tricycle undercarriage, the LA-4 is all metal and seats four. Its distinctive outline with pylon mounted pusher engine, mid fin mounted tailplane with large upturned trim tabs and boat hull make it an identification pushover.

Taken over by Consolidated Aeronautics Inc. in 1962 but retaining the Lake tag, LA-4 production continued, plus the six seat 270 hp Renegade and military Seawolf.

In the last thirty-five years Lake have turned out 1300 amphibians. Three LA4s and two Renegades are on the UK Register.

# LAKE
# LA-4 BUCCANEER

LIGHT AMPHIBIAN
Lycoming, 180 hp

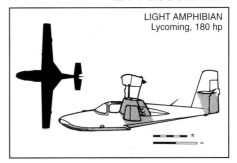

| DATA | IMPERIAL | METRIC |
|---|---|---|
| Span | 38 ft | 11.6 m |
| Wing area | 170 sq ft | 15.8 sq m |
| Aspect ratio | 8.5 | 85 |
| Empty Weight | 1575 lb | 714 kg |
| Loaded weight | 2400 lb | 1089 kg |
| Wing loading | 14.1 lb/sq ft | 69 kg/sq m |
| Max speed | 131 mph | 211 kmh |
| Cruise speed | 125 mph | 201 kmh |
| Stalling speed | 40 mph | 64 kmh |
| Climb rate | 800 ft/min | 246 m/min |
| Range | 627 mls | 1010 km |

A side-by-side two seat amphibian designed and built by Volmer Jensen of Volmer Aircraft, Burbank, California. The Sportsman which first flew in 1958 is available as a PFA approved plans built aeroplane, many sets of which have been sold – mainly in the USA. (two are shown on the UK Register – believed stored in Scotland).

The Sportsman utilises the wings of Aeronca Chiefs or Champions which are 'V' strutted, wooden sparred with metal ribs and fabric covering.

The fuselage/hull is wooden with GRP cladding over a plywood skin. The Bungee sprung undercarriage rotates upwards for water operation, and this is carried out manually. The main wheels are equipped with brakes.

The 'T' tail unit is a fabric covered welded steel structure, akin to the Aeroncas.

A Continental of 85 to 100 hp is pylon mounted in pusher configuration above the mainplane.

Amphibians with their two environments, live a hard life and the forty-year-old Sportsman (the first homebuilt amphibian?), may now be 'putting its feet up'.

# VOLMER
# SPORTSMAN

LIGHT AMPHIBIAN
Continental, 85 hp

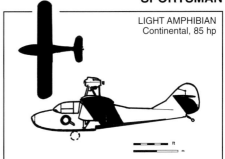

| DATA | IMPERIAL | METRIC |
|---|---|---|
| Span | 36.5 ft | 11.1 m |
| Wing area | 175 sq ft | 16.3 sq m |
| 748 | 7.2 | 7.2 |
| Empty Weight | 1000 lb | 454 kg |
| Loaded weight | 1500 lb | 680 kg |
| Wing loading | 15.7 lb/sq ft | 41.8 kg/sq m |
| Max speed | 95 mph | 153 kmh |
| Cruise speed | 85 mph | 137 kmh |
| Stalling speed | 45 mph | 72 kmh |
| Climb rate | 600 ft/min | 183 m/min |
| Range | 300 mls | 480 km |

The innovative designer George Pereira, who works in the USA, built an 'inland waters' seaplane, the Osprey 1, which first flew in 1971 and was specifically for the home-builder. In 1973 the Osprey 2 appeared - this time an amphibian powered by a Franklin Sport engine.

Construction of the tricky hull was achieved by blocking polyurethene foam over a basic wooden 'boat', then shaping it to form the keel, chine, step etc. and then 'glassing over the finished shape.

The wings, which fold, have a big wooden box spar and an auxiliary rear spar and foam/GRP tip floats.

The wheels are manually operated and, when up, are enclosed behind doors. The water rudder springs up in to the air rudder and the dual controls fitted cockpit has an upward and backward sliding hood.

Over 1000 plans have been sold and over 50 are flying.

The Osprey 2, now powered by a 150 hp Lycoming, is small, sleek, good looking and said to be easy to build.

There are four on the UK Register and one being built.

LIGHT AMPHIBIAN
Lycoming 0-320, 150 hp

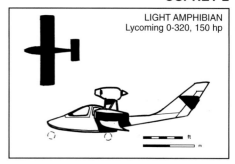

| DATA | IMPERIAL | | METRIC | |
|---|---|---|---|---|
| Span | 26 | ft | 7.9 | m |
| Wing area | 130 | sq ft | 12.1 | sq m |
| 748 | 5.1 | | 5.1 | |
| Empty Weight | 970 | lb | 440 | kg |
| Loaded weight | 1560 | lb | 707 | kg |
| Wing loading | 12 | lb/sq ft | 58.5 | kg/sq m |
| Max speed | 130 | mph | 241 | kmh |
| Cruise speed | 109 | mph | 209 | kmh |
| Stalling speed | 60 | mph | 97 | kmh |
| Climb rate | 1200 | ft/min | 365 | m/min |
| Range | 360 | mls | 576 | km |

In 1972, leading glider builders, Schwiezer Aircraft Corporation acquired the rights of the two seat Teal 1 amphibian from its designer / constructor David Thurston (co designer of the Lake LA-4 amphibian) and transferred all jigs and tools to their plant at Elmira. NY. with Thurston engaged as Engineering Manager.

The Teal, which first flew in 1968, is an metal with some GRP topside fairings, a tractor airscrew, trouser type wing floats and main wheels that simply hinge upwards and backwards but remain, joyously, in the slipstream!

Fifteen Thurston Teal 1s were made plus the Schwiezer Teal 2 and 3 (which has more power and four seats)

In 1976 Schwiezer sold the rights to Teal Aircraft Corp. who built thirty-eight before changing its production base to International Aeromarine in Canada, who have fitted the Teal 3 with a tricycle undercarriage.

There are only two currently on our Register.

LIGHT AMPHIBIAN
Lycoming, 150 hp

| DATA | IMPERIAL | | METRIC | |
|---|---|---|---|---|
| Span | 32 | ft | 9.8 | m |
| Wing area | 157 | sq ft | 14.7 | sq m |
| Aspect ratio | 6.5 | | 6.5 | |
| Empty Weight | 1435 | lb | 651 | kg |
| Loaded weight | 2200 | lb | 998 | kg |
| Wing loading | 14 | lb/sq ft | 68.3 | kg/sq m |
| Max speed | 120 | mph | 192 | kmh |
| Cruise speed | 110 | mph | 176 | kmh |
| Stalling speed | 52 | mph | 83 | kmh |
| Climb rate | 650 | ft/min | 200 | m/min |
| Range | 472 | mls | 755 | km |

This incredibly sleek and futuristic looking amphibian hailed from Seawind International of Ontario, but is now under the wing of Seawind SNA Inc. of Kimberton, Penn. and marketed in Europe by Tony Irwin, Seawind Europe Ltd. of Loughborough, Leics, UK.

This all composites aeroplane is a fast four seater that has been under continual development since it first flew in 1982. Supplied in a comprehensive kit of major pre-constructed assemblies; the method of construction is similar to that of 1/72 plastic models - on a larger scale!

250 and 300 hp. Lycomings are fitted to four sub classifications, De Luxe, Standard, Club and Kit.

The cabin is exceptionally roomy, the undercarriage and flaps are hydraulically operated and the tanks provide a cruise range of 1460 miles at 55% power and 169 mph.

Having natural 'star quality', the Seawind was scripted to be in the James Bond blockbuster Goldeneye.

Twenty are now flying and a 140 kits have been sold, seven on this side of the Atlantic.

### SEAWIND SNA INC
# SEAWIND 3000

LIGHT AMPHIBIAN
Lycoming, 300 hp

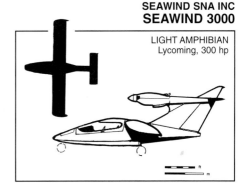

| DATA | IMPERIAL | | METRIC | |
|---|---|---|---|---|
| Span | 52 | ft | 10.65 | m |
| Wing area | 160 | sq ft | 14.9 | sq m |
| Aspect ratio | 7.6 | | 7.6 | |
| Empty Weight | 2300 | lb | 1044 | kg |
| Loaded weight | 3400 | lb | 1542 | kg |
| Wing loading | 20 | lb/sq ft | 97.6 | kg/sq m |
| Max speed | 200 | mph | 320 | kmh |
| Cruise speed | 186 | mph | 300 | kmh |
| Stalling speed | 59 | mph | 94 | kmh |
| Climb rate | 1250 | ft/min | 410 | m/min |
| Range | 1460 | mls | 2336 | km |

This French designed and manufactured Ultralight amphibian is in production at Auray in Brittany by SMAN, a firm of boat builders.

Construction is a mixture of wood, composites, light alloys and carbon fibre with the wings all Dacron covered.

At the time of writing 30 of these pretty little aircraft have taken wing, including one under evaluation by the French Army.

The tricycle undercarriage retracts neatly into the under surface of the lower wing and the nose wheel - protruding a little at the bow - makes an effective fender!

The main wheels are fitted with differential brakes and the nose wheel castors; there are no landing flaps and ailerons on the top plane only.

Open cockpit or bubble canopy versions are available as are the two Rotax engines, the four stroke 912 giving the performance shown below.

SMAN Billie Marine market a kit version and one is on the UK Register.

### SMAN BILLIE MARINE
# PETREL

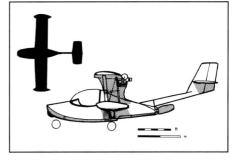

| DATA | IMPERIAL | | METRIC | |
|---|---|---|---|---|
| Span | 27.6 | ft | 8.5 | m |
| Wing area | 220 | sq ft | 20.7 | sq m |
| 748 | 7 | | 7 | |
| Empty Weight | 506 | lb | 230 | kg |
| Loaded weight | 909 | lb | 450 | kg |
| Wing loading | 4.1 | lb/sq ft | 20 | kg/sq m |
| Max speed | 85 | mph | 136 | kmh |
| Cruise speed | 75 | mph | 120 | kmh |
| Stalling speed | 32 | mph | 50 | kmh |
| Climb rate | 650 | ft/min | 200 | m/min |
| Range | 250 | mls | 400 | km |

Rotary Air Force Inc of Saskatchewan are a small team who have made a big impact on the gyroplane scene.

Entering the market in 1987 with the single seat RAF 1000 they have embodied its design principles in the best selling, two seat, RAF 2000.

This neat, Subaru powered, autogyro is produced as an easy build kit (300-400 hours) which comes complete with engine, instruments and rotors, promises to be the shape of the small gyro future! Kits have been sold world wide and thirty or more are currently being built in the UK plus ten already flying.

Unusual for the type, the '2000 has a fully enclosed cockpit with coloured upholstery and carpets, plus a two speed heater, a comprehensive panel and landing lights.

The rotor blades are composites moulded over a foam profiled dural spar, the sturdy main structure also being of dural tube. Water cooled, the Subaru engine runs on unleaded auto gas and drives a three bladed Warp Drive prop.

The design is CAA and PFA approved and Newtonair of Newton Abbot, Devon, the sole UK agents operate a demonstration and training facility at Dunkeswell Airfield.

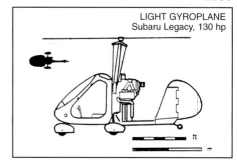

**RAF 2000**

LIGHT GYROPLANE
Subaru Legacy, 130 hp

| DATA | IMPERIAL | METRIC |
|---|---|---|
| Rotor Dia. | 30 ft | 9.24 m |
| Length | 13.6 sq ft | 4.18 sq m |
| Empty weight | 730 lb | 331 kg |
| Loaded weight | 1540 lb | 700 kg |
| Disc loading | 2.18 lb/sq ft | 10.6 kg/sq m |
| Max speed | 100 mph | 160 kmh |
| Cruise speed | 80 mph | 128 kmh |
| Climb rate | 1200 ft/min | 370 m/min |
| Range | 280 mls | 448 km |

The best selling Robinson R22, which first appeared in 1975 has proved a popular two seater, particularly in the training role, with 226 on the UK Register.

The four seater R44 came onto the scene in 1991 and sports 120 on our Register. Its power unit is the Textron Lycoming 0-540, flat six of 225 take off hp. driving a two blade rotor

Though bearing a family resemblance to its smaller sister R22, the R44 is a much bigger aircraft - about the same size as a Bell Jet Ranger!

Although a bigger machine, the R44 continues the Robinson theme of simple, light weight construction, making it fast for its power group and considerably cheaper than its contemporaries.

Produced at the Robinson Helicopter Company's plant at Torrance, California the R44 is in full production.

The floatplane version is typed as the R44 Clipper. Data below for R44.

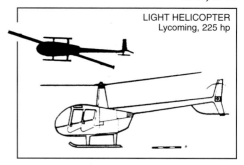

**ROBINSON R22, R44**

LIGHT HELICOPTER
Lycoming, 225 hp

| DATA | IMPERIAL | METRIC |
|---|---|---|
| Rotor Dia. | 33 ft | 8.5 m |
| Length | 38.2 sq ft | 11.7 sq m |
| Empty weight | 1400 lb | 635 kg |
| Loaded weight | 2400 lb | 1089 kg |
| Disc loading | 2.8 lb/sq ft | 13.6 kg/sq m |
| Max speed | 140 mph | 224 kmh |
| Cruise speed | 129 mph | 206 kmh |
| Climb rate | 1000 ft/min | 308 m/min |
| Range | 402 mls | 643 km |

A development of the earlier and very similar, Enstrom F28 of 1960. The Model 280 first flew in 1973 and had a bigger cabin, swept stabiliser fins and a tail skid.

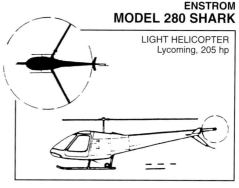

The '280 is sleek for a rotorcraft, with its fully enclosed fuselage, monocoque tail boom, single spindle rotor drive and general lack of protuberances. (The prototype had an open work lattice boom).

The 280s, from B, to F, are three seaters, the only four place being the 280L which first flew in 1978.

The standard power unit is a turbo charged Lycoming H10-360-E1AD of 205 hp. - or 153 kW.

Still in production at the Michigan factory, some 200 have been made to date.

The F28 and Model 280 are physically almost identical, but the fin type tail skid differentiates the '280 from the F28 which has a bent tube skid/tail rotor guard.

There are twenty-one F28s on the UK Register and thirty-five Model 280s.

| DATA | IMPERIAL | | METRIC | |
|---|---|---|---|---|
| Rotor Dia. | 32 | ft | 9.75 | m |
| Length | 29.3 | sq ft | 8.9 | sq m |
| Empty weight | 1495 | lb | 678 | kg |
| Loaded weight | 2200 | lb | 998 | kg |
| Disc loading | 2.74 | lb/sq ft | 13.4 | kg/sq m |
| Max speed | 117 | mph | 188 | kmh |
| Cruise speed | 100 | mph | 161 | kmh |
| Climb rate | 1300 | ft/min | 396 | m/min |
| Range | 237 | mls | 381 | km |

First flown as far back as 1947 the Model 360, or UH-12 was designed by the innovative rotorcraft pioneer Stanley Hiller. The Rotormatic system, which bears his name, has a pair of paddles, on a boom below the main rotor which operate the cyclic pitch control.

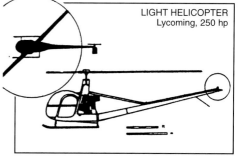

Originally a three seater with a 178 hp Franklin engine and enclosed cabin and engine bay, the first production models appeared with open cockpit and engine bay, and were type approved in 1948. One of these made the first coast to coast flight by a commercial helicopter in the USA.

In 1950 came the 12-A with new type rotor and a 200 hp Franklin, these were ordered by the Army as H23-A Ravens.

The 12-B with minor mods, were again ordered by the Army, 273 being delivered as H23-Bs.

The 12-C introduced the 'gold fish bowl' canopy, going out of production in 1965, but started up again in 1973 with the reformed Hiller Aviation Company.

2000 UH-12s have been built and four are on the UK Register.

| DATA | IMPERIAL | | METRIC | |
|---|---|---|---|---|
| Rotor Dia. | 35.4 | ft | 10.8 | m |
| Length | 26.6 | sq ft | 8.1 | sq m |
| Empty weight | 1700 | lb | 771 | kg |
| Loaded weight | 2750 | lb | 1247 | kg |
| Disc loading | 2.8 | lb/sq ft | 13.6 | kg/sq m |
| Max speed | 95 | mph | 153 | kmh |
| Cruise speed | 87 | mph | 140 | kmh |
| Climb rate | 1290 | ft/min | 393 | m/min |
| Range | 225 | mls | 362 | km |

First flown in 1956, the bug like Model 269 went into production in 1961 at the initial rate of about one hundred a year.

They are in use for both civil and military purposes and have been supplied to various foreign air forces.

The US Army employs the basic 269A - re-designated TH-55-AS Osage - as its standard helicopter trainer and has taken delivery of over 800.

The 300C variant is the model currently in production at Schweizer where it is sometimes fitted with an Allison 250-C20W turbine. The 300CQ is an extra quiet Schweizer built version.

There are fifty-four 269s on the UK Register.

# HUGHES
# MODEL 269

Lycoming, 160 hp

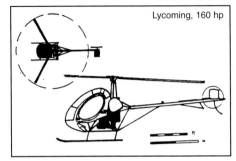

| DATA | IMPERIAL | METRIC |
|---|---|---|
| Rotor Dia. | 25 ft | 7.7 m |
| Length | 22.2 sq ft | 6.8 sq m |
| Empty weight | 910 lb | 413 kg |
| Loaded weight | 1550 lb | 703 kg |
| Disc loading | 3.16 lb/sq ft | 15.4 kg/sq m |
| Max speed | 86 mph | 137 kmh |
| Cruise speed | 70 mph | 112 kmh |
| Climb rate | 1450 ft/min | 446 m/min |
| Range | 200 mls | 320 km |

The Bell 206 A first flew in 1966 and was developed from Bell's losing contender in the Army Light Observation Helicopter trials.

Probably the most successful commercial helicopter ever made, with over 6000 aircraft produced and in use all over the world, there are 130 on the latest UK Register.

The attractively styled fuselage embodies in it's semi monocoque construction, aluminium sheet and honeycomb sandwich. The engine is mounted behind the rotor and above the passenger compartment.

This fast, comfortable and popular helicopter is much used by big corporations for executive travel, and oil and electricity companies for surveillance work.

The first 206A ran to a production of 660 units; in 1971 came the JetRanger 2 with the 400 shp Allison, 1600 of which were made before the JetRanger 3, with 425 shp entered the lists, and is still in production.

A military version with bigger rotor has been delivered in considerable numbers and is typed as OH-58 Kiowa.

Data for JetRanger 2.

# BELL
# JETRANGER

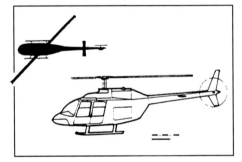

| DATA | IMPERIAL | METRIC |
|---|---|---|
| Rotor Dia. | 33.3 ft | 10.16 m |
| Length | 31.2 sq ft | 9.56 sq m |
| Empty weight | 1455 lb | 660 kg |
| Loaded weight | 3200 lb | 1451 kg |
| Disc loading | 3.7 lb/sq ft | 18 kg/sq m |
| Max speed | 140 mph | 225 kmh |
| Cruise speed | 134 mph | 216 kmh |
| Climb rate | 1260 ft/min | 384 m/min |
| Range | 388 mls | 624 km |

The prototype Model 47, three seat helicopter, first flew in 1945. first production models were for the military and type, named H13 Sioux.

Type designations run to fifty or more and space permits only a few to be mentioned.

The first civil version, the 47B appeared in 1946 and was the worlds first commercial helicopter to be CAA type approved.

All the early models had 178 hp Franklin engines and the well known Bell rotor stabilising bar, car type cabin and covered tail boom. The 'gold fish bowl' cabin came in with Model 47D in 1948 and with it the open frame tail boom. Model 47E was a two seater with a 200 hp Franklin engine and Model 47G of 1953 was similarly powered but had three seats.

From 1955 Lycoming engines supplanted the Franklins, built by Augusta in Italy, Kawasaki in Japan and Westland in the UK. It is the most prolific helicopter in the world. It has been in production for over forty years, with over 4000 being built. There are twenty-five on the UK Register and several in UK museums.

# BELL
# MODEL 47

LIGHT HELICOPTER
Lycoming, 240 hp

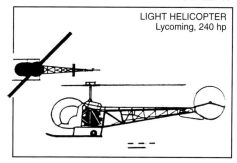

| DATA | IMPERIAL | METRIC |
|---|---|---|
| Rotor Dia. | 37.1 ft | 11.3 m |
| Length | 31.5 sq ft | 9.6 sq m |
| Empty weight | 1650 lb | 748 kg |
| Loaded weight | 2850 lb | 1293 kg |
| Disc loading | 2.64 lb/sq ft | 12.9 kg/sq m |
| Max speed | 105 mph | 169 kmh |
| Cruise speed | 90 mph | 145 kmh |
| Climb rate | 800 ft/min | 244 m/min |
| Range | 290 mls | 467 km |

Developed from a range of towed autogyros by Igor Bensen and his company, Bensen Aircraft Corporation. The first motorised model, the B8-M (M = motorised), first flew in 1957 and was powered by a two stroke 72 hp McCulloch engine. Later power options include the 90 hp McCulloch or a 64 hp VW engine, this model classified as B8V.

A mechanical rotor drive, enabling jump take offs may be fitted and two seats are an option. The B8M may be kit or factory built, the company now however is no longer in existence.

The rotor blades are laminated wood on a steel spar and are controlled in cyclic pitch and yaw only. The overhead control stick is replaced in many models by a 'floor' mounted stick.

Many thousands of Bensen gyrocopters and their powered brethren have been built, mainly in the USA. Over ninety-three are on the UK Register as a PFA approved type.

# BENSEN
# B8 M

LIGHT AUTOGYRO
McCulloch, 72 hp

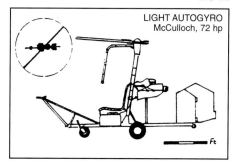

| DATA | IMPERIAL | METRIC |
|---|---|---|
| Rotor Dia. | 20 ft | 6.16 m |
| Length | 11.3 sq ft | 3.5 sq m |
| Empty weight | 247 lb | 112 kg |
| Loaded weight | 500 lb | 227 kg |
| Disc loading | 1.6 lb/sq ft | 7.8 kg/sq m |
| Max speed | 85 mph | 136 kmh |
| Cruise speed | 60 mph | 96 kmh |
| Climb rate | 1000 ft/min | 308 m/min |
| Range | 100 mls | 160 km |

The two seat Brantly B2 first flew in 1953; development continued for six years and production commenced in 1959.

The B2 A is an up-dated version of the original B2, with re-designed cabin and improved equipment. The B2 B has more power with a 180 hp. fuel injected Lycoming. All B2s have dual control and a unique rotor of extruded aluminium which has flapping hinges at the root and half way along the blade. The type approval was issued by the FAA in 1963. In 1989 Japan acquired build rights and, in the same year, the new Brantly Helicopter Industries was formed in Texas.

The flat four engine is mounted vertically and the clean tapered fuselage give the B2 very tidy lines, further enhanced by the minimal rotor pylon.

There are nine B2s on the UK Register of the 400 produced.

Of very similar appearance, the Brantly B305 is a five seater.

## BRANTLY B2A

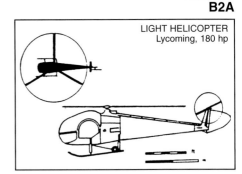

LIGHT HELICOPTER
Lycoming, 180 hp

| DATA | IMPERIAL | | METRIC | |
|---|---|---|---|---|
| Rotor Dia. | 23.9 | ft | 7.4 | m |
| Length | 23.9 | sq ft | 7.4 | sq m |
| Empty weight | 1020 | lb | 463 | kg |
| Loaded weight | 1670 | lb | 758 | kg |
| Disc loading | 3.78 | lb/sq ft | 18.5 | kg/sq m |
| Max speed | 100 | mph | 160 | kmh |
| Cruise speed | 92 | mph | 147 | kmh |
| Climb rate | 1400 | ft/min | 431 | m/min |
| Range | 250 | mls | 400 | km |

A very neat home-built two seat helicopter from the USA. Originally factored by Rotorcraft Aircraft Inc. up to 1990 when all the Corporation's assets were purchased by English businessman John Netherwood who was new to the field. Netherwood's company was named Rotorway International. (Rotorway Inc. had marketed single and two seat kit helicopters in the 70's)

The Executive 162F arose from the combination of this corporate mix - and very successful it has been too.

Powered by Rotorway's own engine, a flat four cylinder unit developing 152 hp. the Executive 162 replaces the earlier '90, and can be built from a complete kit or from quick build ready assembled units.

The Executive 90 established the market for the type and it has been taken up by distributors world wide.

There are forty-two Executives on the UK Register.

## ROTORWAY EXECUTIVE 162

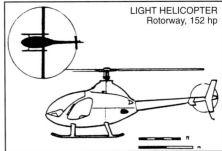

LIGHT HELICOPTER
Rotorway, 152 hp

| DATA | IMPERIAL | | METRIC | |
|---|---|---|---|---|
| Rotor Dia. | 25 | ft | 7.6 | m |
| Length | 22 | sq ft | 6.7 | sq m |
| Empty weight | 925 | lb | 420 | kg |
| Loaded weight | 1425 | lb | 646 | kg |
| Disc loading | 1.9 | lb/sq ft | 7.27 | kg/sq m |
| Max speed | 115 | mph | 185 | kmh |
| Cruise speed | 95 | mph | 153 | kmh |
| Climb rate | 1000 | ft/min | 305 | m/min |
| Range | 180 | mls | 290 | km |

Wing Commander K H Wallis began designing and experimenting with a small single seat autogyro in 1950, and having patented various unique features, the prototype WA 116 first flew in 1961 with a 72 hp two stroke McCulloch drone engine - having experimented earlier with a Triumph motor cycle engine.

In the following year three Beagle built WA 116s were evaluated by the British Army - but no order ensued.

In 1964 Wallis Autogyros was formed and modest production commenced. In 1969 the first two seat trainer flew and a nacelle was added to the, hitherto, exposed seating.

In 1968 the WA 116 broke the world height record for autogyros and a year later the speed record at 111 mph.

The WA 116 became well known as the deadly little 'chopper' in the film 'You only Live Twice'.

To achieve full British certification a 100 hp RR Continental was fitted in 1995 and was later re- typed as WA 117. Twenty WA 116s are on the UK Register.

## WALLIS
## WA 116 AGILE

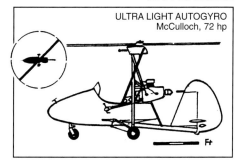

ULTRA LIGHT AUTOGYRO
McCulloch, 72 hp

| DATA | IMPERIAL | METRIC |
|---|---|---|
| Rotor Dia. | 20.3 ft | 6.2 m |
| Length | 11.1 sq ft | 3.4 sq m |
| Empty weight | 2957 lb | 134 kg |
| Loaded weight | 550 lb | 250 kg |
| Disc loading | 1.72 lb/sq ft | 8.4 kg/sq m |
| Max speed | 80 mph | 128 kmh |
| Cruise speed | 60 mph | 96 kmh |
| Climb rate | 1000 ft/min | 308 m/min |
| Range | 100 mls | 160 km |

This helicopter is a civilian development of the US Army's OH-6A Cayuse that first flew in 1963, and was to set several world records for it's class in 1966.

The first '500 flew in 1967 powered by an Allison 736 turbine of 278 shp. driving a four bladed main rotor and seating pilot and four passengers.

The '500 C of 1970 has a 400 shp. Allison and consequently flies faster and higher.

the '500 D has a five bladed rotor and a 'T' tail with small end plates and the '500 E has a more pointed nose and bigger tailplane end plates.

Military versions of the '500 have been supplied to many foreign air forces and Kawasaki of Japan and Nardi SA in Italy are licensed to build the type.

The design of the rotor head is unusual; the opposing blades, of the four, are joined by a laminated stainless steel strap that allows feathering and flapping movement and considerably simplifies the head machinery.

There are thirty-two of the type on the UK Register.

## HUGHES
## MODEL 500

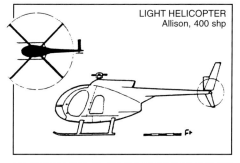

LIGHT HELICOPTER
Allison, 400 shp

| DATA | IMPERIAL | METRIC |
|---|---|---|
| Rotor Dia. | 26.5 ft | 8.05 m |
| Length | 23 sq ft | 7.01 sq m |
| Empty weight | 1320 lb | 598 kg |
| Loaded weight | 3000 lb | 1360 kg |
| Disc loading | 5.4 lb/sq ft | 26.6 kg/sq m |
| Max speed | 160 mph | 258 kmh |
| Cruise speed | 150 mph | 241 kmh |
| Climb rate | 800 ft/min | 244 m/min |
| Range | 335 mls | 339 km |

# INDEX

Manufacturer in italic.